HOW TO READ THE BIBLE

Two Volumes in One

By Etienne Charpentier

Translated by John Bowden

Originally published in separate volumes as
How to Read the Old Testament and *How to Read the New Testament*

GRAMERCY BOOKS
NEW YORK • AVENEL, NEW JERSEY

Originally published in two separate volumes as:
How to Read the Old Testament and *How to Read the New Testament*

English translation copyright © John Bowden 1981
Originally published as *Pour lire le Nouveau Testament* © Les Editions du Cerf, 1981
and *Pour lire le Ancien Testament* © Les Editions du Cerf, 1981.

This 1991 edition is published by Gramercy Books, distributed by Outlet Book Company, Inc.,
a Random House Company, 40 Engelhard Avenue, Avenel, New Jersey 07001, by arrangement
with The Crossroad Publishing Company.

Random House
New York • Toronto • London • Sydney • Auckland

Printed and bound in the United States of America

Library of Congress Cataloging-in-Publication Data

Charpentier, Etienne.
    [Pour lire l'Ancien Testament. English]
    How to read the Bible : two volumes in one / Etienne Charpentier.
        p.   cm.
    Originally published in 1982 in two separate volumes as How to
read the Old Testament and How to read the New Testament which was
translated from Pour lire l'Ancien Testament and Pour lire le
Nouveau Testament.
    Includes bibliographical references and index.
    ISBN 0-517-05590-2 :
    1. Bible – Study.   2. Bible – Introductions.   I. Charpentier,
Etienne. Pour lire le Nouveau Testament. English. 1991.
    II. Title.
BS600.2.C43   1991
    220.6'1 – dc20   90-23841
                                                              CIP

8 7 6 5 4 3 2

How to Read the Old Testament

A Guide to the Bible

This book is for those who want to read the Bible but don't know how to go about it. It has been planned as a modest, yet ambitious guide to the Old Testament. There is a companion volume on the New Testament.

A travel guide

When we go on a trip, we may like to buy one of those guides that we can take with us, suggesting places to visit, telling us the sights to see and giving us a brief history of the country to which we shall be going. This guide is meant to help you to discover the Bible in just the same way.

It is a modest guide. It is very simple. Those who have never opened a Bible or who have tried, but given up, should find no difficulty with it (though they will have to do some work!). Before I wrote it, I tried out its contents for a long time with a great many groups. It is short. Each chapter is divided into sections of two or three pages which can be read on their own.

At the same time, however, it is an ambitious guide, because it sets out to offer you all the equipment you will need for reading the Bible on your own. The plan is as follows.

After a general introduction, there are eight chapters, each constructed on the same lines, and containing:

• A summary of the history of Israel. These two pages (always with a grey border) begin the chapter, but they are also a self-contained whole. You can read them one after another right through the book to have an overall view of the history of Israel.

• An introduction to the biblical writings produced during this period. We shall see the gradual growth of the different traditions which one day will become the Law (sometimes called the Pentateuch); we shall hear the prophets who were active in preaching during the periods concerned; we shall discover the way in which the wise men reflected on the human condition, life, love, death, and how their reflections one day culminate in the great works of wisdom literature.

• Parts of the Bible to read (indicated by 📖). These draw attention to the more important texts that you should read, by yourself or in a group.

• Documentation (contained in the boxes). This varies a great deal and includes explanations of important or difficult words, helps towards reading the texts, ancient texts which can be compared with the Bible, theological and spiritual reflections, and so on.

How to use this guide

You can use this guide by yourself. It can also be used for group study, in schools or churches. That's why it has been divided into eight chapters: a group, meeting only once a month, could use it to go through the Old Testament in a year.

Reading a travel guide before a trip gives us a general idea of what we shall be seeing and whets our appetite; but we know that some of the things it says will not mean anything to us until we actually arrive. We also know that we shall not be able to visit all the monuments listed in the guide. The same thing is true of this book.

You will be well advised to begin by reading each chapter straight through. That will give you a general idea, and you will know the texts that you will be 'visiting', while being well aware that you won't have time to see them all: at least you will be able to note the ones you would like to study. Then go back through the chapter again, Bible in hand. If you are part of a group, the work can be shared between you; thus at each meeting one person will have studied one particular part of the chapter more attentively than others, and will be able to help them to understand this part better.

You have your guide . . . but what specific country are you going to visit? In other words, which edition of the Bible are you going to use?

Which Bible?

There are plenty of good versions of the Bible. Translations vary, and some are more faithful than others. In particular, those which concentrate above all on putting the Bible into a truly modern idiom, like the *Good News Bible* (*Today's English Version*), can be rather free with the original text. However, in the end it does not really matter which edition of the Bible you use. If you have a Bible, you can use this guide.

We had to choose one particular translation of the Bible to quote in the pages which follow, and after a great deal of deliberation, finally decided on the *Revised Standard Version*. This was one of the earliest of the new translations, and is still one of the best – and one of the most widely used. Mention should also be made of the *Jerusalem Bible*, which is a very close contender. If you plan to buy a new Bible, you might well consider the Standard Edition of the Jerusalem Bible, which also has introductions and notes to each book. It will be a good source of extra information, but unfortunately it is not cheap!

Why read the Old Testament...

... especially now that we have the New Testament? If you've bought this guide, you will already have decided that the Old Testament is important. If you still need to be convinced, turn to pages 109–111.

Who is the author of this guide?

Who is the author? Certainly not me! Granted, I produced it, but that would not have been possible without the countless biblical scholars who are my friends, among whom I have worked, and from whom I have 'stolen' ideas or pictures in the course of meetings, lectures, conferences or my own reading. Nor can I forget the friendship of all those peoples in groups both in Chartres and throughout France where I have learned what I would like to share with you. This guide is as much their work as mine. Thank you, everybody!

Étienne Charpentier

This picture from the tomb of a certain Beni-Hassan, in Egypt (about 1890 BC), gives us some idea of the world of the patriarchs. A caravan of thirty-seven Arab nomads is paying its respects to the local governor. Men, women and children all seem to be in glowing health. They are wearing woollen garments in various colours. The men are well armed. Their chief (who does not appear in this part of the picture, but see p. 17) is offering as a present an ibex caught in the desert (see Genesis 12.10).

Getting Ready for our Journey

Suppose you decide to have a holiday in Spain. You have a number of choices. You can spend a couple of weeks in a town or a resort, in which case you will know that place well, but not the rest of the country. You can manage on your own and make no fixed plans. Or you can go to a travel agency which will suggest a choice of package tours: you can cover the whole of Spain by coach in a month.

However, even the last kind of holiday could be organized in two different ways. One way, the itinerary might be completely fixed. The coach stops at such and such a sight, the guide takes you round it, you get back in the coach which puts you down at a particular museum, and so on. Alternatively, the arrangements could be much simpler. The coach stops for two days in one town, three in another; at each stop the agency gives you a leaflet with the things to see and you make your own plans: if you want to, you can make use of the services of the guide suggested by the agency for this church or that museum. The itinerary is marked out: you are offered various options and make your own choice.

This book suggests something like this second kind of holiday. Each chapter makes up one of the eight stops in a journey through the Old Testament. At each stop you will be told what there is to visit, and you will be offered a guided tour of one or other of the more important texts. However, it is up to you to choose. You certainly won't be able to see everything. So choose!

Of course, it's a bit frustrating: we find our mouths watering, we want to see everything, study everything, and there just isn't time. The coach, the next chapter, calls us to join it, and we have to go. . . Obviously, by the end of a trip of this kind we cannot claim to know Spain – or the Bible. But we have got to know it a bit; lots of things have fallen into place, and we can go on to read a particular book, return to a certain city or study a particular prophet. We shall no longer be disorientated, because we shall be able to see where they fit into a whole.

Before beginning a journey, we pack our bags and get ready. We learn a bit about the geography and the history of the place to which we are going, we read up the language of the country and learn one or two essential words and phrases. We gather together our things, and they will differ depending on whether we are leaving for the mountains or for the sea.

So in this first chapter, before we really begin, we are going to gather together some essential ideas so that we don't get too lost.

This is what you will find on the next few pages:

1. *The Bible: book or library?* Some practical advice about getting to know the Bible itself (pages 6–7).

2. *A people rereads its life.* A more theoretical reflection on the Bible: not 'eye-witness accounts' but the reflections of believers (pages 8–10).

3. *Reading and studying a text.* Two methods of analysing a text, and a 'tool box' (pages 11–15).

4. *A people stamped by its geography.* The geographical and historical environment of Israel (pages 16–17).

5. *A people stamped by the mentality of the Near East.* A survey of the thought-patterns of the people with whom Israel is in contact (pages 18–21).

6. *A thousand years of history.* The great moments of Israel (pages 22–23).

1. The Bible: book or library?

We shall begin by getting to know something about the Bible itself. If you are already familiar with it, you can go straight on to page 8.

Names

The word Bible comes from the Greek; it is a plural noun, *ta biblia*, and means 'the books'. When this word was taken over into Latin, it became singular, the Bible.

The Bible is more than a book; it's a library. In it you will find a number of very different works, collected together in two large groupings, the Old Testament and the New Testament (usually abbreviated as OT and NT). The word 'testament' here does not mean what we might take it to mean in modern English: it is the same word as the Latin *testamentum*, which translates the Hebrew word meaning covenant. So the Bible is the collection of books which tells us about the covenant, the agreement, which God made with Israel through Moses (the old covenant) and which he fulfilled in Jesus (the new covenant).

The Bible is often called scripture, the scriptures, or holy scripture. That is important, and means at least two things. First, this is the Word of God set down in writing – so there can be a Word of God which is not written. Furthermore, it is the writings which are the Word of God for us, and not the events or the words spoken before they were composed. We shall come back to this point.

Books

The first part of the Bible, the Old Testament, is common to both Jews and Christians, but with some differences.

The Jews, followed by Protestants, recognize only the books written in Hebrew, forty of them; Catholics also recognize six books written in Greek. Protestants call these latter books 'apocryphal'; Catholics call them 'deutero-canonical', that is, books which entered the canon, or rule of faith, at a secondary stage (see the box on p. 86).

The New Testament, which is identical for all Christians, consists of twenty-seven books.

So the Christian 'library' – the Bible – contains either sixty-seven or seventy-three books. They are usually re-ferred to by means of abbreviations (you will find a list on p. 125). Thus Gen. refers to Genesis and Rev. to Revelation. The system of abbreviations is almost uniform, but you will find slight differences between one edition of the Bible and another, and between different books about the Bible.

Classification

If you are putting books on the shelves of a library, you have several possible ways of doing it.

If you want to be aesthetic, you will arrange them according to size. So in the Bible, the letters of Paul are arranged in order of decreasing length.

If you want to be practical, you will arrange the books according to subject. So in the Bible, we find all the prophets, or all the books of Paul, together.

If you want to follow the development of ideas, you can arrange the books in the order in which they appeared. You might have all the books published before the Second World War, then all the books published before the assassination of President Kennedy, and so on. That is the order we shall try to follow in this book.

The books of the New Testament are arranged in the same way in all Christian Bibles.

The books of the Old Testament are arranged in two different ways.

The Jewish Bible contains three parts: the Law or Torah (which we call the Pentateuch); the Prophets or Nebiim, divided into two groups, the former prophets (which we wrongly call the 'historical' books) and the latter prophets (Isaiah, Jeremiah, Ezekiel and the twelve others); and lastly the Writings or Kethubim. By taking the first letters of each of these Hebrew titles (Torah, Nebiim, Kethubim), the Jews formed the word TaNaK, which is their name for the Bible. This is the arrangement you will find in the Jerusalem Bible, which adds at the end those books which are not recognized by Catholics.

Most Bibles have adopted an order inspired by the Greek Bible, which arranges the books in four parts: the Pentateuch, the historical books, the prophetic books and the wisdom books.

Languages

The whole of the Old Testament is written in Hebrew (there are just a few passages in Aramaic). Like Arabic, these two languages are written with consonants only; the reader has to add the vowels according to the way in which he understands the text. Beginning in the seventh century of our era, Jewish scholars known as 'Massoretes' fixed the meaning of a text by adding vowels in the form of little points above and below the consonants. This is why the Hebrew text is sometimes called the 'Massoretic text'.

The Old Testament was translated into Greek in Alexandria, from about the third century BC onwards. According to legend, seventy scribes working independently all arrived at exactly the same translation. The significance of this legend is important. It indicates that a translation of this kind must have been inspired by God. As a result, the translation is known as the Septuagint (Greek for seventy: the usual abbreviation is LXX). There were other ancient Greek translations, by Aquila, Symmachus and Theodotion.

The New Testament was written entirely in Greek, in the common language spoken at the time. This Greek, which is not the same as classical Greek, is called *koine* (Greek for common, i.e. language).

Specialist scholars work with and translate from the original texts, i.e. Hebrew for the Old Testament and Greek for the New Testament.

Of the other ancient translations or versions I should mention the translations into Syriac, Coptic and Latin. The Latin version known as the Vulgate (*editio vulgata* or popular edition) is the work of St Jerome (end of the fourth and beginning of the fifth century of our era).

Chapters and verses

To make it easy to find one's way around the Bible, Stephen Langton, Archbishop of Canterbury, had the idea of dividing each book into numbered chapters: this was done in 1226. During a carriage journey from Lyons to Paris in 1551, the printer Robert Estienne numbered almost every phrase of these chapters: hence our modern division into verses.

The division into chapters and verses does not always match the meaning of the text; you don't have to take account of it to understand the meaning. However, it is very practical, because all Bibles have adopted it. So to indicate a passage in the Bible, it is enough to give the reference, i.e. to indicate the book, the chapter and the verse, e.g. 2.4. In the box you will find the system of abbreviations and references generally used today.

How a reference works

First comes an abbreviated form of the title of the book (for a list of abbreviations see p. 125).

The first figure indicates the chapter, and the second, separated from the first by a full stop (sometimes a colon), indicates the verse.

Thus Gen. 2.4 denotes Genesis, chapter 2, verse 4.

A hyphen is used in indicating several chapters or verses. Gen. 2–5 denotes Genesis, chapters 2 to 5 (inclusive); Gen. 2.4–8 denotes Genesis, chapter 2, verses 4 to 8 (inclusive).

A semi-colon separates two different references. Gen. 2; 5 denotes Genesis, chapters 2 and 5.

A comma separates different verses in the same chapter. Gen. 2.4, 8, 11 denotes verses 4, 8 and 11 of chapter 2.

An f. added to a figure indicates the following verse (ff. indicates an indeterminate number of subsequent verses). Thus Gen. 2.4f. denotes Genesis chapter 2, verses 4 and 5.

Some verses are particularly long. If you want to indicate just part of the verse, you add letters to the numbers. Thus Gen. 2.4a denotes the first part of Genesis chapter 2, verse 4.

Here is an example: Gen. 2.4–6, 8; 3.5f.; 4.1–6.8 denotes: Genesis, chapter 2, verses 4 to 6 (inclusive) and verse 8, then chapter 3, verses 5 and 6; chapter 4, verse 1 to chapter 6, verse 8.

This system may seem very complicated, but it is no more difficult than looking up a number in a telephone directory. You'll soon get used to it.

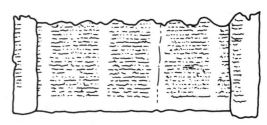

Qumran manuscript. Temple Scroll. Before 70 BC.

2. A people rereads its life

The Bible, and above all the Old Testament, is a disconcerting book. Even those who have never opened it know that it is the holy book of Jews and Christians and expect to find in it the 'word of God in a pure form', a kind of catechism or handbook of morality.

And when they do open it . . . they find stories about the past of a tiny people, which are often quite insignificant, stories of an unedifying and immoral kind which one cannot read aloud without blushing, wars, murders, poems with which it is difficult to pray even if one turns them into 'psalms', the counsels of an antiquated morality, out of date and deliberately misogynist. . .

A disconcerting book. . . But is it in fact a book?

In the first place, it is a library, consisting of seventy-three books, the writing of which extends over more than a thousand years. Put side by side on the shelves of your bookcase *Gawain and the Green Knight* and a collection of Snoopy cartoons, the Canterbury Tales and a mediaeval theological treatise, Winston Churchill's memoirs of the Second World War, some Elizabethan love lyrics and sermons by Newman, the songs of the American Civil War and Tolkien's *Lord of the Rings*, together with some modern books on theology and some on science. You will have representative works written in English over the past thousand years or so, but you will end up rather disorientated. . .

The Bible is in fact more than a fixed library; it is a world we have to enter for ourselves, an adventure to which we are summoned: that of a people seized with a passion for God.

Perhaps a little story will make things clearer.

It was the eve of their golden wedding. When I arrived, they were alone. Their children had already left. We spent the evening together, and it was marvellous.

I thought I knew these old friends well enough: simple people who had lived together for half a century, sharing joys and sorrows. That evening, however, I saw them with new eyes, because they showed me their 'treasure': a plain cardboard box held it all. Of course there were photographs, from the family wedding photograph, posed and very solemn, to snaps of a child's smile or a holiday view. There were postcards, trite and conventional, some in pieces because he had carried them round in his uniform pocket all through the war. As I looked through them, the couple gave me a commentary and explained why they had kept them, and these common objects became sad or happy mementoes of moments in their lives.

And it was their lives which took shape through their family papers. The family genealogy, a monotonous list of old-fashioned names, here became pride at belonging to a line, at having roots in a particular area. A lease was no longer a pretentious and minutely detailed document, but the final realization of a life-long dream of work and savings: they had their own house. Letters exchanged during their engagement ('Hey, you mustn't let him read that,' the old man protested, delighted that it would show me the tenderness of their love) had been put next to prayers composed for the great moments of their life. Their marriage sermon lay next to rather a bad poem sent by a grandchild.

The evening went like a dream. I thought I knew these old friends well, and all of a sudden, with them and alongside them, I discovered the meaning of their life. All these papers and photographs were trivial, valueless. Yet for us they became priceless: they were no longer just objects, but the whole of a life, summed up and interpreted. Each one of these commonplace things had a place in a story of which it formed part of the fabric.

Now we must go back to some of the important points of this illustration.

1. Life turned into a 'text'

This married couple showed me photographs and documents; these objects were interesting, not only in themselves, but above all because they were so to speak the life of the couple in concentrated form. Through them and by means of them, I was able to go a little way into the world of my friends and share in their adventure of love.

Similarly, the various books of the Bible can often seem trite and uninteresting to us. But through them we shall discover the adventure of a people of believers, and will be able to enter into their world.

2. You understand afterwards

'That's our first love letter,' my old friend said to me with a wicked smile. I read it in amazement: it was an algebra problem. At that time he and his future wife were still at school. Because she was away ill, he had been given the task of writing to her with the maths homework. An ordinary enough letter, but it had started something, and it had been followed by others. Taken by itself, the letter would have been completely uninteresting; kept by chance and reread after their marriage, it had really become their first love letter.

So there are events which make no sense by themselves: they make some sense by becoming part of our history. At the moment when they are taken, photographs are not very interesting; looked at afterwards, they become important.

Thus each event can carry within it a number of meanings which we may not see all at once; if, however, it is important, we shall be led to think about it again, and by thinking about it, we shall discover its riches. The more one goes on, the richer the original event becomes.

Describing an event is not the same as giving an exact account, like a photograph of what happened; it is rather like recreating this event and showing the meaning that it now has for us. And as we talk about it later, we discover yet other things. For example, a friend may tell us something; we don't pay too much attention, and then later, often a good deal later, we exclaim, 'So that's what he wanted to tell me. . .' How are we going to describe the friend's original statement – in terms of what he told us or in terms of how we now understand it? In other words, are we going to reproduce his exact words or add the meaning that he truly wanted to convey?

3. Exact or true?

Sometimes we hear people asking, 'Is what is in the Bible true? Did miracles really happen?' Before we answer, we ought perhaps to ask ourselves what we mean by 'true'. It can have a number of meanings. For example, someone might say, 'This story is true, this novel is true, this poem is true. . .' We immediately realize that the meaning of true here isn't always the same. In a novel, everything has been made up, but it can be true if we identify easily with it, if it is a good reflection of the realities of human life. Nothing is exact or historical, but everything is true.

It is always dangerous to use labels, but at least that allows us to see clearly. So let us take these two words, exact and true.

We use the word exact to refer to what actually happened in history: what the camera or the tape recorder might have registered. In this perspective my old friends' first love letter is no more than sending on maths homework: what this friend actually said will be reproduced exactly as it was.

But it is true that these algebra sums are a 'love letter', and the way in which I reproduce the phrase used by my friends will be more true than if it were exact.

Is the Bible, then, true? Yes, but in this sense of the word. Of course we shall find inaccuracies, and the way in which events are narrated or speeches reported will not always be exact, but it will be true because it includes the meaning which has been discovered.

4. Believing in order to understand

The essential reality of the event cannot be seen with the eyes; we have to infer it through the historical features of the event, through what we can see. For example, we might see a man and a woman kissing. That is an exact, historical fact. But we cannot infer anything from it. Sometimes we are obliged to kiss people we do not like or love. If someone tells me that this couple is in love, then the kiss takes on meaning: it becomes a sign of their love. 'If someone tells me. . .': that means that I believe what I am told, and it is because I believe that I understand this kiss as a gesture of love. If we are to understand, we need to believe, and the fact of understanding reinforces our belief. In this way, then, we progress as though up a spiral staircase: we keep going round, but at each turn we progress further.

It is the same with the Bible. That applies to those who wrote it. They told of events, but these events took on meaning because they believed. And that applies to us who read it today: we can study it whether or not we are believers, and we can understand what the texts tell us. But we understand them differently if we share the same faith as the authors, and if we enter on the same quest as theirs.

All that might seem rather complicated, but we shall return to it, and things will become clearer as we go along. For the moment, let us draw one important consequence from what has been said so far. What is the meaning of a text? What is reading?

5. The meaning of a text

When we are confronted with a text, above all an ancient text, we instinctively think rather like this. The author had something to say, a meaning to communicate. He wrapped up this meaning in his own words and his own culture. So our task today consists of unwrapping this meaning and wrapping it up again in our own words. We imagine that there is an objective meaning in the text, a hard core that we have to extract.

By now, we should be beginning to understand that things are not quite as simple as this. As I listened to my old friends describing their life to me, of course I was trying to understand what they wanted to say; but as I listened, I transformed it. After that evening I had a picture of them which doubtless was not quite the picture they had of themselves, and which was not the picture that would have been presented to another friend who might have been there. As we read a text, we reshape it in the light of what we are ourselves. That is quite normal: in that way we continue the life of the event that is being narrated, adding the meaning that we discover in it.

Reading is a matter of getting hold of a text and making it tell us something for today, something that will make us live.

In that case, though, can we make a text say virtually anything? That is where the study of the text comes in, and the use of different methods of study.

A miraculous history?

'Why should the Bible interest me? It tells a miraculous story in which God is talking all the time (to Abraham, to Moses, to the prophets. . .), and in which he is always performing miracles to free the oppressed, heal the sick. . . What has that to do with my ordinary, common, everyday life, or with the life of the world? God chattered on for two thousand years, and now he is silent. But people are still oppressed and wretched. Why doesn't he act any more?'

That's a real objection. But what I have already said should enable you to guess that those who make this objection are comparing histories at two different levels.

The historian who studies the history of Israel will find it to be the ordinary history of a tiny people in the Near East, no different from the others.

The believers who produced the Bible read in these events the word and the intervention of their God, in the same way that the couple I mentioned discovered a love letter in some maths homework.

The history of Israel is as common, ordinary, wretched as our history today. It is the same. And the unbeliever will not discover any trace of God in it.

But to read the Bible should lead us to reread our existence with the eyes of the believer. If we do, we shall discover that God continues to speak to us as he spoke to the prophets, and he continues to act. And the whole of our life will appear to us to be a history full of miracles.

3. Reading and studying a text

What I have just said suggests that we should distinguish between reading a text and studying it.

Reading a text is making it produce a meaning for its present-day reader. That's what we do naturally; we say, 'That's what this text says to me... What strikes me about this text...', and that is the kind of reading that we must finally achieve. But there is an obvious danger: can you make a text say virtually anything? That is where study comes in.

Study, that is, working on the text with the help of different methods of analysis, is aimed at helping us to discover that there is a distance between us and this text, that we cannot just rush straight into it, and that it is dangerous to project our feelings and our psychology on to it too quickly. This study should also make us read the text very carefully. There are texts which we know so well (or think that we know so well), from the Gospels, for example, that we no longer actually read them: we skip over them and repeat what people have always told us about them.[1]

Two methods of analysis

In fact, when confronted with a text, we instinctively use two ways of studying it. Let me give you a trivial example.

Old aunt Bertha has written to you. As you read her letter, you imagine her there and interpret the text from what you know of her.

Suppose for a moment that your aunt is complaining; if you know that she moans all the time, you will not pay much attention, and will simply say, 'That's just like her!' On the other hand, if you know that she is a very tough person, you may wonder why she is complaining, and feel that perhaps she is really ill. Or again, when you read a sentence in which she is attacking the young or a particular social group, you may say, 'It's her age,' or, 'It's the way she was brought up.' Here, then, you go beyond the text to imagine your aunt, and you try to see what she is trying to convey in the light of what you know of her.

Now suppose that while reading you come across a phrase you can't understand. For a few moments you stop looking for the meaning and pay attention to the grammar, that is, you try to sort out the elements which allow a phrase to make sense: 'Where is the subject? What is the object?' Once you have these elements in place, you read the text to make sense of it. Or again, you note that the letter begins in a pessimistic tone and ends in a better frame of mind; the atmosphere has changed a bit. You read the text once more to see what has caused this transformation (for example, it could be quite simply the fact of telling her troubles to someone). Here, you do not leave the text behind, but try to understand it in itself.

Specialists have taken up these two major ways of studying a text and have perfected them. We are now going to see how they use them, and how we can make use of them too.

1. Historical analysis

If you were reading a letter from aunt Bertha, you would ask yourself, 'What does she want to say?', and to find an answer, you would set the letter against the background of her life, past or present.

That is also the question that we ask when confronted with a biblical text: 'What does Luke want to say? What does the author of Genesis want to say?'

However, things are rather more complicated than that. You know your aunt Bertha. I don't, and if I read her letter I shall get some idea of her from her writing, the references she makes to particular events, the mentality she displays. I shall be able to put an age to her, detect something of her background and ideas, and I shall interpret the letter in terms of this person I have begun to imagine. Of course that's rather dangerous, and we have to be aware of that: I am inventing a person from the text and then interpreting the text in the light of what I think I know of the person.

Similarly, we know Luke or the author of Genesis only from their texts. So we must tread carefully, and constantly check what we are saying.

1. For example, we always talk about the 'adoration of the shepherds' in connection with Luke 2.1–20. But read the text! You will see that the shepherds do not come to adore, but only to deliver a 'sermon' to Mary!

11

How to place an author

It is easy enough to place aunt Bertha, because she is a contemporary. But as soon as she refers to the 1914–1918 war, I am obliged to recall what I have read in books. The books of the Bible were put together two or three thousand years ago. To place them, we shall have to use, among other things, information coming from:

- **History** which we know from the Bible and also from the documents of other peoples.

- **The literature** of the time: the Jews, exiled in Babylon, heard the great Mesopotamian legends about the flood; Jewish sermons from the time of Jesus show us how people understood scripture in those days.

- **Archaeology:** the city of Jericho was in ruins when Joshua took it; the pool with five porticos, mentioned by John, has been discovered in Jerusalem.

This work is obviously restricted to specialists. Fortunately, however, they are concerned to pass on the most important results of their research. There are plenty of excellent popular accounts, some of which are mentioned on page 115. And you can use the introductions and notes in your Bible, which will provide essential information.

How to place a story

We imagine all too easily that the author of a story is no more than a tape recorder giving an exact rendering of words and actions. Now an author speaks to us as much about his life and about his age as about the event which he reports. Here are some examples.

Luther lived in the sixteenth century. Suppose we read two books about him by Catholics, one written about 1900 and the other today. The first will say something like this. By his pride Luther, a defrocked monk who seduced a nun, set Europe and the church on fire and caused a great deal of bloodshed. The second will say: Luther had his failings, like all of us, but above all he was a monk with a passionate concern for God, haunted by the question of man's salvation. He saw that the church needed to be reformed and to return to the Bible, and the church pushed him out. We can learn things about Luther from these two books, but above all we shall learn how ecumenism has made its mark on Catholics between 1900 and today!

The old couple I mentioned earlier were describing their marriage on the eve of their golden wedding. To understand that marriage, I have to put it in the context of 1930.

But I also have to put it in the context of 1980, because they were also describing it in terms of the half century which has since passed.

Similarly, a biblical author tells the story of Abraham differently, depending on whether he is writing in the happy days of David or, five hundred years later, in a camp of exiles in Babylon. The words of Jesus must be understood in the light of the history of the thirties, but also in the light of the communities who wrote them down towards 80 or 90.

That, very briefly, is the concern of historical analysis: to put a text back in its historical context, in the different moments of history when it came into being, in an attempt to see what the author wanted to say. (The method is sometimes called historical-critical, to show that we keep a critical point of view when putting ourselves in the context of this history.)

Materialist analysis

'That shows the way she was brought up', we might think in reading some remark in aunt Bertha's letter. That means that when we speak, although we imagine the words are ours, they are often our social background and our education talking through us.

In placing texts in their historical context, materialist analysis is attentive to this aspect. A text is also a product of the social, economic and political conditions of its day. This method is called 'materialist' because it deliberately uses the analytical framework developed by Marxism. (You can use this framework without being compelled to accept all Marxist theory.)

2. Structuralist analysis

Let's go back to aunt Bertha's letter. Faced with an incomprehensible sentence, we shall stop looking for its meaning for a moment to sort out the elements in it (subject, object and so on) which allow a sentence to have meaning.

Now from the beginning of the twentieth century a new science of the study of language has come into being: semiotics (from a Greek word *semeion*, meaning sign) studies these signs, which are the elements of language or the conditions of meaningful language.

Specialists in semiotics teach us that there is not only a grammar of phrases but also a grammar of the text. Just as when writing a sentence we respect a certain number of rules (fortunately, without thinking about them!), so when we write a text (a letter, a story. . .), we respect other rules. We cannot study them here. You will find some of them in the explanation given on page 15.

We must note just one of the chief characteristics of this method. With the historical method, we go beyond the text to interpret it in the light of what the author wanted to say. Here, we try not to go beyond the text, but to study it in itself, independently of the intentions of the author ('the author is dead!'); we move around the text, in every direction, forgetting what we already know (or think we know) of it, and leaving aside what we want to find there, looking at it only for itself. For us, that is the chief advantage of this method.

Imagine a couple of friends taking a walk in the woods. One loves mushrooms. That's all he sees; for him, woods mean mushrooms. His friend is unaware of them, and treads on them without noticing; for him woods mean birds, or stones, or trees. It is the same when we read a text. Unconsciously, we already have some idea: we are in search of a particular piece of information or we are looking for some form of comfort, and that is all we see. That explains why we so easily misunderstand one another. You might imagine these friends beginning by paying as comprehensive a visit as possible to the woods, each forgetting their own interests: they will try to see everything, birds, trees, mushrooms. . . After that, if they so wish, they can go out looking for mushrooms. They will no longer be tempted to say that woods mean mushrooms; they will know that they have chosen to look for mushrooms, but that woods offer other possibilities.

The advantage of structuralist analysis, even practised in a very rough and ready way, is to force us to look at the text from the greatest possible number of perspectives, forgetting our own viewpoint as we look at the text. After that, in our own personal reading, we may perhaps retain only one perspective, but we shall know that others exist. And our reading will be enriched.

3. A parable

I shall sum up what I've just said with the help of a parable. I am listening to a record with a friend – say it is a Mozart symphony. Each of us will hear it differently; I may find it joyful while my friend finds it sad. Each person listens as they are, as they are feeling at that moment, and they project their feelings on to the work.

Our interpretations are so different that we decide to study the symphony, so that we are better able to come to some agreement. With the help of a score, we study the work itself, analysing the movements, the entries of the various subjects, the instrumentation, and so on. Then we leave the work and read a book on the life of Mozart, to see what he wanted to do. By using these two methods we shall discover a great deal, and dispense with certain personal interpretations. That's interesting. But a symphony wasn't written to be studied, but to be listened to.

Now we put the record on again, to listen to it anew. Our study will have helped us to do that better, but now we forget this study and simply devote ourselves to the pleasure of hearing the symphony. We give it a meaning, we discover in it a new delight in life. And that is the essential thing.

Substitute read for listen and book for record and you have the essentials of what I have tried to say in this section.

Seal belonging 'to Shema', servant of Jeroboam'. Found at Megiddo (eighth century BC)

A 'tool box'

First contact

Read the text. Note your spontaneous reactions: what strikes you, what you like, what amazes you, what raises questions for you.

Studying the text

Go back to the text without any explanatory notes from your Bible or any other help. If it is not too long, you might copy it out. Go through it (if necessary, using coloured pencils) and mark:

The text itself

- words or expressions which keep recurring, correspond or contrast.
- those involved in the action (people or things): note what they do, what they say, what happens to them.
- places and movements. Are certain places connected with a particular person or idea?
- indications of time: the tenses of verbs, other pointers.

As a result of all this, see what is happening in the text. Who is doing or looking for what? Who (or what) is helping in this search? is getting in the way? What happens between the beginning and the end of the text? Can you see any change? In whom or in what? How does it happen? What stages are involved? Who or what brings about this change?

The text put back in its context

This text is part of a larger whole (book, chapter). How does it fit into this whole? What is its place? What does it contribute?

The text in the setting of its time

With the help of the notes in your Bible or other aids, you can ask yourself:

- When was this text written? What was the situation of the people or the author at that particular time?
- Do some words or expressions have a meaning peculiar to that particular time?
- What is the literary genre of this text (see page 25)?
- Are there similar texts to this period, in the Bible or outside it? Does this OT text take up themes from the Bible? What does it add? Does it take up themes known in Egyptian or Mesopotamian literature? What are the similarities? What are the differences? Does this NT text take up Jewish themes from the time of Christ? or OT texts? In that case, how do they illuminate it?
- If there are similar texts in the Bible, in particular in the Gospels (you may often find references in the margin of your Bible), compare them. Note the similarities and the differences. How does this help you to understand the text better?
- This text was produced by a community for a community. Who is talking to whom? What question are they answering?

A check

Go back to the questions you noted down at the beginning. Can you answer them?

Reading the text

Now put aside this book and your 'tool box', and read the text. What does it say to you? How does it help you to live?

...hen you get out your tool box, the aim is not to use ...e tools but, say, to strip down an engine. Here I have ...ought together a number of tools which may help you ...strip down a text: the aim is not to use all of them.

First contact

...is first reading is too often the only one that we do. ...allows us to discover a little about the text, but above ...to discover ourselves: what are our chief interests, ...r preoccupations.
...f you are working as a group, put down the questions ...t do not try to answer them straight away: you will run ...e risk of getting bogged down in minor problems. ...ke them up again after your study.

Studying the text

...re we make use of the important methods I men-...ned above. The first questions are inspired more by ...ucturalist analysis, and the later ones by the historical ...thod. The aim is not to make the method work per-...tly, but to study a text.

The text itself

...ese questions may seem to be too scholarly or too ...ldish. Their chief concern is to make you look at the ...t very closely, forgetting preconceived ideas. Do not ...sitate to spend time on them: you will find that this ...ys off.
...bove all, pay attention to all the contrasts. We can ...y think by means of contrasts. Saying that a house ...arge makes sense, only because we compare it – in ...minds, at any rate – with an apartment and not a ...er block.
... story begins when there is a need, and it ends when ...need has been met. The whole aim of the story is ...show us the stages which are gone through for this ...to be achieved, and the obstacles that have to be ...mounted on the way. The various elements in the ...on (people or things) are organized around this ...rch for what is lacking; they can be rearranged into ...categories:

...ender → object → recipient
↑
...upport → subject ← opposition.

Here is a trivial illustration. I see that my neighbour Paul is thirsty: the object that he lacks is a drink. I ask Peter to go and get him something to drink. As the sender, I set up Peter as the subject to go to look for what Paul, the recipient, needs. If Peter is truly to be the subject, he must be willing (he might refuse), know-ledgeable (where to find the drink) and able (he must have some money). He will find support from those who tell him what he needs to know (where the refrigerator is), or what he needs to have (money), and opponents who may put obstacles in his way. A number of people may be in opposition, help one another, lack something, but they will form a single group.

You must remember that at this point we are not yet looking for meaning: we are trying to sort out the ele-ments which allow a text to make sense. Be ready to spend time on this research: you will find that as a result the text says much more to you.

The text in its context

We have become far too accustomed to reading texts in tiny fragments, particularly as a result of lectionaries at the mass or in other services. Put them back in their proper contexts; they will often take on a new flavour.

The text in its time

This is the point at which we use the historical method. Now is the time to read the introductions and notes in your Bible, or other aids (commentaries, which go through a text verse by verse); usually you will find that they provide all the information you need. You may also find an atlas of the Bible useful.

The last question is important: do not forget to ask why people wanted to report this event or these words; they do not do so as a matter of course, but in answer to a question that was raised at the time.

Check

By now you should have found an answer to the ques-tions you asked at the beginning. If not, write them down and ask someone with more knowledge when you have a chance.

Reading the text

This is the object of all the work that you have been doing so far. Spend time on it. You might like to try to rewrite the text in such a way that it speaks to you now.

4. A people stamped by its geography

Look at the map of the Near East on the opposite page. Note where there are seas and deserts. That explains how civilizations grew up and developed in three main regions, in the plains and the valleys.

The great civilizations

To the south, in the Nile valley, from about 3000 BC Egypt becomes an important people, governed by dynasties of kings (Pharaohs) living sometimes in the north (Memphis) and sometimes in the south (Thebes). The history of Egypt is usually divided up in terms of dynasties. Thus the Exodus probably took place under the Nineteenth Dynasty (about 1250).

To the north, on the plains of Asia Minor, the Hittites flourished. They were extremely powerful for about 1500 years, but had virtually disappeared by biblical times.

To the east we have the expanses of Mesopotamia (from the Greek, meaning the area between the rivers). This region is also called the fertile crescent. Magnificent civilizations grew up there side by side and gave way to one another, disappearing only to return to power some centuries later. Chief of these in the south are Sumer, Akkad and Babylonia, with Assyria in the north. This is the region which is now Iraq. Further east, in present-day Iran, the Medes emerged, to be followed by the Persians.

Other peoples later came from the west, from present-day Europe, to invade the Near East: the Greeks, three centuries before Christ, and the Romans, in the first century BC.

What happens when great peoples are neighbours? They fight! 'At the return of spring, when kings set out to war,' says the Bible, as naturally as we say, 'At the return of autumn, when people go out hunting again. . .' But in order to fight, they have to make contact with or to invade one another, and to do that it was necessary to move through the narrow corridor between the Mediterranean and the Arabian desert.

The one problem was that the tiny people in whom we are interested, Israel, lived in this corridor! So we can understand how much its life depended on the power of other nations. As a buffer state between the great powers, it served as a forward post for now one, now another. And it was tempted to make alliances with one or the other.

To have an idea of the way in which these powers succeeded one another, you should now read the contents of the boxes in the map on the right. The numbers indicate the order in which they intervened in the history of Israel. If you want more detail, look at an atlas or a chronological table of the history of Israel. There may be one in your Bible.

Canaan

In the Bible or in extra-biblical texts the word Canaan sometimes denotes a people and sometimes a country.

The country of Canaan is roughly equivalent to present-day Palestine. You will find a schematic map of it on page 44. Look at the map. The country is divided, vertically, into several regions.

A coastal plain extends along the Mediterranean, divided by Mount Carmel.

The central region is made up of a plain (Galilee) and hill country (Samaria Judah).

Finally, to the east we have the strange valley of the Jordan. Look at the indications of height: the source of the river, at the foot of Mount Hermon, is about 200 metres above sea level. At Lake Huleh, it is still 68 metres above sea level, but by Lake Tiberias, about 15 kilometres lower, it is already 212 metres below sea level and it flows into the Dead Sea at 392 metres below sea level.

This is the country in which, in the twelfth century BC, those tribes settled which, around 1000 BC, became the kingdom of David and Solomon. On Solomon's death the kingdom divided into two: in the south, the kingdom of Judah, with Jerusalem as its capital, and in the north, that of Israel, the capital of which was Samaria.

Also round about the twelfth century the Philistines settled to the south, on the Mediterranean coast. Some centuries before the birth of Christ the Greeks gave their name to the country: Palestine, or the land of the Philistines.

Another small kingdom was to play an important role in the history of Israel, that of Damascus.

We can already imagine to what extent the history of Israel would depend on that of other peoples. It remains for us to see how its thought and ideas would be stamped by other civilizations.

MACEDONIA

GREECE

Athens Ephesus

⑤ GREECE
Alexander of Macedon
conquered Palestine in
333. After him his generals
were dominant in turn:
LAGIDS of Egypt, 320 – 198.
SELEUCIDS of Antioch,
198 – 63.

• Bogazkoy (or Hattu)

HITTITES

Tarsus • Issus

⑤

⑥

⑥ ROME
Pompey triumphs over the
Seleucids in 63 BC.
From then on Palestine
is under Roman rule.
Titus captures Jerusalem
in AD 70.

Antioch
Hamath

④ ②

Tyre Damascus

Samaria
Jerusalem

Alexandria

① EGYPT
Controlled Canaan long
before Israel settled
there.
After its zenith under
the Ramessids (Nineteenth
Dynasty) it steadily declined
but still caused Israel trouble.
The LAGIDS (or
Ptolemies, descendants
of one of Alexander's
generals) ruled there
till 63 BC. They
dominated Palestine from
320 to 198.

①

• Cairo
Memphis

SINAI

MIDIAN

• El Amarna

Nag Hammadi
• Karnak
Thebes • Luxor

ARABIA

② ASSYRIA
Expanded during ninth century.
Captured Samaria in 721.
Declined rapidly after
being defeated in Egypt
in 660. Nineveh captured
by Babylon 612.

ASSYRIA

• Haran

Carchemish

Nineveh • Khorsabad

Mari Assur **BABYLONIA**

③

AKKAD

Babylon

SUMER

• Ur

• Ecbatana

④ PERSIA
A great power from
Cyrus on (550 – 529).
Conquered the Middle
East. Conquered by
Alexander 330.

• Susa

PERSIA

③ BABYLON
Supreme in 18th century
BC with Hammurabi.
Then subject to Assyria.
All powerful after 625.
Captures Jerusalem in 597
and destroys it in 587.
The Persians destroy
Babylon in 538.

0 50 100 150 200 250 miles

0   100   200   300   400 km

5. A people stamped by the mentality of the Near East

Throughout its history, Israel was in contact with neighbouring peoples and was familiar with their chief literary works. We shall have occasion to reread some extracts from them. Here I shall try to put these great civilizations in context.

Egyptian hymn to the sun god Aten

Here are some extracts from this hymn, composed by Pharaoh Akhenaten.

You shine out in beauty on the horizon of heaven,
O living disc, the beginning of life.
When you have appeared on the eastern horizon,
you have filled every land with your perfection.
When you set on the western horizon,
the earth lies in darkness as in death.
The earth lies in silence,
for the one who created it has gone to rest on his horizon.
Then the earth becomes bright: you have arisen on the horizon.
As solar disc, you shine by day.
Men awaken and stand on their feet.
Their arms are bent in worship, because you appear.
The whole land goes to work.
All beasts are satisfied with their pasture,
the trees and plants become green.
The birds flutter in their nests,
raising their wings in worship before your spirit.
The ships sail upstream and down.
The fish in the river dart before your face.
You make the seed grow in women,
make fluid into mankind.
How manifold are your works!
They are hidden from the face of man,
O sole God, apart from whom there is no other.
You have made people for yourself,
the Lord of all of them,
wearying himself with them,
the Lord of the whole land, rising for them.
You are in my heart. . .

(from *Near Eastern Religious Texts relating to the Old Testament*, SCM Press and Westminster Press 1978, pp. 16ff.)

Egyptian thinking was shaped by the country. The Egyptian lived in a radiant part of the world: he felt a degree of anxiety as he watched the sun setting in the evening, though experience had taught him that it would appear the next morning, having conquered the powers of the night. ·Divinized under various names, the sun was the first of the gods, who had engendered other gods and men. In the adjacent box you can read some passages of the great hymn to the sun god composed about 1350 BC by Pharaoh Akhenaten; the author of Psalm 104 may have been inspired by it.

The Nile tended to flood, but this happened at fixed times and the floods brought the fertile alluvium and the water needful for life.

The Egyptian temperament was naturally optimistic; the gods were good and watched over men. After death, a new and splendid life awaited the faithful, even if this life was somewhat impersonal.

In contrast, **Mesopotamian thinking** was by and large fundamentally pessimistic. Those who lived in this area inhabited a valley in which the floods were unpredictable, sometimes producing real 'deluges' of which many traces have been found in archaeological excavations. There were frequent invasions of nomads from the Arabian desert, or surging in from the plains of Iran.

So, too, the Mesopotamian gods were usually capricious, constantly struggling among themselves: man tends to appear as a terrified mortal seeking to avoid the repercussions of their anger. According to the Gilgamesh epic, the gods have given him death for his portion and they have filled him with deceit. The kingdom of the dead is a sorry one: the shades of the dead are reunited for a joyless destiny.

Here are some of the great myths from which we shall have occasion to quote extracts.

The epic of Atrahasis (which means the very intelligent) is known to us from a copy found in Babylon and dating from 1600 BC. In this long poem of 1645 lines, we are shown the gods wearied by all the chores they have to do. They decide to create man to do the work; they form him of clay mixed with the blood of a god whose throat has been cut. But mankind proliferates, makes trouble and wearies the gods, who inflict various scourges, culminating in the flood. However, the god Ea warns a man who builds a boat, and puts his family in it, along with a pair of every animal.

The poem Enuma Elish (named after its first two words, meaning 'when on high') is also very ancient; in its present form it must have been written about 1100 BC. At the very beginning there were two sexual principles, Apsu, the sweet water, and Tiamat (whose name can be found again in the *tehom* – abyss – of Gen. 1.2), the salt waters of the sea. All the gods take their origin from these. Because they annoy her, Tiamat wants to kill them, but Marduk overcomes her, divides her in half like an oyster, and makes her into the vault of heaven. Then he creates man from the blood of a rebel god.

The Gilgamesh epic is beyond question the most famous work from ancient Mesopotamia. Created in Sumer, it developed over more than a thousand years in Assyria and Babylon, and was known by the Hittites, having been copied again in Palestine. In its present form it is composed of twelve cantos.

Gilgamesh, a Sumerian hero, becomes unbearable to the gods because of his pride. They produce a rival, Enkidu, a monster living with the wild beasts. He is humanized by a woman and becomes a friend of Gilgamesh: together, they accomplish all kinds of exploits. However, one day Enkidu dies; Gilgamesh discovers the atrociousness of death and sets off in search of immortality. The hero of the flood gives him the secret of the herb of life. Gilgamesh succeeds in getting hold of it, but a serpent snatches it from him, and Gilgamesh has to resign himself to death.

Canaanite thought has been better known since the discovery, in 1929, of the library of the city of Ugarit, present-day Ras Shamra in Syria. The heyday of Ugaritic civilization was in 1500 BC, about the time of the patriarchs: Abraham, Isaac and Jacob.

The chief god is called El, often presented in the form of a bull. (One of the names for God in the Bible is Elohim, a solemn plural of the word El – the equivalent of our 'royal we'.) This religion pays homage to the deified forces of nature: Baal, god of storm and rain, sometimes called 'the rider on the clouds' (like God in Ps. 68.5), and Anath, his sister, later called Astarte: she is the goddess of war, love and fertility.

Israel, and above all the kingdom of Samaria, was to be attracted by Canaanite religion and the sexual cult offered to the naked goddess in the high places, with its rites aimed at obtaining fertility for land and flocks.

The organization of the universe in Babylon

The poem Enuma Elish tells of the birth of the gods through Apsu, the male principle, and Tiamat, the female principle. Tiamat wants to destroy the young gods, who are disturbing her. They delegate their power to Marduk (the god of Babylon). He kills Tiamat and the gods allied with her. Then he forms the world from her body.

Marduk strengthened his hold on the vanquished gods,
and turned back to Tiamat whom he had bound.
With his unsparing mace he crushed her skull,
then the lord rested and contemplated her corpse,
intent on dividing the form and doing skilful works.
He split it like a dried fish,
set up one half and made it the firmament,
drew a skin over it, posted guards
and instructed them not to let its water escape.

(*Near Eastern Religious Texts*, p. 83)

One might compare this myth with the story in Gen. 1 and also with a different myth often represented in Egyptian sculpture.

The organization of the universe in Egypt

Shu, the god of the air, separates Nut, his daughter, the heavenly vault, from Geb, his son, the earth (Egyptian papyrus from between 1100 and 950 BC).

A hymn, written about 1400 BC, celebrates the sun god Amon, who goes through the night to rise upon sleeping humanity. He is father of all the gods, and they sing his praises:

They say to you, 'Welcome, father of the fathers of all the gods,
who raised the heaven and laid out the earth,
who made what is and created what will be,
we offer hymns to you because you have wearied yourself with us.'
(*Near Eastern Religious Texts*, p. 15).

We shall discover the nature of **biblical thinking** as we go along. However, it is good to emphasize here a basic feature which distinguishes it from the other patterns of thinking to which I have referred.

Shema Israel, Adonai hedad! Hear, O Israel, the Lord is one! That is the essential faith of the people as Deuteronomy puts it (6.4). Israel is aware of being addressed by its God, and the people respond to him in love. By way of a caricature, we might represent mythical thought by an arrow which begins with man and returns to him: man projects a deity on to the beyond and then, by means of ritual, he tries to gain control over this deity, to enlist his service.

deity

ritual

man

In the Bible, the arrow goes the other way. God addresses man and man responds. Here ritual becomes the expression of the response.

God

ritual

man

The ritual may be the same, but it has changed its meaning. Here is an example. A child may give its mother a bunch of flowers in order to be allowed to go to the cinema; the same child may give the same bunch of flowers to its mother on Mothering Sunday. In the latter case this is a disinterested gesture meant to express a response to its mother's love. It is a form of recognition. That is the basic attitude of eucharist, thanksgiving, to which we shall have occasion to return later.

However, now that we have put these various tools in our luggage, it is time to set off to discover the Bible.

The god Hadad (called Baal in the Ugaritic texts) standing on a bull which serves as a pedestal. He is holding bolts of lightning in his hand (eighth century BC). This calls to mind the cult of the Baals and the bulls which were installed by king Jeroboam at Dan and Bethel.

Nature myths in Canaan

A poem found at Ugarit celebrates Baal and Mot. Baal is the god of storms and rain, Mot is the god of death. So here we have an evocation of the agonizing problem of fertility. Baal aids men by making the soil fertile with his rain; in this way he has been absorbed by Mot, the god of the underworld. Will the water remain captive in the earth, bringing about a drought?

This extract from the poem shows El, the supreme God, guessing that Baal will be reborn, that the rain will return.

Someone announces the dream that El is going to have:

If the all-powerful Baal is alive,
if the prince, the lord of the earth, exists,
in a dream, kindly El benign,
the heavens rain down fat,
the torrents flow with honey.

El has this dream and rejoices:

In a dream, the kindly El benign,
in a vision the Creator of creatures sees
the heavens rain down fat,
the torrents flow with honey.
Joyfully the kindly El cries out,
'Now I can sit and rest,
for all-powerful Baal is alive,
the prince exists, the Lord of the earth.'

In the Bible we can find the formula 'a land flowing with milk (or fatness) and honey' (see, for example, Ex. 3.8). We shall come up against this problem of fertility – to whom is it to be attributed, to the Baals or to God? – when we study the northern kingdom (page 47).

Towards the end of this book (on p. 115), you will find a list of others which will help you to make a fuller study of the subjects covered in this guide, if you so wish. However, remember that the essential thing is to read the texts themselves. You can sort things out very well with a good Bible, its introduction and notes, and this book.

You will find Walter Beyerlin, *Near Eastern Religious Texts relating to the Old Testament*, a useful source book for exploring the thought world of the peoples of Mesopotamia, Ugarit and Canaan (SCM Press and Westminster Press 1978, 299pp.).

MYTH

On a number of occasions we have come across the word 'myth'. What does it mean?

The ancient myths appear as stories presenting gods, goddesses and ancient heroes. On a first reading we may be somewhat disconcerted, but we shall very soon be caught up in them, because we can see that they are concerned with the great questions that we ask ourselves and which are taken further here. Where does the world come from? Why does man exist at all? Why is there suffering and death? Why is there this mysterious attraction between the sexes? What relationship do human beings have with the divine?

However, instead of discussing these problems in profound and difficult books, as happens today, the myths discuss them in 'strip cartoons'.

Let's take a present-day example: the Miss World contest. In a time when royalty hardly exists any more, a queen is chosen and surrounded by her courtiers.

Our existence is often a grey one, with all the tedium of daily life; this queen is crowned and receives magnificent presents. All this helps to put this contest in another world, a dream world, an unreal world. But it expresses the desire of every woman to be beautiful, to be rich, to succeed, and the desire of every man to admire feminine beauty. However, there is another side to it. A woman might be alienated by this myth, might no longer be free to be herself. For example, we can see how girls copy the hair-style of Miss World or try to reproduce her measurements, though it may not suit their kind of beauty. The photo-romances in some magazines in which the secretary marries the boss's son play the same role: they allow the secretary to dream, perhaps enable her to live, but she does so in a dream world, and in the end she neglects her work and thinks of nothing but how to seduce her boss's son.

Putting it at its simplest, we might say: myth consists of taking a great question that we ask ourselves and projecting it, in the form of a story, on an unreal world, on a time before time began, the time of the gods when man did not yet exist. This history of the gods is our own, transposed into another setting. In that way it becomes the model that man must copy.

For example, people ask about the meaning of the attraction between the sexes or how to obtain fertility. They imagine a world outside time, in which gods and goddesses fall in love, have intercourse, and produce children. If they are fertile, our soil and our flocks will also be fertile, since these deities are simply the unreal transposition of our existence. It is therefore necessary to compel them to be fertile: the aim of religious rites is to force the gods to come together in intercourse. Union with sacred prostitutes, in Babylon or the high places of Canaan, was not an orgy, but a religious rite aimed at securing the fertility of the soil.

So all these mythical stories are extremely serious: they are the first reflections of humanity. We can understand why the Bible took up this language to express its own reflections. However, it transformed the language profoundly. To put it briefly, one might say that it made the photo-romance into a psychological novel.

If we read a good psychological novel, a romance, we will find a couple, with their joys and their problems. . . At first sight it may look just like a photo-romance, but in fact it is the opposite. It does not offer us escape into a dream; on the contrary, it recalls us to our everyday life because it is made up of a thousand and one observations by the author, taken from the lives of different couples. So he compels us to reflect on our existence and take it in hand.

Inspired by these great myths, notably in the creation stories, the Bible rethinks them as a function of its faith in a sole God who intervenes in our history and wills for man to be free.

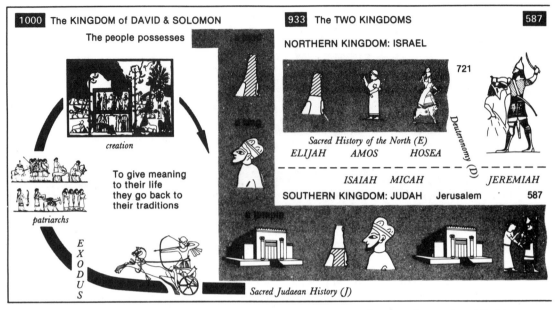

| 1000 The KINGDOM of DAVID & SOLOMON | 933 The TWO KINGDOMS | 587 |

The people possesses

creation

patriarchs

To give meaning
to their life
they go back to
their traditions

E
X
O
D
U
S

NORTHERN KINGDOM: ISRAEL

721

Sacred History of the North (E)
ELIJAH   AMOS   HOSEA

Deuteronomy (D)

ISAIAH   MICAH   JEREMIAH

SOUTHERN KINGDOM: JUDAH   Jerusalem   587

Sacred Judaean History (J)

The diagram above is meant to help you to place the great moments in the history of Israel.

The drawings reproduce paintings or sculptures from different periods. You will find them again, with a brief description, at the head of each chapter, and on pages 4, 20 and, above all, 122.

The diagram is a summary. It is important, because it indicates the route we are going to follow.

The kingdom of David and Solomon

About the year 1000, David captured Jerusalem and made it the capital of a kingdom bringing together the tribes of the south and the north. His son Solomon provided an organization for it.

In this way there was a land, a king and a Temple where God made himself present to his people.

This was also the beginning of literature. People began by writing down their memories of the past: the Exodus, or liberation from Egypt, became the fundamental experience in which God was discovered to be the liberator, the saviour; the story of the patriarchs (Abraham, Isaac and Jacob) was written to show how the promise of God to Abraham had been realized with David. The story even went back to the beginning of the world: God did not want only one people to be free, but all humanity.

The two kingdoms: Judah and Israel

On the death of Solomon in 933, the kingdom broke into two: in the south that of Judah, with Jerusalem as its capital; in the north that of Israel, whose capital was Samaria.

Judah remained faithful to the dynasty of David. The king made the nation a unity and represented it before God, this God who lived in the midst of his people in the Temple. The traditions begun under David and Solomon ended up in a Sacred Judaean History (or Sacred History of Judah). The prophets Isaiah and Micah preached.

Israel broke with the dynasty of David: the kings did not therefore have the same religious importance. It was the prophets who gathered the people together and maintained its faith, threatened by contact with Canaanite religion which revered the Baals (here you can see one riding on a bull). The traditions begun under David and

22

or the great moments of Israel

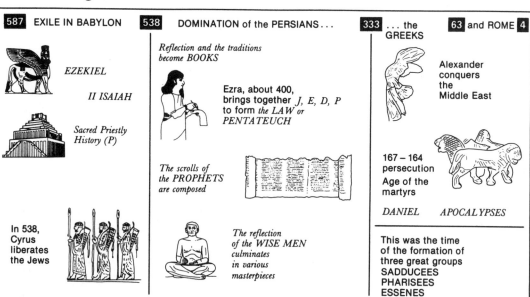

587 EXILE IN BABYLON **538** DOMINATION of the PERSIANS... **333** ... the GREEKS **63** and ROME **4**

EZEKIEL

II ISAIAH

Sacred Priestly History (P)

In 538, Cyrus liberates the Jews

Reflection and the traditions become BOOKS

Ezra, about 400, brings together *J, E, D, P* to form *the LAW or PENTATEUCH*

The scrolls of the PROPHETS are composed

The reflection of the WISE MEN culminates in various masterpieces

Alexander conquers the Middle East

167 – 164 persecution Age of the martyrs

DANIEL   *APOCALYPSES*

This was the time of the formation of three great groups
SADDUCEES
PHARISEES
ESSENES

Solomon ended up in a Sacred History of the North. The prophets Elijah, Amos and Hosea preached.

Collections of laws were made in the North. When they were taken up later in Judah, they were to become Deuteronomy.

In 721, Israel was destroyed by the Assyrians.

In 587, Judah was deported to Babylon.

Exile in Babylon

The people lived in exile for half a century. They had lost everything, their land and their king; would they also lose their faith in God? Prophets like Ezekiel and a disciple of Isaiah revived their hopes: the priests presented them once again with their traditions, to help them find meaning in their sufferings. This development ended up in the Sacred Priestly History.

Under Persian domination

In 538, the Persian king Cyrus freed the Jews. They settled in Palestine again. The community, purified by the sufferings of the exile, had a wretched existence.

Over the five previous centuries, the people had gone over their history several times, to find meaning and hope in each situation. These three sacred histories, which had already been composed, together with Deuteronomy, were brought together by Ezra, the priest-scribe, to form a unique book: the Law.

In addition, the reflection of the wise men, begun at the time of Solomon and even before, ended up in the production of masterpieces like Job, Proverbs and Tobit.

Under Greek and then Roman domination

In 333, Alexander conquered the Middle East and Greek language and culture spread there.

In 167, a successor of Alexander, king Antiochus, sought to force the Jews to renounce their faith, on pain of death. This was the time of the Israelite martyrs and the people who are known as the Maccabees. These events prompted the reflection of the authors of apocalypses: they awaited the end of time, when God would intervene.

In 63, Rome took over the Middle East. King Herod reigned from 40 BC to 4 BC.

1 The Exodus: A People Expresses its Faith

Pharaoh Ramses II at the battle of Kadesh (about 1200 BC)

We are setting out on a journey through the Old Testament: we are going to pass through the key moments in the history of Israel and see how Israel expressed its faith throughout its existence. However, when we leave for a foreign country, before getting into the coach it is a good thing to pause for a moment to review the route that has been suggested to us, to see the reasons for this or that excursion, to gather some information about the customs of the country and the way in which people express themselves. Similarly, before undertaking our journey we are going to stop, in this chapter, at a passage from the book of Exodus. That should get us into practice by discovering a number of things.

First, we are going to familiarize ourselves with reading and studying texts. This may seem a bit complicated, but that is only because we shall try to take an overall view by looking at everything at once. Don't be frightened! Everything will become clear as we go along.

We are going to make the acquaintance of what are called literary genres, or different ways of expressing the same thing. You don't write to your friends in the way that you write to the tax man.

We shall discover that the texts as we now read them in the Bible have a long history: they are made up from even earlier documents. That explains the apparent zig-zag course that we shall follow.

However, this study will not be purely intellectual. We shall discover that for Israel the liberation from Egypt was the foundation event which created Israel as a people. Israel kept going back to it, meditating on it in order to make sense of the present and find hope for the future.

Reading Exodus 12.1 to 13.16

First reading

Begin by reading the text straight through. Do not bother about the titles and notes in your Bible. If there are words and phrases that you don't understand properly, don't worry. We shall come back to them second time through. For the moment, just read the text and ask yourself:

What event is it talking about?

How is it talking about this event? Is it 'narrating it' (in which passages)? Is it deriving laws from it (in which passages)? Is a liturgical celebration being organized to celebrate this event (in which passages)?

Having read the text, try to give a title to the different parts you have discovered. That will compel you to be more precise about the 'literary genre' of these parts.

An Egyptian scribe (fifth dynasty, 2500–2350 BC)

Second reading

You can now take up certain points with the help of the notes in your Bible, or with other aids.

As you will discover, the texts were produced at different times. Don't spend too much time on this question now; you will understand it better at the end of the chapter.

These are liturgical texts. They show us how to preserve the memory of the event by celebrating it, and what meaning it gives to life today.

Israel took over two already existing festivals, but it changed their meaning and their connection with a historical event. There are, in fact, two kinds of festivals: some celebrate nature and recur every year (we celebrate New Year's Day, the beginning of the year); others celebrate an event which once took place

Literary genres

There are different ways of talking about the same thing. For example, we talk about the illness of a close friend in different ways to the sick person's family, the doctor and the social welfare people; we also talk about it after the friend is better in a different way from when he or she was hanging between life and death.

At a deeper level, these different ways of presenting things (or 'literary genres') correspond to different needs in the life of a group. Every group produces a certain number of texts. Take, for example, a small angling club: this will compose documents of a legal kind (the club rules); slogans or short phrases to advertise itself (Relax and go fishing. . .); stories, sometimes embellished stories, real 'epics', in which the catching of a roach is described as though it were the catching of a whale. There are also celebrations: drinks at the bar or the annual dinner.

Thus in order to exist, every society has to create a literature. A nation has its laws, its speeches, its celebrations, its stories about the past, its epics, its poems and its songs.

Consequently, the fact that Israel existed as a people gave rise to a whole literature of different kinds. Here are some of them.

Stories. We have to recall the past to give everyone a common mind. By hearing stories about our ancestors we become aware of belonging to the same family.

Epics. These, too, are accounts of the past, but their chief aim is to arouse enthusiasm and to celebrate heroes, even if it is necessary to exaggerate details in order to do so.

Laws give organization to a people and allow a common life.

The liturgy, celebrations, ritual (sacrifices, for example) express this common life, just as celebration meals bind the family together. Religious actions show the link between men and God.

Poems, canticles and psalms are the expressions of the sentiments and the faith of the people.

The oracles of the prophets – solemn words said to come from God – recall people to true faith.

Teaching by prophets and priests may be given under the form of instruction, but also as stories and tales (parables).

The wisdom writings are reflections on the great human questions: what is life, death, love? Why evil? Why suffering?

Be careful to distinguish literary genres

Each mode of expression, each genre, has its own kind of truth. One does not expect a collection of Asterix cartoons to be as exact as a history book. You don't read the creation story (Gen. 1) as a scientific account. It is a liturgical poem. Similarly, the account of the crossing of the Red Sea is not a newspaper account (Ex. 14): it is an epic.

Thus whenever possible, we should ask what literary genre a particular text is, and what kind of truth it conveys.

---

in history (in France they celebrate July 14, the Storming of the Bastille).

Every spring the nomads celebrated passover: they ate a lamb and used its blood to mark the poles of their tents, to ward off evil spirits. Israel took over this festival (Ex. 12.2–11, 21–22), but made it a remembrance of the liberation from Egypt (12.25–27).

Every spring, peasants celebrated the feast of unleavened bread: they rejoiced over the new crop, doing away with anything which recalled the old one. Israel took over this festival (12.15), but made it a remembrance of the liberation from Egypt (12.17, 39; 13.3–10).

Christians took over these festivals and extended their meanings: they celebrated the definitive freedom brought by Christ.

Israel did the same thing with the old custom of offering the very best to the deity: the firstborn of animals and sometimes of human beings. For them, this custom too became a remembrance of the liberation from Egypt (13.2, 14–15).

Studying a text: Ex. 13.17–14.31

Studying the account of the crossing of the Red Sea will allow us to discover what are called the Pentateuchal traditions.

First reading

Begin by reading this text in your Bible. At first sight it is a story which reads well enough. However, if you look closer, you will notice some strange things. What form does the 'miracle' take? In one instance the wind dries up the sea and the Egyptians get bogged down in the quicksand. In the other, God divides the sea so that the Hebrews can pass through. Sometimes, God himself fights; sometimes he gives orders to Moses, and Moses is the one who acts. The styles differ: sometimes the description is very specific and God is presented as a man who fights, puts spokes in the chariot wheels (in that case we say that the account is anthropomorphic, from a Greek word meaning 'in the form of a man'), and sometimes the story becomes very abstract: God speaks and it is his word which acts.

Observations of this kind made throughout the Pentateuch have led scholars to construct a hypothesis: the Pentateuch was composed from four traditions or documents, at one point collected together to form a single whole.

We are going to try to check this hypothesis by the account given here.

Second reading

Look at the story as it is laid out on pages 28–29. It is set out in three columns: I have taken the text out of a box so that the three traditions can be seen clearly (the fourth is not used here). Of course, there is some guesswork in this division, and sometimes it is by no means clear whether we should put a verse in one column or another. However, even if there are errors in detail, the general impression is important.

When it is laid out in this way, you can read the following text by going from one column to another and keeping to the order of the verses, or you can read each tradition separately by taking only one column. In this story the Elohistic tradition is less important, so to simplify our task, we shall study only the Yahwistic and the Priestly traditions.

Yahwistic tradition

Read this text, which is in the left-hand column. Who are the main characters (you can underline them in different colours)? What do the Egyptians want? Do they know how to get it? Have they the power? What do the Hebrews want? Who will show them how to get it? Who will give them the power?

What is the nature of the event?

Underline the words which keep occurring. Does the word 'see' always have the same meaning (see with one's eyes or with one's faith?)? Has 'fear' the same sense in vv. 1 and 13 as it has in v. 31 (with what other words is it in parallel in this verse)?

The aim of the text seems to be to show how the Hebrews passed from one kind of fear to another. How did this transformation come about? What significance does it have for the faith of the Hebrews and for our own?

Priestly tradition

Read the text, which is in the right-hand column. Here there is only one main character: who is he? What does he want? How does he act? Note all the expressions which keep occurring. Some of them will doubtless cause you problems (God hardened their heart): don't bother about that for the moment; we shall come back to it later (p. 63).

What God seeks is to glorify himself, to make himself known as Saviour. This is not vanity. 'The glory of God is for man to live', said St Irenaeus. God's glory consists in saving his people, and then he appears in the eyes of others as a God who saves, the Lord who protects. But the people have to allow themselves to be saved, to have confidence in God: this is the way in which man can sanctify the name of God, i.e. allow him to show that he is holy, the Lord. We shall see that again when we study the prophet Ezekiel (p. 66).

What is the nature of the event? Note the repetitions: God gives an order, then there is an account of how the order is carried out; this procedure is often used by the Priestly tradition (see the first account of the creation in Gen. 1). Here the important thing is the word of God which creates what it says. Compare the 'miracle' with Gen. 1; a similar theme emerges: God divides the waters and dry land appears (Ex. 14.16, 22, 29; Gen. 1.9, 10).

What meaning does that give to the story of the crossing of the Red Sea? To the creation narrative?

Pentateuchal traditions

Let's begin with a simple example: we have four different texts which tell us about Jesus: the four Gospels.

People have always wanted to bring them together to make a 'life of Jesus', putting into one narrative all the details that we find throughout these four books.

Suppose I ask a literary critic who knows nothing about the existence of the Gospels to study this 'life of Jesus'. He will soon sense that the book does not come from a single hand; for example, he will notice the changes in style (the very detailed descriptions given by Mark and the well-constructed speeches from John), the differences in vocabulary, and so on. And he will put forward the hypothesis that the 'Life' was composed from different documents. He will then try to rediscover these documents by dividing the text back into several columns, corresponding to our four Gospels.

If we now compare the result of his work with our Gospels, we shall doubtless note two things.

'Holes': when Mark and Luke, for example, describe the same episode, the 'life of Jesus' will keep only one version and the other will get lost.

Mistakes: it is not always easy to recognize whether a small fragment of text comes from Matthew or from Luke, and our critic may make mistakes.

Now let's go back to the Pentateuch. These five volumes (which is what the Greek word Pentateuch means) form a single work. However, for a long time scholars have guessed that it was composite, and they have produced the hypothesis that the whole work was a collection of four main traditions written at different times.

Thus the Pentateuch would be written in several stages:

1. Underlying it is the personality of Moses and the events of the Exodus.

2. Subsequently, small units were composed and handed down, orally or perhaps already in writing: stories, laws, speeches, meditations on the event, liturgical celebrations etc.

3. At different periods, scribes (prophets, priests, wise men) collected together these small units to make connected narratives: the four documents.

4. Finally, these four traditions were collected together in a single five-volume work.

We shall have occasion to study these documents in detail. For the moment, it will be enough to put them quickly into context.

1. The Yahwistic tradition (denoted by the letter J) is so called because from the beginning it calls God Yahweh (explaining why it is known as J and not Y is rather a complicated business – ultimately this goes back to a less accurate way of reproducing the Hebrew equivalent of Y with a J). It doubtless comes from the time of Solomon, about 950 BC, and originated in royal circles in Jerusalem. The king has an important place there; he is the one who gives the faith unity.

2. The Elohistic tradition (denoted by the letter E) calls God Elohim. It came into being, perhaps around 750 BC, in the northern kingdom, after the united kingdom of David and Solomon had split into two. Clearly stamped with the message of prophets like Elijah and Hosea, it attaches great importance to prophets.

These two traditions were brought together in Jerusalem, about 700 BC. This fusion, which is sometimes called Jehovist (JE), was not a simple addition; it was the occasion for completing and developing certain traditions.

3. The Deuteronomistic tradition (letter D) is contained above all in Deuteronomy, but it has influenced other books. It was begun in the northern kingdom and completed in Jerusalem.

4. The Priestly tradition (letter P) came into being during the Babylonian exile, in the years 587–538 and later. After the deportation, the priests reread their traditions to keep up the people's faith and hope.

These four traditions and their developments were in turn collected together in a single volume: the Pentateuch. This work seems to have been finished about 400 and has often been attributed to Ezra the priest.

In this first chapter we shall simply try to familiarize ourselves with these traditions. In subsequent chapters we shall take each of them up again, one by one. That will take us through the Pentateuch four times, each time keeping to a single tradition.

For further detail about the Pentateuchal traditions, see 'How Israel Became a Nation' by Ernest Nicholson, in *A Basic Introduction to the Old Testament*, edited by Robert C. Walton, SCM Press and John Knox Press 1980, pp. 42–58.

Exodus 13–14

Yahwist	*Elohist*	Priestly

13

[17]When Pharaoh let the people go, God did not lead them by way of the land of the Philistines, although that was near; for God said, 'Lest the people repent when they see war, and return to Egypt.' [18]But God led the people round by the way of the wilderness toward the Red Sea. And the people of Israel went up out of the land of Egypt equipped for battle. [19]And Moses took the bones of Joseph with him; for Joseph had solemnly sworn the people of Israel, saying, 'God will visit you; then you must carry my bones with you from here.'

[20]And they moved on from Succoth, and encamped at Etham, on the edge of the wilderness. [21]And the Lord went before them by day in a pillar of cloud to lead them along the way, and by night in a pillar of fire to give them light, that they might travel by day and by night; [22]the pillar of cloud by day and the pillar of fire by night did not depart from before the people.

14

[1]Then the Lord said to Moses, [2]Tell the people of Israel to turn back and encamp

[2b]in front of Pi-hahiroth, between Migdol and the sea, in front of Baal-zephon; you shall encamp over against it, by the sea.

[3]For Pharaoh will say of the people of Israel, "They are entangled in the land; the wilderness has shut them in." [4]And I will harden Pharaoh's heart, and he will pursue them and I will get glory over Pharaoh and all his host; and the Egyptians shall know that I am the Lord.' And they did so.

[5]When the king of Egypt was told that the people had fled,

[5b]the mind of Pharaoh and his servants was changed toward the people, and they said, 'What is this we have done, that we have let Israel go from serving us?' [6]So he made ready his chariot

[6b]and took his army with him,

[7]and took six hundred picked chariots

[7b]and all the other chariots of Egypt with officers over all of them.

[8]And the Lord hardened the heart of Pharaoh king of Egypt and he pursued the people of Israel as they went forth defiantly.

[9]The Egyptians pursued them,

all Pharaoh's horses and chariots, and his horsemen and his army,

and overtook them encamped at the sea, by Pi-hahiroth, in front of Baal-zephon. [10]When Pharaoh drew near, the people of Israel lifted up their eyes, and behold, the Egyptians were marching after them; and they were in great fear. And the people of Israel cried out to the Lord;

[11]And they said to Moses, 'Is it because there are no graves in Egypt that you have taken us away to die in the wilderness? [12]Is not this what we said to you in Egypt, 'Leave us alone and let us serve the Egyptians? For it would have been better for us to serve the Egyptians than to die in the wilderness.'

28

¹³And Moses said to the people, 'Fear not, stand firm, and see the salvation of the Lord, which he will work for you today; for the Egyptians whom you see today, you shall never see again. ¹⁴The Lord will fight for you, and you have only to be still.'

¹⁵The Lord said to Moses, 'Why do you cry to me? Tell the people of Israel to go forward. ¹⁶Lift up your rod, and stretch out your hand over the sea and divide it, that the people of Israel may go on dry ground through the sea. ¹⁷And I will harden the heart of the Egyptians, so that they shall go in after them, and I will get glory over Pharaoh and all his host, his chariots, and his horsemen. ¹⁸And the Egyptians shall know that I am the Lord, when I have gotten glory over Pharaoh, his chariots and his horsemen.'

¹⁹Then the angel of God who went before the host of Israel moved and went behind them;

and the pillar of cloud moved from before them and stood behind them, ²⁰coming between the host of Egypt and the host of Israel. And there was the cloud and the darkness; and it lit up the night;

and the night passed without one coming near the other all night.

²¹Then Moses stretched out his hand over the sea,

^{21b}and the Lord drove the sea back by a strong east wind all night, and made the sea dry land,

^{21c}and the waters were divided. ²²And the people of Israel went into the midst of the sea on dry ground, the waters being a wall to them on their right hand and on their left. ²³The Egyptians pursued and went in after them into the midst of the sea, all Pharaoh's horses, his chariots, and his horsemen.

²⁴And in the morning watch the Lord in the pillar of fire and of cloud looked down upon the host of the Egyptians, and discomfited the host of the Egyptians, ²⁵clogging their chariot wheels so that they drove heavily; and the Egyptians said, 'Let us flee from before Israel, for the Lord fights for them against the Egyptians.'

²⁶Then the Lord said to Moses, 'Stretch out your hand over the sea, that the water may come back upon the Egyptians, upon their chariots and upon their horsemen.' ²⁷So Moses stretched forth his hand over the sea,

^{27b}and the sea returned to its wonted flow when the morning appeared; and the Egyptians fled into it, and the Lord routed the Egyptians in the midst of the sea.

²⁸The waters returned and covered the chariots and the horsemen and all the host of Pharaoh that had followed them into the sea; not so much as one of them remained. ²⁹But the people of Israel walked on dry ground through the sea, the waters being a wall to them on their right hand and on their left.

³⁰Thus the Lord saved Israel that day from the hand of the Egyptians; and Israel saw the Egyptians dead upon the seashore. ³¹And Israel saw the great work which the Lord did against the Egyptians, and the people feared the Lord; and they believed in the Lord and in his servant Moses.

In this text, the Exodus has become a poem, a song for celebrating all liberations, of yesterday or today.

Begin by reading this song (aloud – it's better!). You will soon see that there are as it were two choruses responding to each other:

one sings of the power of God in general: vv. 2–3, 6–7, 11, 18;

the other celebrates the specific acts of God: vv. 1, 4–5, 8–10, 12–17.

What impression is made on you by the images they use, particularly in talking about God? Some of them may astonish you, like that of God the warrior (the Greek Bible, two centuries before Christ, turned this into 'God, breaker of war' in the translation). Here we come up against symbolic language (see p. 109); speaking of God the warrior is a way of saying that, 'God is not distant; he is not absent from human struggles for justice and liberty.'

What specific actions of God are celebrated:

in vv. 4–5, 8–10?

in vv. 12–17? The names of the peoples mentioned (Edom, Moab, Canaan, the Philistines) make up an itinerary. What is it? 'The holy abode', 'on thine own mountain', 'the place which thou hast made for thy abode', clearly refers to a building. Which? To what period should we date this stanza?

At this period it was thought that God had a precise purpose in liberating his people (v. 17): what was it?

What does v. 18 teach us about the faith of Israel and its political system?

The Exodus is today

This text leads us to make certain important observations about our faith.

The God celebrated here is not an abstract God, an idea, however lofty. This God is known because his action can be recognized in specific events.

These events are those of today, but the presence of God in them can be discovered only by meditating on the events of former times. Go back to vv. 12–17: we are in the time of the monarchy, the people is settled in Canaan, the Temple has been built, and

God is ruling in the midst of his people. Compare this stanza on the passage through the peoples (vv. 12–16) with that on the drowning of the Egyptians (vv. 8–10): it is in the light of what he has just experienced that the author describes the events of the Exodus, and they allow him to decipher that experience.

So this poem is open to the prayer of future centuries: each believing community over the ages is invited to add its own stanza! That is precisely what John does in Revelation, as he shows us the elect, in heaven, singing the song of Moses (Rev. 15.3). Catholic Christianity sings this song during the paschal vigil; it is an invitation to us to extend it by adding other verses celebrating the interventions of God and Jesus in our present-day history, the history of the world and our personal history.

Hebrew poetry

We should look in passing at some features of Hebrew poetry.

Imagery. Hebrew is a very concrete language. In it, objects and things become symbols, suggesting a rich but invisible reality. Rather than develop abstract ideas, the poet prefers to accumulate concrete images, enriched by all his experience. Instead of saying that God is powerful, he shows him wielding a thunderbolt; he is a warrior; his right hand, which wields the sword, is a strong one; he is a guide, gardener, architect etc.

Parallelism. The two parts of a verse often take up the same idea, but with expressions which are complementary or in opposition. For example,

This is my God, I will praise him;
the God of my father, I will exalt him.

Look for other examples in this poem.

The foundation event

'Each one, from generation to generation, must feel as if he himself has come out of Egypt, for it is written: On that day (the day on which the departure from Egypt is celebrated) say to your son, 'That is why the Lord intervened for me, when I came out of Egypt. . .' This extract from the Jewish passover ritual indicates how important this event was for Israel. Throughout its history, the Jewish people – and Christians in turn – have not ceased to meditate on it and discover its significance.

Here we can only evoke some aspects of this richness, but the whole book will allow you to go on discovering it.

The foundation event

'Israel has always considered the departure from Egypt as a special moment in its history, an event which puts it on a different footing from everyone else.' Of course the people existed with Abraham, but only in promise. The Exodus is really the moment when it was created as a people.

When people wanted to understand the meaning of other events (the crossing of the Jordan, the union of the twelve tribes), institutions or rites, and when they wanted to explain the very existence of the people, it was to the Exodus that they turned.

The encounter with God

In this event, Israel began to discover who was its God, and what his name was. It discovered that God is liberator and saviour before recognizing him as creator. That is so important that we shall come back to it. God is 'the one who has brought us out of the house of slavery'. That is his principal title, almost his proper name, used time and again throughout the Bible.

At the time of the vision of the burning bush, God gave his name to Moses, Yahweh, and he explains it by a phrase which can be translated, 'I am who I will be', that is to say, you will discover who I am in what I shall be and do with you, and with your people, in history (Ex. 3.14).

Thus God and his people are united by a blood-tie (cf. the rite in Ex. 24.3–8), by a covenant.

'From servitude to service. . .' This title, given to a commentary on Exodus, is a splendid summary of the essential movement. The people is aware that God has freed them from slavery in Egypt; from now on they may freely put themselves at his service, a service which consists primarily in a daily life led in covenant with God, which is given expression in worship.

A past that is always present

The Jewish passover expresses very well that the Exodus is not just a past event; it is an event which accompanies Israel throughout its existence. When people celebrate it in worship, it becomes present and they participate in it. Reference to this past allows them to understand the present: the whole of life is seen as an exodus, a march towards the kingdom of God. It makes it possible to keep faith in the terrible times of catastrophe or deportation; if God has freed us before, he can do so again. This maintains our hope by turning our attention to the future.

The first Christians continued this meditation. They interpreted the life of Christ as an exodus, and texts like the First Letter of Peter, the Epistle to the Hebrews or Revelation show that all Christian existence is an exodus, following Christ to the definitive kingdom.

As we think of all that, we have gone beyond the texts of the book of Exodus, but as we shall see, everything that meditation on this event has prompted in the course of time also makes up the event and allows us to understand it.

However, can we go back through all this richness of meaning to the event itself? Can we answer the question, 'What actually happened?' That is what we shall now try to see.

What is a historical event?

Before trying to see 'what happened at the Exodus', we must see more clearly what a historical event is.

The answer to this question might seem obvious: a historical event is made up of facts which you can see, or could have seen. However, that definition needs to be qualified.

There are no such things as 'brute' facts, facts which one can account for in an objective way: there are only interpreted facts. Two people describe the same event: they do it in two different ways. That is to say, they do not report the fact in itself, but 'the fact as they saw it', and the same gesture might seem mockery to one and encouragement to the other.

Facts are historical because they are interpreted and given a meaning. There are past facts which have been forgotten immediately because they have no meaning: they are 'in history' but not historical. I open the door, I pick up a pencil . . . these facts exist, but they do not have any special meaning. A historical event is one which leaves a trace in the memory of a person or a group, a fact which lasts in history because it is found to have meaning.

In this sense, however, the meaning is not perceived until afterwards, sometimes long afterwards. As we see the new era which has begun for the Catholic church, we can see the importance of the decision of John XXIII to hold a council; again, the manifold declarations about the 'rights of man' which the French Revolution provoked around the world help us to understand it. So it is by going through history and seeing all that a fact has led to down the ages that we begin to grasp its significance.

Sometimes, too, we have to go back through history: certain events, perhaps minimal ones, have this power of becoming a symbol for a whole development. Suppose we take a well-known example: the fact that insurgents entered the Bastille to free two or three prisoners guarded by a few easy-going soldiers is a modest enough fact in comparison with other dramatic or glorious events. When did this fact become 'historical'? On 14 July 1789? Or after the revolution had succeeded, when it became the symbol of it? Both together! This is because there was a fact on that day which could be made into a symbol; however, only by taking on value as a symbol did it become historical.

With this last example we have come very close to the epic. In an epic narrative, the facts get mixed up; different events are combined, embellished and interpreted to form the account. We cannot tell whether all the events narrated are exact, and yet, beginning from real facts and concentrated on the personality of a number of people, they express something very true: what the people has discovered in depth about its origins, its values, about what it is. The Song of Roland could not have been produced without the personality of Charlemagne, of Roland, and the expedition across the Pyrenees; but its truth is also its expression of the soul of the people at the time it was produced and its vague feeling of being what it is thanks to these heroes.

The Exodus. What happened?

Moses

Underlying these stories is the personality of Moses. Born in the reign of Horemheb (1334–1306) or Seti I (1309–1290), he was educated in a school of scribal interpreters, needed by Egypt in its relations with the Asiatics.

He bore the marks of his time in the desert, in Midian: there he was in contact with a group – of which his father-in-law Jethro was priest – which seems to have been deeply religious and to have worshipped a god Yahu.

Two exoduses?

Some texts present the departure from Egypt as an expulsion, others as an escape. There were probably two exoduses which were then combined in popular memory.

The expulsion will have taken place about 1550. Semites, the Hyksos, had taken power in Egypt round about 1720. They were expelled in 1552. At that time, sons of Jacob, who were also Semites and had profited from the presence of the Hyksos, were also expelled. They took a northern route, and then went down towards the oasis of Kadesh. One day, they entered Canaan from the south.

The escape took place about 1250. Another group of Semites had stayed in Egypt. Galvanized by

Moses, they took advantage of a spring festival to escape (and perhaps some catastrophes had fallen on Egypt, bringing about the death of the children). They took the northern route. Near Lake Sirbonis, an Egyptian detachment caught up with them, but the chariots got bogged down in the quicksand. Safe, the Semites left this dangerous route and went down towards Kadesh.

The 'crossing' of the sea

In the Yahwistic tradition, it is not a matter of crossing 'through' the sea: the wind dries up the waters and the Egyptian chariots get bogged down under the amazed eyes of the Hebrews. We know from ancient historians that the shores of Lake Sirbonis, formed of a narrow band of sand which divides the lake from the Mediterranean, were very dangerous.

It is only in the Priestly account that God divides the waters and makes dry land appear, as at the beginning of the world he divides the primordial waters to produce dry land! The Exodus is presented as an act of creation, and the creation narrative is presented (Gen. 1) as an act of liberation.

ITINERARY OF THE EXODUS

1 Route of the Philistines
2 Direct route to Kadesh
3 Caravan route to Akaba
4 Traditional itinerary
5 Possible itinerary

Sinai

Depending on the tradition, this mountain is called Sinai or Horeb. Where was it?

Was it Mount Musa, in the south of the Sinai peninsula? This southern itinerary has been traditional only since the fourth century AD; the settlement of monks at the foot of Mount Musa may have influenced this choice.

Near Kadesh, at Mount Hor?

In Midian, east of the Gulf of Akaba?

A theology in epic style

You may be disappointed that everything is so uncertain. That is the result of the nature of these accounts: they are epic, and their importance is primarily theological.

An epic. Different clans claiming the same origin – those who stayed in Canaan, those which were expelled from Egypt, those who escaped with Moses – formed a federation at the time of the assembly at Shechem (Josh. 24). In allying with the rest, each clan contributed its traditions, which were fused to form the common heritage of the new group. The various remembrances were played off, one against the other. So, for example, the remembrance of the 'crossing' of the Jordan contributes towards making the skirmish by the lake into a 'crossing of the sea' (compare Josh. 3.13c with Ex. 14.15a). A number of events marked the settlement in Canaan: the crossing of the Jordan, the capture of fortified cities, the victory at Taanach celebrated by Deborah (Judg. 5). From among these, one event emerged to become the symbol of all the others, the symbol of liberation: the Exodus.

A theology. These remembrances were worked on, not to give us a course in history or geography, but to tell us about God. These stories show us the face of a liberating God, who wants people to be free, to serve him freely and to live their lives in covenant with him. That is the essential element, the motive power throughout the life of Israel and then of Christianity.

This fundamental experience will allow people one day to discover that God does not just want to liberate a people, but mankind: they will then be able to write creation stories which extend this gift of life and liberty to all mankind.

33

2 The Kingdom of Jerusalem

A reconstruction of the Temple of Solomon

Round about the year 1000 BC, David became king and captured Jerusalem, which he made his capital. This was a new starting point for Israel. How was it reached?

From the Exodus to David

About 1200, the group which had left Egypt under the leadership of Moses and then of Joshua settled in Canaan. The country had already been occupied by various clans, grouped around small fortified towns on the hilltops. These clans made their living from agriculture and trade, and fought among themselves.

By force or by stratagem, sometimes by treaty, the Hebrew group became established in the centre of the country. Later, the book of Joshua came to describe this settlement as a marvellous epic, above all to teach a lesson: the Hebrews had conquered the country, but God had allowed them to do so; the conquest was a gift.

At a great assembly held at Shechem, a religious bond was established between various tribes, which made a covenant with God (Josh. 24).

During what is known as the time of the Judges (between 1200 and 1000), the tribes centred on Yahweh – of which there were now twelve – were divided into three groups: in Galilee, in Samaria and south of Jerusalem. The link between them was very loose, and was principally religious. Sometimes, however, when danger threatened one tribe or another, a saviour (or judge) arose and called the people to arms: then everyone returned home after the victory (Book of Judges).

However, pressure from the Ammonites in the centre and above all from the Philistines, good warriors and mighty beer-drinkers, who had settled in the south near the Mediterranean, made the various tribes aware that they needed a strong central power. The central tribes

A Canaanite king. Ivory (Megiddo, between 1350 and 1150)

had an unfortunate venture into monarchy with Abimelech; the southern tribes did not fare very well with Saul.

In the religious sphere, the inhabitants of Canaan worshipped a God El, but above all they practised a nature religion: they worshipped Baals, who were divinized forces of nature (storms, the earth, etc.), and their consorts, the Astartes, goddesses of love and fertility. The Hebrews who worshipped Yahweh as their God were often tempted by the sensuous cults of the Canaanites in the high places.

David

Profiting from the fact that the three great powers of the Near East were helpless at that time (these were the Hittites, who had virtually disappeared, the Egyptians and the Assyrians), and relying on his personal valour, David succeeded in having himself chosen king successively by the tribes of the south and then the tribes of the north. He conquered the city of the Jebusites situated between the two groups of tribes and made it his capital: Jerusalem. That created a completely new situation for Israel.

So in the political sphere Israel had a king like other nations. That raised a question for some believers: was not Yahweh the only king?

The prophet Nathan then came to play a key role. To consecrate the king in Babylon or Egypt, the priest would proclaim an oracle from the national god over him, in these terms: 'You are my son; I am your father'. Through Nathan, God declares that he will take responsibility for a formula of this kind: on the day of his consecration, the son of David – that is, each of his legitimate successors – becomes the son of God.

We can see how the king, as God's representative, has an essential role: he appears as the one responsible for the well-being of the nation before God; political and religious unity are realized around him.

In the religious sphere, David performed an action with political significance: he decided to install the ark of the covenant in his capital. From the time of the Exodus this ark had been the place of the divine presence for his people. By establishing it in Jerusalem, David bound the presence of God to that of the monarchy. It is not surprising that the faithful challenged this action, because here were two ways of representing God. There was either a static God, installed in a particular place, under man's control, at the disposal of the king and the people; or God remained free, a God who had guided his people, who went where he willed, whose presence and whose action were always unforeseeable (this is shown, in symbolic language, by the itinerary of the ark narrated in I Sam. 5–6). And God, again through Nathan, rejected David's offer to build him a house (II Sam. 7).

These are two ways of conceiving of God that we shall find right through the Bible (cf. Acts 7.48), and which still remain possible even today.

In the administrative sphere, David began to organize his kingdom. Different functions appear: army leaders, priests, secretaries, a ministry of information (II Sam. 8.16–18). And David even held a census (II Sam. 24).

David's foreign policy also had religious consequences. Through his victorious campaigns, David brought a number of tribes into his kingdom; other kingdoms submitted to him. By becoming vassals of the king, these people could also benefit from the covenant with God. The scribes who came to write the history of the people tried to show that this universalism had already been proclaimed in the person of Abraham.

Solomon

Solomon inherited his father's kingdom. Endowed with God-given wisdom (I Kings 3), that is to say, with the art of governing well, he took advantage of peace to organize the kingdom. A more developed government came into being (I Kings 4–5): the country was divided into twelve districts, each charged with providing for one month the provisions and the manpower for his great projects. Imposing stables were built at Megiddo and elsewhere. A fleet sailed over the seas. Riches deriving from trade with Egypt and Syria flowed into Jerusalem, where Solomon built a magnificent Temple for his God and an even larger palace for himself. He was a great king!

And yet there was a darker side to his kingdom. Solomon played the great lord too much, acting like any other king of the time and not as God's representative. The Bible credits him with 700 wives and 300 concubines. Perhaps that's too much! But Solomon had several wives (one of them a daughter of Pharaoh) from foreign nations: they brought their gods with them and the risk of idolatry was great. Solomon exploited his people, and although he succeeded in containing a potential revolt, it broke out after his death. His son, politically incompetent, was the cause of the division of the kingdom into two: the northern tribes went their own way. The united kingdom had lasted only seventy years.

The two kingdoms

From 933 there are two kingdoms:

The southern kingdom, or Judah, with Jerusalem as its capital. All its kings were descendants of David and thus benefited from the promise handed on by Nathan: saints or sinners, they are sons of God.

The northern kingdom, or Israel, with Samaria as its capital. Its kings were not descended from David (of the nineteen, eight were assassinated!). In this kingdom the king was not the one who was held responsible for the salvation of the people before God.

The beginnings of a literature

Because there was peace, because Solomon had organized his court along the lines of that of Pharaoh, a start was made on editing the sacred traditions. The Bible refers to two books which have been lost, 'The Book of the Upright' and 'The Book of the Wars of Yahweh'. Doubtless at that time a history of the ark (I Sam. 2–5) and a history of the Davidic succession (II Sam. 9–20) were composed. Poems were collected together: the song of the bow and the elegy on Abner, doubtless composed by David (II Sam. 1; 3), perhaps some psalms, and sayings later collected in the book of Proverbs.

Above all, a start was made on the Sacred Judaean History which we call the Yahwistic tradition. That is what we are going to read next.

The Sacred Judaean History

Solomon organized his court along the lines of that of Pharaoh: scribes had an important place in it. Trained in the craft of writing, they were also wise men, people endowed with discernment who had learned the art of living: their wisdom was considered to be a divine gift.

The Sacred Judaean History (the sacred history of the kingdom of Judah) is doubtless their work. It is called the Yahwistic tradition (or document) because from the beginning God is called Yahweh. To make things simpler, the author of this tradition is called 'the Yahwist': the word can denote a scribe or group of scribes. It is denoted by the letter J (see p. 27 above).

This tradition was begun in the time of Solomon and continued under his first successors in the kingdom of Judah. The king, son of David and son of God, is the divine representative and brings about the political and religious unity of the nation. The Yahwistic tradition is at the service of the monarchy and shows that this realizes the divine promise to the patriarchs: thus it is also a political writing which supports the monarchy. At the same time, however, the Yahwist criticizes it and calls it to order: the king is not an absolute monarch, but is in the service of God and his people, and even of other nations.

I shall suggest that we read some texts from this tradition, following the theme of the blessing as a guideline. Then we shall study the creation story in more detail.

Some characteristics of the Yahwist

He is a marvellous storyteller. His stories are very vivid, always concrete and full of imagery. God is often represented as a man (anthropomorphism): in the creation story he is in turn a gardener, a potter, a surgeon, a tailor. That is the Yahwist's way of telling us about God and man; he proves to be a profound theologian.

He is a very human God. He walks with Abraham as with a friend (Gen. 2); he invites himself to a meal with Abraham and bargains with him (Gen. 18). Man lives on familiar terms with him and meets him in everyday life.

His is a God who is utterly different. However, this God is the master: he commands or forbids (Gen. 3.16); he calls. 'Go, leave,' he says to Abraham and Moses. He has a plan for history. His blessing will bring happiness to his people and through them will extend to all people. (It is remarkable to find such universalism at this period.) Man must respond to this divine call and obey God.

Man's sin is to want to take God's place. This sin draws down the curse on him: Cain, the flood, the tower of Babel.

His is a God who is always ready to forgive, particularly when men like Abraham (Gen. 18) or Moses (Ex. 32.11–14) intercede with him, and always ready to renew his blessing.

📖 *A key text: Gen. 12.1–3*

[1]*Now the Lord said to Abram,*
'Go from your country and your kindred and your father's
house to the land that I will show you.
[2]*And I will make of you a great nation,*
and I will bless you, and make your name great,
so that you will be a blessing.
[3]*I will bless those who bless you,*
and him who curses you I will curse;
and by you all the families of the earth will bless
themselves.'

Who are the main characters here?

What words seem to you to be important and keep occurring (how many times)?

Note the tenses of the verb: imperative and futures.
The word nation denotes a people organized and settled in a territory.

What does this text tell you?

Read Gen. 12.6–9. What new promise is made to Abraham (v. 7)?

Reading some texts

The cycle of creation stories

The table on the right shows you the probable division of the verses of Gen. 1–11 between the Yahwist and the Priestly writer. Here we shall be reading only the J texts. We shall be studying the creation story in more detail later on (page 39).

These chapters are not history but theology expressed in images: they are the reflection of wise men. The author tries to reply to the great questions which people ask about life, death, love, our origins. His starting point is his faith in God, and he reuses ancient myths (see page 21).

The story begins in an optimistic way, but soon the history of mankind appears as that of the proliferation of evil. The curse falls five times in succession (3.14, 17; 4.11; 5.29; 9.25). Each time, God forgives or promises salvation, except on the last occasion. The story of the tower of Babel expresses the feeling that we live in a broken world, in which men no longer understand one another. So is our history accursed?

How does the story of Abraham appear as a response?

Note the reversal of 11.4–12.2 and the five blessings.

The Abraham cycle

The genre here is not yet historical. We have legendary traditions based on a historical foundation and given a religious interpretation in order to provide teaching.

Abraham appears as the guardian of the divine blessing for all peoples. What does he do with it

in Gen. 12.10–20?

in Gen. 18.16–33? Note vv. 17–18.

in Gen. 22.15–18?

If you wish, you can see how the New Testament continues the line of Abraham: Gal. 3.8; Heb. 11.8f.

The Jacob cycle

Here we have the same literary genre as that of Abraham. Traditions about two different clans, those of Jacob and Israel, have been fused together and the two names have been given to the same person, who becomes the grandson of Abraham.

Read Gen. 28.13–16. Why does God make promises to Jacob? What are they?

Gen. 32.23–33. For this episode of the struggle between Jacob and God, see the notes in your Bible or a commentary.

Chapter	J	P
	The creation	
1		1–31
2		1–4a
	4b–25	
3	1–24	
4	1–26	
5		1–28
	29	30–32
	The flood	
6	1–8	9–22
7	1–5	6
	7	8–9
	10	11
	12	13–16a
	16b	17a
	17b	18–21
	22–23	24
8		1–2a
	2b–3a	3b–5
	6–12	13a
	13b	14–19
	20–22	
9		1–17
	From Noah to Abraham	
	18–27	28–29
10		1a
	1b	2–7
	8–19	20
	21	22–23
	24–30	31–32
11	1–9	10–27a
	27b–30	31–32

Benediction

Benediction – the word comes from the Latin – or blessing means saying good things to someone. When God says good things to someone, good things happen to him, because the word of God is all-powerful and does what it says.

By contrast, cursing – malediction – is to say bad things and thus bring them about.

The good things that God says or does can be in the order of having (riches, fertility), but they are above all in the order of being: the very life of God.

The Moses cycle

Moses remains the key figure in the Old Testament. However, his person appears differently in each of the traditions.

For the Yahwist, he is present everywhere, from the departure from Egypt to the arrival in Canaan. But God is the true leader of the people, the only liberator. Moses does not perform miracles, is not a leader in war, does not found a religion; rather, he is the shepherd whom God inspires to make his will known to men.

♥ *Exodus 3.1–8 God calls Moses*

Look at the reaction of Pharaoh in Ex. 8.4; 10.17; 12.31–32. Compare Moses' role as intercessor with that of Abraham in Gen. 18. The people of God must forgive and bless even their worst enemy!

The Balaam cycle

Israel found themselves confronted with the people of Moab. The king of the country brought the seer Balaam from the east to curse Israel. What does Balaam do (Num. 24.1)? It would be a good thing to read the whole of Num. 24.1–19, but you should at least look at vv. 7 and 17.

Here is the way in which Num. 24.17 was understood at the time of Christ, according to the explanatory translation (or targum) which was made then:

Hebrew text	Targum
A *star* shall come forth out of Jacob, and a *sceptre* shall rise out of Israel.	A *king* shall arise from the house of Jacob and a *saviour* (or *messiah*) from the house of Israel.

Does this explanation help you to understand Matt. 2.1f.? What is this star, for Matthew?

The patriarchs

When we want to construct a family tree, we begin with ourselves and go back to our ancestors. We are guided simply by ties of blood. Of course that is important, but sometimes there are ties of friendship or companionship which are stronger than blood ties. A friend becomes a 'brother'. So we can understand how, even now, in certain tribes, when an alliance is made everything is shared: traditions and ancestors. Since now there is only one group, the fact is expressed by setting up ties of kinship between ancestors.

This is what Israel seems to have done in the case of the patriarchs. Round about the eighteenth or seventeenth century BC, various nomadic clans settled in Canaan: those of Jacob, Isaac, Israel, Abraham. . . They adopted the same local god, El. They made an alliance. Once they became brothers, their respective ancestors also became kin: in this way Abraham became the father of Isaac and the grandfather of Jacob was identified with Israel.

There is nothing disturbing about this hypothesis which scholars have put forward. It simply makes us rather more careful when we claim to be reconstructing the history of the patriarchs. However, that is not the essential thing.

The essential element is the religious significance which Israel saw in this history. In this celebration of the deeds of its ancestors, in each generation it found food for meditation and a new strength for its faith. Here the Yahwist discovers a promise of blessing which is given to the king, the son of David: he must pass it on to everyone. The Elohist shows his contemporaries, who are tempted to abandon God for Canaanite idols, that their fathers Abraham and, above all, Jacob were models of faithfulness towards God. The Priestly writer lived in exile: everything seemed to have fallen apart; there was no more possible hope. To strengthen his faith and his hope, he relied on the promise of God to Abraham: God once pledged his faithfulness; he will save us despite our sins.

Paul sees Abraham as the very embodiment of faith: it is not that he wants to be righteous before God through what he does, his works; he puts his whole trust in him. The Letter to the Hebrews invites us to set out in the steps of Abraham, without wanting to know the way in advance.

What are we going to discover in Abraham to enable us to live in faithfulness to God today?

♦ *The Creation Story. Gen. 2.4 – 3.24*

First read this well-known text carefully. Note your reactions and your questions.

Then go through it again asking certain questions (you can underline the text in different colours):

Who are the main characters? What are they doing?

Try to distinguish different parts: what is each one of them about?

Select the themes or expressions which keep occurring. In particular, where is there mention of the tree of life? Of the tree of the knowledge of good and evil? Which expressions explain what one gets from eating its fruit?

Wisdom reflection

What is the literary genre of this text? Clearly it is not an eye-witness account, nor is it instruction in history or geography. Rather, it is the reflection of wise men who are raising the great human questions. Where do we come from? Where are we going? What is the reason for life, suffering, death? Why the mysterious attraction between the sexes? What is the relationship between man and God, man and nature (work), man and his fellows?

To try to reply to these questions, the author relies on his own reflections, but also on those of the wise men of other civilizations. Above all, the starting point for his reflection is his faith: believers before him had already meditated on the Exodus and the entry into Canaan; in these events they discovered something of the aspect of their God. And it is above all in terms of what he already knows about his God in this way that the author tries to respond.

We shall take up some of the questions, and put them back in the context of the thought of the time.

Adam and Eve. First, let's get one difficulty out of the way. You sometimes hear people say, 'Adam and Eve never existed.' That shows that they haven't understood the literary genre of this text. Humanity certainly started one day. With whom? Where? How? Science has to answer these questions, not the Bible. But the Bible calls the first couple, or the first couples, that science may present to us as the first human beings, 'Adam and Eve'. In Hebrew these names mean Mr Man and Mrs Life; thus they are symbolic names representing both the first human beings and every human being: everyman.

The formation of the earth. What scientific idea (of the time) underlies this story? (We shall see that the science of Gen. 1 is different.) Doubtless here we have the underlying experience of the nomad, for whom an oasis in the desert is a paradise.

The creation of man. Of what elements is man formed? Read the passage below taken from a Babylonian poem: what similarities and differences can you see between the two texts? How are the pessimism of Babylon and the optimism of the Bible expressed?

This text does not contradict in any way the theory of evolution, according to which man's origins lie in animal life. It gives a religious significance to the appearance of man. What significance?

The Atrahasis epic (Babylon, before 1600 BC)

The gods are worn down by the tasks that they have to perform:

When the gods laboured in the fashion of men
and were subjected to toil,
the toil of the gods was great,
burdensome their labour, immense their distress. . .

The gods rebelled. To be rid of their buden, they decided to create man. The god Ea advises:

Cut the throat of a god,
with his blood and his flesh
let Nintu (the mother goddess) mix clay,
so that god and man are mingled
in the clay. . .

Man and nature. What is the role of man towards nature (2.15)? Towards the animals (2.19: to name is to give a new being)? Is it not to proclaim that science is legitimate?

The creation of woman. Why was woman created? In what way is the idea expressed that man and woman are of the same nature and that they differ from animals?

For us, to be 'side by side' signifies equality: perhaps we have the same image here. Perhaps, too, the passage takes up an old play on words: in Sumerian, side and life can be written in the same way.

Deep sleep: the Hebrew here has a rare word which expresses a supernatural experience, a kind of ecstasy, as the Greek Bible translates it.

Perhaps here we have the old myth according to which man becomes man only in loving relations with woman. See the text below.

The Gilgamesh epic

Gilgamesh is the hero of the city of Uruk. To counterbalance his power, the gods create a monster, Enkidu, who lives with the wild animals. On the advice of a huntsman, a sacred prostitute offers herself to him. He goes with her for six days and seven nights, and then sated, he wants to return to the wild animals, but they flee. Enkidu wants to follow them, but this is impossible. He has lost his strength, but he has become a man.

Enkidu has no strength,
his knees remain motionless
when he wants to follow his herd.
Weakened, he can no longer run as before,
but his heart and his spirit are lightened.
He returns to sit at the feet of the courtesan
and begins to gaze at her face,
and now he understands
what the courtesan says. . .

The serpent. This creature played a prominent role in mythology. In Egypt the serpent opposed the sun god during the night, trying to prevent him from rising. In Canaan, it was a sexual symbol in certain cults. According to the Gilgamesh epic, it was the serpent which stole the herb of life (see below). All this could have influenced the choice of the serpent. However, the essential concern of the text is to show that sin does not come from within man, that it is not part of his nature: it comes from outside. Thus man is responsible for his actions (compare this view with the Babylonian text below).

Babylonian theodicy (second millennium)

The king of the gods, creator of mankind,
the god Ea who modelled their clay,
the goddess who fashioned them,
gave man a perverse spirit,
they gave him for ever,
not truth, but the lie.

The Gilgamesh epic

Haunted by the idea of death, Gilgamesh leaves in search of immortality. The hero of the flood reveals to him the existence of a herb of life. Gilgamesh succeeds in plucking it from the abyss and wants to take it to his city. He goes for two days and then stops.

Gilgamesh saw a well whose water was cool.
He went down into it to bathe in the water.
A serpent snuffed the fragrance of the plant.
Silently it came up from the earth
and carried off the plant; immediately
it shed its old skin.
Thereupon Gilgamesh sat down and wept,
his tears running down over his face.

The tree of the knowledge of good and evil. Of course, this tree and its fruit are symbols (it's not a matter of an 'apple'), in the same way as we might say that 'we enjoy the fruits of sleep or of our labours'. What does the tree represent?

We must dispose of a wrong interpretation: this is not the tree of knowledge or of science, as though they were forbidden to man. The text affirms the contrary: God gives man the world for him to cultivate, animals for him to name, and thus science for him to create.

In reading this text you will have noticed that this tree was often connected with expressions like, 'You will be like God, knowing good and evil' (3.5); this tree is 'to be desired to make one wise' (3.6); see also 3.22.

If you have time, you might read Ezekiel 28: the prophet takes up the same imagery (Eden or paradise, being like God, cherubim, and so on); the sin of the king of Tyre is to say 'I am god' because he has acquired wisdom.

What is forbidden man, then, is to refuse to be man, to want to make himself God. Only God is 'wise', knowing the roots of happiness and misfortune. One cannot steal this wisdom; God has given it to those who love him with respect or, as the Bible puts it, to those who 'fear' him (see, for example, Prov. 3.18).

The wisdom which man thought he could steal finally left him naked; he discovers that he is only a man, and he shares the serpent's state: naked and crafty are the same word in Hebrew.

Suffering and death. Did man suffer and die before the advent of sin? That is not a good way of putting the question. The author looks closely at the human condition in his day; he knows that there is suffering and death, and tries to make sense of them. And he comes up against the wisdom of God which men cannot know. To want to steal this wisdom is to find oneself naked again, paralysed by this sorrowful human condition. So he discovers a link between suffering and sin. Before sin, Adam would have suffered and died, but he would have gone through this without anguish, trusting in God. (We shall return to this word 'before'.)

Original sin

What Christians call 'original sin' does not appear in the text of Genesis, but in Paul's Letter to the Romans (Rom. 5).

We understand by Genesis that if Adam is man, everyman, his sin is that of everyman, the sin of the world. In this sense, each of our sins forms part of this sin of Adam, increases it and gives it its particular character.

For Paul, the affirmation of original sin is simply the consequence of a much more important fact: we are all saved in Jesus Christ. We are all saved, he goes on, because we all need to be. He then tries to prove this, first of all in terms of statistics, by showing that both Jews and Gentiles are sinners (Rom. 1–3). He then resumes his demonstration in a symbolic way: since Adam represents all of us, and Adam sinned, we are all sinners in him. However, that is merely a consequence. The essential thing is that we are saved in Jesus Christ. Where sin abounded, grace abounded even more. In other words, he tells us that we are not 'gracious', but given grace: sinners who have been reprieved. And that is miraculous. When we survive an accident that could have been fatal, our scars are a miraculous sign: each time we see them, they remind us that we are still alive. The dogma of original sin ought also to encourage us: it reminds us that God saves us in Jesus Christ, that we are more than conquerors in him who loved us (Rom. 8.37).

The tree of life. This appears for the first time in 2.9. According to 2.16, man can eat of it. It reappears in 3.22f. Here we discover the goodness of God. He is not jealous, as the serpent claims. He and he alone has the power of life, and he is ready to give it to man on condition that man wants it: 'I have set before you life and death ... therefore choose life' (Deut. 30.19–20).

Paradise: a task to be performed

The author wants to express two things which are hard to put into words without losing touch with them. The first is an inference from his faith: God created man to be happy and free; God did not create sin and evil. He knows the second from experience: all men are sinners; all men want to make themselves God, and always have done.

If we pick up a coin, we cannot see both sides at the same time; to do that, we have to cut the coin in half across its circumference, and then it is no longer a real coin. The Yahwist does something like that here. His two affirmations are the two sides of human reality; he separates them to put them side by side, 'before' and 'after'. That's clear enough, but it stops being man! This 'before' is not a historical tense but a theological image; it is simply meant to express God's concern, a concern which is never in fact realized as such.

Some time after the Yahwist, the prophet Isaiah took up the same images again, but projected them on to the end of time: this is what God will bring about one day (Isa. 11.1–9). Perhaps the Yahwist and Isaiah are telling us the same thing: paradise is not in the past, a beautiful dream that we have lost; it is before us, and is a task to perform.

Which God? Which man?

I began this study by saying that the Yahwist is trying to answer the great questions we ask ourselves. Finally, what help has he given you?

What picture of God do you find here?
What is man?

For an explanation of this fresco see p. 122.

Prophets of the Kingdom of Judah

We are now going to make the acquaintance of the first prophets to preach in the kingdom of Judah.

Nathan

He has left no writings, but he played an important role alongside David.

II Sam. 7.1–17. Read this text and put it in the context of the religious and political situation of David's kingdom (see p. 34).

Note the contrasts: dwell in a house/move about in a tent; house (to live in) / house (dynasty); my name / your name. Can you rediscover the two notions of God which were mentioned on p. 35? Can you make them more precise?

What is the role of the king in Israel? Look at the titles given to David: servant, shepherd, king.

If you have time, read I Chron. 17.1–15. The book of Chronicles was written after the exile, more than five centuries after this text from Samuel. Compare II Sam. 7.14 with I Chron. 7.13 (people no longer believed that this son of David could sin), and II Sam. 7.16 with I Chron. 17.14 (the possessive adjectives have changed). This shows that in five centuries the figure of this son of David has increased in importance. Read Psalm 2: now he is said to be king over the whole world. That allows us to understand the sense in which this title son of David could be given to Jesus.

Nathan's other interventions can be found in II Sam. 12 (David's sin) and I Kings I.

Isaiah

Isaiah preached in Jerusalem between 740 and 700. He was a great poet and an acute politician, but above all he was a prophet. He exerted considerable influence on his time. Two centuries later, some disciples inspired by him laid claims to his name, and their work was added to his. So we have to distinguish between the book of Isaiah (which has 66 chapters) and the prophets: Isa. 1–39 is partly the work of Isaiah; Isa. 40–55 comes from a prophet living at the time of the exile, and Isa. 56–66 from a disciple after the exile.

The political situation at the time of Isaiah was a complicated one. The two kingdoms of Jerusalem and Samaria were prosperous (at least as far as the rich were concerned – they were grinding the faces of the poor!), but Assyria was threatening. About 734, the kings of Damascus and Samaria tried to force Jerusalem to join a coalition against Assyria: this Syro-Ephraimite war was to be the occasion for the main oracles of Isaiah. Notes to your Bible or commentaries will give you more details about this social, economic and political context.

To make yourself familiar with Isaiah you might begin by reading the first twelve chapters, or even just Isa. 6–12; 28.16–17; 29.17–24.

The call of Isaiah (Isa. 6) explains his message. Coming to the temple, he experienced the presence of God. He became aware that he was only a man and that he was a sinner: he felt lost. But God made him persevere and purified him. Isaiah saw that the great sin is pride (people think that they can cope by themselves, make themselves God), and salvation lies in faith (putting oneself wholly and humbly, with trust, in God's hands).

Isaiah tries to give his people the same experience. God is like an enormous rock on the way: the people have to choose. Pride is to bump into it (8.14) and

---

'No one can see God and live'

This phrase recurs often in the Bible, and it reflects the experience of Isaiah. It is not that God is wicked, but that he is utterly different from us! Electric current is a good thing, but if we touch a high-voltage transmission cable we are burnt to a frazzle, because we cannot take such power. Similarly, we cannot take God who *is* life, when we only *have* life. That is why God veils his glory when he shows himself: for example, it is a vision of his back which is shown to Moses (Ex. 33.12f.).

Furthermore, of course, we are sinners and cannot stand before the holy God, the God who is both utterly different and perfect. God has to purify us and hold us. But in the end it is only through his Son Jesus that we may 'dare' to call him Father.

find death (5); faith is to rest upon it (10.20–21), or upon this rock which is the Messiah (28.16). Sadly, this preaching will succeed only in hardening the hearts of the majority, but it will also lead to the formation of a small remnant of faithful (6.9–11).

Isaiah was a Judaean. For him the king was son of David/son of God, the guarantor of the faith of the people and their representative before God. He is also tormented by king Ahaz's lack of faith. Panic-stricken at the coalition between Damascus and Syria, Ahaz sacrificed his son to the false gods (II Kings 16.3), thus endangering God's promise to David. Isaiah came to him to announce that despite everything God would keep his promise, that another child was already on the way and that the young woman (Ahaz's wife) was pregnant. And Isaiah put all his hopes on this child, the little Hezekiah, Emmanu-el, God with us (Isa. 7). Isaiah celebrates the era of peace which he foresees when Hezekiah becomes king, becomes son of God (Isa. 9), and he even celebrates in advance the coming of the true son of David who will appear one day to establish universal peace (Isa. 11). These various oracles are important, but they are sometimes difficult to understand. Look at the notes in your Bible or in a commentary.

Micah

Isaiah was an aristocrat. Micah is a peasant: he suffered personally under the policy of the great which led to war and the injustice practised by the rich. One day he went to Jerusalem to proclaim God's indignation.

If we were to keep only one verse from him, it should be Micah 6.8, in which he succeeds in making a magnificent combination of the message of the three prophets of this period: in the northern kingdom Amos, who preaches justice, and Hosea, who preaches God's tenderness; in Jerusalem Isaiah, who preaches a humble faith:

He has showed you, O man, what is good;
and what does the Lord require of you
but to do justice, and to love kindness,
and to walk humbly with your God?

But you might also read his cries against social injustice (2.1–5; 3.1–12; 7.1–7), the announcement of a Messiah who will not be the son of David, king of Jerusalem, but the son of David, the little shepherd of Bethlehem (5.1–5, quoted by Matt. 2.6), or his message of hope (7.1–10, quoted by Luke 1.73).

Prophets

A prophet is not someone who announces the future, but rather someone who speaks in the name of God, someone who has been made privy to God's plans (Amos 3.7) and now sees everything through God's eyes.

Are we to think in terms of extraordinary revelations? That is by no means impossible, but it seems in fact that the prophets discover this word of God in two moments or places: at their calling and in their life. Their calling is the determinative factor: this is the moment when they have the experience of God, as with Isaiah on a visit to the temple, as with Jeremiah in continued prayer, and as with Hosea in an unhappy marriage. This is the light which enables them to discover this word, to read the signs of the times, in life, in great political events and in day-to-day living.

From the time of their calling, everything speaks to them of God: the branch of an almond tree in flower or a boiling pot (Jer. 1.11f.), married life (Hos. 1–3; Ezek. 24.15f.) or enemy invasion. And in this way they teach us to read in our own lives this same word which continues to address us.

The prophets express themselves through words: oracles (declarations made in the name of God), exhortations, stories, prayers, but also through actions. Prophetic actions communicate the Word, and even make history.

If you are working as a group, you clearly cannot study everything suggested here in a month. So why not share out the work? Everyone could read the whole of the chapter, and then individuals could study just one part, looking for particular features. So when the group meets, each person will be able to make his or her own contribution, and you will discover where certain agreements become obvious.

It is in fact important to have a general idea about this period. People were not just at work composing the creation story or the Sacred Judaean History. Prophets were preaching, and wise men expressing their reflections (particularly in Gen. 2–3); people were praying (even if we cannot be sure which psalms go right back to this period). In this enormous period of gestation, the Bible is slowly coming to birth.

3 The Northern Kingdom 935–721

King Jehu pays homage to the Assyrian king Shalmaneser III

Only fifty kilometres separate the two rival capitals, Jerusalem and Samaria. Yet in many respects, the kingdom of Israel is very different from its brother and enemy, the kingdom of Judah.

Geographical situation. A look at the diagrammatic map on the right will tell you more than a long explanation.

Jerusalem is in the middle of the hills, near to the desert of Judah. The stony ground produced some cereal crops and allowed the cultivation of vines and olives, as well as the rearing of sheep. The kingdom had no access to the sea – the rich plain of the Shephelah was occupied by the Philistines – and focussed more on the Jordan valley and the Dead Sea.

By contrast, the northern kingdom occupied the hill country of Samaria with its verdant valleys, together with the plains of Sharon and Jezreel. The transfer of its capital gives an indication of its development: Jeroboam, its first king, installed himself at Tirzah, facing the Jordan. One of his successors, Omri, bought the hill of Samaria and built his capital there: the northern kingdom was now focussed on the sea, and had easy links and commerce with the Canaanite princes of the north (present-day Lebanon and Syria). That partly explains its economic and religious situation.

Economic situation. You need to read the description of the inhabitants of Samaria, with their ivory- and ebony-panelled walls, given in the book of Amos (3.12; 5.11; 6.4) to see the prosperity of the country. But you will also see the social injustice which it generated: excavations at Tirzah, the first capital, show a group of well-built houses, separated by a wall from a mass of shanties.

An official in the king's presence. Hittite bas-relief (eighth century BC)

NB that some heights on this map are indicated + or − because a good deal of the land is below sea level.

44

Religious situation. Israel had more contact with the Canaanites living in its territory than did Judah, and also with the princes of Tyre, Sidon and Damascus. We shall be looking more closely at some of the features of Canaanite religion, which was attractive to an agricultural people because it was centred on a cult of divinized forces of nature, Baals and Astartes, who were thought to give fertility to the soil, to the flocks and to human beings. Israel was tempted to insure itself by backing two religions at once, limping on both feet, as Elijah put it: worshipping Yahweh while serving the Baals.

To prevent his people from going to the Temple at Jerusalem, Jeroboam had set up two bulls (two calves, as the prophets mockingly put it), one at Dan and one at Bethel (I Kings 12.26f.). These bulls were probably meant to serve as pedestals for the true God Yahweh, offering him a place where he could make himself present, as did the ark of the covenant in Jerusalem. However, because the bull was the symbol of Baal, the danger of idolatry was great.

Political situation. The system of monarchy, inaugurated by David and Solomon, continued in Israel. Here, however, the kings were no longer the legitimate descendants of David: eight out of nineteen were assassinated, and one dynasty gave way to another. The king was not son of David and he could not be son of God. 'They made kings, but not through me,' complains God (Hos. 8.4). So the king was not the guarantor of the unity of the people and their representative before God, as he was in Judah. In Israel, the prophet came to play this role, and often opposed the king.

The kings themselves were neither better nor worse than those of Judah, and some of them were great men.

International politics. Israel was deeply involved in the politics of its time.

Egypt was in decline, while Assyria, a powerful nation, made several incursions into Canaan.

To the north of Israel, the small Aramaean kingdom of Damascus prospered. Because of its Semitic origin and its power, it was a near neighbour to Israel and Judah and was ally or enemy in turn. For example, an Assyrian document shows us that in 853, Assyria was confronted with a coalition of Aramaean kingdoms including Ahab of Israel, with two thousand chariots and ten thousand soldiers.

The two kingdoms of Israel and Judah reached the zenith of their power round about 750. Assyria wanted to extend its empire towards the Mediterranean. The first

obstacle in its way was Damascus. That was marvellous for Israel and Judah; Damascus was preoccupied with this second front and no longer attacked them. Indeed, as long as it resisted, it served as a buffer against Assyria. It is not necessary to have much knowledge of politics to realize that this situation could not last long. However, for the moment, governed by intelligent kings each of whom reigned for about forty years, the two kingdoms profited and enjoyed their prosperity. This was the time when the prophets Amos and Hosea were preaching in Israel.

However, in 732 the Assyrians captured Damascus, and in 721, Samaria. Some of the inhabitants were deported to Assyria, where they became assimilated: we lose track of them. That was the end of the northern kingdom.

The Samaritans after 721. All the inhabitants were not deported; some of them remained in Samaria. The Assyrians brought colonists to Samaria, deported from other provinces of their empire, who arrived with their traditions and their gods.

This gave rise to a new population, of mixed blood, who served both the God of Israel and other gods. (See the spicy and biased account in II Kings 17.24–41.)

We shall have occasion to look at the disputes between the Samaritans and the Jews who returned from exile in Babylon (pages 74, 79).

We can understand why, in the time of Christ, Jews and Samaritans mistrusted each other.

Literary activity

The Elijah traditions (I Kings 17–19; 21; II Kings 1–2) were certainly brought together after the ninth century, and, about 750, the tales about Elisha (II Kings 3–9), along with fine historical accounts like the story of Jehu's revolution (II Kings 9–10).

The oracles of Amos and Hosea were set down in writing.

The Sacred History of the North, which we call the Elohistic tradition, was doubtless also written down about 750.

Finally, this period also saw the formation of codes of law, to adapt the old legislation to the new social situation. Influenced greatly by the message of the prophets, particularly Hosea, these codes eventually formed the kernel of Deuteronomy.

Prophets of the Northern Kingdom

In the northern kingdom, the prophet, not the king, was the guarantor of faith. So we shall begin by listening to three great prophets.

Elijah

Like Nathan in Jerusalem, Elijah has left us no writings. However, he and Moses are the two great figures of Jewish faith. The New Testament, and above all Luke, presents Jesus as the new Elijah.

His name is a message in itself: Elijah is a version of Eli-yahu, my God is Yahweh. He appears in the ninth century, in the reign of Ahab. Ahab married Jezebel, daughter of the king of Tyre. This alliance contributed to the prosperity of Israel, but Jezebel brought with her her religion, her Baals and her prophets. And the people worshipped God while serving Baal . . . Elijah made his choice.

Read the pages in which he appears: I Kings 17–19; 21; II Kings 1–2. Try to sort out the main features. Here are some of them.

Man before God. The expression 'my God whom I serve' or 'to whom I bow' appears often. Elijah made an unequivocal choice and wants the people to do so as well.

Transported by the spirit. Look at the comic response of Obadiah in I Kings 18.12. This is the source of Elijah's strength of purpose and inner freedom.

His undivided faith. At the time of the sacrifice on Carmel (I Kings 18) he wants to force the people to choose between the living, personal God who intervenes in history, and the divinized powers of nature, the Baals (see the box on the next page). Like us, Elijah believes without seeing; because God asks it of him, he announces the coming of rain . . . but without seeing any on the way (I Kings 18.41f.)!

His intimacy with God. Along with that of Moses (Ex. 33.18f.), his vision of God (I Kings 19) has remained the model for the mystical life: this is the maximum that mankind is allowed to see. However, Elijah remains a man like ourselves, discouraged and afraid (19.1f.). Verse 12 of ch. 19 should be translated, 'there was the sound of a silence': God is not in the divinized forces of nature, he is the mysterious God whose presence one senses in silence and emptiness, a hidden God. Like Moses, in his prayer Elijah does not give himself over to mystical effusions: he tells God of his mission.

Defender of the poor. Confronted with the king and men of power, he defends the poor (I Kings 21).

His universalism. Because he believes in God unequivocally and allows himself to be guided by the spirit, he is completely free to move among the pagans (I Kings 17). However, he asks the pagan woman for unconditional faith (17.13).

A tale of Elijah (II Kings 1). Unfortunately, this popular tale, like all those told of Elisha, has helped to make Elijah into a judge who calls down fire from heaven upon sinners.

The ascension of Elijah (II Kings 2). Probably because people did not know of a tomb of Elijah, they came to think that he had been taken up to God. Luke was inspired by this text to write the account of the ascension of Jesus (Acts 1.6–11); because Elisha sees Elijah ascending, we know that Elisha is to receive his spirit to continue his mission, just as the disciples receive the spirit of Jesus since they see his ascension.

In Luke, Jesus is the new Elijah

Read the texts where Luke refers explicitly to the Elijah story: 4.26 (the sermon in the synagogue at Capernaum); 7.12, 15 (the resurrection of a young man at Nain); 9.42 (the healing of a child); 9.51, 54, 57, 62 (Jesus goes up to Jerusalem); 22.43, 45 (the agony in the garden, Jesus is comforted by an angel). Note, too, that Luke has left out the saying of Jesus which identifies John the Baptist with Elijah (Matt. 11.14; 17.11–13).

In the light of this, you can see how the features that we noted in the case of Elijah help us to discover the character of Luke's portrait of Jesus: his relationship to the Father, frequently expressed in prayer; his inner freedom granted through the spirit; his universalism and his tenderness towards the poor, the sinners, the outcast, the women; his demand that the disciples should place unconditional trust in him. Again like Elijah, Jesus is a man with a single aim: he is going towards his being 'received up' (9.51), which is at the same time his being lifted up on the cross and his ascension into the glory of the Father.

Amos Act justly

Amos was originally a shepherd from Tekoa, near Bethlehem. He was sent by God to the north at the time when Samaria prospered under king Jeroboam II. A popular preacher with a vigorous turn of phrase, he was struck by the luxury of the houses of the rich, but above all by their injustice. For example, see 3.13–4.3 (luxury); 2.6–16; 8.4–8 (social injustice).

Amos was a prophet; on two occasions he speaks of his call. In 7.10–17 he describes it, and in 3.3–8 he tries to make sense of it. A prophet is someone who is taken into the counsel of God, and thereafter sees everything in the light of it, trying to decipher God's plan in his life and the events of his time.

His social teaching, too, is based on the covenant. The covenant is not an assurance which allows people to live in any way they like. It is a responsibility. 'You only have I known of all the families of the earth,' God declares, 'therefore I will punish you for all your iniquities' (3.1–2).

If God punishes people, it is to bring about their conversion. Amos foresees that there will be a small 'remnant'; some will be saved from the disaster (3.12), and that is a reason for continuing to hope (8.11–12; 9.11–15).

The God of Amos is no longer just a national God: he also watches over the morality of other nations (1.3–2.3, fine examples of oracles). He can do this because he is Creator: Amos quotes a poem (perhaps inspired by a Canaanite hymn): 4.13 + 5.8–9 + 9.5–6.

Hosea Love tenderly

Hosea came from the north and preached at the same time as Amos. He discovered the tenderness of God through personal experience. Hosea loved his wife, although she behaved badly towards him; through his love he succeeded in restoring to her the feelings she had had when she was young. This is how God loves us: not because we are good, but so that we can become good (Hos. 1–3). God loves us as a husband loves his wife: this theme occurs often in the Bible and gives a new meaning to faith. The law given at Sinai seems more like a marriage contract, an agreement between spouses, and sin is more like adultery, prostitution, a failing in love.

Hosea has an inexorable view of the sinfulness of his people: there is no trust, no tenderness towards one another, no knowledge and love of God. We shall be studying a text from him in more detail, but as we read the whole book, we should stop at those passages which present the love of God (1–3, like that of a husband; 11, like that of a father) or which call for a loving response from the people (4.1–3; 6.4–6, a phrase which Matthew quotes twice: 10.12; 12.3–7). And we can see how sin is the opposite to this (4.4–10; 5.1–7; 7.1–2).

If we are interested in what makes up the life of the people, we might note everything that is said about the institutions of the law, the cult, the land and the prophets. Their importance exceeds that of king and judges. The ideal time was when Israel lived in the desert after the Exodus, under the leadership of the prophet Moses.

God of history or gods of nature?

Israel believed in a God who had intervened in her history: the God of Abraham, Isaac and Jacob, the God-who-brought-us-out-of-slavery. This God guided the people when they were wandering in the desert and he brought them into the land of Canaan.

Now, however, Israel has settled down: the people have fields and towns. What concerns them is how to make sure that the soil and their flocks are fertile. To whom should they pray to have rain in due season? They found an established religion which was well equipped to answer these needs: the Baals, divinized forms of the storm and the rain, and the Astartes, divinized forms of sexuality and fertility (look again at what was said about Canaanite thought on page 19 above).

A God who intervened in history – that was all very well. But one had to make a living, and it was safer to rely on the Baals.

We should not imagine too quickly that this problem is an obsolete one: the Baals have simply changed their name. The Christian may easily experience the same conflict: he believes in a God who has intervened in history and in his son Jesus, but what does this faith have to do with economic necessities? Is it not safer to rely on the 'powers' of nature (one's bank balance, one's own skills and power)?

📖 *Studying a text: Hosea 2.2–23*

Begin by reading this text, paying no attention to the annotations in the margin. Who is it talking about? With what imagery? What does the text say to you?

Note what you like about it, what surprises you, what makes you ask questions, etc.

2　*Plead with your mother, plead –*
　　for she is not my wife, and I am not her husband –
　　that she put away her harlotry from her face,
　　and her adultery from between her breasts;
3　*lest I strip her naked*
　　and make her as in the day she was born,
　　and make her like a wilderness,
　　and set her like a parched land,
　　and slay her with thirst.
4　*Upon her children also I will have no pity,*
　　because they are children of harlotry.
5　*For their mother has **played the harlot**,*
　　she that conceived them has acted shamefully, for she said,
　　'I will go after my lovers,
　　who give me my bread and my water,
　　my wool and my flax, my oil and my drink.'
6　**Therefore** *I will hedge up her way with thorns;*
　　and I will build a wall against her, so that she cannot find her paths.
7　*She shall pursue her lovers but not overtake them;*
　　and she shall seek them, but shall not find them. Then she shall say,
　　'I will go and return to my first husband,
　　for it was better with me then than now.'
8　*And **she did not know** that it was I who gave her*
　　the grain, the wine and the oil,
　　and who lavished upon her silver and gold which they used for Baal.
9　**Therefore** *I will take back*
　　my grain in its time, and my wine in its season;
　　and I will take away my wool and my flax which were to cover her nakedness.
10　*Now I will uncover her lewdness in the sight of her lovers,*
　　and no one shall rescue her out of my hand.
11　*And I will put an end to all her mirth, her feasts, her new moons, her sabbaths,*
　　and all her appointed feasts.
12　*And I will lay waste her vines and her fig trees, of which she said,*
　　'These are my hire, which my lovers have given me.'
　　I will make them a forest, and the beasts of the field shall devour them.
13　*And I will punish her for the feast days of the Baals*
　　when she burned incense to them
　　and decked herself with her rings and jewellery
　　*and went after her lovers and **forgot me**, says the Lord.*
14　**Therefore**, *behold, I will allure her,*
　　and bring her into the wilderness and speak tenderly to her.
15　*And there I shall give her vineyards, and make the Valley of Achor a door of hope.*
　　And there she shall answer as in the days of her youth,
　　as at the time when she came out of the land of Egypt.

Annotations (right margin):

God *husband* / *accused* / *judge*
Baals *lovers* / *accused*
People *wife* / *mother* / *land*

First accusation

punishment

Second accusation

punishment

Third accusation
'punishment'

Exodus

16 **And in that day**, *says the Lord,*
  you will call me 'My husband'
  and no longer will you call me 'My Baal'.
17 *For I will remove the names of the Baals from her mouth,*
  and they shall be mentioned by name no more.
18 *And I will make for you a covenant* **in that day** *with the beasts of the field,*
  the birds of the air and the creeping things of the ground;
  and I will abolish the bow, the sword, and war from the land;
  and I will make you lie down in safety.
19 *And I will betroth you to me for ever;*
  I will betroth you to me in righteousness and in justice,
  in steadfast love, and in mercy.
20 *I will betroth you to me in faithfulness, and you shall know the Lord.*
21 **And in that day**, *says the Lord,*
  I will answer the heavens and they shall answer the earth;
22 *and the earth shall answer the grain, the wine, and the oil*
  and they shall answer Jezreel;
23 *And I will sow him for myself in the land.*
  And I will have pity on Not pitied,
  and I will say to Not my people, 'You are my people';
  and he shall say, 'Thou art my God'.

Gen. 2.23

Peace of paradise
Gen. 2.18–23;
Isa. 11.6–8

See Hos. 1.8
This is the negation of
Ex. 3.14

Who are the main characters here? What are the images which represent them?

What are they doing? What are they looking for?

Note the expressions which keep occurring, the words which seem important to you, the play on possessive adjectives (e.g. the grain, my grain. . .).

In these divorce proceedings, which are presented as an ultimatum, note the three accusations made by God (what are they?) and the punishments which he has in mind (what is the third?).

Pay attention to the contrasts: loved / not loved; give / receive; wilderness v. 3 / wilderness v. 14 (is the meaning the same? why?); does being married mean being supported, at the beginning, and also at the end?

Set this text in the context of the thinking of the time (see the box on p. 47); the crucial issue is to know who gives fertility, the divinized powers (the Baals) or the God of history. How does Hosea refer to history (see the references given in the margin)?

What face does God present here? Is he part of nature? He is the one who gives meaning to everything, but nature has its laws which are discovered by science.

What does he expect of man? Note the words which indicate man's response.

The language of love

Tenderness (Hebrew *hesed*) is a key word in Hosea, signifying the bond of love between two partners.

Love (*rahamim* in Hebrew) is a word reserved for God's love towards us. It is the plural (which means, in Hebrew, the superlative) of the word for mother's breast. This is a mother's love, which goes to the roots of one's being.

Faithfulness, fidelity. Words which all come from the same root in Hebrew ('*emet,* '*emuna,* '*amen*) denote solidity, permanence in an accord between two beings: they can put complete trust in each other.

Knowledge. People know with all their being, with heart and body as well as with understanding (the word can also express the sexual union between man and wife).

Be gracious (*hanan*): a mother's action in leaning over her baby. (In Hebrew the name John is Johanan, God is gracious.)

These are the names which God writes on his 'visiting card': 'The Lord, a God loving and gracious, abounding in steadfast love and tenderness' (Ex. 34.6).

The Sacred History of the North: The Elohistic Tradition

The northern tribes separated from Jerusalem and its king, the successor to David. However, they had the same past and the same traditions. Very soon, in the kingdom of Judah, these traditions were collected together to produce the Sacred Judaean History (or the Yahwistic tradition). Two centuries later, perhaps about 750, in the kingdom of Israel, the same traditions were brought together in the writing of a Sacred History of the North. The tradition is called Elohistic, because in it God is first called Elohim. It is denoted by the letter E.

We have here the same history as that produced in the south, but because the context is different, the history is different also. As we have seen in our study of the prophets, in Israel there was a great temptation to abandon the true God and serve the Baals, or at least to make certain by backing both sides. It was no longer possible to count on the king for the maintenance of the true faith, because he was no longer a descendant of David.

The prophets vigorously reminded the people that there was only one possible covenant: that which God had made with his people. The writers who produced this history had been brought up on the thinking of the prophets and the wise men. For them, to remind the people of their traditions was one way of involving them in the covenant.

This is probably the reason why this history does not begin, like that of the south, with the creation stories, but with the covenant with Abraham.

The religious feeling needed to keep the people faithful to this covenant was the fear of God – not fear as we know it, but respect combined with trust.

We are going to start with a careful reading of two texts in which the Elohist gives good expression to his main convictions: the making of the covenant on Sinai (you will find the text on the opposite page) and the story of Abraham's sacrifice of Isaac, which you can read in your Bible.

We shall then go quickly through this Sacred History of the North, taking as a guideline two elements which are very closely connected: the covenant and the fear of God.

Some characteristics of the Elohist

These characteristics will be clearer if you compare the Elohist with the Yahwist (see p. 36).

He tends to be less vivid, less concrete.

God is utterly different from man. The Elohist usually avoids anthropomorphisms, or ways of talking about God as though he were a man. This inaccessible God reveals himself through dreams. When he speaks in person, he does so through theophanies, or spectacular manifestations. One cannot make any image of the deity.

The Elohist is very interested in moral questions, and he has a developing sense of sin. For example, he explains that Abraham never lied (compare Gen. 12.10f. (J) with Gen. 20 (E)). The law given by Moses is less concerned with how to celebrate the cult than with morality, duty towards God and one's neighbour.

Real worship consists in obeying God and observing the covenant, rejecting all covenants with false gods.

The true men of God are no longer the king and the priests but the prophets: Abraham, Moses (the greatest), then Elijah, Elisha, etc.

The reflections of the Elohist are rooted in the prophetic tradition and the reflections of the wise men.

One possible way of using this guide

We are following a series of great moments in the history of the people and trying to put in context all the texts produced during each period. This necessary backcloth should make it possible for you to follow several courses.

You can follow the approach I have already indicated.

You can also follow a number of great figures: Abraham, Moses and so on. I have tried to indicate the main texts in each chapter. You will find a list of references on p. 120.

The covenant on Sinai. Ex. 19–20

Here are the verses attributed to the Elohist.

19.2 And there Israel encamped before the mountain.³ And Moses went up to God.

⁹And the Lord said to Moses, 'Lo, I am coming to you in a thick cloud.¹² And you shall set bounds for the people round about, saying, "Take heed that you do not go up into the mountain or touch the border of it; whoever touches the mountain shall be put to death; ¹³no hand shall touch him, but he shall be stoned or shot; whether beast or man, he shall not live." ' ¹⁶All the people who were in the camp trembled. ¹⁷Then Moses brought the people out of the camp to meet God; and they took their stand at the foot of the mountain. ¹⁹Moses spoke, and God answered him in thunder.

20.1–17. The Ten Elohistic Commandments (Decalogue).

¹⁸Now when all the people perceived the thunderings and the lightnings and the sound of the trumpet and the mountain smoking, the people were afraid and trembled; and they stood afar off, ¹⁹and said to Moses, 'You speak to us and we will hear; but let not God speak to us, lest we die.'

²⁰And Moses said to the people, 'Do not fear; for God has come to prove you, and that the fear of him may be before your eyes, that you may not sin.' ²¹And the people stood afar off, while Moses drew near to the thick cloud where God was.

20.22–23.33. The Book of the Covenant. This is also Elohistic.

24.3 Moses came and told the people all the words of the Lord and all the ordinances; and all the people answered with one voice, and said, 'All the words which the Lord has spoken we will do.' ⁴And Moses wrote all the words of the Lord. And he rose early in the morning, and built an altar at the foot of the mountain, and twelve pillars, according to the twelve tribes of Israel. ⁵And he sent young men of the people of Israel, who offered burnt offerings and sacrificed peace offerings of oxen to the Lord. ⁶And Moses took half of the blood and put it in basins, and half of the blood he threw against the altar. ⁷Then he took the book of the covenant, and read it in the hearing of the people; and they said, 'All that the Lord has spoken we will do, and we will be obedient.' ⁸And Moses took the blood and threw it upon the people, and said, 'Behold the blood of the covenant which the Lord has made with you in accordance with all these words.'

Read this text carefully.

Note all the characteristics of the Elohist (see the box opposite). What is the role attributed to Moses? Note the various features: prophet, mediator, priest.

Fear: what kind of feeling is this? What is its purpose? For God, the trial is a way of testing the faithfulness of the people.

The covenant: note the ritual; here we have a bilateral contract. God gives his law and the people promise to obey it (in Hebrew, the word understand also means to obey, see Deut. 6.4). Blood is sprinkled on the two parties to the contract; on the altar, which symbolizes God, and on the people. This rite has two aspects: it signifies that if one of the parties infringes the covenant, their blood will be shed, and above all, it shows that the two are 'of the same blood'.

 Abraham's sacrifice of Isaac. Gen. 22.1–13,19

Read this account in your Bible, leaving out vv.14–18, which come from the Yahwist.

Without question, the basis of this is an old story which shows that God does not want the sacrifice of children (a practice sometimes to be found at that time). The Elohist takes up this old story to show us a particularly impressive portrait of Abraham.

Note the features characteristic of the Elohist.

Note the features which we find in both this text and in the account of the making of the covenant.

Put yourself in the place of an Israelite hearing this story: how would Abraham appear to him as the model of what he should be and do?

How is he our model?

Human sacrifice

First fruits are much sought after: what we have first seems to us to be best. And from the beginning of time, the deity has been offered the first fruits of the harvest.

It also happened, at least among the Semites living in Canaan, that the firstborn could be offered in sacrifice, for instance in dramatic cases (invasion, and so on). This was fairly rare, and the Semites coming from the East (Mesopotamia), like Abraham, knew nothing of this rite.

Israel rejected this kind of sacrifice: the firstborn was redeemed; that is, an animal was offered instead.

A survey of the Sacred History of the North

It is difficult to read this sacred history straight through; when the two parallel traditions, the Sacred History of the South and the Sacred History of the North, were amalgamated after the return from exile in Babylon, in cases of overlap the northern history was usually sacrificed, to such a degree that it now exists only in a fragmentary state. We shall pause for the more certain texts.

Abraham cycle

This history almost certainly began with Abraham and not with the creation narratives, as did the Yahwistic version. The first text is the account of God's covenant with Abraham (Gen. 15). Because it is now extremely entangled in the Yahwistic account, we shall be reading it later (see p. 60).

Abraham and Abimelech (Gen. 20). Here we find the main characteristics of the Elohist: his concern for *morality*. Abraham does not have a very good role, but he did not lie! And only he, as *prophet* (v. 7), can intercede for the king (v. 17). He discovers that the *fear of God* (v. 11) can also be found in a pagan. Furthermore, the pagan did not sin: God, in a *dream*, prevented him (v. 4).

Hagar and Ishmael (Gen. 21.9–21). God intervenes in favour of the oppressed.

Abraham and Isaac (Gen. 22.1–14). We have read this important text. In Jewish tradition the Akedah (or binding) of Isaac to the stake is important. See the box on the right, about the Targum on Gen. 22.10.

Jacob cycle

Jacob's dream (Gen. 28.10f.) is partly to be attributed to the Elohist, with the dream (vv. 11–12), fear before the God who is utterly different (vv. 17–18), and God's protection of the weak (vv. 20–22).

Jacob's journeys (Gen. 29–35). During these chapters we see Jacob visiting the chief sanctuaries of the northern kingdom. Thus the origin of these sanctuaries is given roots in the history of the patriarchs.

The Joseph story

Here again it is difficult to distinguish between the Elohistic and the Yahwistic narratives. Joseph was the father of two northern tribes (Ephraim and Manasseh), and he was buried at Shechem (Josh. 24.32). That explains the interest in this patriarch.

In this story we can discover characteristics of the Elohist. For example, the test (Gen. 42.16), the fear of God (42.18), God's protection of the weak (45.5; 50.20). God pursues his aim of saving men, even through suffering and sin.

Targum on Gen. 22.10

At the beginning of our era Jews read the scriptures in the synagogue in Hebrew, the sacred language; but the people who spoke Aramaic no longer understood it. So a translation had to be made. Instead of translating the text word for word, the Jews made a free translation, which was called a Targum (see p. 81). These Aramaic translations are very interesting, because they show us how scripture was understood at the time of Christ. Sometimes there were small changes, sometimes explanations were added. This was the case with the account of the sacrifice of Isaac. After v.10 the Targum adds:

Isaac answered and said to his father: 'Bind me well so that I may not struggle at the anguish of my soul, and that a blemish may not be found in your offering. . .' The eyes of Abraham looked at the eyes of Isaac, but the eyes of Isaac looked at the angels on high: Isaac saw them but Abraham did not see them. The angels on high answered, 'Come and see these two unique men in the earth; the one slaughters and the other is slaughtered. The one who slaughters does not hesitate, the one to be slaughtered stretches out his neck.'

The binding (Akedah in Aramaic) that Isaac asks for expresses his own inner offering: in struggling, he does not want to risk wounding himself, because in that case he would no longer be a victim that could be offered.

In their moments of anguish, the Jews ask God to remember this Akedah and because of it, to pardon their sins and save them.

Moses

The role of Moses in the formation of the people is more important here than in the Yahwistic history (see p. 38). He has the power to perform miracles; he plays the role of intermediary between God and the people, he acts as a prophet, and his prayer is efficacious; he even appears as a priest.

The midwives and the birth of Moses (Ex. 1.15–2.10). The midwives fear God and prefer to obey him rather than Pharaoh. And God saves the weak, the baby Moses. The author was probably inspired by a story, known in Egypt, about the birth of Sargon of Agade, who lived in Mesopotamia more than 2,300 years before Christ.

The burning bush (Ex. 3–4). God shows himself in an amazing way. He reveals his name to Moses, in a phrase which is difficult to translate. Perhaps the best rendering is 'I am who I will be', that is, 'It is by seeing what I shall prove to be and shall do with you, in your history, that you will discover who I am.' So we can only see who this God is through those who serve him. He is the God of Abraham, of Moses, of Jesus Christ . . . of Mr or Mrs or Miss Smith. The aim of the liberation from slavery in Egypt is for the people to put themselves at God's service (4.23, a phrase which occurs often). Here Israel is called God's firstborn, not the king, as in the Yahwistic history.

The birth of Sargon of Agade

I am Sargon the mighty king, king of Agade.
My mother was poor; I never knew my father. . .
My mother, the poor woman, conceived me, in secret she
*   bore me.*
She set me in a basket of rushes, with bitumen she sealed
*   my lid.*
She cast me into the river which rose not over me.
The river bore me up and carried me to Akki, the drawer
*   of water.*
Akki, the drawer of water, lifted me out as he dipped
*   his ewer.*
Akki, the drawer of water, took me as his son and
*   reared me.*
Akki, the drawer of water, made me his gardener.
While I was a gardener, Ishtar granted me her love.
For fifty-five years I exercised kingship.

Moses and Jethro (Ex. 18). Moses' father-in-law helps him to organize the people; he gives him a good position as representative of the people before God (v. 19); one of the criteria for choosing assistants is to be that they fear God.

At Horeb We have already read Ex. 19–20 and later we shall be reading the two law codes (Ex. 20–23: see p.60). In the northern kingdom, the mountain of God is called Horeb and not Sinai.

The golden calf and the vision of God from behind (Ex. 32–34). Here against the Yahwistic and Elohistic traditions are entangled. The sin of the people and of Aaron is obviously idolatry, since they had worshipped an idol; the bull (the calf) is probably the pedestal of the true God (32.5); the people want to force God to make himself present by offering him a throne; in that case he would be a deity under their own control (look again at these two conceptions of God on p. 35). Moses reveals himself as intercessor (33.30f.). He is charged with guiding the people to an encounter with their God: read the impressive account in Ex. 33.7–11. With Elijah, Moses is the one who has advanced furthest towards being intimate with God. However, even he can see only God's 'back' (Ex. 33.18–23).

The gift of the spirit to the elders (Num. 11.16–17, 24–30). We have seen that in the northern kingdom the prophet is the one who maintains the true faith, and Moses is the first and greatest prophet. But the author's ideal is that all the people should be prophets, being guided by the spirit which inspired Moses.

For your work
Remember what I said earlier: when you read a travel guide, you find a general account of what there is to see, but you know that you can't see everything . . . It's the same here. The essential thing is that you should have some idea of the conditions and the ways of thinking in the northern kingdom. Choose the texts that you are going to study. And don't be upset if you can't study them all!

4

The Last Period of the Kingdom of Judah 721–587

A prisoner being led away by an Assyrian warrior
(Nineveh, seventh century BC)

When we began our journey, we paid particular attention to the united kingdom of David and Solomon (pp. 34–35). Then we spent some time in the northern kingdom (pp. 44–45). Now we must return to the southern kingdom, Judah: we are in the last period of its existence, which extends from the fall of the northern kingdom (721) to the capture of Jerusalem (587).

Judah from 933 to 721

A tiny kingdom, squeezed between Israel and the Philistines (see the map on p. 41), Judah spread over the hills around Jerusalem and into the Negeb desert. It lived from agriculture and the rearing of livestock, chiefly sheep, and also trade with Arabia and Egypt.

In the political sphere it was, of course, subject to the repercussions of the international situation. For a great deal of this period, the great powers, Egypt and Assyria, were weakened. So political and military activity was concentrated on the territory of Canaan: struggles, alliances, victories and defeats among the little kingdoms of Judah, Israel and Damascus.

The situation changes from 745 with the return of Assyria to the scene. Damascus and Israel formed a coalition to resist Assyria, and wanted to force Judah to join them; this was the Syro-Ephraimite war, the occasion for Isaiah's oracles (see p. 39). The young king of Judah, Ahaz, preferred to appeal to the king of Assyria for help. This came, Damascus was taken in 732 and then Samaria in 722–721.

The repercussions for the kingdom of Judah caused by the fall of Samaria are important both politically and psychologically.

Judah between 721 and 587

All the territory north of Jerusalem (the old northern kingdom) became an Assyrian province. King Ahaz, who was

A Canaanite king.
Ivory
(Megiddo, between
1350 and 1150)

partly responsible for the destruction of the united kingdom because of his appeal to Assyria, remained loyal to Assyria until his death.

Hezekiah, his son, reigned for about thirty years in his own right; his total reign amounted to more than forty years, since for twelve years his father shared the responsibility of government. Despite Isaiah's advice, he adopted a complicated policy of alliances with Egypt, and with a king of Babylon who at one point rebelled against the king of Assyria.

In 701 Sennacherib, the new king of Assyria, embarked on a campaign against Judah. Hezekiah fortified his capital and had 'Hezekiah's canal' dug in the rock. This was a kind of tunnel which brought the waters of the source of the Gihon as far as the pool of Siloah, within the ramparts. However, Sennacherib shut him up in Jerusalem 'like a bird in a cage'. Sennacherib ended by lifting the siege (perhaps because an epidemic ravaged his army), contenting himself with exacting heavy tribute from Hezekiah.

Manasseh, a violent and impious king, reigned for forty-five years, submitting without a fuss to the king of Assyria. The Assyrian king was now Assurbanirpal: this literate and artistic king has left us a library consisting of more than 20,000 tablets of baked clay on which are engraved the annals of the kingdom and the great literary works of the Middle East. However, towards the end of his reign the political map began to change: a new dynasty appeared in Babylon; further east, in present-day Iran, the Medes became powerful, and in the west Egypt began to awaken once more.

It was in this context that Josiah began to rule in Jerusalem. His reign was to last thirty years. After two impious kings, Manasseh and Amon, the accession of this pious king was hailed with fervour, all the more since Josiah succeeded in recovering some of the territory of the northern kingdom. Was Josiah going to be a new David? During his reign, in 622, a scroll was discovered in the Temple containing laws which had their source in the old northern kingdom: when completed, this collection of laws was to become Deuteronomy. The discovery was to serve as the basis for the great reform which Josiah undertook, with political and religious aims in view (II Kings 22–23).

A new generation of prophets preached in this period: Zephaniah, Nahum, Habakkuk and above all Jeremiah.

There was a dramatic turn of events in 612: Nineveh, the Assyrian capital, was captured. All the peoples of the Middle East applauded the downfall of the enemy. Unfortunately they failed to realize that they had merely changed masters: the victorious Babylonian general was called Nebuchadnezzar, and his first concern would be to set off on a campaign against Egypt.

King Josiah sought to bar the way to Pharaoh Necho, and he was killed at Megiddo. This tragic death of the godly king was a great blow to the faithful: why should someone who trusted in God meet such a lamentable death? It marked the end of the reform launched by Josiah, which did not have time to make a deep impression on the hearts of the people.

In 605, Nebuchadnezzar's victory at Carchemish opened up the way to Palestine for him. He captured Jerusalem in 597 and deported the king and some of the inhabitants. These included a prophet priest, Ezekiel. Nebuchadnezzar had installed a vassal king in Jerusalem, but when his back was turned, this king made an alliance with Egypt. Furious, Nebuchadnezzar returned. On 9 July 587 (or 586) he captured the city, destroyed it, burnt the Temple and the ark of the covenant, and deported the inhabitants to Babylon . . . That was the end of the kingdom of Judah.

The capture of Jerusalem was a considerable psychological shock for believers, as we shall see at our next stage. For the moment, we must go back to the first shock – the capture of Samaria: this partly explains the reflection which began in Judah after 721.

The shock of the fall of Israel in 721

The Germans today know well the trauma brought about by the division of their nation, and they always keep alive the hope of seeing their people reunited.

The faithful in the kingdom of Judah experienced the same trauma, as they saw Assyria destroy Samaria and annex its territory. The trauma was all the greater because it was a blow not only to their patriotic feelings but above all to their religious faith. Granted, the two kingdoms were separate nations, and fought against each other. But they had the same God, the same traditions and the same certainty of being the 'people of God', to whom God had given a country. The annexing of Samaria called in question the two poles of this faith: the people and the land. Was this people to be reduced to Judah alone? Thanks to the prophets and the wise men, there was still a lively hope that one day God would be seen to bring about the reunification of the people: the true people is made up of Israel and Judah.

This political and religious context explains to a large degree the intense literary activity which went on in the kingdom of Jerusalem under kings Hezekiah and Josiah.

Literary activity

The Levites of the north took refuge in Jerusalem, bringing with them the literature that had been produced in their kingdom: the Sacred History of the North (the Elohistic tradition), the collections of laws, the oracles of their prophets etc.

The laws seemed to be too much stamped with the spirit of the north, so for a century they lay dormant in the Temple library until Josiah made them the basis for this reform. Confronted with these laws, scribes undertook a fusion of the two histories, the Judaean history (the Yahwist) and that of the north (the Elohist); this fusion, sometimes called the Jehovist (JE), seemed to be the common property of the tribes of both north and south.

Josiah's reform brought to light the laws which came from the north; when completed, they became Deuteronomy.

In the light of the teaching discovered in Deuteronomy, people began to organize the traditions about Joshua, the Judges, Samuel and the Kings. Rewritten in this way, these books became an illustration, in imagery, of what Deuteronomy was trying to express in theory.

Finally, the oracles of the prophets – Zephaniah, Nahum, Habakkuk and Jeremiah – were put down in writing (see Jer. 36). Many psalms were certainly composed at this time, and the reflection of the wise men continued, above all on the death of the godly king Josiah.

Deuteronomy

The place, Jerusalem. The year, 622. On the orders of king Josiah, work is going on in the Temple. The high priest discovers 'the book of the law' (II Kings 22) and Josiah makes this 'Book of the Covenant' (II Kings 23.2) the basis for the great reform which he undertakes. That was how the central core of what was to become Deuteronomy was discovered.

The book itself has a complex history, and the editing of it stretched over several centuries. So it represents a current of thought we have to note, since this way of reflecting on the history of Israel recurs in a number of books of the Bible.

Deuteronomy as we have it, and its history

The book is presented as a series of speeches by Moses. Before he dies, he gives the people laws, and his last advice on the way in which they should live in the country that they are going to conquer.

The book as we have it now is the culmination of a long history, the main stages of which we can reproduce with some degree of probability.

In the northern kingdom, so before the fall of Samaria in 721, people were becoming aware that the law once given by Moses did not match up very well with reality: this law had been made for a nomadic people, and now Israel had become an organized nation.

New problems had appeared, of a greater or lesser degree of seriousness. For example, the conscription of young married men, the danger of the pagan cults practised in Canaan; the injustice of the rich, who ground the faces of those without rights . . . So it was necessary to read just the law, to make as it were a 'second edition'. This is how, little by little, the laws and customs which one day formed the core of Deuteronomy, the second law, came into being.

The Levites who collected and interpreted these laws and customs were influenced a great deal by the preaching of prophets like Elijah, Amos and above all Hosea. They discovered more clearly that the law given by God to his people was not just any kind of contract, but a covenant, a bond of love like that which unites the betrothed with the one whom he loves (see Hosea 1–3).

After the fall of Samaria in 721, Levites took refuge in Jerusalem, where Hezekiah was king. They

---

Some characteristics of the Deuteronomist

At a formal level:
- the style is very emotional. The author is not content to teach; he wants to convince people that they should obey.
- numerous repetitions, for example: The Lord your God . . . Hear, O Israel, remember . . . Keep the commandments, laws and customs . . .
- a constant mixture of the second person singular and the second person plural. This is doubtless the sign of two stages in the editing. In the book as it is now it becomes the affirmation that the people is a single body, but that each believer among this people keeps his own personality.

Some key ideas:
- The Lord is the sole God of Israel.
- He has chosen a people for himself. In response to this election, the people must love God.
- God has given the people a land, but on condition that they remain faithful to him, remember his covenant with them, today.
- It is above all in the liturgy that the people, an assembly called by God as at Horeb, remembers and understands the word of God.

---

brought these laws with them; they organized them and completed them. They also reflected on the causes of the ruin of their kingdom; what should they have done to remain faithful to God? So their laws are sometimes purely theoretical: they seek more to express a spirit than to make rules which cannot, or can no longer, be applied. Thus, every seven years debts must be remitted and slaves freed (Deut. 15); when a city is captured, all the inhabitants must be killed so that the conquerors are not contaminated by their religion (Deut. 16); people must go up on pilgrimage to Jerusalem for the three great annual festivals (Deut. 16), and so on. This last law is particularly significant: to reconstitute the unity of the people, the Levites want to re-centre the faith upon the sole place where God makes himself present, the Temple in Jerusalem, thus relegating to a secondary level the ancient sanctuaries like those at Shechem and Mount Gerizim.

This first arrangement, made in Jerusalem by the Levites who brought their traditions from the north, forms the old core of Deuteronomy (the passages written in the second person singular between chapters 5 and 26). The reign of the impious king Manasseh made this 'book' sink into oblivion. It was deposited in the Temple, and found there again in 622.

Josiah made it the basis for his great political and religious reform, through which he sought to recreate a people united around Jerusalem. It was perhaps at this period, or later, that the passages written in the second person plural were added, along with the chapters at the beginning and the end.

Finally, after other modifications, this book took its place in the great composite work produced about 400 BC: the law in five volumes, or the Pentateuch.

Because those involved in this work were concerned to be faithful to the thought of Moses; or in other words, because they were certain that the laws they produced were those which Moses would have enacted had he been alive at this time, they put them on his lips as great speeches which he delivered before his death.

'You only had to. . .'

It is all too easy to rewrite history, to say after the event, 'You should have . . . You only had to do that . . .' One wants to retort, 'I would like to have seen you in my position . . .' But if it is God, as it is here, who says it to us . . .?

In their account of the temptations of Jesus, Matthew and Luke show us how, in Jesus, we have seen God in our position! The devil revives in Jesus the temptations of the people and our own temptations. And Jesus retorts with verses from Deuteronomy: he replies as the people should have done. So in him, it is the history of the people and our own history which at last prove successful.

Is it possible to love God? asks Deuteronomy. The New Testament replies: in Jesus, from now on, everything is possible.

A current of thought

However, Deuteronomy is not just a book. People talk about the Deuteronomistic tradition (designated by the letter D): that indicates that we have a current of thought, a way of re-reading history in a precise context, i.e. of the obstacle posed by the fall of the northern kingdom.

In 587 the southern kingdom was destroyed in its turn. Other theologians also meditated on this setback and reread the history that had already been written. As they put the final touches to the books of Joshua and Kings – and also, but in a rather less tidy way, to the books of Judges and Samuel – these writers tried to show how people should have lived in faithfulness to God if they had wanted history to take another course.

Some texts from Deuteronomy

Of course you need to read the whole book to see the love of God for his people, to understand the appeal to respond to him by loving him with all one's being for all one's life, and loving one's brothers and sisters also. However, we can begin with some important texts.

The election (4.32–40). This divine choice is based above all on his love. It is not a privilege but a mission.

'Shema Israel . . .'(6). The beginning of this chapter has become the prayer of every Jew and forms the heart of his faith. 'Hear/obey (the word has two senses), Israel, the Lord is one!' This is the fundamental affirmation, and its consequence is, 'You shall love the Lord with all your heart . . .'

Daily life is like an examination (8.1–5). God tests us to see whether we put our trust solely in him. This text is taken up again in the story of the temptations of Jesus.

The law is not an external code, but a demand to respond to love with love (10.12f.).

The Temple: this is the unique place where God makes himself present to his people (12.2–28); people have to go up on pilgrimage there three times a year (16.1–17).

The true prophet (18.15–22). God announces the coming of the definitive prophet. The first Christians recognized Jesus in this text.

Cursed is anyone who hangs on the tree (21.22). This verse was to play a great role in the thought of Paul about the crucified Jesus (see, for example, Gal.3.13).

Social sense (24.14–22). Here and in many other places we can see the tenderness of Deuteronomy and its love for the insignificant.

The 'eucharist' of the firstfruits (26.1–11). We shall be studying this text on the next page.

The word of God in our heart (30.11–20).

Studying a text: The 'Eucharist' of the Firstfruits. Deuteronomy 26.1–11

Israel had now been living in Canaan for several centuries. The people worshipped a God who had intervened in history; this is recalled by the 'creed' inserted at the heart of the text. Now, however, the Israelite has become a peasant farmer, a trader: what interests him is the fertility of the soil and his livestock. We discover once again the conflict that was there in the time of Hosea (see p. 49): 'The God of history or the gods of nature?' Every year, at harvest time, the Canaanites celebrated a festival in honour of Baal, the god of fertility and vegetation. Israel took over this rite, but what sense did they give to it?

If we don't mind anachronisms, we could say that this text follows a pattern still used in our eucharistic liturgies: offering, narrative (a 'creed', which narrates a history or the account of the last supper), adoration and communion. In what way does the fact of telling a story over our gifts, our life, transform it?

All this, and other things as well, this text invites us to discover.

Begin by reading it carefully, without paying attention to the notes in the margin.

1   *When you come into the land which the Lord your God gives you for an inheritance,*
    and have taken possession of it and live in it,
2   *you shall take some of the first of all the fruit of the ground,*
    which you harvest from the land that the Lord your God gives you,
    and you shall put it in a basket,
    and you shall go to the place which the Lord your God will choose,
    to make his name to dwell there,   The Jerusalem Temple
3   *And you shall go to the priest who is in office at that time,*
    and say to him, 'I declare this day to the Lord your God
    that I have come into the land which the Lord swore to our fathers to give us.'
4   *Then the priest shall take the basket from your hand,*
    and set it down before the altar of the Lord your God.
5   *And you shall make response before the Lord your God:*
    'A wandering Aramean was my father,   Creed = a narrative
    and he went down into Egypt and sojourned there,   Object: a land
    few in number;   The Lord is absent
    and there he became a nation,
    great, mighty and populous.   Object: a land of freedom
6   *And the Egyptians treated us harshly,*
    and afflicted us,   The Lord at the service of his people
    and laid upon us harsh bondage.
7   *Then we cried to the Lord the God of our fathers,*
      and the Lord heard our voice,
      and saw our affliction, our toil and our oppression;
8   *And the Lord brought us out of Egypt with a mighty hand and an outstretched arm*
    with great terror, with signs and wonders;
9   *and he brought us into this place and gave us this land,*
    a land flowing with milk and honey.   Object: happiness in a land one does not possess
10   *And behold, now I bring the first of the fruit of the ground,*
    which thou, Lord, hast given me.'
  And you shall set it down before the Lord your God,
  and worship before the Lord your God;
  and you shall rejoice in all the good which the Lord your God has given
  to you and to your house,
  you, and the Levite, and the sojourner who is among you.   The Lord recognized as Lord

Begin by reading this text carefully, with the help of the 'tool box' (p. 14).

Who are the main characters? What are they doing? What are they offering? Is the Lord present everywhere? In what places? What are the expressions which recur? Note the play on pronouns: I/you . . . we.

At the beginning of the text, we have only the worshipper as an individual: you. At the end, this 'you' is joined by the Levite and the stranger. What do these three main characters have in common, so that they can be grouped together? How does this grouping change the relationship between the worshipper and his land?

Put this text in the religious context of its time (see p. 44): how does it resolve the conflict between the God of history and the powers of nature?

Some guidelines in case you get stuck (don't read them immediately).

A story begins when someone lacks an object and ends when the object is obtained. Here we can find three stories each inside the other.

v. 5b. The lack of a land has been satisfied since Israel became a great nation. But the way the text continues makes it clear that something has gone wrong. So the object has to be made more precise: a land of freedom. Why have things gone wrong? This is the only passage in the text from which God is absent. Does that imply that a quest without God cannot come to a firm conclusion?

vv. 6–9. Instead of the Egyptians, who bring slavery, God gives the land of liberty (note the appearance of 'we' in a difficult situation).

However, here God seems to be at the service of his people, like the gods of nature.

vv. 10–11, which resume vv. 1–4. Because its history is told, the produce of the soil changes its significance. At the beginning this was 'my fruit which I give you'; it becomes 'the fruit which you give me to grow'. Here God is recognized as Lord.

The relationship to the land is also changed. The Levite and the stranger enjoy a land which does not belong to them. It is the same with 'you'! Our goods do not belong to us; they are to serve our happiness and that of all men.

The former prophets

The Jews gave a different name to the books that we call 'historical': Joshua, Judges, Samuel and Kings. They called them the former prophets, thus putting them on the same level as the latter prophets, Isaiah, Jeremiah and the others.

Here there is more than a change of title. When a modern author chooses to have his book published in a collection of history or philosophy, he indicates something about his concern and shows how he wishes us to read it.

So these books are not history books. They do not seek to give an exact reconstruction of events, and it is not important if, for example, the archaeologists tell us that Jericho was virtually in ruins when Joshua captured it. The author is not a reporter photographing a battle, but a prophet looking for the meaning of the event.

Prophetic books. This indicates that the authors meditated on the traditions which reported events to them, in order to discover what word of God they conveyed. The authors sought less to narrate the events than to discover what these events mean for us. So over the years their work could be taken up again, meditated upon, narrated, in a different way, so as to bring a new word of God in a new historical situation.

In reading Deuteronomy, we have discovered above all a current of thought. The definitive editing of these former prophets was probably carried out by scribes stamped by this current. They had already edited versions of these narratives at their disposal. They took them up and brought them together to derive a lesson from them. After the catastrophe of 587, the account of the failings of Israel and its kings became an appeal for conversion. God remains faithful to his promise to give the land, but this is on condition that the people are faithful to him. God remains present to his people, as he was in his Temple, but on condition that the people return to him. In this meditation on the past, the prophets look above all for light on the present and a hope for the future.

The Jehovist tradition (JE)

This is the name sometimes given to the fusion of the Yahwistic tradition (J), composed under David and Solomon in the southern kingdom, and the Elohistic tradition (E), brought together in the northern kingdom. This fusion was more than a straightforward literary operation; it represents a decision of faith, a reflection in depth on the new situation created by the fall of the northern kingdom.

We are in Jerusalem. King Hezekiah, supported by the prophet Isaiah, is on the throne. He is the successor to David and Solomon, to whom God promised a land, a people, a dynasty. However, for two centuries this united kingdom has been split in two: into the northern kingdom, Israel, and the southern kingdom, Judah. They are aware that both of them, together, are the people with whom God made a covenant on Sinai, and that they inherit the promise made to Abraham.

Now in 721 the northern kingdom was destroyed by Assyria. This event shook the faith of the people seriously, on two fundamental points: the land and the people. The land once given to David had been increasingly invaded by the enemy, who were now encamped almost at the gates of Jerusalem. Was the people from henceforth to be reduced to the tribes of Judah and Benjamin, who made up the southern kingdom?

The faithful among the Israelites from the north who had escaped the massacre took refuge in Jerusalem, bringing their traditions with them. King Hezekiah wanted to stimulate a national and religious renewal, and in his reign an intense theological and literary activity began to develop. The Jehovist tradition was to prove a fine example of it.

This fusion is a response in faith to the agonizing problem raised by the situation of the land and the people. The fundamental hope continued (and has always continued) that the people is made up of both Judah *and* Israel. To show this, the two traditions which had grown up separately were put together in a single work. It was a tricky business, because the two traditions often had the same narratives presented from slightly different perspectives. Those who brought them together tried to respect each of them – which is how modern scholars can rediscover the traces of each – while making sure that the new narrative hung together. They succeeded very well in keeping the hope of the Yahwist, centred on the David dynasty, while incorporating into it the moral and spiritual demands of the Elohist. The result, then, was a work which could be the common property of the tribes of both the north and the south, showing their faith in the God of Israel and their hope in the future. We shall now look quickly at two texts from it.

The covenant with Abraham. Gen.15

This story is probably the beginning of the Elohistic tradition, but it has been amalgamated with a Yahwistic narrative to such a degree that scholars do not even attempt to distinguish the two, being content to pick out the ideas dear to each tradition.

Thus the promise of descendants and a land is added to the blessing of Gen.12.2;13.14, from the Yahwistic tradition. The covenant is a favourite theme of the Elohistic tradition.

As it is now, the text is not without its rough patches, but it is a splendid illustration of the total faith of Abraham. The covenant ritual is important. Normally, the two partners to the covenant would both pass between animals which had been cut in two, signifying that if one or other broke the covenant, they would suffer the same fate as the animals. Here, God alone passes between them, because the promise is his alone. That is essential for Israel, as it is for us; our history as believers starts with this unconditional promise by God, who throws the weight of his faithfulness on to the scales of history. In its sorriest moments, when it was aware of being unfaithful, of being justly punished for its sins, Israel could always turn towards this covenant. God has given an unconditional promise, and he will keep it.

The Book of the Covenant. Ex.20.22–23.19

This is an ancient text, going back to the very beginnings of Israel. It came into being at a period, probably that of the Judges, when there was neither king nor priest. The economy was based on the rearing of livestock, with little agriculture. The text was preserved in the northern kingdom, and Deuteronomy was inspired by it. By paying attention to all the specific sectors of daily life, it teaches that all life must be lived under the eye of God.

At the time of the Jehovist fusion, it was incorporated into the Exodus narrative, and breaks up the framework of that account. However, in this way it contributes by giving the whole narrative the structure of a covenant alliance, in which, this time, both partners commit themselves.

Prophets of Judah in the Seventh Century

Nobody knows quite when the voice of Isaiah fell silent. According to Jewish tradition he was martyred by king Manasseh. But another generation of prophets arose, whose words we are going to hear.

Nahum

You should read his hallucinating vision of chariots fighting at the overthrow of Nineveh. Long before it actually happened – he was probably preaching round about 660 – Nahum 'sees' the ruin of the Assyrian capital in 612. This is an amazing act of faith in the power of God which is evoked in the psalm which begins the book. In fact, at this time Assyria was at the height of its power.

Zephaniah

When Zephaniah was active, the reign of the wicked king Manasseh had just ended: the young king Josiah who was enthroned in 640 had not yet begun his great religious reform.

The first part of the book (1.1–3.8) is a tragic recognition of the situation. The same Hebrew word keeps recurring, though in English it is translated by a longer phrase: draw near . . . in the midst. Zephaniah is dismayed; however hard he looks, in the midst of the people there is no one who is righteous, save God: but he stands alone! Jerusalem does not draw near to her God (3.2). And, the great day of the Lord's wrath is near (Dies irae, dies illa . . . 1.14f.).

Since powerful men, kings, prophets and priests have gone wrong, the prophet turns to those who are poor in heart, those who do not pride themselves in their own strength, but put their trust in God (2.3). In this way Zephaniah is the pioneer of a theme – that of spiritual poverty – which will develop further in the New Testament.

However, the love of the Lord is strongest of all. For the future, God at last sees the time when he will finally be able to be in the bosom of the daughter of Zion, in the midst of his people, and of all the peoples purified by his love. God has only to think of this to begin to dance with joy!

Habakkuk

Habakkuk preached about 600, when the Babylonians were beginning to sweep down on Palestine. For him, they are the instrument of God destined to punish the Assyrians who have oppressed Israel. However, that raises a question for him. How can God use such impure instruments? Why do the wicked always prosper? Habakkuk raises the question of evil at a national level. God replies to him in a phrase which Paul will one day make a summary of his message: the righteous shall live by faith (2.4).

The prayer of Habakkuk (ch. 3) expresses his faith and his joy in God in the midst of the worst trials.

Daughter of Zion

It has been traditional in all civilizations to use a female figure as a symbol for a nation (think, for example, of Britannia!). Hosea compared his people with an unfaithful wife whose heart is transformed into that of a young woman by the love of God.

Micah was the first to use the strange expression 'daughter of Zion'; it probably denotes the northern quarter of Jerusalem, the summit of the hill of Zion where those who escaped the catastrophe of the fall of Samaria regathered after 721. So it indicates a small remnant purified by suffering.

Zephaniah has a vision that in the future this remnant of Israel will be so purified that God can live in their midst, and all the nations who have been purified will join with them (Zeph.3.9). So this image is important for us: it indicates the destiny of each one of us, since here we have the people of the last days.

Jeremiah puts more stress on the sorrowful mystery of the purification that will be needed (4.11; 6.23); so does Lamentations. However, when she is finally purified, this 'woman' will once more search for God, her husband (Jer.31.22).

The disciples of Isaiah who preach at the end of the exile show this virgin of Zion, the Lord's bride, giving birth to many sons (Isa.54.1; 60; 62: 'Rejoice, daughter of Zion . . .'). She will even be giving birth to the new people (Isa.66.6–10).

The first Christians took up this theme once more in order to present the mystery of the church, the woman who was to give birth to Christ through the sorrows of Calvary and throughout history (John 16.21f.; Acts 12). And for Luke, Mary is the image of this church, filled with grace in the last days (Eph.1.6), and welcoming the Saviour into her midst (Luke 1.28–31).

Jeremiah

'Without this extraordinary being, the religious history of humanity would have taken another course, and Christianity would never have happened.' So wrote Ernest Renan, author of a famous Life of Jesus, in the last century.

Jeremiah experienced the terrible drama in which his people were involved, in 597 and then in 587. Furthermore, he had foreseen it, and tried to prepare the people. However, they were thoughtless and simply persecuted him.

Jeremiah began to preach in the time of king Josiah. At that time his preaching was no different from that of the prophets who had preceded him. He wanted to make his people aware that they had gone astray, that the life they were leading would only end in catastrophe. In the first six chapters, which sum up this preaching, two key words recur: the people have *abandoned* God – they must *return* to God, and be converted.

Strangely enough, Jeremiah was silent during the religious reform undertaken by Josiah, though he certainly approved of it.

In 605 the Babylonian king Nebuchadnezzar defeated the Egyptians at Carchemish, in the north of Syria, and in 603 he advanced as far as Jerusalem, which surrendered. Jeremiah understood that the enemy would come from the north, from Babylon. He foresaw the catastrophe and prepared his people for it. When a mishap befalls us (an illness or an accident) and there is no more that we can do about it, there is nothing for it but to try to make sense of what has happened. 'It is afterwards that we understand,' I said at the beginning of this book (p.9). This is what prophets like Ezekiel, and some disciples of Isaiah living in exile in Babylon, tried to do (see the box entitled 'God will punish you . . .'). The great merit of Jeremiah is that he understood beforehand, and made sense of the disaster before it happened. Of course, the people did not listen to him, but rejected him and persecuted him, preferring to follow the false prophets, who reassured them. However, when events proved Jeremiah right, his message was remembered. Thanks to him, the people who endured catastrophe had the possibility of making sense of it as it happened. To a great degree this enabled people to endure the exile in faith and hope, not being overwhelmed by their misfortunes, but rather discovering a new meaning in life.

Of course you won't be able to read all of Jeremiah. But here are at least a few texts that you could read.

True religion. The people are good at practising their religion; they revere the ark of the covenant and go to the Temple; they offer sacrifices, observe the sabbath and circumcise children. They practise their religion, but their heart is not in it. They think that because they respect the ritual, God will have to protect them, along with Jerusalem, the holy city. They have made their practice of religion a matter of security which relieves them of the obligation to love. Jeremiah announces that God will destroy all these false securities: the ark of the covenant (3.16); the Temple (7.1–5; 26); Jerusalem (19), for what God demands is not an outward circumcision, of the flesh, but an inward circumcision, of the heart (4.4; 9.24–25). These attacks seemed so blasphemous that Jeremiah barely escaped death. In this way he prefigures Jesus' attacks on our senseless practices.

The new covenant. Chapter 31 is the climax of his message. He preaches hope beyond misfortune: God will pardon and make things new.

What is this security based on? Read 31.20.

Personal responsibility (vv.29–30): Ezekiel develops this aspect at length (Ezek.18).

What features make the covenant a new one (31.31–34)? Luke (22.20) and Paul (I Cor.11.25) see it realized in the blood of the Last Supper.

Prophetic actions. Like all the prophets, but to an even greater degree, Jeremiah preaches his actions as well as his words. These symbolic gestures are often more than a simple announcement: because the prophet bears the word of God, the effective word, in some sense they make the event announced become present in advance. In this sense the actions of Jesus at the Last Supper are also prophetic actions.

Jeremiah's personal journal. With Paul, Jeremiah is the person in the Bible whom we know best. In fact he gives us his personal reactions; he tells us of his faith and doubts in passages which are extremely personal. They are sometimes called his confessions. Read at least 12.1–5; 20.7–18: how do these 'prayers' help us to understand God? ourselves? our relationship with God?

Jeremiah's call (1.4–19). The way in which a prophet describes his call, his vocation, often sheds a great deal of light on his message. In the case of Jeremiah, there is nothing extraordinary: everything seems to take place in the intimacy of prayer. Using this text as a starting point, try to discover the nature of the mission entrusted to Jeremiah and some features of his character. On what is his certainty based? The two visions (vv.11f.,13f.) show us how a prophet 'sees' God in events. How can that help us to discover the word of God in our life and in world events?

God will punish you . . .

The message of the prophets may well shock us. They often present us with a God who threatens his people with punishment because they have sinned. So are natural catastrophes, wars, human injustice, all punishment from God? We find such a picture of a vengeful God intolerable.

Here is a parable. Imagine a young man, crazy about his motor cycle. One day he has an accident: hospital, long months of convalescence, doctors, nurses . . . and one nurse who soon begins to look after him with more than professional care. One day they get married. This boy might well say to the nurse who became his wife: 'It's lucky that I got smashed up; otherwise I would never have come to know you.' We might accept this remark, but we would find it objectionable if the chaplain went up to him and said, 'You were lucky . . .' Why? In the first case, it is the person involved who himself, out of his own feelings and after the event, makes sense of his accident; it is not imposed on him from the outside. Furthermore, the accident remains a misfortune for him; the good luck is the happy outcome to his troubles.

Now let's change the story and apply it to the prophetic books. Suppose that before his accident this boy had led a dissolute and selfish life. His suffering, the long months of loneliness led him to reflect on the emptiness of his life, and the boy who came out of the hospital was a changed person. He decided to transform his life and to put himself at the service of others. If he even rediscovered faith, one could imagine him saying one day to God, 'It's a good thing you allowed this accident, because as a result I've found meaning in my life.' We can accept this prayer, but we would find objectionable the chaplain who said, 'You see, God's punished you . . .'

The prophets are the boy, and not the chaplain. Ezekiel was deported with the people; Jeremiah was persecuted and bore in advance the sufferings of the people. They reflected on events which for them remained a misfortune. However, from within and after the event (or before it, in the case of Jeremiah), they tried to make sense of these events and to see the good effect that they might have. They led the people to recognize that they had lived badly and had to change their lives. For them, even if the language which they use is sometimes rather abrupt, these events are less divine punishments than occasions for discovering the love of God which invites them to a new life.

An Assyrian warrior cuts off the head of a prisoner (Assyrian painting, eighth century)

5 *Exile in Babylon 587–538*

Winged bull with a man's head.
Assyria (eighth century)

July 587: after a siege lasting one year, the army of Nebuchadnezzar, king of Babylon, captured Jerusalem. That was the end of the kingdom of Judah.

Ten years of madness. 597–587

Nebuchadnezzar had already captured Jerusalem in 597. At that time he was content to accept substantial tribute, to deport some of the inhabitants (including the prophet Ezekiel) and to leave behind a vassal king.

It might have been hoped that that would teach the people a lesson. However, led astray by false prophets who nurtured their illusions and made them feel that they were just having a bad time for the moment, the people experienced ten years of madness. They continued a carefree existence, and made an alliance with Egypt against the Babylonians.

In Jerusalem, the prophet Jeremiah preached the need for submission to the Babylonians. For him, the essential thing was not whether the nation was free or politically subject, but whether it was just and spiritually free, serving its God and acting rightly. The voice of Jeremiah, declared a traitor to his country, was muted by the mud-filled cistern into which he was thrown.

In Babylon, Ezekiel spoke in the same way to the fellow-countrymen who had been deported with him, but to no effect. They were secretly making flags to welcome their brothers who would come to deliver them. In 587, they saw these brothers arrive – at least those who had not been put to the sword – not as liberators, but with ropes round their necks, exhausted by the 1,500 kilometre march, following a king whose eyes had been put out, and retaining in his empty sockets a last sight – that of his sons having their throats cut.

Reconstruction of a ziggurat. The tower of Babel was thought to be like this

The miracle of the exile

The people had lost everything that went to make up their life:

● the land, the concrete sign of God's blessing on his people.

● the king, through whom God handed on this blessing, the guarantor of the unity of the people and their respresentative before God.

● the Temple, the place of the divine presence.

In the last resort, Israel had even lost its God. At this time, it was thought that each country was protected by its national God, the power behind its armies. So the God of Israel had been defeated by Marduk, the god of Babylon. And one did not go on serving a conquered god.

The great miracle of the exile was that instead of proving the ruin of the faith of Israel, this catastrophe brought about a change in this faith and purified it. The miracle occurred thanks to the prophets, like Ezekiel and a disciple of Isaiah known as Second Isaiah, together with the priests: these led the people to reread their traditions in order to discover there a foundation for their hope. Together, they discovered a new and more spiritual way of living out their faith. Temple and sacrifices were a thing of the past. But it was possible to meet on the sabbath to worship God and to meditate on his word. The king was no more. But was not God the only true king of Israel? The land was lost. But circumcision in the flesh could mark out the bounds of a kingdom with spiritual dimensions. In this way, in exile, what we call Judaism came into being, i.e. a way of living out the Jewish religion which would be that of the time of Jesus and of our own time.

By the waters of Babylon . . .

What was the situation of the Jews who had been deported? That question is not very easy to answer. The people had undergone a terrible psychological and moral shock, and they had also experienced physical suffering. In this period, the capture of a city and deportation meant that women were raped, small children were dashed against the rocks, warriors were impaled or burnt alive, eyes were gouged out and heads cut off. We can read an echo of this suffering in Ps.137. However, we should not imagine that life in Babylon was like that in a concentration camp. The Jews enjoyed relative freedom (though that did not exclude forced labour); Ezekiel was free to visit his compatriots, who could devote themselves to agriculture. At the end of the exile, some of them preferred to stay in Babylonia, where they formed an important and prosperous group. The archives of the bank of Murashu in Nippur (south of Babylon) show us that a century after the exile a certain number of Jews had quite substantial accounts.

The Jews were impressed by the city of Babylon and its traditions. The city had the form of a vast square, covering about thirteen square kilometres, with the river Euphrates running through it. The gate of Ishtar, adorned with multi-coloured enamelled bricks, opened on to the sacred route, flanked by temples, in the midst of which rose the ziggurat (a kind of stepped tower). This was the tower of Babylon, or Babel. Annually, at New Year, they would listen to the recitation of the great poems (Enuma Elish, the Gilgamesh Epic) which told how the god Marduk, god of Babylon, created the world, and how the god Ea saved mankind from the flood. They discovered the thoughts of the wise men about the human condition. In this way the Jews were in contact with a type of thinking which was widespread in the Middle East, and this will clearly have helped them to reflect.

Cyrus the 'messiah'

On 29 October 539, Cyrus seized Babylon without firing a shot, probably thanks to the help of Babylonians who were exasperated with the incompetence of their king Nabonidus.

Cyrus was a petty king of Persia, one of the provinces of the empire of the Medes which extended to the north and east of Babylon. In 550 he seized power in Media, went as far as Asia Minor to seize the fabulous treasure of king Croesus, and returned to Babylon. His amazing rise was followed passionately by the Jewish exiles and Second Isaiah; was not this the man whom God had chosen, had marked out through his anointing (*messiah* in Hebrew) to liberate them?

And in fact in 538 in Ecbatana, his distant summer capital, Cyrus signed an edict allowing the Jews to go home. He even granted them substantial war damages to rebuild their country. Was this because of his natural benevolence, or his political sensitivity? He was actually interested that the Jewish nation, an advance bastion of his empire in the direction of Egypt, should be utterly devoted to him. Whatever his motives, for the Jews this was the end of their nightmare, and at that time a large number of them returned to 'the land'.

Literary activity

The Jews had lost everything. They had nothing left but their traditions. So they began to read these again with great concern.

The prophets Ezekiel and the Second Isaiah preached, one at the beginning of the exile and one at the end.

Priests reassembled the collections of laws which had already been put into writing in Jerusalem towards the end of the monarchy: the Holiness Code (Lev.17–26). Augmented after the return from exile, this law was to become Leviticus.

Above all, in order to sustain faith and hope among the people, the priests once more reminded them of their origins. This rereading of history is known by the name of the Priestly tradition, and is the fourth of the documents which make up the Pentateuch. So all the elements of the Pentateuch were complete: it remained only to bring them together in a single work. This happened around 400.

Disaster, suffering, and also contact with Babylonian and then Persian thought, led the wise men of Israel to deepen their reflection on the human condition. In the centuries after the exile this reflection culminated in works like Job.

We can also easily imagine that the prayer of believers would take on a new tone. Psalms (for example 137 or 44; 80; 89) could be composed at that time as appeals to the God who keeps faith.

In Jerusalem, some Jews spared deportation voiced their lament in the book of Lamentations, wrongly attributed to Jeremiah.

Prophets of the Exile

Ezekiel

Ezekiel was one of the first group to be deported, in 597. For ten years, in Babylon, his message was couched in the same terms as that of Jeremiah, who remained in Jerusalem: he censured the people of God (Ezek.3–24) and the nations (Ezek.25–32) for their wicked conduct.

From 587, when the catastrophe had come about and the people had lost all hope, his preaching became a message of hope: God would restore his people (33–39). Ezekiel was so sure of this that he gave a description, in futuristic terms, of the Jerusalem of the future, transformed by God (40–48).

A disconcerting figure

Ezekiel can never be like anyone else. Like his predecessors, he has visions, but his are flabbergasting: for example, read the account of his call (ch.1). He performs prophetic actions, but sometimes these go beyond the bounds of good taste: see chs.4–5. Some passages in his allegories would make a guardsman blush – so don't read chs. 16 or 23!

However, it is by means of this very excessiveness that Ezekiel achieves the solemn effect he makes, and when he wants to , he can become a very great lyric poet: see his cry against the prince of Tyre (ch.28). Compare it with Gen.2–3: you will see that these two texts exploit, in different ways, the same mythological traditions.

The father of Judaism

Ezekiel's message served as the foundation of what came to be called Judaism, that is to say, the Jewish way of living before God and with others as it took form after the exile.

Ezekiel has a very lively sense of the holiness of God, and he wants this to be expressed with all men's being. Hence the importance he attaches, because he is a priest, to regulations and ritual.

In this way he is inspired by the Holiness Code (Lev.17–26), created by the priests at Jerusalem before the exile (see p.68).

Jeremiah insisted on the inward aspect of religion; his ideals were sustenance for the piety of God's poor. The danger here was that religion might become detached from day-to-day living. Ezekiel also preaches an inward-looking religion, but insists on a complementary aspect: this faith must be expressed through the body, in ritual. The danger here is that people observe the regulations without having their heart in what they do.

◗ Some texts from Ezekiel

The holy presence of God
God made himself present in his temple. However, first Nathan (II Sam.7, see p.42) and then the other prophets had sensed that God does not want to dwell materially in a place, but spiritually, among a faithful people. Ezekiel, living in exile, shows how this can be realized, in his own person.

Read, one after the other, Ezek.9.3; 10.4–5; 11.22–23; then Ezek 1; and finally Ezek.37.26–28; 43.1–12. What is Ezekiel trying to say by means of these extraordinary images? Where is God present? How? (Perhaps Luke was thinking of Ezek.11.23 when he put the Ascension on a mountain facing east, the Mount of Olives.)

I am the good shepherd. Ezek.34; 37.15–18
Who are the shepherds of the people? How have they behaved? Who will be the true shepherd?

Jesus was inspired by these texts (Matt.18.10–14; Luke 15.1–7; John 10). Who is the shepherd? What force and what significance does this give to the words of Jesus?

Behold, I make all things new. Ezek.33.1–11; 37.1–14. The people are in exile, and desperate; they are like old carcases drying out in the sun . . . What does God announce in the vision of ch.37? God recreates his people by his word and gives them life through his spirit. What can this say to Christians today? Ezek.36.16–38; 47.1–12. What is the spirit doing? Whence does it spring? Jer.31.31–34 makes that plainer: how? How do these texts help us to understand John 7.37–39; 19.34, or Gal.5.22–25?

Second Isaiah. 'The voice which cries.' Isa.40–55

Here is something amazing! To be in exile, scorned, humiliated, having lost everything, toiling without hope, a foreign labourer . . . and then to begin to sing of the God who does miracles, in a voice which is so convincing that it brings hope to a whole people. Where did this disciple of Isaiah, who hides behind his mission and simply calls himself 'the voice which cries', find such strength? In his faith in God. God is always 'the-one-who-brought-us-out-of-the-house-of-slavery' at the Exodus, so he can still free us. He has the power to do so, because he is the creator. And he will do so because he is faithful and loves us more than a mother.

Before we study an important text, let's single out some of the major themes of this moving prophet.

The gospel
Three times, there rings out this good news or gospel, that God will at last establish his kingdom, show himself to be the true king, and make evil, suffering and injustice disappear (40.9; 41.27; 52.7. See also 35.3–6, which comes from the same period). By performing miracles and pronouncing the beatitudes, Jesus proclaims that this is realized in him: the poor will be happy, because from now on their poverty is ended.

God's tenderness. 43.1–7; 49.14–16
This is one of the finest sayings about the love of God, whose feeling for us is the gut-feeling of a mother.

The new exodus
The liberation is seen as a more marvellous exodus than the first. See, for example, 40.3; 41.17–20; 43.16–23; 44.21f.; 48.17–22. The first Christians interpreted the life of Jesus and our own in the light of the Exodus (see the references in the margin of your Bible, if it is an annotated version).

Cyrus the messiah
Here is a fine example of the interpretation of history. Cyrus captures Babylon for personal aggrandisement. He himself interprets this as a call from Marduk, God of Babylon (see the adjacent box). For Isaiah, it is the God of Israel who has called him and anointed him (41.1–5,25–29; 42.5–7; 44.27–28; 45.1–6,11–13; 48.12–18). Faith, and faith alone, allows us to see a meaning in events.

🕮 The Servant of God. Isa.52.13–53.12

This text is the climax of the message. There is some controversy over how it should be interpreted.

Begin by looking at those who speak:
God announces the glory which awaits his servant (52.13–15).

The nations who have persecuted this servant are amazed and confess their mistake (53.1–6).

The prophet meditates on the fate of this servant, an innocent victim who has been put to death (53.7–9).

Then he prays:
Lord, ground down as he is by suffering, may he please you; make him a sacrifice of expiation,
so that he may see his descendants and prolong his days,
and fulfil the good pleasure of God.
God hears this prayer. 53.11–12.

This servant is probably the personification of the people of Israel, humiliated, scorned, put to death. Calamity has come upon them and they cannot do anything but try to make sense of it (look again at 'God will punish you . . .', p.63).

How is this situation of the death of the servant transformed? What is the final outcome? Why? (Look at the two aspects, the attitude of the servant and the action of God.)

This servant did a great deal to help the first Christians understand Jesus. How does he help you to discover the meaning
of the mission of Christ (53.12)?
of his death for the many (Mark 10.45; Rom.4.25; the accounts of the Last Supper: Matt.26.28; Mark; Luke)?
The mystery of Easter? Read Phil.2.6–11.

How does this help us to make sense of our lives?

The Cyrus Cylinder

On a clay cylinder discovered in Babylon, Cyrus gives his interpretation of events:

Marduk, the great Lord (of Babylon), the protector of his people, beheld with pleasure the good deeds of Cyrus and ordered him to march against his city, Babylon. He made him set out on the road to Babylon, going at his side like a real friend. Without any battle, he made him enter his town Babylon.

Leviticus

This is a marvellous book, full of sexual tabus and blood! But you need to be brave to venture into it: there are constant repetitions, a boring tone, strange and pettyfogging rules – everything is calculated to put us off. And yet . . .

We need ritual

Because we are physical beings, we express our feelings through specific actions. Watch a family laying the table before a dinner party; everything is set out in accordance with a fixed pattern, with custom, but that is the way in which we show our friends how pleased we are to see them. However, that is also the possible danger of ritual; in a restaurant, the waiter who lays the table may do so with complete indifference.

We also need ritual when we are preparing to meet God. As the fox said to the little prince in Saint-Exupery's story, it's a way of 'dressing up the heart'. For Israelite believers, meeting God was an important matter, the one thing that was worth while. So for them the minute details in ritual were one way of expressing their sense of living in the presence of the holy God.

'Be holy because I am holy'

Many of the regulations in Leviticus belong to a culture which is no longer our own and it would be stupid to want to apply them. But what they tell us is still essential: God is present, and we live before him. God is mentioned constantly (more than 350 times), and 'before him' recurs like a refrain (more than 50 times). Read ch.19: one motivation underlies all the regulations, from love of neighbour (v.18) to justice for the hired labourer (v.13), and taking in all the situations of everyday life: 'I am the Lord your God'. So it is in his love for God that the believer sees the way in which he should live in the world and with others.

This God is the holy God; that is, he is utterly different from us. He is the living God, he is Life. And that explains the mysterious respect there is for blood and sexuality.

'The blood is the life' (Lev.17.11,14)

Blood is sacred because it is life, the very life which comes from God and which flows in our veins. So the blood of men may not be spilt. One may not drink the blood of an animal (much less that of a man); that would be to claim to fortify one's life by human means, whereas God alone is the master of life. So this is not a culinary regulation (don't eat black pudding!), but a matter of respect for life. By contrast, offering blood in sacrifices is a way of recognizing the gift of life which God makes to us. In these sacrifices what is offered is not the victim –

Sacred – sacerdotal – sacrifice

Sacerdotal is an archaic word, meaning 'priestly', but by using it here we can see how the notions of the sacred, priesthood and sacrifice are all connected with the same root. In all religions, the sacred is the sphere of the deity, completely separate from the profane (*pro-fanum*, Latin for 'before the holy place'). Israel largely shared in this mentality. God was the Holy One, that is, the one who is utterly different.

Furthermore, Israel had a keen sense that man exists only in relationship, with others and above all with God. But how was it possible to bridge the gap between the holy God and man?

This was the responsibility of the priest. To fulfil it, he had to enter the sphere of the sacred, and that was achieved through consecration, i.e. separation: separation from the people to be reserved for the cult; separation from the profane and from everyday activities to enter the temple. The culmination of the priest's activities was sacrifice. The word does not mean deprivation, but transformation: to sacrifice is to make sacred: what one offers passes into God's domain. In return, the priest can hand on God's gifts to the people: pardon, instruction, blessings.

With Jesus Christ, this conception was to be completely transformed. In him the sacred became profane. It was no longer possible to make a distinction between the two; through him, everything was sanctified. And he is the only priest, the perfect mediator: his sacrifice is the unique sacrifice (the Letter to the Hebrews develops this aspect at length). However, the temptation of the church is always to express sacrifice and the priestly ministry by going back to the Old Testament pattern: this explains the present difficulties connected with priesthood in the Catholic church today.

---

which is no more than a carcase – but the hot (literally, 'living') blood, i.e. the very life of the victim. We should get into the habit of replacing this word blood by its equivalent, the life which is offered; these texts from Leviticus or the Letter to the Hebrews then become terribly evocative.

The same applies to the sexual prohibitions. Over and above the tabus (which certainly exist), the principal element is the impressive feeling of sharing, through sexuality, in the handing on of the life which comes from God, and which explains the sacred character of sexuality.

The composition of Leviticus

The Holiness Code (Lev.17–26) was composed in Jerusalem before the exile. At the time when Deuteronomy, which came from the north, was being edited, and everything was centred on the covenant and election on the part of God, the Jerusalem priests wanted to codify the customs practised in the Temple, all centred on the cult, to remind people that God is holy, utterly different.

The law of sacrifice (Lev.1–7) and the law of purity (Lev.11–16) were edited after the exile, as was the law of festivals (Num.28–29).

Some texts from Leviticus

Of course you can't read the whole book. But it would be a pity to miss some texts.

Lev.19.1–17: God's holiness is the source of brotherly love and life in society.

Lev.23 reminds you how time is sanctified by the sabbath and the great festivals.

Lev.16 presents the great day of forgiveness, Yom Kippur: this was the only time in the year when the high priest could penetrate behind the veil of the temple, to obtain remission of sins. The author of the Letter to the Hebrews used this liturgy to express Christ's sacrifice. This chapter also takes up an old custom with a touch of magic to it, that of the scapegoat.

Finally, if you want to discover about the various kinds of sacrifices, read Lev.1–7.

Impure or sacred?

For us, purity and impurity are moral notions.

In the Bible, as in all religions, they are notions which come very close to those of tabu or the sacred. A person is impure when he has made contact with a mysterious power which can be good or evil. In that case it is necessary to perform a ritual which purifies, which removes the contagion of this power.

Some illnesses, for example, can make people impure because at that time they are thought to be under demonic influence.

Conversely, contact with God can bring 'impurity'. Thus, only a short while ago, one could read this rubric in Catholic liturgical books: 'After communion, the priest purifies the chalice' (with a linen cloth called a 'purificator'). Had this chalice become impure (in the moral sense) through having contained the blood of Christ? No, it had become sacred because it had entered the divine sphere, and its purification was a rite of desacralization, allowing it again to be put to some profane usage. A woman who has just given birth must also be purified. We might ask whether this, too, is not an act of desacralization: because she had come into contact with God, the source of life, by giving life, she has to undergo a certain ritual in order to return again to everyday life.

This question of purity and impurity is very complicated, and the object of much discussion by scholars. Here I have over-simplified it almost to the point of falsification. However, it's worth at least remembering several points:

- the notions of purity and impurity often have no moral content, but are more closely connected with ideas of tabu and the sacred;

- sometimes, however, these same words take on a moral significance;

- confusion between the two senses of these very words is doubtless partly responsible for the discredit into which sexuality is brought: we have given a moral sense to impurity in places where the Bible gives it a ritual sense.

The Priestly History

In exile, the people had lost all that made them a people. There was a risk that they might become assimilated and disappear, which had been the fate of the northern kingdom 150 years earlier, when they had been deported to Assyria. Who would help them to withstand this test? Prophets like the priest Ezekiel and Second Isaiah, but above all the priests. In Jerusalem these formed a solid group, well organized and with a deep piety. They were the ones who would sustain the faith of the exiles. They succeeded in adapting religion to the difficult situation and giving it a new future.

They invented new forms of practice or gave religious practices a new significance. The sabbath, as a sanctification of time, and circumcision, as a mark of belonging to the people, would become primordial symbols (reread p.64). Sacrifices were replaced by assemblies (or synagogues) where people prayed and meditated on the word of God: this is the origin of what was later to become synagogue worship.

The Priestly History, denoted by the letter P, came into being in this context. The priests reread past history to discover in it a reply to agonizing questions. Why is God silent? How can we believe in God in this Babylonian world which celebrates the god Marduk as creator? What is the place of other nations in God's plans? So this tradition invites us to continue its reflections, and to see how we today, in a new situation, can live out our faith and respond to the world's questions. God's promise is always valid; but we have to work to fulfil it.

A key text: Gen.1.28

And God blessed them, and God said to them,
'Be fruitful and multiply, and fill the earth and subdue it; and have dominion over the fish of the sea and over the birds of the air and over every living thing that moves upon the earth.'

This is an extraordinary blessing, which expresses the faith of the priests in exile. The five verbs are an

---

Some characteristics of the Priestly writer

The style is dry. The Priestly writer is not a storyteller. He loves figures and lists. He often repeats the same thing twice: God says. . .God does. See, for example, his version of the crossing of the Red Sea (p.26 above); the creation (Gen.1); the building of the sanctuary (Ex.25–31;35–40).

The vocabulary is often technical and has to do with the cult.

Genealogies appear often. They are important for an exiled people without roots. They give the people roots in history and connect up this history with that of the creation (Gen.2.4; 5.1; Num.3.1).

Worship has pride of place. Moses organizes it; Aaron and his descendants are made responsible for continuing it through pilgrimages, festivals, and worship in the temple, which is the holy place in which God makes himself present. The priesthood is an essential institution which assures the existence of the people; it replaces the role of the king in the Yahwist and the prophet in the Elohist.

Laws are usually put in a narrative context. So they are attached to historical events which give them significance. See, for example, the law of fertility (Gen.9.1) in the story of the flood, or the law of the Passover (Ex.12.1ff.), attached to the tenth plague.

Because of all these characteristics, the Priestly texts are the easiest ones to identify in the Pentateuch.

---

exact contradiction of their present situation. They express the will of the creator God which will be fulfilled one day, and put an end to evil and to the exile.

You can see how this blessing underlies the book of Genesis, giving a new colouring to the events which are narrated: Gen.8.17; 9.1–7 (the flood); 17.20 (Abraham); 28.1–4; 35.11 (Jacob); 47.27 (Joseph). In Ex.1.7 this is no longer a promise, but a reality which has to be pursued throughout history.

A survey of the Priestly History

Like the Yahwistic tradition, the Priestly History begins with creation and goes as far as the death of Moses (Deut.24.7). On the next two pages we shall be studying the creation story. Here we shall read one or two texts.

The covenant with Noah and the flood. Gen.6–9

The two traditions, the Yahwistic and the Priestly, have been fused in the present account of the flood. Both closely follow the mythical account of the flood told in the Gilgamesh epic. The Priestly tradition stresses the construction of the ark, built with three storeys, like Solomon's Temple: it is in the sanctuary that man finds salvation (6.16).

This narrative ends with the covenant with Noah, with his descendants and with the whole earth (9.8–17). Thus the God of Israel is the universal God and his covenant relates to all men. All nations have a place in God's plan.

But does Israel have a particular place?

The covenant with Abraham. Gen.17

The law of circumcision is attached to a narrative which is made up of four speeches by God. Try to see how the thought progresses from one to the other. What does God ask of Abraham? That he should go in his presence (remember Leviticus) and be whole, without fault or blemish, like the offering for sacrifice (Ex.12.5; Lev.1.3). Circumcision becomes the distinctive sign of the people (compare this text with Gen.15, p.60).

In exile, Israel becomes aware that the people have sinned and broken the bilateral covenant made on Sinai. According to the terms of this covenant, it is natural that God should have let it lapse. As we shall see, the authors pass quickly over Sinai, to return to the covenant with Abraham. Here it is a matter of a promise to which God alone is committed. Whatever its sins, Israel (and we too in our turn) can have recourse to it.

This tradition is interested in Abraham's purchase of land at Hebron to bury Sarah in (Gen.23). This is important for the exiles: their ancestor bought a piece of land and is buried in it (25.9). So they have a right to this land!

The Exodus

These exiles stressed the harsh servitude in Egypt (Ex.1.13–14; 2.23–24) and the promise made by God to Abraham (Ex.6, the calling of Moses). The priests remember the way in which this liberation was celebrated: the cult makes present for each generation the action of the Lord who gives freedom (Ex.12.1–20). The crossing of the sea becomes a powerful act of the creator God (see p.26); he is capable of renewing it for his exiled people. The law of the sabbath is attached to the gift of manna (Ex.16), so the people can cease work on that day without being afraid that God may let them die of hunger.

The covenant on Sinai

This covenant was too important for the exiles to pass it by in silence. However, they transformed its meaning. No actual covenant is made here (as with the Yahwist and the Elohist: Ex.24). God simply announces that he will make Israel a kingdom of priests and a holy nation (Ex.19.5–6). Israel is not governed by kings, like other nations, but by priests.

God does not give a law for his people, but orders to build a sanctuary (Ex.25–27), to establish priests and the cult (Ex.28–29); the only law is that of the sabbath (Ex.31.12–17).

Faced with the failure of the covenant on Sinai, people turned to God's promise to Abraham. And the priesthood was the institution charged with reminding the people of their sin and of God's forgiveness.

The holy presence of God. Ex.25.10–22; 40.34–38

You should read at least the beginning and end of Ex.25–31; 35–40. 'Let them make me a sanctuary, that I may dwell in their midst' (25.8). The text focusses our attention on the mercy seat (the plate of gold which covered the ark), and on this empty space between the mercy seat and the two cherubim. It is there that God makes himself present for his people; and it is on this mercy seat that once a year the high priest sprinkles blood to obtain the divine forgiveness (Lev.16).

To indicate that Christ is the real presence of God and that his blood brings forgiveness, Paul was to write: God put him forward as an expiation by his blood (Rom.3.25).

✦ *The Creation Story. Gen.1.1–2.4*

To study this well-known text, you can use the tool box from p.14.

In these two pages, you will find some help towards answering the questions in the order in which they are given. However, don't read them now. If you try to answer all the questions on p.14 you won't even have to read what follows; you will find it all out by yourself.

So go back to the tool box and your Bible.

When you have finished your study, you can read this next part if you want to.

Here are some of the words or expressions which keep occurring:

God said . . . ten times. These ten words remind us of the ten commandments. God creates the world in the same way as he creates his people on Sinai.

God acts (various verbs). This opposition between creation by the word and creation by action is perhaps an indication of an earlier twofold narrative; or perhaps it is the Priestly Writer's usual style.

And the evening . . . Creation is assigned to six days, culminating in the sabbath. So this is a liturgical arrangement and not a scientific one, to establish the importance of the sabbath.

People tend to forget that this text was produced during the exile. That helps to give it the significance of being an act of faith. At first sight it seems to be poetry, an escape from reality: 'All the world is good.' Now the author is writing in exile, in a broken world. He goes beyond scorn, evil and suffering to affirm his faith in a God who wants a good and just world.

Some expressions or realities had a special sense at that time.

We have seen the importance of the sabbath for the exiles. To show that God himself observed it gives it a sacred character.

The text does not speak of the sun and the moon, but of the two 'lights' (Gen.1.16). This word was part of the cultic vocabulary of the priests; it denotes the lamps shining in the temple (see for example Ex.25.6; 27.20). So the sun and moon are not gods, as they are in Babylon, but signs to indicate a presence (like the light before the sacrament in a Catholic church) and to indicate the times for festivals. The Temple of Jerusalem might be destroyed, but the whole universe was God's temple.

It is interesting to compare this text with the Babylonian myths. There God does not create from nothing; he creates by separation. These accounts took up the old myth which was as well known in Babylon as it was in Egypt; reread the texts on p.19. In Hebrew, the word for abyss is *tehom*, and recalls the Babylonian *Tiamat*. However, there is no trace of struggle here: God is the one God.

We could compare this narrative with many other bibilical texts; however, let's be content with two.

1 The Priestly creation story (Gen.1) **and the Yahwistic creation story** (Gen.2).

The 'science' (as accepted then) underlying the two stories is different. In Gen.2 the land appears like an oasis in the middle of the desert. Here it is an island in the midst of the waters. By successive separations, God makes dry land appear and puts man on it.

In Gen.2, the male is created first to cultivate the earth: then comes the female. Here, humanity (man and woman) is created last. This is another way of showing human dignity; in a liturgical procession, the most important figure comes last. This is mankind, which is created. Only at a second stage is it shown that mankind is made up of males and females.

2 The creation and the crossing of the Red Sea (Ex.14).

We noticed the similarities between these two texts when we studied Ex.14 (p.26): God speaks and acts (directly, or through Moses); he separates the waters so that dry land appears. So the liberation is shown as an omnipotent act of the creator God, and creation as an act of the liberator God who wants not only a people, Israel, but all peoples, all mankind, to be free.

We must now take up some features of these texts in rather more systematic fashion.

A liturgical poem

We should not look for instruction in science or history here. This is a poem expressing the extraordinary faith of priests in their God. The world was created in six days to legitimize the sabbath. This sabbath has a twofold significance. It is the time when God keeps sabbath, that is, ceases to work himself; so the seventh day is the time of human history, the time given to man to work and continue creation; after this will come the eighth day, the last day. However, this sabbath is celebrated by stopping work in order to sanctify time, pay homage to God.

From the liberator God to the creator God

The God whom Israel discovered first was the God who freed them from slavery in Egypt; a God who acts in history. And the exiles in Babylon now turned again to this God in hope of a new liberation. However, as Second Isaiah forcefully puts it, this God is capable of acting in history because he created history.

Man in God's image

How is man the image of God? The story lays stress on two aspects.

Man was created a creator. Man shows God's power through his mastery of the world by science. So he has the responsibility of organizing the universe and making it habitable. That is his concern.

Man is a loving relationship. The image of God who is love cannot be found in a single individual: it is found in a couple, a man and a woman, who love each other and whose love produces life. It was necessary to await the revelation of Jesus to discover all that this image could evoke of the very mystery of God himself. Conversely, however, the human couple are the sacrament of this God who is Trinity.

A God without a name

To give someone a name is to have some power over them; to reveal one's own name is to give something of oneself. So God does not have a proper name (see Gen.32.23–33: God refuses to give his name).

El, Elohim. The first way of naming God was to use the common noun *el*, god. Semites were already addressing their chief god in this way in the third millennium: he was 'the God'. Moslems have kept this usage: Allah comes from *al-Ilah*, the God. People would simply talk about the El of Abraham, of Isaac . . . And that is a first lesson: God remains unknowable. We can only discover things about him through what he is to those who worship him: the God of Abraham, of Jesus, of Mr and Mrs So-and-So. The plural Elohim denotes his majesty, like the royal 'we'.

Yahweh. God seems to give his name to Moses (see p.53). In fact, this is less his name than an indication of a presence. And in any case, we don't know how to pronounce it. As a mark of respect, the Jews never pronounced this divine name. They wrote the four consonants of the word YHWH (you will sometimes hear people talking about the Tetragrammaton, Greek for four letters), but they read it as Adonai, the Lord. The Massoretes (see p.7) put the vowels of Adonai on the consonants of Yahweh producing the barbarism Jehovah, which we find so often in old translations, hymns and prayers.

The Septuagint, the Greek Bible, translated the Tetragrammaton by Kyrios, the Lord. And the first Christians imitated this. Out of respect for the Jews, who are very shocked to hear us pronounce God's ineffable name, we should do the same thing and always read YHWH as 'the Lord'. That happens in RSV, but unfortunately not in the Jerusalem Bible.

6 Israel under Persian Domination 538–333

Persian royal guard. Susa (fifth century)

In 538 the edict of Cyrus allowed the Jews to return to their ancestral land and to rebuild their Temple (see this edict in Ezra 1.2–4). This fitted in well with Cyrus' spirit of tolerance and also with his political plans: it was necessary for Jerusalem, the last bastion of his empire in the direction of Egypt, to remain faithful.

For two centuries, the Jews formed part of the Persian empire with its enterprising kings, while Greek power grew. We must find some fixed points in this turbulent history. (For the successions of kings and events, see the chronological table on pp.118–19, and the maps in your Bible.)

The Persian empire

After capturing Babylon, Cyrus pursued his conquests in the east. He died there in 530. His son Cambyses captured Egypt, but came to grief in Ethiopia.

During a long reign, Darius I (522–486) began to organize his immense empire. He divided it into twenty provinces called satrapies, governed by a satrap, a chancellor and a general: they had to pay heavy taxes. He established a remarkable network of roads, including the 'Royal Road', which went from Susa as far as Ephesus on the Mediterranean coast. He conquered Thrace and Macedonia, in the north of Greece, but met his match at Marathon (490).

After Xerxes I, who was also beaten by the Greeks in the sea battle of Salamis (480), Artaxerxes 1 (464–424) first had to pacify Egypt, which had rebelled. The Jew Nehemiah, a royal official at the Persian court, was sent to Jerusalem; having formerly been dependants of Samaria, the Jews became an independent prefecture.

At that time Greece was experiencing its golden age

Assyrian scribe. Assyrian wall painting (eighth century)

– the century of Pericles – in art (the Parthenon), in literature (Sophocles and Euripides), and in philosophy (Socrates and Plato).

Darius II (424–404) had to fight in Egypt. On the island of Elephantine, near to the present-day Asswan dam, there was a Jewish military colony with a temple to the God Yahu. Correspondence with the Jerusalem authorities and the Persian court tells us something about its religion.

When Artaxerxes II became king (404–359), Egypt regained its independence. The province of Jerusalem again became important as a forward bastion of the empire. In 398, the king sent Ezra there. He tried to re-establish peace between Jews and Samaritans, who were to enjoy a special status in the empire: they had to obey the 'Law of the God of heaven' (Ezra 7.21) under the direction of the high priest. This fragile union between Jews and Samaritans only lasted for about twenty years.

The last Persian kings were faced with rebellions in various satrapies before being swept away by a new power, that of Macedon. In 338, Philip of Macedon reunited Greece, to his own advantage. When his son Alexander came to power in 336, a new era in history had begun.

The return from exile

Cyrus put an end to fifty years of exile in Babylon. We can work out that about 50,000 Jews took the opportunity to return home, in two main waves.

In 538, a first convoy led by Sheshbazzar included many priests, a few levites and a great many secondary figures: slaves and Temple servants. Those with less religious motivation, who had made good in Babylon, preferred to stay where they were.

74

It was difficult to settle in Judah again. The territory had been put under the control of the Samaritans (see p.45), who looked askance at the arrival of the time-honoured owners of the land which they had come to occupy. They wanted to help in rebuilding the Temple, but the Jews rejected the offer because Samaritan religion was not pure. By contrast, the Samaritans were opposed to the reconstruction of the walls of Jerusalem. These difficulties, not to mention the drought and the lack of money, caused an interruption to work on the Temple. It was probably during this period that a disciple of Isaiah whom we call the third Isaiah, Trito-Isaiah, delivered his message.

In 520, in the reign of Darius, a new convoy of exiles led by the prince Zerubbabel and the high priest Joshua arrived from Babylon. Under their direction, and with the support of the prophets Haggai and Zechariah, the Temple was finally rebuilt in 515.

515. The era of the Second Temple

After five years of struggle, the Temple was finally rebuilt. The old men who had known the splendour of the Temple of Solomon could hardly hold back their tears because the new one seemed to be so shabby (Ezra 3.10–13; Hag.2.3). No matter: there was a Temple. Enlarged and decorated by Herod from 19 BC to AD 64, it was destroyed by the Romans in AD 70.

It is important to remember the expression 'Second Temple': it denotes a building, but even more an age, which extends from the return from exile down to AD 70. This is the period of Judaism.

The two missions of Nehemiah (in 445 and 432) made possible the rebuilding of the walls of Jerusalem and mark independence from Samaria. Round about this time the prophet Malachi tried to revive the faith of the people.

In 398, Ezra was charged by king Artaxerxes with reorganizing the area (this is one possible date; the chronology here is very complicated). He re-established purity of faith with an iron fist; he dissolved marriages contracted with non-Jews, and imposed the 'Law of the God of heaven' as the state law. This law was probably the Pentateuch as we now have it, which Ezra edited on the basis of the various traditions.

The solemn ritual described in Neh.8–10 is one of the most important moments in the history of Israel: this is as it were the official birth of Judaism. The gathering does not take place in the Temple, but in the public square. It does not consist of bloody sacrifices, but of reading the law and prayer. Here is the birth of synagogue worship.

Some important aspects

Many details of the history of Israel still remain obscure. However, we can at least note some more general points.

The power of the priests

The priests reorganize the people. They become the real religious and political leaders.

The Jews in the world. The 'Diaspora'

Many Jews remained in Babylon, and formed a lively community there. We know of the existence of a community in Elephantine, in Egypt. The community in Alexandria, also in Egypt, was soon to prove important. So here we see a dispersion (Greek *diaspora*) of Judaism: Jerusalem remains the centre, but other important centres take shape elsewhere.

A common language: Aramaic

Aramaic, which is close to Hebrew, was the international language of the Persian empire for trade and diplomacy (rather as English is today). In Judaea, this language gradually took the place of Hebrew, which simply remained as a liturgical language. At the time of Christ, people spoke Aramaic and no longer understood Hebrew.

This common language and the Diaspora contributed towards opening up the Jews to universalism.

Literary activity

Prophets like Haggai, Zechariah, Malachi, Obadiah and above all Third Isaiah were preaching at this time.

However, this period is characterized above all by the influence of scribes and wise men.

Scribes like Ezra read the scriptures once more, brought them together (the Pentateuch), and completed them (Chronicles, Ezra and Nehemiah).

The wise men brought together earlier reflections and began to produce great works like Ruth, Jonah, Proverbs and Job.

The psalms began to be brought together in collections which soon turned into a book.

Prophets of the Return

Haggai

In 520, Haggai addressed a brief but scathing message to those who had returned from exile: 'What's this? You've been back twenty years. You've rebuilt your own houses, but the house of the Lord is still in ruins.' He wanted to know whether Israel was going to reconstruct its national life with or without God. Always a valuable question!

First Zechariah. Zech.1–8

The fourteen chapters which make up the book as we now have it bring together the preaching of two prophets. We shall read the message of the second of these prophets in the next chapter.

First Zechariah takes up the preaching of Haggai, but he does so in a language of his own which is already that of the apocalypses (see p.89).

Malachi

When Malachi was preaching, the Temple had been rebuilt. Worship had begun again, sacrifices . . . and also the bad pre-exilic habits. The rites were performed, but in any old way, and at the same time people were unjust, unfaithful.

Malachi reacted vigorously, and his message had a great influence, right down to the New Testament.

His book takes the form of a dialogue between God and his people, a prelude to the definitive dialogue of the gospel. 'I was hungry . . . When, Lord, did we see you hungry? . . .' I love you, says God. And you say, In what way do you love us?. . . 'And you say'. This refrain occurs eight times, directed against a nation of arguers. It is repeated eight times to lay bare the sin which is carefully tucked away: the sin of those who offer their left-overs to God (1.6f.), of priests who do not preach the word of God (2.1f.), of those who repudiate their wives (2.10f.: a splendid meditation on marriage), of those who cannot even distinguish between good and evil (2.17f.).

God finally announces that he will send the prophet Elijah to earth before the day of judgment. This text helped to give Elijah a position of considerable importance in Judaism. Jesus declared that John the Baptist filled this role (Matt.17.9f.)

Joel

We do not know when this 'ecological' prophet preached. The pollution everywhere seemed to him to be a sign of the coming of the day of the Lord, the day when God would lay bare men's sins. However, God would put his spirit into those who had been stripped in this way. Peter quotes Joel 3 on the day of Pentecost (Acts 2).

The word of God

Some people lay themselves open to disappointment: they read the Bible in search of the word of God and it seems more and more to be the words of men.

People sometimes have a rather magical view of the word of God, as though it is something which falls from heaven. Whereas God reveals himself in a history, through the events of human life, and these are what we have to decipher.

Doesn't the Christian feel the same bewilderment when faced with Jesus? Christians see him as the Son of God, the Word, whereas his contemporaries saw him as a man like they were. John does not write 'We have seen the word', but 'That which we have seen and heard concerning the word' (I John 1.1); that is, illuminated by faith and the Spirit, we have perceived the word through what we have seen (human actions and words like our own).

God acted in just the same way in the Old Testament. The Jews experienced ordinary events, but believers, primarily the prophets, read in them a word of God, just as we can see words in actions: 'What he did spoke volumes', 'His smile said it all'.

However, we can fool ourselves. Are we sure that the prophets and other believers didn't fool themselves too? It is here that faith in the Holy Spirit which enlightens the believer becomes important. 'The spirit will lead you into all truth,' said Jesus (John 16.13). To look for a word of God which falls from heaven can simply be to reject the spirit and to refuse to live in faith; in such a 'word' we would have God at our disposal, whereas he reveals himself to us, humbly, in human forms.

Third Isaiah. Isa.56–66

Galvanized by the promises of the new Exodus announced by Second Isaiah, the exiles went home. But the happy future to which they looked forward never materialized, and their enthusiasm waned. The resettlement was a sorry affair. But how was it possible to reconstruct a nation when people no longer believed in their destiny? A disciple of Isaiah tried to give them faith in their mission.

The task was difficult, because his audience was divided: people repatriated from Babylon, Jews who had remained at home; strangers who had settled in the meantime, Jews in the Diaspora. Dissension and hatred crept in, together with mistrust of strangers; idolatry threatened, and hopes were shattered. The prophet tries to communicate his enthusiasm to all these groups, despite all the problems.

The book as we have it now takes the form of a fine curve, with matching texts on either side of a peak in chapter 61. Before we study that chapter, we must run through the rest of the work.

56.1–8. Strangers can belong to the people of God because his house of prayer is for all peoples. 66.17–24. God will gather all the nations together again for a new creation.

56.9–57.21. The prophet laments those who think that they are automatically part of the people of God. 66.1–16. By contrast, he shows God giving the daughter of Zion power to bring forth the new people (see p.61 again).

58. True religious practice, true fasting which pleases God, is to share your bread, do away with injustice, free the oppressed . . . 65. Blessings and curses: those who allow themselves to be loved by God and those who refuse.

59.1–15. The prophet's accusation bears fruit: the people confess their sins. 63.7–64.11. A fine psalm of supplication, anticipating the 'Our Father': an appeal to the tenderness of God, asking him to rend the heavens and come down. For Mark, this is realized at the time of the baptism of Jesus (Mark 1.10).

59.15–20; 63.1–6. God is not mocked. Like a vine-presser, he will trample on his enemies. Revelation (19.13) applies this tragic text to Christ: in the last resort, the blood which flows is his own blood, shed for our sins.

📘 *Studying a text: Isaiah 60–63*

Isaiah 61 is the climax of the book. However, it forms a whole together with chs. 60; 62, which match each other. So we have to study the three together.

Rejoice, daughter of Zion. . .Isa.60; 62
Read these two chapters and try to see how the different protagonists are presented.
God. What aspect does he present? Note the imagery which expresses his feelings. The daughter of Zion. Whom does she denote? Note the imagery which expresses the change in her situation. The sons. . . Who are they? Where do they come from? Who attracts them?
Here we have an extraordinary image of the people of God (and now, of the church): like a cathedral, bathed in floodlights, shining out over the city in the darkness to guide those who are going through the shadows, the people form a luminous sign set up in the world to give a sense of direction. However, the light does not come from the people, but from the God who is in them.

The spirit of the Lord is upon me. Isa.61
This chapter is divided into three parts.

61.1–4. The prophet introduces himself.
How did his vocation come about? What is his mission? To whom is he sent, and what is the news (evangel, *euangelion*, Greek for good news) that he brings? Note the imagery which expresses transformation.

61.5–9. The prophet speaks to his audience.
He speaks, and the Lord speaks through him (v.8) about the future. What promise is given? What will be the people's role?

61.10–11. The prophet or the people express their enthusiasm. Perhaps it is both of them together. Why? What is its source?

Now look back over the whole of Isa.60–62. What is this good news which is capable of bringing new enthusiasm to these discouraged returnees?
Read Luke 4.16–21. In what way could Isa.61, according to Luke, express Jesus' mission? How does it help us to understand the significance of Jesus' miracles and the message of the Beatitudes?

The Law or Pentateuch

When Ezra arrived in Jerusalem in 398 (?), his mission was to reorganize the community and to settle the differences with the Samaritans.

The Law

As a state law, he imposed 'the Law of the God of heaven' (Ezra 7.21) upon everyone. There is agreement that we should see this law as the Pentateuch in its present form, as Ezra had organized it. He had a vast collection of texts at his disposal for doing this:

The Sacred Judaean History (the Yahwist) (see p.36);

The Sacred History of the North (the Elohist) (see p.50).

These two traditions had already been fused into a single account (see p.60: the Jehovist).

Deuteronomy (see p.56).

The Priestly History (see p.70), and Leviticus (see p.68).

Independent traditions, notably laws on sacrifices and festivals, which had been edited by the priests on their return from exile (cf. p.69).

With these texts Ezra succeeded in producing a work which, if it is not always coherent, is at least unified.

The resultant sacred history runs from creation to the death of Moses and brings into relief the two figures of Abraham and Moses.

After the creation narratives (Gen.1–11), the rest of Genesis (12–50) presents the patriarchs, with Abraham in first place. The father of believers, he is the bearer of the divine promise (the covenant: Gen.15; 17); he is the intercessor before God (Gen.18); he has complete trust in God, even when God asks for his son (Gen.22).

With the book of Exodus, Moses comes on stage and occupies it almost to the end. After the reminder of slavery in Egypt and the call of Moses (Ex.1–15), the lion's share is given to the covenant on Sinai, framed by two accounts of life in the wilderness (Ex.16–18; Num.11–12). The Covenant Code has a central position (Ex.20–23, see p.60). Prominence is also given to the various priestly laws: Ex.25–31 and 35–40; Leviticus; Numbers 1–10. Amidst all this, the story of the golden calf (Ex.32–34) is meant to provide a reminder of the ever-present risk of breaking the covenant. The last part presents the march to the promised land (Num.13–36) and the last speeches of Moses on Mount Nebo (Deuteronomy).

Thus Moses is presented as the mediator. He is completely on God's side, his instrument for freeing the people from slavery and leading them to serve God through the law which he gives. Moses is completely on the side of the people, in a solidarity so total that mysteriously it extends even to sin. And along with the people who die in the wilderness, Moses will die before entering the promised land, but, as the rabbis rendered it so magnificently, 'with a divine kiss' (Deut.34.5).

The Law, written and oral

For the Jews, the word of God is essentially the Law (Torah in Hebrew) which God gave his people on Sinai.

It has been set down in written form in the Pentateuch: that is the heart of scripture. However – and the rabbis stressed this very strongly – it has also been handed down, in parallel, by word of mouth. For the Jews, the oral traditions are as important as scripture.

The Prophets are also the word of God, but not quite to the same degree. In the liturgy, their role is above all that of illuminating the Law.

The Writings are revered without having the same importance as the Law and the Prophets.

So we can understand the importance of Ezra, who gave definitive form to the Law. 'If the Law had not been given to Moses,' said one rabbi, 'Ezra would have been worthy to receive it.' Moses and Ezra remain the two great figures of Judaism.

The Samaritans

It looks as though Ezra was successful in imposing the 'Law of the God of heaven' not only on the Jews, but also on the Samaritans, whose origins, as we saw on p.45, were very mixed. In fact, however, this religious union did not last long and soon the Samaritans parted company with the Jews for ever (perhaps in the time of Alexander). They even built their own temple on the summit of Mount Gerizim. However, they kept the Law (or Pentateuch), and their text of it is virtually identical with the Jewish text. That is the only scripture they recognize.

So relations between Samaritans and Jews are very complicated. We know from the Gospels how tense relations between the two communities were at the time of Christ. However, they recognized the same common destiny.

A Samaritan community has survived until today, and every year it is possible to go and see the sacrifice of the paschal lamb on Mount Gerizim.

I & II Chronicles – Ezra – Nehemiah

This work was probably composed at the beginning of the Greek period. The author is unknown. He is usually called the Chronicler. His plan was an ambitious one, to write a history from Adam to Ezra. He was a learned man and quotes his sources: about twenty books, of which some (like Samuel and Kings) are known to us, others not. The two parts of his work have been divided into four books: I and II Chronicles, Ezra and Nehemiah.

It would be fascinating for you to compare some passages in Chronicles with those in Samuel and Kings: you would see how a midrash was written (see p.81 and the brief comparison of passages about Nathan's prophecy on p.42). I shall single out some features of the Chronicler.

First, he offers us a theology of history. In order to show what the life of his contemporaries should be like, he idealizes a period of past history, that of David and Solomon. He moves very quickly from Adam to David (largely by means of genealogies). When it comes to David he spreads himself, chooses his sources, and eliminates episodes which do not favour his hero (David's sin, the luxury and idolatry of Solomon). David is the king after God's heart, the representative of God, who remains the only king of Israel. David had been able to provide his kingdom with a capital, Jerusalem, and to prepare for the building of the Temple and the organization of worship.

The Chronicler passes over the history of the northern kingdom in silence. He is chiefly interested in the history of the Temple and its worship. Priests and levites are very important for him.

He knows how to show that when kings and the people are faithful they are fortunate, and when they are unfaithful they are unfortunate. In a rather simplistic way, then, he tries to show by means of imagery what experience might be like of the kingdom of God on earth.

You might read Nehemiah 8–9

Neh.8. What are the features of this worship? Where does it take place? Who presides over it? What is new about it compared with temple worship?

Neh.9. What points of history are touched on in this confession of sin? What does the speaker rely on: his own merits? God? What qualities are recognized in God? How can this inspire our own prayer?

Wisdom

You and I, indeed all of us, are wise men, but we are not all writers producing wisdom literature.

The wise man is in fact someone who tries to live a good life and discover, in his existence and that of the world, those things which enhance life and those which lead to death. So he reflects on the great human questions: life, death, love, suffering, evil. Does human existence have a meaning? What meaning? Everyone has a philosophy, at his or her own level: the young child and the old man, the professor and the manual worker or the housewife; each of them develops a wisdom, a way of living.

And sometimes poets and philosophers take up all this diffuse reflection, brood on it and produce great works.

That is what also happened in Israel. All the time the people existed, they sought the meaning of their life, reflected on its great problems. We have seen, for example, that the creation stories are 'a wisdom reflection' (pages 39,72). Throughout its existence Israel expressed its reflection in proverbs, kinds of popular sayings; in prayers, in sketches of works.

However, it was only after the exile that writers began to take up all this reflection and, after a long period of gestation, to compose the great works which we are about to read.

So we must be on guard against one possible danger in this study. Over the five previous stages we have listened to the prophets and seen how the Pentateuch gradually developed; we have come to the wisdom books only at this sixth stage. That might suggest that Israel first lived and wrote its history and did not get down to thinking until eight or nine centuries later! Of course, that's not the case. We shall now be reading books, literary works produced at this period. However, we shall see how they take up a long period of earlier reflection, just as the Pentateuch took up elements composed earlier.

Who were the wise men in Israel?

Every Israelite. Wisdom is popular wisdom. For example, many proverbs take up ancient wisdom in a compressed form, with well-constructed maxims.

The king. He was responsible for governing the people and therefore for seeing what was good for them and what was not. He was thought to share in the divine wisdom.

The scribes. Wisdom is popular wisdom, but it is also learned. It was taught at school. The scribes, most often court officials, were the first wise men, and it was thanks to their political acumen that they held power. There were often conflicts between the prophets who defended the weak, and this class of scribes.

The wise men living after the exile are the heirs of all these currents. Having learned to reflect and write, they produced wisdom which was human wisdom, but at the same time they saw this as a gift of God, who alone was wise.

Some features of wisdom

Wisdom is the art of living a good life, seeking what leads to life and not to death. It is a reflection on the great human questions: life, death, love, suffering, evil, men's relationship with God and with one another, social life, etc.

Wisdom is universal and timeless. Suffering and death, life and love, know no frontiers. The sick man who gives vent to his suffering in Babylon or in Israel two thousand years before Christ reacts in just the same way as someone in agony in a modern hospital.

Thus the wise men of Israel drew abundantly on the reflections of other civilizations: Egypt and Babylon, and then Greece. However – and this is where they were original – all this reflection was put into the melting pot of belief in the one God. In the last resort, the true source of wisdom is God, and the only way of getting it is to have a close and respectful relationship with this God, which the Bible calls the fear of God.

Wisdom writings in the Persian period

We shall begin with two books included in our Bibles. One of them is to be found either in the Writings (Jerusalem Bible) or the historical books (RSV); the other in the Prophets. However, both of them belong to wisdom literature.

Ruth

God's sense of humour! To restore the purity of Jewish faith, Ezra had just required Jews who had married foreign wives to repudiate them. Of course God was obliged to approve this, but found that Ezra was going a bit too far, so he inspired this charming story. Boaz, a pious Jew from Bethlehem, marries Ruth, a foreign woman from Moab. They have a son, Obed, father of Jesse and grandfather of . . . David!

This is a lesson in universalism, and a humorous reminder from God to all of us who think that we love him because we observe his regulations: 'You need to love me without fanaticism. Be intelligent, and don't confuse the end with the means . . .' Ruth is mentioned in the genealogy of Jesus (Matt.1.5).

Jonah

Here is a prophet who disagrees with God's methods: Jonah, the hero of this miraculous tale. God sends him to preach to Nineveh, the capital of the Assyrians, that terrible enemy. Nineveh is in the east. Jonah embarks in a boat westwards. He is running away, sleeping in the hold of the ship, out to sea. However, God gets him back by means of a great fish which spews him out in the direction of the east. So off he goes . . .

When he gets to Nineveh he preaches that God is going to destroy the city and is very pleased about that. But the inhabitants repent, and God does not destroy them.

This is a magnificent lesson in universalism. God loves all men. 'He does not want the death of a sinner, but rather that he should repent and live' (Ezek.33.11).

For Jesus, Jonah is a sign of the call to conversion (Luke 11.29; Matt.16;4), and for Matthew, an image of the resurrection (Matt.12.40).

Midrash and Targum

Very soon the Jews were faced with the question how to bring scripture up to date. This word of God had been given in a situation different from that in which they now lived. So scripture had to be reread to see how it might make sense in the present.

Midrash (from the root *darash*, search) is a word used for both the method of interpretation and the works composed by this method.

We can distinguish two kinds of midrash:

Midrash *halakah* (from a root meaning way, road). This is concerned with rules of conduct, laws. In Judaism, *halakoth* (the plural form) is synonymous with laws.

Midrash *haggadah* (from a root meaning to tell). These are chiefly concerned to edify.

The Priestly History, which rereads the traditions in the context of the exile to find meaning and hope in them, and the work of the Chronicler, who looks to history for a way of experiencing the kingdom of God, are the beginning of midrash *halakah*. Ruth and Jonah are more types of midrash *haggadah*.

The Targum is the oral translation of scripture into Aramaic. Hebrew always remained the sacred language. However, a time came when people no longer understood it because they spoke Aramaic. In the liturgy, scripture was read in Hebrew and then a scribe translated it into Aramaic. Instead of making a literal translation, though, he developed the meaning as it was then understood (see the examples on pp.38,52).

At the service presided over by Ezra (Neh.8–9), after the reading of scripture, the Levites explained it to the people. This is perhaps one of the first pieces of evidence about this practice.

The chief targums were fixed in writing towards the beginning of our era. They allow us to see how certain texts were understood at the time of Christ.

The first Christians took over this way of interpreting scripture. They often read it in the light of the targums and they sometimes wrote Christian midrash (the infancy stories in the Gospel of Matthew, for example).

Job

At the time when the great tragedians of Greece were writing plays about history and human life, like *The Persians* and *Antigone*, a Jewish poet began to produce the drama of a believer coming to grips with suffering: Job.

The book of Job as we now know it has a long history. It consists of an old tale in prose (the beginning and end of the book), perhaps already known at the time of Solomon, which from the time of the return from exile served as the framework for dialogues between Job and his friends. Further additions were made at a later date.

The drama of Job is that of every believer who suffers without cause. Job believes in God who is just and omnipotent. He suffers, and when he examines his conscience (in connection with justice and his love for others), he finds that he is innocent.

The task of his friends is to present the traditional arguments: 'If you're suffering, that's because you have sinned . . .' or, 'It's because God loves you: he always chastises those whom he loves . . .' 'That's all eyewash,' cries Job. Confronted with God's silence Job shouts out, rebels, blasphemes.

Finally, God speaks. To explain, or to provide consolation? No! To overwhelm Job by the splendour of his creation and to ask him just one question: 'By what right do you ask me to give an account of myself?' And Job prostrates himself in adoration.

In the end, this does not tell us any more about the reason for evil. However, it is a good thing that in this way a book could express our revolt against evil. We now know that rebellion and blasphemy can be prayers ('Only Job has spoken well with me,' says God, 42.7), that pious explanations are worthless, and that the only possible attitude for the believer is that of trust. 'The terrible moment when God isn't true and yet I still love him,' as one believer wrote. This is the attitude of Christ on the cross.

You might read at least these passages:

Job's despair: 3.6–7; 29–30 (God's absence and silence).

The poem about the wisdom of which God alone has the secret: 28.

Job's examination of his conscience: 31.

God's 'reply': 38.

Proverbs

The book of Proverbs give us a good idea of the wisdom literature and the way in which it developed.

Proverbs appears as a group of nine collections of sayings, differing in length, style and period. The earliest proverbs may very well go back to the time of Solomon (these are in chs.10–22). Two collections (30; 31) are attributed to foreign wise men, which is an indication of the universalism of wisdom. There are affinities between the collection of the wise men in 22.17–24.22 and an Egyptian text, The Wisdom of Amenemope. The beginning (1–9) and the end (31.10–31) were composed after the exile.

You might begin with the earliest collections. It's not a matter of reading these chapters straight through, but of taking them in small doses, rather as you might dip into an anthology of quotations. You might amuse yourself by composing a personal anthology of your own – one easy way of doing this is to mark various themes with different colours. Here are some ideas to help you begin:

The fear of God, the source of wisdom: 10.27; 14.2,26–27.

God is sometimes mentioned. What does he do? 10.22,29; 11.1;12.2,22.

Educational methods: 10.13; 12.1; 19.29.

Some virtues (love, humility, justice . . .): 10.2; 11.2;12.28.

Women (a splendid collection for misogynists!): 11.22; 18.22; 19.13; 21.9,19; 27.15.

Moral vignettes: adultery: 7.6–27; laziness: 19.24; 24.30–34; the businessman: 20.14; the drunkard: 23.29–35.

Sumerian proverbs (from the end of the second millennium)

It is better for the poor man to be dead than alive.
If he has bread, he has no salt;
if he has salt, he has no bread . . .

Anyone who has never had wife or child
has never been led by the nose.

Man's life is like a jug of water in the desert.
His wife is a man's future.
His son is a man's refuge.
His daughter is a man's salvation.
And his daughter-in-law is sheer hell!

Lady Wisdom. Prov. 1–9

Like 31.10–31, the first chapters were composed last, probably in the Persian period. The author takes up the message of Deuteronomy, Jeremiah and Second Isaiah. A master is speaking to his son or disciple; he is teaching him to live in accordance with wisdom, to love his neighbour (3.27f.) and to keep away from debauchery. Human love is celebrated with accents which anticipate the Song of Songs (5.15–23).

In some passages wisdom is personified: Lady Wisdom (contrasted briefly with the foolish woman: 9.13f.). Wisdom is a prophet (1.20–33), a hostess offering a meal (9.1–6), and even daughter of God (8.1–31). We are now going to study a very characteristic text (8.22–31). In the next chapter we shall see how the wise men continued this line of development: wisdom became more and more someone who came from God himself. These texts enabled the first Christians to express the divinity of Christ as God's wisdom (I Cor.1.24).

📖 *Studying a text: Proverbs 8.22–31*

22. *The Lord created me at the beginning of his work,*
    the first of his acts of old.   Before creation
23. *Ages ago I was set up*
    at the first, before the beginning of the earth.   or *consecrated*
                                                                             See Prov. 8.15; Ps.2.6
24. When there were no depths I was brought forth,
    when there were no springs abounding with water.
25. Before the mountains had been shaped,
    before the hills, I was brought forth;
26. Before he had made the earth with its fields,
    or the first of the dust of the world.
27. When he established the heavens, I was there   During creation
    when he drew a circle on the face of the deep,
28. *when he made firm the skies above,*
    when he established the fountains of the deep,
29. *when he assigned to the sea its limit,*
    so that the waters might not transgress his command,
    when he marked out the foundations of the earth,
30. *then I was beside him, like a master workman;*   or *small girl*
    and I was daily his delight,
    rejoicing before him always,
31. rejoicing in his inhabited world,
    and delighting in the sons of men.

Who are the main characters? How are they distributed through the text? Look at words and expressions which correspond.

What does God do? What does Wisdom do? What is the situation for God (see the verbs)? for creation? for men? What is the role of Wisdom?

Some of the expressions are difficult, and you may need a commentary to help you.

At the end of this study you might ask yourself: how does this text help us to understand the role of Christ? See Col.1.15–20.

'amen – 'amon – 'amun

Verse 30 is a good point at which to note the richness – and the complexity – of Hebrew. In Hebrew, as in Arabic, people wrote only the consonants. Vowels were added when the text was read, depending on the meaning. Here we have three consonants making up the root 'mn, which evokes something solid. In the liturgy, 'amen means, 'That sure, that's certain'. Here we can read a present participle, 'amon, the one who founds or who supports, hence architect, master workman; or one can read the passive participle, 'amun, one who is carried, hence baby, small girl.

7

Israel under the Greeks (333–63) and Romans (from 63 BC)

In 333, by his victory at Issos, north of Antioch, Alexander the Great opened up the way to the Middle East. In 332 he arrived in Egypt and founded Alexandria. In 331 he took Babylon, Susa and Persepolis. In 327 he reached the frontiers of India. And in 323, this young king died in Babylon at the age of thirty-three. In ten years he had won victories during a march of 18,000 kilometres; he had founded more than seventy cities in his immense empire (many of which were called Alexandria); he had spread Greek culture with its art, its baths and its stadiums, and provided a common language as means of unity. This *koine,* or common language, which at that time was spoken in Greece, was to be spoken throughout the Mediterranean basin for eight centuries, down to about AD 500, when it was replaced by Latin. This was the language into which the Old Testament was translated – the version known as the Septuagint – and in which the New Testament was written.

Israel under the Lagids: 333–198

On the death of Alexander, his generals, known as the Diadochi, quarrelled about the future of his empire. In the end they divided it into three, founding dynasties which each bore the name of their first king. So there were the Antigonids in Greece, the Lagids in Egypt and the Seleucids in Syria (their kingdom in fact stretched from the Mediterranean to India).

For more than a century, Palestine was under the thumb of the Egyptian Lagids. These kings, who mostly bore the name of Ptolemy, usually respected the various nationalities and allowed the Jews to live in peace, according to the statute which had been fixed by Ezra. So the Jews enjoyed a considerable degree of autonomy.

During this period the three main centres of Judaism began to go their different ways.

We know little about the community in Babylon, but it continued to survive. Over the next few centuries it produced some important works for Judaism, in particular the Babylonian Talmud.

In Egypt, the Jewish community in Alexandria developed rapidly. At the time of Christ it made up about a fifth of the city. It gave birth to a form of Judaism which was compatible with Greek thinking. It was here that the Bible was translated into Greek (the Septuagint), that books like Wisdom were written, and that in the time of Christ the Jewish philosopher Philo tried to rethink the faith in Greek terms.

In Palestine, the community was divided. Some were tempted by Greek civilization, by its games, its baths and its athletics; some even went so far as to disguise their circumcision by a surgical operation. Others were very disturbed at this tide of Hellenism (or Greek civilization). They were very attached to their Jewish faith and to the way in which it had hitherto been expressed in practices and rituals, and were concerned to show that it allowed people to develop; however, to maintain Jewish faith it was necessary to preserve its particular forms of expression as well. (We know that this is a perennial problem, which can provide an explanation for contemporary clashes within the church.) This is the context in which books like Koheleth, Tobit and Sirach appeared.

The persecution which struck this community at the time of the Seleucids accentuated the division and threw the people into utter confusion.

Israel under the Seleucids: 198—63

In 198, Syrian elephants broke up the Egyptian army, and the age of the martyrs began for Israel. At Paneion, near the source of the Jordan, the Seleucid king Antiochus III wrested control of Palestine from Egypt.

Unlike the Lagids, the Seleucids wanted to impose Greek culture and religion on the Jews by force. In 167, Antiochus IV abolished Jewish privileges, did away with the sabbath and circumcision, desecrated the Temple and installed in it the abomination of desolation, i.e. a statue of Zeus. The crisis was all the greater because the high priests were not in agreement: some of them supported Hellenization.

A priest gave the signal for revolt by killing an emissary of Antiochus who had come to enforce sacrifices to idols. With his five sons he took to the hills. The fifth of these sons was Judas, who was to give his surname to the family; he was known as the Maccabee (Latin, Maccabaeus), the Hammer. By some lucky moves, Judas succeeded in liberating Jerusalem. Temple worship was restored on 15 December 164. Thereafter the event was celebrated by Hanukkah, the feast of dedication. Two of Judas' brothers, and then their descendants, succeeded him, thus founding the dynasty of the Maccabees, also known as the Hasmonean dynasty. They even took the title of king, for a while restoring the monarchy in Israel.

Unfortunately, the history of the Hasmoneans, which began in the blood of martyrs, ended in a morass. The successors of Judas managed to have themselves nominated as high priests by the Seleucids, often resorting to bribery to gain this end; some crucified faithful Jews who were hostile to their actions.

In 63 the Jews, who were divided into rival groups supporting two different kings, were reduced to appealing to Rome for arbitration. Roman authority arrived in the Middle East in the person of the general Pompey. Supporting one side, Pompey captured Jerusalem after a three-month siege. This was the beginning of Roman rule, which was to last until the seventh century AD, the time of the Arab invasions.

The Jewish sects

The religious groups in Judaism are known as sects – not in any derogatory sense. Most of them came into being at this time.

The Pharisees ('the separated ones') belong to the current of Hasidim (derived from the root *hesed,* see p.49), or pious Jews, who from the time of Ezra on wanted to reconstruct the nation on the basis of spiritual values. The Pharisees were profoundly religious, devoted to the Law and the practice of it. As a result of their profound piety and their knowledge of the scriptures they were to become the conscience of Judaism.

The Essenes, who are better known since the discovery of the Qumran manuscripts, were also Hasidim. They probably took refuge in the desert at the time of the Maccabean revolt, forming a community of the new covenant near the Dead Sea. Here they prepared for the coming of the Messiah in prayer and meditation. They were intransigent and broke even with the Pharisees, whom they found too lukewarm.

The Sadducees were made up of high-ranking priests. They supported the Hasmoneans and seemed concerned above all to defend their power by all available means. We should not confuse with this priestly aristocracy the many 'grass-roots' priests who were often very pious and connected more closely with the Pharisaic movement.

Literary activity

A prophet now known as Second Zechariah preached at this time.

Hellenization was to provoke various reactions of defiance or sympathy: Koheleth, Sirach, Tobit, the Song of Songs, Baruch and Wisdom. The scriptures were translated into Greek: the Septuagint.

The persecution of Antiochus and the Maccabean epic inspired several works: Esther, Judith, I and II Maccabees, and the development of a literary genre which began to emerge with the last prophets. This was the apocalyptic trend, represented in the Old Testament by Daniel.

The last psalms were written, and the Psalter came into being.

Prophets of the Greek Period: Second Zechariah

Scholars have divided Isaiah into three; they have also divided Zechariah into two: chapters 9–14, they say, are by a prophet from the time of Alexander.

The arrival of this young king, who overthrew the powerful Persians, raised people's hopes: perhaps God was at last going to intervene. For the prophet, however, radical change could come only from God. So he revived messianic hopes, that is to say, the expectation of a Messiah, one anointed with holy oil (Greek *christos*), by whom one day God would establish his kingdom. The portrait of the Messiah which he draws is unique in the Bible: he combines the features of the royal Messiah, son of David or son of God (see p.42), with those of the suffering servant in Isaiah (p.67). In particular, there are four poems that you can read which were all applied to Jesus by the first Christians. Here they are.

The Messiah king, lowly and peaceful. 9.9–10.

9.1–8 clearly describes Alexander's expedition to Palestine and Egypt in 333. Would he be the Messiah? 'No,' said the prophet.

Read 9.9–10. How is this king introduced? What does he rely on: his strength? on God? What does he bring?

Read Matt.21.5.

The shepherd sold by his people. 11.4–17; 13.4–9

The different images in this story are not easy to decipher. This is probably what they mean. The sheep are the people and the shepherds are the kings or high priests; the merchants or traffickers are the false prophets, wicked priests who hand people over to the enemy. Those who buy are the enemy; the three shepherds who are destroyed are possibly three high priests; the breaking of 'Grace' and 'Union' is probably a recollection of past invasions and the schisms between Judah and Israel in 935 and between Israel and the Samaritans. The author is trying to understand present events in the light of the past.

The shepherd is the prophet, but also God (11.13). To make mockery of him, people pay the price of a slave.

Read Matt.26.31; 27.3–10. Thus Jesus is identified with the good shepherd and with God.

God transfixed. 12.10–13.1

This is the most extraordinary oracle of all: God declares that he himself is afflicted through the person who is pierced.

What is the unexpected result (13.1)? Read Ex.36.25f.; 47.1–12. Who represents this spring? Where does it flow from?

Read John 7.38; 19.34: How does Zechariah help us to understand who Jesus is? Where does the spring come from? John does not claim to give medical information (on which side Jesus was pierced); he is making a theological point. Jesus is the true temple from which the Spirit flows.

Deutero-canonical and Apocryphal books

There is one small difference between Catholic Bibles and those of other Christian churches, in the content of the Old Testament. Catholic Bibles have seven or eight extra books which they call deutero-canonical and others call apocryphal.

The word canon means 'rule': a book is canonical if it is recognized as a rule of faith. The canon of holy books is the total recognized as a rule of faith.

Christians followed the Jews over the Old Testament. However, two different canons had been established. Round about AD 90, the Palestinian rabbis recognized only the books written in Hebrew. The Jews of Alexandria accepted others which were written or known in Greek.

Christians who read the Bible in Greek adopted the canon of the Alexandrian Jews. However, St Jerome, who translated the Bible into Latin early in the fifth century, opted for the Hebrew canon.

At the time of the Reformation in the sixteenth century, the Protestants followed Jerome by printing the disputed books at the back of their Bible (from which they had disappeared by the nineteenth century): they called them apocrypha (kept secret).

At the Council of Trent, the Catholics held that these books had the same level of inspiration as the rest, but they called them deutero-canonical (admitted into the canon at a secondary level). The most important of the books concerned are Judith, Tobit, I and II Maccabbes, Wisdom, Sirach, the Greek passages of Esther, Baruch and the Letter of Jeremiah.

Wisdom Literature

I shall now introduce the wisdom literature composed during the Greek period. Probably you won't be able to study all of it. If you're working as a group, each person could read one work and share his or her discoveries with others.

Koheleth or Ecclesiastes

This is a strange book. The author applies acid to all our security and certainty: action, politics, love, pleasure. All vanity, says Koheleth. One thing matters, and that is to eat well. Is there a God? Yes. But God is in heaven and you are on earth, so stop your stupid chatter.

The author hides behind a pseudonym. Koheleth clearly represents the assembly. He is perhaps the voice of the assembly, listening to a good sermon in which everything is foreseen, God is just and good, and the world goes on in accordance with his plan . . . the voice of the assembly which dares to say: 'That's all rubbish!'

He is an austere counsellor who suggests that we should not take ourselves too seriously, that we should shed our illusions, and act. Since you don't know which of two things will succeed, do them both!

Tobit (deutero-canonical)

This is a very attractive story: a midrash *haggadah*. The author rereads the story of the patriarchs and derives from it an edifying story which he sets at the time of the exile.

Old Tobit, a holy man who has gone blind, is in despair; young Sarah, a virtuous girl, finds that all her fiancés die, and she wants to die herself. Why this absurd evil? Is God absent, or indifferent?

The author shows us how God is present in the life of each one of us, but in a hidden way. We have to know how to discover him.

The story is at the same time a splendid testimony to marriage and human love.

You should read at least the fine prayers (eucharists): the prayer of Tobit in despair (3.1–6), of Sarah on the verge of suicide (3.11–15), of Sarah and Tobit in their marriage chamber (8) and of Tobit when he is cured (13.1–10).

Song of Songs

This is a marvellous poem which celebrates human love in all its physical dimensions, with a realism which modern poets would not dismiss.

The text as it is now has a long history. It probably takes up old love songs sung on the wedding night of a couple; perhaps it is inspired by pagan rites, but without ever mentioning God, it is also a meditation on Gen.2.23–24, Mal.2.14 and those prophetic texts which celebrate God's love for his people in the imagery of betrothal.

The text was to go on to have a long history, also; it became the symbol of the love between God and the people (or the believer) and inspired not only Jews but Christians like St John of the Cross.

At a time when women were men's slaves, these songs in which a couple love each other equally, in the freshness of a tenderness which does not ignore difficulties, are quite extraordinary compositions.

Sirach or Ecclesiasticus (deutero-canonical)

A model grandson translated into Greek a book written by his grandfather round about 190. The temptations of Hellenism were great, and many young men will have been tempted to abandon their ancestral traditions. This book, which has an old-fashioned attraction because of its middle-class piety, seeks to show that faithfulness to the Law and its practices allows a man to gain true wisdom.

As with Proverbs, you might like to make a small anthology of texts (there are some very appealing ones); however, there are some passages on which you should spend time:

The hymn to the fear of God (which is as fine as the hymn to love in I Cor.13): 1.11–20. Wisdom was imparted to us at our mothers' breasts: everyone is born with a grain of it.

The joy of those who seek wisdom: 4.11–19.

Lady Wisdom introduces her role in creation and in history:24. She is identified with the Law. This famous passage inspired John (John 1).

You can find marvellous passages in the praise of creation (42.15–43.33) and above all in the praise of famous men (beginning at ch.44). At least read the portrait of the high priest Simon (50), which inspired Luke 24.50–52.

Literary Offshoots of the Epic of the Maccabees

The epic story of the Maccabees is a brief one (it spans a period of only three years, from 167 to 164), but it left a profound mark on Judaism. Confronted with the firm purpose of Antiochus IV to impose Greek religion by force, believers were led to make a decisive choice between apostasy and martyrdom. The action, and above all the religious concern, of Judas the Maccabee, and his success which led to the purification of the Temple, brought about a revival of faith. However, as we have seen, his successors soon became bogged down in political intrigues and intoxicated with the taste of power.

For a century, this epic provoked three kinds of reaction which we can find in literature. Roughly speaking, they might be classified like this.

1. Sword in hand. The epic story is told in I Maccabees, which supports the combatants. Judith and Esther, written as romances, express feelings at the time.

2. Joined hands. Other believers, especially after seeing the development of the Maccabean dynasty, are very reticent. Only God can bring about liberation. The true religious attitude is not to take up the sword, but to join hands in prayer, asking God to intervene. II Maccabees represents the Pharisaic view: faith leads to martyrdom, and martyrdom will make God act.

The apocalyptic trend, along with Daniel, takes this direction and looks for the intervention of God at the end of history.

3. The outstretched hand. When the storm had passed, and also because he lived in Alexandria, far removed from the dramas of Palestine, a wise man wrote the Wisdom of Solomon, in which he tried to express his Jewish faith in such a way that it would be meaningful to cultured Greeks.

We shall go through this literature, and pause over two texts: Daniel 7 and Wisdom 7.

Judith (deutero-canonical) – Esther

These two edifying stories (in the form of midrash) express the enthusiasm engendered by the Maccabean epic. They stress one essential point: it is God who acts and who saves. To do this he chooses the weakest instruments: the hands of women.

II Maccabees (deutero-canonical)

This book is not the sequel to I Maccabees. It was even written earlier, about 124. It is a summary of another work in five volumes composed by Jason, who lived a short time after Judas the Maccabee.

Underlying these pious stories we find the spirituality of the Pharisees and their total commitment to God. Let me bring out several points.

A holy war. In relating the exploits of Judas, the author stresses that it is God who gives the victory; hence the prayers before every battle, the miraculous interventions (chs.8ff.).

The martyr. Total commitment to his faith may lead a man to witness to God in the most decisive way possible, that of martyrdom. The martyrdoms of old Eleazar (6.18–31), and above all that of the seven brothers (7), are famous.

The resurrection (7.9,23,29). Here the author takes up, even more exactly, the doctrine already presented by Daniel (Dan.12.2), which was shared by the Pharisees. We shall come back to it when we study Daniel.

Prayer for the dead (12.38–45). This text has played a key role in the Catholic theology of 'purgatory': if we pray for the dead, we should pray that they have not fallen into nothingness, and that they can be pardoned after their death. Protestants, who do not recognize this book, simply commit the fate of the dead to God's hands, without seeking to penetrate the mystery.

Creation from nothing (7.28). Hitherto, it had not been demonstrated that God created from nothing (ex nihilo); he was thought to have ordered primordial chaos by separating the elements (Gen.1; see p.72).

I Maccabees (deutero-canonical)

The author, who is probably writing about 100 BC, is well-disposed towards the Maccabean dynasty. He tells the history of the first three Maccabees: Judas (3–9); Jonathan (9–12) and Simon (13–16). He wants to write a sacred history along the lines of the former prophets (see p.59), and shows us God at work liberating his people by saving them from the disaster in which sin has involved them.

The Apocalypses

All through our lives, we come up against happy and sad events. We try to get the better of them, to make the best of them, to make sense of them. And we ourselves change when we realize that we are going in the wrong direction.

This is what the prophets did: they interpreted events and discovered a word of God in them: they called on people to change, to be converted.

Sometimes, however, it happens that evil is so great, that a situation is so hopeless, that there is no way out. One cannot hope for better days. And if anyone could then tell us how things would turn out, we would see the light at the end of the tunnel and be given courage to hold on.

The apocalypses are more this kind of material. They generally came into being at a time of crisis. The authors of them had a pessimistic view of the world, believing that it was entirely under the sway of the 'prince of this world' (or a devil). To offer hope, they proclaimed that in the end God would come and create all things new. Until then, people would simply 'cross their arms' and pray. We can see the ambiguity in this trend, which was both pessimistic and optimistic, evoking faith and running the risk of not being involved.

In modern language, apocalypse has become a synonym for catastrophe. It's a pity that only this aspect has been retained, since apocalypse also signifies light and hope.

The Greek verb *apokalyptein* can be translated into Latin as *re-velare*, remove the veil, hence our 'reveal'. History is thought to unfold in a straight line, the end of which is hidden in God's secret. To uphold his people's hope in dramatic times, God lifts the veil which hides the end, revealing the happy outcome to history as a result of God's victory.

The long-jumper

But how does the author of an apocalypse have such a revelation? His technique is rather like that of a long-jumper. The long-jumper wants to jump forward as far as he can; to do that, he first goes back: then he runs as fast as he can for thirty or forty yards and when he arrives at the take-off, he jumps forward, carried by his impetus.

Some characteristics of apocalypses

The author uses a pseudonym. He attributes his book to a holy man of the past. This gives him two advantages. This holy man is near to God, so he can reveal God's secrets. And he is a man from the past, so he can proclaim the future!

Composed in times of crisis, apocalypses are pessimistic about a world doomed to perdition because it is wholly in the hands of the devil, 'the prince of this world'. In the end they are optimistic: God will create a new world.

Their vision of God is somewhat deterministic: everything has been foreseen in advance, and has been written in the heavenly books.

They call forth a total faith in God, but they risk encouraging a lack of involvement: nothing can be done except to wait for God to act.

They are concerned above all to maintain hope.

Restricted to the initiated, they use a special code, expressed in both words and images (see p.90).

The author of an apocalypse is like us. He does not know the future. But he is sure of one thing. God is faithful. To discover how he will bring history to an end, it is enough to see how he has guided it in the past. So the author goes back: he pretends to be writing three or four centuries before the time in which he is living, runs rapidly through history and then, when he comes to his own time, he leaps forward, projecting what he has discovered in his reading of history on to the end of time.

A very widespread trend

There are only two apocalypses in the Bible: Daniel and Revelation. However, many texts in the latest of the prophets already belong within this trend (Isa.24–27; 34–35; Zech. 1–8).

Between 150 BC and AD 70, this trend produced numerous books. It made a deep mark on the minds of believers, making them live in hope and expectation of the end.

The Book of Daniel

This book is very closely bound up with the Maccabean epic. The author is writing about 164. The book itself is classed either with the Writings, as in the Jewish Bible, or with the Prophets, as in the Greek Bible and most modern versions. It makes use of two different literary genres: pious histories and apocalypse.

Pious histories – or black humour! Dan.1–6

In time of war, the morale of the troops is important, and good stories are effective in keeping it up. By introducing fictitious figures, they make it possible to laugh at the expense of the enemy without his taking account of it. Thus it would have been rather dangerous to say that God would make Antiochus IV 'one with the beasts who eat the grass of the earth'; so this description is applied instead to Nebuchadnezzar, who lived four centuries earlier (Dan.4).

However, these stories go beyond humour. They are edifying tales (like midrash *haggadah*, see p.81), aimed above all at strengthening faith. Here are some examples.

Jewish rules about food are very strict. They appeared ridiculous to pagans and even to certain Jews who were tempted by Hellenism, and Antiochus forbade his subjects to observe them. The story of the young people exiled in Babylon is a reply to this: fed on raw carrots and fresh water, they are in better shape than those who eat meat (Dan.1)!

Israel was trampled underfoot by Antiochus, as it had been formerly by others: Babylonians, Medes, Persians, Greeks with their offshoots in the persons of the Lagids and the Seleucids. They felt powerless before this colossus. 'Don't panic,' says Daniel, 'this colossus has feet of clay.' A mysterious stone becomes detached from the mountain and grinds the colossus to dust (2.34). Thus it is God, and not the sword of the Maccabees, who will put an end to history and establish his kingdom.

To those Jews who 'set at nought the king's command, and yielded up their bodies rather than serve and worship any god except their own God' (Dan.3.28), the author tells the story of the three young men thrown into the furnace: 'Do not fear. God will send his angel into the fire with you, to keep you from evil!' (Dan.3). To this story has been added, in Greek, the magnificent 'Song of the Three Children in the Furnace'.

'And even if they kill you, God is capable of bringing you out alive from the tomb.' That is the teaching of ch.6. Daniel is thrown into the lions' den; a stone seals it like a tomb, and the king puts on mourning. Daniel is dead! But he comes out alive. He is the image of the whole Jewish people, put to death by their persecutors but brought to life by their God.

Features peculiar to apocalyptic already appear in some of these texts: the stone symbolizing the intervention of God, visions and dreams. However, it is above all in chs.7–12 that the author deliberately uses the literary genre of apocalypse.

A theology in images

The apocalypses use a system of images which have to be deciphered. Here are the main ones.

Colours
White means victory, purity.
Red means killing, violence, the blood of the martyrs.
Black means death and impiety.

Figures
Seven is the perfect figure, and signifies fullness.
Six (seven minus one) is imperfection.
Three and a half (half seven) is imperfection, suffering, the time of trial and persecution. Be careful! Three and a half can appear in various forms, but its symbolic value remains the same: thus three and a half, or a time, times and a half a time (perhaps 1 + 2 + ½), or three years and half a year all have the same significance as three and half days or forty-two months or 1,260 days!
Twelve means Israel (because of the twelve tribes).
Four signifies the world (the four points of the compass).
A thousand is an incalculable quantity.

Other images
A horn signifies power.
White hair signifies eternity (and not old age: the 'ancient of days' in Dan. 7 is not old, but eternally young!).
A long robe often signifies priestly dignity.
A golden girdle signifies royal power.
The goats are the wicked.
The sheep are the people.

An apocalypse. Dan.7–12

It was the apocalyptic part of Daniel (7–12) which was above all to stamp Israelite thought. The author, as we have seen, is writing in 164. He pretends to be writing at another time of persecution, that of the exile, four centuries earlier, and he takes the name of Daniel, a Canaanite pagan hero mentioned by Ezekiel. So he has no difficulty in 'foretelling' the future between the exile and the time of the Maccabees! However, he does this to discover the broad outlines of the way in which God acts and thus to discover how he will bring history to an end. We shall now study the most important text.

📖 *Studying a text. Dan.7*

First read this text straight through. You will be completely out of your depth! However, this will help you to see how apocalyptic literature works.

Now identify the different parts. Usually there is a vision, which is then interpreted by an angel.

The vision is narrated in 7.1–14, but an important detail is highlighted in 19–22. So read 7.1–8, then 19–22, then 9–14.

The interpretation is given in vv.15–18 and then 23–28.

We shall now go through this in more detail.

There is a contrast between the beasts and a man (in Hebrew, 'son of' is a generic term, so son of man means man); the beasts come out of the abyss, the resort of evil powers, and man appears from heaven. So before we know what these figures represent, we know that the former are evil and the latter is good, on God's side.

What do the four beasts represent? Look at the interpretation given in 7.17. Why is there special interest in the fourth? The most terrible beast represents Antiochus IV, who is persecuting the Jews. See v.25. Who does the man represent? See vv.18,27.

How do the beasts change? How does man change?

How is this vision a message for the Jews under persecution, who accept death rather than deny their faith?

Resurrection of the dead. Dan.12.1–4

This text is the first text in the Bible to give us a clear presentation of belief in the resurrection of the dead. The vision in Ezek.37 was still only an image of the resurrection of the people. Here we have personal resurrection. This text expresses in a different way what is affirmed in Dan.7. Let us look at the situation again.

Antiochus IV persecuted the Jews. Some of them preferred to die rather than to renounce their faith. That raised a serious question: hitherto, people of Israel did not have any conception of a life after death. The only life you had was earthly life. Now these martyrs were prepared to lose all that they had for the sake of God. And God responded. 'You are persecuted and accept death,' writes Daniel. 'That is the visible side of things. Now I shall show you the invisible side of things. Those of you who accept death in this way, people of the saints of the Most High, will be led into glory for a completely new life, in a marvellous kingdom which will last for ever.'

So here we find two ways of speaking, two very important means of expressing the resurrection.

Daniel 12 puts it in terms of before and after. 'Before death, you were alive. Death made you fall asleep, into a deep hole. After death, you will come out of this hole and wake up.' Those who awoke would be the same people as before. However, the new life would not be just the same as what had gone before; the author uses cosmic imagery to describe it: the splendour of the firmament.

Daniel 7 stresses this further dimension. It puts it in terms of below and above. On earth (below) you are put to death. However, above you are brought near to God for a completely new form of life.

We need to remember this imagery when we study the resurrection of Christ: the first Christians used it as a means of expression.

One important detail: man here is an image, a collective figure representing all those who trust in God, even to death. We should remember it when Jesus is presented as Son of man.

**Three lions.
Persepolis (sixth
to fifth century BC)**

Wisdom in the Diaspora

We are going to end with two books which were written in the Diaspora, one in Babylon (Baruch) and the other in Egypt (Wisdom).

Baruch (deutero-canonical)

This book is attributed to Baruch, secretary to the prophet Jeremiah; in fact it is made up of four sections coming from different periods and different authors. As it is now, it is a fine expression of penitence. It begins with an affirmation: our sins have broken our relationship with God (1.1–14). Then comes a reflection on sin as being exile far from God; the only recourse we have is to the tenderness and the faithfulness of God (1.15–3.18). So one can meditate on the wisdom of God which is none other than the Law; by practising the latter one acquires the former (3.9–4.4). The last part, the tone of which suggests Second Isaiah, gives consolation to Jerusalem and tells her that God grants her his light and his mercy. Reconciliation is achieved (4.5–5.9).

It is worth reading the fine prayer of the exiles (2.11–3.8), and above all the meditation on God's wisdom: 'It has appeared on earth and lived with men' (3.32–4.1). John says precisely this when he speaks of Jesus.

Jesus the Wisdom of God

To simplify things: the prophets helped Christians to discover the mission of Jesus, what he had to do; the wisdom literature helped them to perceive his being, who he is.

In the Old Testament, the Wisdom of God is sometimes personified, but the language remains figurative, as when I say, 'my heart's in the Highlands'; I personify my spirit as though it were capable of going somewhere without me, but I am well aware that it is my own self, so that I can attribute all my good points and my failings to it. Similarly, the Wisdom of God is God's own self; it is God as he is wise. So one can attribute to Wisdom all the powers of God, like the power to create, and so on (Wisdom 7).

When Christians came to say that Jesus is the Wisdom of God, that made it possible for them to attribute to him the qualities of this wisdom, i.e. the very qualities of God.

Wisdom (deutero-canonical)

This book was written in Greek, in Alexandria in Egypt, about 50–30 BC, and is the last work in the Old Testament to be composed.

The author is a Greek who knows his classics well; he is also a Jew. Living far from upheavals experienced by the community in Palestine under the Hasmonean dynasty, he practises the policy of the outstretched hand. Like the Jewish philosopher Philo of Alexandria at a later date (Philo was a contemporary of Jesus), he tried to think out his Jewish faith in terms of Greek culture.

His book can be divided into three parts.

1. Human destiny in God's plan. 1–5

What is the meaning of life? With a good deal of psychological skill, the author portrays two different attitudes. We were born by chance, say some; life is short and there is nothing after it. And he shows the practical consequences to which this can lead: enjoy life and trample on others to get what you want. In reality, these are friends of death and they forget that God has created man incorruptible by making him an image of his own nature. On the other side there are those who trust in God, who remain firm in his love. They often suffer and are sometimes persecuted, but when they have accomplished their task they will live with God.

The first Christians used these texts, combining them with passages from the prophets to express the death and the crucifixion of the Righteous One.

2. The praise of wisdom. 6.1–11.3

We shall return to one passage from this section, but you should read all these chapters, where the author urges us, like him, to seek the Wisdom of God which is the friend of men, to make it a companion in our lives and to become lovers of his beauty. Then, in an amazing midrash, he takes up the important moments of sacred history to show that Wisdom was in control. Wisdom formed Adam, piloted Noah's ark, allowed Abraham to be braver than a father concerned for his child; it led Moses, and so on.

3. A meditation on the Exodus. 11.4–19.22

Here Wisdom almost disappears. The plagues of Egypt are punishment for some and salvation for others.

Studying a text: Wisdom 7.21–30

It is difficult to single out a precise text, because the argument is a developing one. You should really read all chapters 6–10.

The author pretends to be Solomon, the wise king, and he shows that he owes everything, not to his birth, but to the fact that he prayed and the spirit of Wisdom came upon him. He was instructed by the craftsman of the universe, who organized it (7.22).

Read this text. How does Wisdom appear? She is seen to be endowed with all the qualities, like a beloved. (In 7.22–23 there is a list of three times seven attributes, the superlative of perfection!) In the Bible, some of these qualities are confined to God, while others were attributed by the Greek philosophers to the divine principle which animates the universe: you might try to identify them – but without arguing, as they are not always clear, and the matter is not very important.

As you look at these attributes, try above all to see the relationship between Wisdom and God.

Verse 26 is very strong. For a Jew, the Greek word *eikon*, image, designates a kind of identity, a presence.

As you look at these attributes, try to see the role of Wisdom towards creation and towards men.

Now you might read Gen.1.26–27, God creates man in his image, and Wisdom 2.23. In Wisdom 7.26, Wisdom is the image of God. Does that mean that man reproduces the features of this Wisdom?

Read II Cor.4.4; Col.1.15, then I Cor.11.7; II Cor.3.18; Col.3.10. What does this teach us about Christ? About men's vocation?

You might end by reading all these chapters again, replacing the word Wisdom in your mind by Jesus.

The Septuagint (LXX)

Septuagint (Greek for seventy, hence the symbol LXX) is the name given to the first Greek translation of the Old Testament.

The name derives from a legend told in the Letter of Aristeas, a Greek work from the end of the second century BC. Seventy-two Jewish scholars, working separately, ended up producing, after seventy-two days, translations which were alike in every respect. This is a way of stressing that this translation is miraculous and inspired by God.

In fact the translation was made by various authors between 250 and 150 BC.

The Jewish community in Alexandria spoke Greek and no longer understood Hebrew. Just as in Palestine the Hebrew text was translated into Aramaic (the Targum, see p.81), so in Egypt it was translated into Greek. This translation was probably liturgical in origin, and is often less a literal translation than an adaptation. It is a rereading of the scriptures, bringing them up to date. One example is famous: Isaiah proclaimed, 'The young woman is pregnant and will bring forth Immanuel' (Isa.7.14). The Septuagint translated this 'The virgin is pregnant', which allowed Christians to apply the text to Mary (Matt.1.23).

This translation is very important.

First, it made it possible to acclimatize Jewish belief to Greek culture and provided a language in which it could be expressed. In fact it uses the common language *(koine)*, but colours it with various phrases borrowed from Hebrew. The New Testament often uses this language.

The Septuagint became the Bible of Christians, who adopted its list of contents (see the deutero-canonical books, p.86), and often took over its method of interpreting the scriptures. Thus it was a vital link in the preparation for expressing Christian belief.

8 The Psalms

An Egyptian musician
celebrating the Sun God
(about 1000 BC)

We shall end this 'holiday trip' through the Old Testament with the book of Psalms.

Why put them all together in the same chapter? Hitherto we have tried to read texts at the time when they were composed. Why treat the psalms differently? There is a simple reason: it is almost impossible to date them. Prayer is the same at all times. Texts are reread and rewritten, so it is wiser to study them together.

That will help us to understand better how Israel prayed, and it will also be a good way of summing up our journey: the essential features of the experience of this people, their discovery of God and their own situation in the world, is all expressed in their prayer.

In fact the psalms are essentially prayer, the response of human beings to the God who addresses them in every situation of their existence.

Human cries

'We are born with his book in our bellies,' wrote a Jewish poet. 'It is not a long book: 150 poems, 150 steps set up between death and life; 150 reflections of our rebellions and our fidelity, our agonies and our resurrections. This is more than a book; it is a living being who speaks, who speaks to *you*, who suffers and cries out and dies, who is raised again and who sings, on the threshhold of eternity.'

A blind harpist

We find all our human cries here: hymns of wonderment at nature or human love, anguish in the face of suffering and death, oppression by society, rebellion against the absurdity of the world or the silence of God. All these cries are here, and they are our own, given to us as the word of God. They teach us that even at the darkest moments of our rebellion, God is present and cries with us, through us, and that both blasphemy and praise can be prayers if they are true and express the way we live.

Two kinds of language

To be brief, we might distinguish language which conveys information, the language of science, from the language of relationships. For example, a child is in bed and calls out to its mother, 'Mother, I'm thirsty.' What kind of language is this phrase? Perhaps it conveys information, that is, the words 'I'm thirsty' give an exact description of the situation; the mother responds in the same key: 'Get up and get yourself a glass of water', and the child goes to sleep. If the phrase expresses some kind of relationship, after having had a drink, the child will say, 'Mother, I'm still thirsty,' or, 'I'm hot'. 'I'm thirsty' here means, 'I need you, I want you to come.'

In scientific language, which seeks to convey information, the words say exactly what they signify. In the language of relationships they seek to convey something else: the lover who addresses 'her pet' or 'his angel' is not expressing a situation but a kind of relationship, like the psalmist who calls his God 'my rock, my fortress'.

This distinction between two kinds of language is important when we are using the psalms in prayer, and even more generally, when we are reading the Bible. In fact, the word of God is always expressed in the language of relationships and not that of conveying information. Granted, the Bible is concerned to teach us certain things, but above all it seeks to enable us to enter into a personal relationship with God. It addresses us. The language of information is directed towards our intelligence, but often it does not bring about any personal change in us. If a child is really thirsty, the mother is not very bothered. By contrast, the language of relationship changes us. The words 'I'm thirsty' disturb the mother and arouse her maternal instincts.

When we are confronted with an object or an action, our scientific sense makes us ask, 'What *is* it?' The poet

94

or the man of the Bible asks, 'What does it *mean*?' If the science teacher hands a flower to a girl pupil, he is obviously asking 'What is it? What kind is it?' But if a boy gives a flower to the same girl, the question is very different.

So when we open the book of Psalms, indeed when we open the Bible, it is important to remember that we are reading a language of relationships. There are certain images or expressions which we are not to understand in a scientific sense, as information, but which we have to interpret as though they were addressed to us. And they speak to us in terms of our personal experience. The same word means one thing to the country farmer who has just broken his ploughshare on an outcrop of rock; it means something different to the walker in the Alps who, having panicked on a crumbling surface, at last gets a footing on solid rock. These two aspects can also be found in the Bible. God is the 'rock' on which men are broken if they fail to respect him; he is also the solid 'rock' in whom we can trust.

The language of an era

Poetic imagery changes with civilization. 'The solemn action of the sower' might move our grandparents; it is meaningless in an age of automated farming.

The Bible speaks in terms of the culture of its time; its language is no longer ours, and that sometimes presents real difficulties. The notes in your Bible, or those in commentaries, will help you to understand the significance of certain symbols.

The forms of biblical poetry are also different. I have already said something about them (p.30). You may like them, or find that they put you off. However, you might say exactly the same thing about some modern poetry.

The numbering of the psalms

The Greek Bible, followed by the Latin version and the Catholic liturgy, does not have quite the same numbering as the Hebrew Bible, which is followed by the majority of modern Bibles. When the numbering differs, the liturgy always has one figure lower.

So you need to be careful when you are given the reference to a psalm.

The numbering of the Hebrew Bible is being adopted more and more, and I have followed it here.

Very often, two figures are given, e.g. Ps.51(50): this is 51 in Hebrew, 50 in the liturgy.

Literary genres

Scholars have tried to define the various literary genres of the psalms. This is important as we try to understand them, and even more important when we use them in prayer: we don't prepare for a celebration with friends in the same way as we do for a day of mourning. To know the literary genre of a psalm is to know how to prepare to meet God.

The classifications suggested by scholars differ in detail, but broadly speaking they agree. In any good introduction to the Psalter you will find a classification of the psalms into these various genres.

This chapter is meant above all to help you to enter into the prayer of the psalms. That is why I have grouped them according to themes rather than according to literary genres (though the two often coincide).

I am not going to pretend that we can make a complete study of the Psalter. However, simply by reading psalms, some for pleasure and others because of their theological importance or their difficulty, we shall try to discover how these old prayers are still our own.

Some themes of prayer

Praise to God the Saviour and Creator.

Praise to the God who is near: he dwells among his people (in Jerusalem, in the Temple), indeed dwells in his people (the Law).

Prayers of hope. God is king and will establish his reign of justice; he will do this through his king-messiah, of whom the earthly king was a figure.

Prayers of petition and thanksgiving. For Israel, these two aspects were inseparable.

Prayers for living. Here we can include several themes which arose out of the reflections of the wise men: how do we live in our difficult human situation?

Before this, the Psalms of Ascent will give us a first introduction to the Psalter.

For each theme, you will find general comments on the left hand page and suggestions for reading psalms on the right.

The Psalms of Ascent: Pss.120–134

It is easy to find a marvellous small collection within the Psalter: fifteen short psalms, fresh, and all bearing the same title. They are called Psalms of Ascent, probably because they were recited during the ascent to Jerusalem for the three pilgrim feasts. The psalms concerned are Pss.120–134. (Ps. 132 is in fact different, and may not have been part of the collection.)

These psalms belong to different families. They will help us to discover the character of psalms, to see the style of Hebrew poetry, and above all to understand the religious feelings of the authors.

Begin by reading the psalms, simply for pleasure.

After that, you can go back to them and study them from different perspectives.

Literary genres

In which family would you classify each of these psalms? Classifications suggested include prayers of trust, individual or corporate appeals for help, a prayer of recognition, a song of Zion, some psalms of instruction and a liturgy.

Try to discover some of the features of each family, while realizing that the borderlines are sometimes blurred: it is possible to pass from supplication to confidence in the same prayer.

Hebrew poetry

Rhythm. In classical English or French poetry, each verse ought to have the same number of syllables. Hebrew works on a different principle. In fact the voice rests or pauses on certain syllables: only these count. They can be the same number in every verse (for example, 3 + 3), or they can vary (3 + 2). Here is an example:

Out of the *depths* I cry to *thee*, O *Lord!*	(3)
Lord, *hear* my *voice!*	(2)
Let thine *ears* be *attentive*	(3)
To the *voice* of my sup*plications.*	(2)

In this strophe the voice pauses on the syllables printed in italics: there is an alternation between three stresses and two stresses.

Parallelism. This consists in repeating the same thing twice in a different way. It happens a great deal. Try to find examples in these psalms (e.g. Ps.122.8–9).

Key words. Sometime each phrase begins by taking up a word from a previous phrase, which it uses as a kind of peg. See, for example, Ps.121.

The imagery

You can study this on two levels.

What imagery is used? What social, economic or cultural milieu does it reveal? It may evoke family

---

Praying together with a psalm

It's clear that there are no fixed ways and that everyone must invent their own way, whether individually or in a group. I can only describe what happens in some places.

The group meets (the atmosphere counts, the way people sit, some focal point of attention). Someone reads the psalm out aloud and then everyone reads it silently: once, twice, ten times, and broods on it. After a longer or shorter period of silent prayer, one person and then another repeats a verse which has made an impression, either reading it straight or re-phrasing it in his or her own words. Many verses, words, images of the psalm repeated in this way, rewritten, filled with the life provided by each individual, take on a new significance and renew prayer. Don't be afraid of periods of silence: they are not dead times, but moments when the word of the Bible becomes the word of a brother or sister which resonates within us and calls forth our own words.

Sometimes the refrain of a well-known canticle can be said spontaneously.

Sometimes, too, verses from the Gospels can be included, expressing the certainty that the psalms are also Christ's prayers.

Some editions of the Psalter provide prayers after each psalm which take up the psalm's main themes.

life: mother and child, mistress and servant; or the life of village people in close contact with nature: the herdsman, arrows, building a house, gathering in the harvest; or the stunned gaze of the countryman as he discovers the great city with its enormous buildings and those who live in them. The psalms also display a popular spirit which sometimes verges on truculence: 'they would have swallowed us up alive.'

Try above all to see what they are saying.

What aspect of God appears in these psalms? What is his relationship with man? A simple expression like, 'The Lord will keep your going out and your coming in from this time forth and for evermore' (121.8) is a magnificent expression of what we call providence, the presence of God in the space and time of human history.

What is man's response to this love of God, in ordinary life, in the trials of the everyday world, in anxiety? What sense of sin is expressed? Notice how in every moment of his life, with the family or in his daily work, man lives in union with his God: for him, everything is a sign of God's love.

What is the meaning of pilgrimage, the importance of Jerusalem and of the Temple, the place where God makes himself present?

A link with the scriptures

You might also notice how these psalms take up the spirituality of Ezekiel and the Priestly History, a piety centred on the presence of God in his temple; how they accord with the Deuteronomic code in expressing the presence of God in everyday life; how they take up, in a very simple way, the imagery of the faith of Second Isaiah in God the Creator brought near to man through his love, or again the eucharistic freshness of Tobit.

In depth, the Psalms of Ascent work on four levels. They celebrate an actual ascent to Jerusalem; but this pilgrimage is also a way of reliving the first ascent from Egypt at the time of the Exodus and the ascent from Babylon at the end of the exile. And it is already an anticipation of this ascent of the people towards Jerusalem at the end of time (see Isa.60–62).

Christian prayer

How was Jesus able to use these psalms in prayer? How can we use them today?

God's Poor

In the Bible, poverty can have two significances, which should not be confused.

First, poverty is a specific situation of deprivation. It is an evil and even a scandal, because it shows that the kingdom of God has not yet arrived, since there are still unfortunates who suffer injustice. The prophets of the exile, in particular, announce the coming of the kingdom of God: when that happens, no one will be poor (see p.67). This is the tradition taken up by the beatitudes in Luke.

Poverty is sometimes envisaged as a spiritual attitude: the attitude of the person who submits himself totally to God because he has experienced his own impotence and his poverty. This poverty is a poverty of heart. These poor, the *anawim* (plural of *anaw*, poor), are the ones whom the Gospel of Matthew declares happy.

This idea of spiritual poverty appears clearly with Zephaniah (see p.61). It developed after the return from exile, and led to the formation of this stratum of simple people, with a deep faith, far removed from the political and religious quarrels of the high priests, whom we find at the beginning of our era in the persons of Zechariah, Elisabeth, Simeon, Anna and Mary.

The Psalms of Ascent, composed after the exile, express this spirituality well.

The life of these poor people, these insignificant men and women who were poor in spirit, was very simple. Country folk, close to nature, they enjoyed the simple pleasures of family life, friendship between brothers, and peace. Although they are incapable of expressing themselves in learned words, the imagery they use reveals the depth of their religious feelings: everything speaks to them of God, and is a message of his love. This is the way in which Jesus will speak in the parables.

This God is personal and close to man. He protects him in all his activities and watches over him; he pardons his sins! And the poor man responds to him with a complete and utter faith and confidence.

This God lives in the midst of his people, in his Temple at Jerusalem. So the life of the poor is one long pilgrimage. Israel is a people on the march to the place where their God lives. They have been on the march since the Exodus, because God freed them then; they have been on the march since the departure from Babylon. They will continue on the march until the time when all the people reassembles united by the same faith, in joy and communion with the one God.

Praise to God the Creator and Saviour

There are times when you want to sing, because the world is beautiful, because someone loves you, or because a friend forgives you and takes a great load from your mind. There are times when a jubilant people wants to sing, when there is a great national victory at sport, or a royal wedding. Songs, an explosion of collective joy fuelled by refrains or slogans, praise in one form or another, have been part of festivals all down the ages.

In Israel, praise blossoms or explodes in most of the psalms; it appears in pure form in the hymns, but it is also present in songs of supplication. Here we have one of the essential characteristics of biblical man confronted with God: whatever his particular situation, whether it is joy or sorrow, in the depths of suffering or sin the believer sees his existence as being in the presence of a God whose beauty and goodness he cannot help celebrating.

This praise is not the logical culmination of a process of reasoning. It is an expression of wonderment and joy of one who knows himself to be loved because God has told him, 'You are precious in my eyes, and honoured, and I love you' (Isa.43.4).

God the liberator

As we have seen, Israel's first religious experience was of liberation and salvation: their God was the one who brought them out of slavery. Other books than the Psalter have preserved some very ancient songs: the brief refrain of Miriam dancing for joy with the people at the time of the Exodus (Ex.15.21), or the magnificent hymn of the prophetess Deborah celebrating the victory won at the foot of mount Tabor about 1225 BC (Judges 5).

By celebrating the wonders of God during liturgical festivals, the people make them present once again, and share in them. They revive their awareness of being the people whom God has chosen, renew their faith in the covenant, and their hope. In fact they remind God of past liberations and call upon him to complement them with new ones.

God the creator

Israel then discovered that if God can intervene in history, it is because he is Lord of it, because he has created the world. The prophet Amos was able to quote a fine hymn to the Creator God (Amos 4.13; 5.8–9; 9.5–6: see p.47). Second Isaiah will make this the basis of his theology.

The structure of these prayers

The structure of these psalms is very simple. They begin with an invitation, an exhortation to praise. The development, beginning with 'for', 'because', 'who', proclaims the wonders that God has performed in history, or his qualities. The conclusion takes up the invitation in a more developed or personal way, and often ends with a blessing to an acclamation: 'Hallelujah' (Praise God!), 'For ever!'

Our prayer

We shall probably find it easy to pray these psalms. The only problem is likely to be a cultural one: some images seem rather strange to us (however, the creation stories have already made us familiar with them), and certain allusions to historical events escape us. That is not very important. We do not feel cut off from our grandparents simply because there are things that we don't know about their lives. Similarly, details apart, these hymns should strengthen our conviction that the history of the people of God is our history, and that it is there, in these divine wonders, from the Exodus to the new exodus in Jesus Christ, that we have our roots.

The titles of the psalms

At the beginning, most of the psalms have indications of the author and of the type of psalm, which are often difficult to understand.

The Hebrew preposition which precedes the name can signify that it is attributed to this author or that the psalm is part of a collection made under his name. When rereading the psalms, people wanted to put them in the context of the life of a great personality.

There is often also an indication of the instrument which is to accompany the psalm, and this may indicate its genre.

◆ The God of Exodus. Ps.114

Invitation: Hallelujah. Praise God!

Development

vv.1–2. The purpose of the first Exodus: God wants to make the people his sanctuary, he wants to dwell in a faithful people (see Ezekiel, p.66, and Nathan, p.42).

vv.3–4. The wonders of the first Exodus.

vv.5–6. The author speaks and makes us ask ourselves about these wonders.

vv.7–8. The wonders of the second exodus, the liberation from Babylon. This is at least one possible meaning: inspired by Second Isaiah (Isa.41.15; 42.15; 43.20, etc.), the author celebrates the new exodus.

Jesus' prayer

It was easy for Jesus to take up this psalm (which was recited in the passover liturgy) to celebrate 'his exodus which he was to accomplish in Jerusalem' (Luke 9.31).

Christian prayer

How can we use this psalm today? The New Testament talks of our life in terms of an exodus (John, I Peter, Revelation); what meaning does that give to our existence? We can also apply it to Christ, our rock and the source of living water (see I Cor.10.4).

◆ The God of the oppressed. Ps.113

Invitation

vv.1–3. Who is called on to praise God? Where?

Development

vv.4–6. Which of God's qualities are praised?

vv.7–9. Compare these verses with I Sam.2.1–10, the 'gospel' proclaimed by Second Isaiah (see p.67), and the beatitudes. What do these verses proclaim?

Jesus' prayer

This psalm is the first of a group (Pss.113–118) called Hallel (praise) which were sung in the liturgy of the three great festivals: so Jesus will have sung them on the evening of Maundy Thursday (Mark 14.26). How could he make this his prayer?

Christian prayer

How does God want to show his greatness? How would we translate vv.7–9 today (the dignity of the poor and the oppressed)? Can we pray this psalm without trying to realize in our own actions what is asked for?

◆ The glory of God: living man. Ps.8

Invitation. v.2

This is taken up again at the end, in v.10.

Development

vv.3–5. The psalm celebrates the greatness of God. Perhaps the beginning should be translated like this:

I want to hymn your glory above the heavens in a better way than with the mouths of babes and sucklings.

These babes are probably the stars which sang in the morning of the world (Job 38.6; Bar.3.35): man celebrates God's glory in an even better way than they did. God's abode is heaven: as in Gen.1, creation is seen as God's victory over chaos.

vv.6–9. Man was introduced in v.5. Now he is the centre, but God remains the subject of all the verbs. To proclaim the greatness of man is to proclaim the greatness of God.

With this hymn we are half-way between the two creation stories (Gen. 2 and 1).

The psalm is quoted several times in the New Testament (see the references in the margin of your Bible, if you have an annotated one).

◆ Creation, God's glory. Ps.104

The author is inspired by an Egyptian hymn to the sun god composed about 1350. The few extracts from that hymn quoted on p.18 will enable you to make a comparison. So a human prayer can become a prayer to the living God, just as our daily bread can become the body of Christ. However, the psalmist rethinks his prayer in terms of his faith and of the creation story in Gen.1.

Invitation v.1

Development, vv.2–30

First of all read this text just to enjoy it. Then compare it with the Egyptian hymn: what connections can you see? Compare it with the story in Gen.1: can you see how it follows the days of creation?

Conclusion, vv.31–35

Personal praise, with joy, and hope for a world that will finally be freed from evil.

Christian prayer

God created all things by Christ and for him (Col.1.15–18). He gives us life through his breath, the Spirit. And the bread and wine become symbols of a world made new in the Spirit.

Praise to the God who is Near

God is the God who is utterly different, Lord of history, the Creator. However, the wonder which Israel never ceased to extol was that God had come very near. He dwells *among* his people: in Jerusalem and in his Temple, the place of his presence to which people go on pilgrimage. He dwells *in* his people. 'For this commandment is not too hard for you, neither is it far off. But the word is very near you; it is in your mouth and in your heart, so that you can do it' (Deut.30.11ff.). Here I have brought together psalms which scholars classify into various genres: psalms of Zion, of pilgrimage, of instruction.

Immanu-el: God with us

Some psalms celebrate the joy of being invited to God's house, of being his guest, sharing an intimate relationship with him. So we should watch out for expressions like 'be with', 'with you', 'be your guest', 'dwell in your house', 'be sheltered by God', 'God before us', 'under your wings'.

It is worth studying Ps.139.

God present in his Temple

Jerusalem – or Zion, the hill on which the city is built – and the Temple are the places where God makes himself present to his people. As we read Isaiah's call (p.42) or the priestly texts about the presence of God upon the ark (p.71), we could see the extraordinary impression it made upon the people.

People went up to Jerusalem three times a year, on the pilgrimage feasts (Passover, Pentecost and above all the Feast of Tabernacles). In this way they once again had the experience of being a community around God. However, there was a danger: the presence of God might be thought to be a piece of magic, dispensing righteous living. Prophets like Jeremiah disabused the people of this idea (p.62), and the exile and the destruction of the Temple forced them to understand that this presence of God was not an automatic assurance. God does not live primarily in a place, but in a faithful people.

Christian prayer. The presence of God is a real fact in Jesus Christ, our true temple. And the church is his body, animated by his spirit. These prayers remind us that the church is a people on the march to the heavenly Jerusalem, the ultimate city where evil will disappear because God will be wholly in us.

God present through his Law

The law gets a bad press. So does obedience!

For Israel, the law is not a matter of orders and commandments. It is the word, a tender word like the smile of a woman responding to her lover, brusque, like a team leader organizing his group for work; precise, like a guide indicating the only firm hold on crumbling rock. And this word – Shema Israel! Listen and obey, Israel! – simply says: 'I love you. . . Do you love me?'

As the etymology of the word reminds us, obey *(ob-audire)* means to get in a good position to listen to someone who is talking, to prepare with all our being to receive his words so that they may resonate in our heart and produce a response which will stem from our whole being. In this sense, the conversation between two lovers is mutual 'obedience'.

It is essential to remember this when you read these 'prayers of obedience' if you are to understand how these believers could sing of the law with such tenderness, as happens, for example, in Ps.119.

Christian prayer. It is easy for us to pray these psalms now. For us the law has taken human form, Jesus Christ, word of God laid down in our hearts by the spirit. And these old words can help us to tell him once again of the passion which inspires us.

With abounding love hast thou loved us, O Lord our God, and great and overflowing tenderness hast thou shown us. O our Father, our King, for our fathers' sake, who trusted in thee, and whom thou didst teach the statutes of life, be also gracious unto us and teach us. O our Father, merciful Father, ever compassionate, have mercy upon us; O put it into our hearts to understand and to discern, to mark, learn and teach, to heed, to do and to fulfil in love all the words of instruction in thy Torah. Enlighten our eyes in thy Torah, and let our hearts cleave to thy commandments, and unify our hearts to love and reverence thy Name . . . Thou hast chosen us from all peoples and tongues, and hast brought us near unto thy great Name for ever in faithfulness. Blessed art thou, O Lord, who hast chosen thy people Israel in love. . .

A prayer from the Jewish liturgy.

📖 Lord, you have known me. . . Ps.139

At some time we have all dreamed of being known as we really are, with our personal qualities and failings, and being loved for what we are. This is the way in which believers know themselves to be known and loved by their God.

However, this intimacy is not entirely a tranquil matter. As in the case of Jeremiah (p.62), the temptation may be that we find this word too heavy to bear, and may seek to evade it.

Verses 1–18. Note the imagery and expressions which indicate proximity and intimacy. Humility is also a matter of recognizing ourselves as the most marvellous gift which God gives us: 'Thank you, Lord, for making me in such an amazing way.'

Verses 19–22. However, this believer still has a sorry question: why evil? In what we may feel to be rather a simplistic way, he asks God to destroy whatever is opposed to him.

Verses 23–24. His final prayer is even more moving: he is no longer sure that he is going on the right way and asks God to protect him.

Christian prayer
God has freely bestowed grace on us through his beloved (Eph.1.6). In him, we can become sons and know something of his intimacy with the Father through the Spirit, which makes us pray, 'Abba, Father!' And we know that the Son protects those whom the Father has given into his care (John 17).

📖 My whole being cries out with joy. . . Ps.84

This hymn of a pilgrim arriving at the temple expresses his passionate love for God.

Look for the imagery and expressions which speak of the march, the habitation (dwelling, house, nest), the happiness (joy, rampart, shield). It is worth looking for those images which express the same realities for us; if we do that, we shall already be half way towards composing a prayer for today.

Christian prayer
From now on the real temple is the body of the Risen Christ. So we can celebrate it in the same words.

And his church is his body all through history. We can celebrate the joy of living as brothers, but ask at the same time that this church should be purified, should become more like what it ought to be, and also ask that God allow us to work in it.

📖 I am thirsty for God. . . Pss.42–43

Originally, these two psalms were one; a refrain (42.6,12; 43.5) divides it into three strophes of equal length.

A temple servant is in exile in Lebanon and cries out in his suffering. In his exile he feels only one pain: being far from God.

42.2–6. What is his desire? (See Ex.34.23.) What is his suffering? What comforts him?

42.7–12. One can pray to God from exile, from any place of exile. This psalm takes up the classic imagery.

43.1–5. The prayer.

Look for images and expressions which are nostalgic (thirst, faint . . .) – water – light – joy – salvation.

📖 The wonders of your Law. . . Ps.119

176 verses! 176 verses to say one thing: 'Lord, I love your law.' Twenty-two strophes, one for each letter of the Hebrew alphabet; the eight verses of each strophe all begin with the same letter which is successively every letter of the Hebrew alphabet. And one of the eight names of the Law appears in each of these eight verses: law, precepts, commandments, and so on. This psalm – which it is better to use in small sections – is as bewitching as an incantation. Just as the lover keeps telling the beloved of the same love in a thousand ways, so the psalmist constantly tells God that he loves him, this God who has brought himself near through his word: 'Thou art near, O Lord' (v.151).

In this loving conversation between the God who speaks and the believer who listens, we might look for those images and expressions which present God: the Law is God, who makes himself near (it comes from his mouth, it teaches him) . . . but remains mysterious.

We should also look at the images and expressions which present man and his attitude: he is turned towards God (he examines, meditates, cherishes, studies . . . the law), he obeys, goes, seeks . . . He is brought back to God, because, in the past, he has sinned.

Christian prayer
You can use this psalm as a prayer by putting Jesus instead of law, for he is the word of God which has been set in our hearts by the Spirit: Jesus, 'the way, the truth and the life'.

Prayers of Hope. God the King. The Earthly King

Two different genres of psalms have been brought together here: common to both is that they celebrate the kingdom, in one case of God, in the other of the earthly king. They direct our attention towards the future, to that moment when God will finally show himself as he is, a faithful and just king, through the intermediary of the one whom he will establish as Messiah king.

The Lord is king

In Israel, God alone is king: the earthly king is only his representative. That was the faith from the beginning.

During the exile in Babylon and afterwards, there was no longer a king. So belief in the kingdom of God developed. Thus Second Isaiah shows that God is king because he is Creator (Isa.40.12–31) and liberator of Israel (41.21; 42.15; 44.6 . . .). The prophet calls on all the people to recognize God as king by celebrating him (42.10–12). He announces that God will finally come to establish his kingdom (52.7).

Five very similar psalms celebrate this kingdom of God: Pss.93,96,97,98,99.

There is an outburst of rejoicing; you might think that it was a festival. Israel, the most distant peoples (the islands) and all the elements of the universe share in this universal joy.

Taking up the good news, the gospel, of Second Isaiah, these psalms proclaim the time when God will bring an end to all wretchedness and poverty (see p.67). Ps.47 probably has the same origin. Ps.24.7–10 is perhaps an ancient psalm celebrating the entry of the ark into Jerusalem at the time of David: verses 1–6, added after the exile, take up the whole theme from a universalist perspective.

These songs were formed in the liturgy: in the cult, the eternal kingdom of God begins to become effective on earth.

Christian prayer
By proclaiming the beatitudes and performing miracles for the poor, Jesus shows that in him the kingdom of God has begun. However, it has only begun: the disciples must realize it. So these psalms reinforce our expectation ('Thy kingdom come') and invite us to work for it.

The 'birth' of the king

Seven psalms (2,21,45,72,89,101,110) and perhaps some others celebrate the king of Israel.

Unlike other peoples, Israel never divinized its kings. However, as the prophet Nathan announced to David (p.42), they became son of God in a special sense on the day on which they were enthroned. On this day of their birth as kings, they were begotten as sons of God.

Perhaps some of these psalms are very old. At all events, they were reread after the exile, at a time when there was no longer a king. At that time they became the bearers of a new hope: one day, God will send his Messiah king to establish his kingdom.

Christian prayer
The Christian recognizes Jesus as this Messiah king; so he is invited to celebrate him and to pray that his Lordship over mankind may increasingly be realized.

Psalm 2 in the New Testament

This psalm helped people to understand and express:

The resurrection of Christ: this is the time when he was begotten (his birth) as son of God, messiah king and Lord of the universe (Acts 13.32; Rom.1.3; Heb.1.5; 5.5; Rev. 12.5). This is not his birth at Bethlehem, and the expression 'son of God' does not have the meaning we attach to it today: it does not denote his divinity but his establishment as king and Lord of the universe.

The death of Christ: he is rejected by the leaders of the people; so these are the 'evil men' of the psalm, who rebel against the Lord and against his anointed (Acts 4.23–31 and probably also Matt.26.3–4).

His coming at the end of the world: one day he will be definitively enthroned as Lord of the universe (Acts 19.15; 21.1–5). Here is the ultimate foundation of our hope, and John promises that we shall share in his glory (Rev.21.7; 2.26).

📖 God is king! Ps.96

It is worth noticing how this psalm makes the message of Second Isaiah into a prayer (as do other royal psalms). Here are some connections:

vv.1–3. An invitation to all the earth to sing a new song (Isa. 42.10). In bringing liberation from the exile, God shows his salvation, his justice, his glory before the nations (Isa.45.14–25; 52.10).

vv.4–6. That shows that God is God and the other deities are nothing (Isa.41.21–29; 43.9–13).

vv.7–9. All the people are invited to praise God.

vv.10–13. In proclaiming God as Creator, vv.11–12 say why God can finally reign as a just king (vv.10–13).

Note the images and expressions which evoke glory and creation, peace and social justice, universal praise.

📖 My son – sit at my right hand. . . Pss.2; 110

It would be a good thing for you first to reread Nathan's prophecy to David (II Sam.7, see p.42).

Ps.2, vv.1–3. The 'wicked' ones, kings and peoples, plot against God and his messiah; thus they make common cause (as in I Chron.17.14).

vv.4–6. God mocks them; he has his plan against which revolts are of no avail.

vv.7–9. The Messiah king recalls this plan: on the day he ascended the throne, God made him his son. However, this monarchy goes beyond Israel: it now extends to all the people of the universe. So this is not just an earthly king.

vv.10–12. A warning to the rebels. Be still!

Ps.110 takes up the same themes with different (and sometimes obscure) expressions.

Sit at my right hand: the image begins from a specific situation, since the royal palace was on the right of the temple; it thus evokes a unique, almost divine position accorded to this king.

You are priest . . . In Israel, as with other peoples, the king is also a priest. In fact he is above all the patron of the priests, and the two functions tended to be kept separate.

Christian prayer
See the boxes: Pss. 2 and 110 in the New Testament.

📖 Faith in the faithless God! Ps.89

'The terrible moment when God isn't true and yet I still love him'. This phrase applies not only to personal situations (like that of Job, p.82), but also to collective situations, as here.

In 587 the monarchy disappeared. Now God has promised always to maintain the dynasty of David. Might he then be faithless? Might he have perjured himself?

vv.2–3. This praise of the love and faithfulness of God is an act of total faith, made in the dark: apparently everything tells against it. That is why the author clings desperately to these two words which he keeps repeating: tenderness and faithfulness (*hesed* and *emunah*, translated steadfast love and faithfulness by RSV). They occur in vv. 2,3,9,15,25,29,34,50 (see the box about the language of love on p.49).

vv.4–5. God is reminded of his promise to David.

vv.6–19. God is Creator and he is king. So he is all powerful. He has no excuse for not keeping his promise!

vv.20–38. A detailed recollection of God's promise to David and his descendants.

vv.39–46. With a bold leap of faith, the author shows that God is unfaithful.

vv.47–52. An agonized appeal for God to act.

v.53. The prayer began with a sheer act of faith. It ends with thanksgiving, for a work which God has not yet performed!

Christian prayer
First of all we learn an attitude: to rebel against situations which makes God false, in prayer, in sheer faith, and in confidence.

Now we can experience this attitude in Jesus' prayer in Gethsemane and on the cross.

Psalm 110 in the New Testament

Jesus applies this psalm to himself when he is before the Sanhedrin (he does the same with Dan.7, the passage about the Son of man).

Jesus is seated at the right hand of God: so the creed affirms. Peter proclaims this on the day of Pentecost to express what happened at Easter (Acts 2.34). The theme is often taken up again in the New Testament: Acts 5.31; 7.55; Rom.8.34; Col.3.1; Eph.1.20; I Cor.15.25; I Peter 3.22.

The Letter to the Hebrews makes v.4 the basis of its argument: Jesus is high priest (Heb.5.6).

Prayers of Petition and Thanksgiving

More than a third of the psalter consists of intercessory prayers, supplications, appeals for help. Scholars distinguish between individual supplications and collective supplications. The only difference lies in what is asked for, so we can study the two together.

These prayers are usually made up of four parts (the order of which may vary): invocation of God and cry for help – an account of the situation – reasons for being heard (above all the love, the faithfulness and the glory of God, and also the confidence of the person who prays) – conclusion, which is often a confident prayer, a thanksgiving in the certainty of being heard and a promise to offer a sacrifice out of gratitude.

The situations which call forth prayer can be very different. Here are the main ones:

- Prayers of sick people who already feel on the edge of the grave.
- Cries of the poor who are oppressed by injustice.
- The prayer of exiles.
- Prayer for victory for the armies of Israel.
- Prayers against the enemy. These cursing psalms raise a particular problem, which we shall study separately.
- Confession of sin.

Christian prayer

It is both easy and difficult for us to pray these psalms.

It is easy to take them up, because they express our own situation at one time or another.

The difficulty comes from several sides.

These prayers are expressed in imagery which will often be strange to us. Sometimes the notes in our Bible or a commentary may help. And in poetry, we need not always understand everything!

Fortunately, we are not always in such situations. The psalms, which are as it were universal prayers, compel us to come out of ourselves, to take into our prayer all those who are in such a situation. The first person in the psalms is almost always a collective; here we are the voice of suffering humanity.

Intercessory prayer bothers us. God is not a stop-gap for our inadequacies. That's true. But love between two people can also be expressed by asking: we know very well that this does not prevent us from acting: on the contrary, we draw on our love for others to find strength to take action ourselves.

Prayers which express only thanksgiving or trust are quite rare; that is because these themes appear in almost all the psalms of supplication. We may keep finding the same parts, but often there is mention of the lesson which is drawn from the event: 'See the power and love of God, which are capable of drawing us, though we are sinners, out of this hopeless tangle.'

Cursing psalms

Some passages in the psalms, and sometimes whole psalms, scandalize us. How can we ask God to kill our enemies, to disembowel them, to break their teeth? Perhaps there are two ways of using these psalms in prayer.

Sometimes they are the only true prayer that we can utter. When we feel incapable of finding our place in the New Testament ('Father, forgive them'), we can at least take up these prayers, which are a step in that direction. So to pray them, humbly, can be one way of making scriptures warm our hearts, so that one day the word of God may take us to the foot of the cross.

However, with Christ, these prayers have changed their meaning and have become prayers of consecration. Read the terrible poem of the divine vintner (Isa.63.1–6, see p.77). God tramples on all his enemies, their blood spurts on to his garments. When Revelation takes up this poem and shows us Christ in bloodstained garments (Rev.19.13), we understand that Jesus had taken upon himself all the sin of the world (II Cor.5.21), and that the blood which flows is henceforward his own.

Praying these psalms today, Christ continues to take on himself this sin of the world, to suffer death and to destroy it by exorcizing it with his love.

Praying these psalms with him, we say in a sense to God, 'Put me on the cross with your Son and blot out all this sin in me, all this sin of the world in which I share. With your Son, I consecrate myself so that all men may be consecrated in the truth.'

My God, why have you forsaken me? Ps.22

vv.2–3. Invocation of God and cry for help.

vv.4–12. The believer begins by giving the reasons why he should be heard: God is near; he has delivered those of former times; he has protected the believer since his birth.

vv.13–22. An explanation of the situation with the help of expressive imagery.

vv.23–27. Thanksgiving. Whether in reality, or whether in hope, he has been heard. He urges the people to join him in praise and invites the poor to share in the sacrificial meal which he is offering.

The opening individual's prayer probably stops here. When it became a collective prayer, by being taken into the psalter, vv.28–32 were added. The announcement of the conversion of the nations and the kingdom of God is dependent on the message of Second Isaiah and corresponds to the psalms which celebrate God as king. Verse 30, which recalls the worship given to God by the dead, must be dependent on Dan.12 (cf. p.91). Thus the prayer becomes the expectation of eternal life.

Christian prayer
According to Matthew and Mark, on the cross Jesus expressed his anguish with the first verse of this psalm, and the passion narrative takes up some of its imagery.

Having become a prayer of Christ, this psalm can become our own, with him and in him.

 Lord, slay them all. . . Ps.109

This psalm is probably the worst of the cursing psalms. People have tried to tone it down by putting the curses of vv.6–19 in the mouths of the enemy, directed against the faithful. It is better to accept it as it is: even a saint like Jeremiah could resort to such 'prayers' (Jer.17.18; 18.21–23; 20.11–12). It is easy to identify the different parts of this psalm.

Christian prayer
First of all, remember that Jesus used this psalm in prayer like all the rest. So it must be possible to turn it into a Christian prayer. You might find inspiration in the box on the left, or in some other way. However, we cannot suppress this psalm and those like it, and exclude them from liturgical usage, because they too are the word of God.

Lord, be merciful (Miserere). Ps.51

vv.3–4. An invocation of God and an appeal for forgiveness.

vv.5–8. I have sinned against you. . .

vv.9–14. A request for purification.

vv.15–19. A promise of thanksgiving: the sacrifice which the believer is going to offer will be himself, with his humbled pride.

vv.20–21. A prayer for Jerusalem. These verses, with their mention of physical sacrifices, do not fit in well with what has gone before and have probably been added.

The believer uses three main types of language to weave together his confession: that of sin (see the box below), that of purification, and that of love (see p.49. Tenderness, love, thanksgiving in v.3). Try to identify them all. What colouring do they give to this prayer?

You might also note how this psalm takes up the message of Ezekiel: the believer has the feeling of belonging to a people of sinners (Ezek.16; 20; 23); he knows that only God can give him a pure heart (Ezek.36.26f.); this will be the work of the Holy Spirit (Ezek.36.26f.; 37.14; 39.29; 47).

What are the themes on which the sinner relies in asking for pardon?

Christian prayer
If Christ could only pray this prayer in solidarity with us, it is easy for us to take it up. Love fully revealed in Jesus Christ, and the Spirit spread abroad in our hearts, allow us to use it in complete trust.

The language of sin

Fault (*hatta*). The root denotes 'to go wrong', 'not to attain one's end'. So to sin is to lack God and therefore to lack happiness (vv.4,5,6,7,9,11,15).

Revolt (*pesa'*). This is the deliberate transgression of another's rights, whether individual, people or God. The prophets often use it to reproach the people for refusing to obey God (vv.3,5,15).

Perverseness (*'awon*). The root signifies to twist, to deviate. The twisted heart of the sinner needs to be converted (vv.4,7,11).

Evil (*ra'*). This is the most common name for sin; it denotes wickedness and immorality (v.6).

Prayers for Living

The reflections of the wide men after the exile led to a deepening of all these themes and the appearance of new subjects like the praise of the righteous, or of the law, or the difficult problem of retribution.

We can also find these subjects in prayer.

Praise of the righteous, or the cult of the saints

It is enough to read the description of the perfect housewife (Prov. 31.10–31) or the ancestral portrait gallery in Ben Sirach (Sir.44ff.) to know how fond the wise men were of this kind of portrait.

Read Ps.111: this is a fine eulogy of God (each verse begins with a different letter of the alphabet, in alphabetical order). Now read Ps.112 (constructed in the same way): is it not amazing that much of the praise given to God is applied to the righteous man? Or take Ps.1 or 26 ('I will wash my hands in innocence. . .'): how can we truthfully say these prayers? There are perhaps two ways in which we can use them.

First, with the simplicity of Mary extolling the work of the Lord within her: 'The Lord has done wonders for me . . .' Sin is not a matter of recognizing one's qualities, but of failing to see them, and refusing to give glory to God for them.

And secondly, with humility. I know very well that I am a long way from having allowed God to realize in me the dream which he cherishes for me. To say these psalms again is to put before one's eyes an ideal, to recognize that one has yet to attain it, and to ask God to show the way to it.

The cult of the Law

We have already read the magnificent Ps.119, with its 176 verses in honour of the Law. You can go on to read Ps.19.

We have seen how, for the Jew, the Law is the word of God, his wisdom (Sir.24; Bar.4.1). Paul could move from 'The Law is my life' to 'Christ is my life'; he was only giving the same reality its true name.

For the Christian – and we shall return to this on p.109 – the Law has not perished. Now that Christ enables us to understand it (Luke 24.25), it remains the way which leads us to him by making our heart burn to recognize him.

The problem of retribution

'If you do good, you will be rewarded; if you do evil, you will be punished': there is nothing to be said against this principle, which is so vigorously recalled by the Deuteronomist, except that the facts often contradict it! Noble souls try to defend it even today by appealing to heaven: the balance will be restored after death. That is open to discussion, but at all events it was an unthinkable view in Israel until people belatedly came to believe in life after death. Meanwhile, they found consolation by hoping to survive in their children, or explaining misfortune as being the result of collective solidarity. It is always easy to say to someone who has suffered unjustly, 'That's because of your grandfather's sin!' Ezekiel (ch.18), and then Job and Koheleth, challenged these easy ways out.

About twenty psalms deal with the problem. We can see in them four main stages in deepening faith.

1. Peace through lack of awareness
People were happy to affirm the traditional doctrine (for example, Ps.138). By transposing what is hoped for into spiritual terms, can we perhaps express a hope for heaven?

2. Astonished suffering
'If God existed, would he let innocent children die?' These psalms (e.g. 10; 94) express the question; sadly, without giving an answer. This may sometimes be our prayer. It is the prayer of many people. These psalms may, fortunately, disturb our security as believers who too often have the answer to everything.

3. Peace in faith
The wicked are seen to prosper; it is said that this prosperity is unreal. Man's dignity lies elsewhere. God will certainly triumph over present trials. Pss.49; 91; 139.

4. Joy in love
Psalm 73, which we are going to read, is a climax. Nothing is explained. The believer has utter confidence, despite the darkness, in God, because he is sure of God's love and also of our own. And it is in this magnificent act of faith, in this self-abandonment to God, certain of his love, that we find joy. Despite everything.

📖 Mankind, beasts to the slaughter. . . Ps.49

You should read Koheleth again before praying this psalm. You will find there the same disillusioned tone, the same way of applying acid to our big ideas and our illusions. 'The satisfied man is like a beast for the slaughter' (vv.13,21).

This psalm is a good counterbalance to those which praise the righteous. It invites us to look elsewhere than in human success for the dignity of mankind. It was the greatness of Koheleth to reject false solutions, even though he did not have others to put forward. Man is greater than all the embellishments with which he bedecks himself. This is the austere lesson of a believer. A necessary lesson.

Christian prayer

We should not be too confident that we know better, that the Christian has an answer to everything. By living as a man, Jesus taught us that one could make sense of human life, but he lived it out in all its harshness, without anaesthetics. And he invites us, with him, to live out our human role with courage.

📖 I am always with you. . . Ps.73

Here is an honest believer who does not disguise the scandal of belief. He affirms with simplicity, 'I was within a hair's breadth of falling. . .'

What he finds scandalous is that because he believes in God and loves him, he wears himself out trying to live an honourable life. The result is that he is poor and scorned, while those who do not believe in anything are fat and sated. 'What is the use of being honest?' (v.13).

All this is too sad, too difficult to accept. So the believer feels that he is stupid, a great beast, before God (the actual word he uses is *behemoth*, the most amazing animal in the Israelite menagerie).

But now he understands: 'I am always with you. You hold me by the hand. You will direct me according to your plan. And one day you will receive me in glory. What else can I want, seeing that I have you?'

Here we have reached a climax: love has the last word, even if the psalmist does not use the term. The believer cannot explain. But he loves, and knows that he is loved. That enables him to hold fast, with joy, to this great certainty: 'I do not know what is to happen, but I love you too much now not to be able to continue to go on loving you.'

Hippopotamus in enamelled pottery (between 2000 and 1800 BC, Egypt). It is decorated with the lotus flowers on which it feeds. Along with the rhinoceros, it is the biblical Behemoth.

Journey's End

Our year's 'holiday' travelling through the Old Testament has come to an end. A companion volume to this one is available, inviting you to a similar journey through the New Testament.

Before we say good-bye, it might be useful, at the end of our journey, to sum up what we have discovered. Along the way, a number of questions have probably occurred to you; now we shall look at them. Why read the Old Testament now that we have the New? Is the Bible the Word of God or the words of men? Finally, on a more personal level, I shall try to say what I hope you have discovered en route; I shall sum it up under the term 'eucharist'.

1. Finishing the course

You have just entered this world of the Bible; you have come to know something of the history of Israel and the surrounding nations; you have met numerous persons, some already known to you and some not; you have read or glanced through texts and books on some of which you would have liked to spend more time. Now that you've come to the end, you probably have the feeling that you've seen a great many things – and forgotten them all. That's natural, but not quite true.

You may well have forgotten facts and dates; you may no longer know at what period a particular book was written. But that doesn't matter too much; when you need this information, you will easily be able to discover it in this book or elsewhere.

That is because – and this is perhaps the first thing this book will have taught you – you have learned to make use of your Bible, to go back and find texts, and to use the notes or to refer to commentaries and other books.

And you've acquired a degree of background. The various dates, and above all the great moments in the history of Israel which were summed up in the diagram on p.22, will allow you now to give some body to the story of the life of Israel, and to place a book within that life.

More important, perhaps, you have acquired a certain way of approaching the Bible. Probably you have now lost the capacity to approach it freshly and naively. However, you should also feel that you have gained in truth. You have seen that the Bible is not an eye-witness account of a history, but an interpretation made by believers. You have acquired certain reflexes. When you read a text, you don't first ask, 'What happened?', but rather, 'What do these believers tell us about what happened? What word of God have they perceived?' Now you are no longer at the level of the event, but at the level of its being put into writing.

I could list all kinds of other discoveries: texts which have become familiar, figures who have become friends, a new aspect of God, a way of relating ourselves to the world. I shall leave you to draw your own conclusions. What we must now do is to take up some questions which you may still want to ask.

2. Why still read the Old Testament?

Do we have to spend time on this question? The course has surely persuaded you that the Old Testament is interesting. It should be enough simply to bring together what you've discovered yourself.

Why still read the Old Testament? There are, in fact, three main reasons. We need it to understand the New Testament. It is a reflection of our own life. The promise which it announces has yet to be realized.

1. We need the Old Testament to understand the New Testament

It is always illuminating to begin a book by reading the Contents page. If it has been put together well, we immediately have an overall view of the subjects to be discussed. However, it is obvious that each chapter title will mean much more when we have read the chapter in question.

The New Testament, the Contents page of the Old Testament

It's the same with the Bible. In the New Testament we come across many terms which are not explained because they form part of the culture of the time. If anyone talks to us, twentieth-century Westerners, using terms like Pentagon, Oval or Red Cross, we know that they are not referring to geometrical figures; these words are part of our culture and are all symbolic, with profound historical connotations.

Similarly, many of the words used by Jesus or his disciples are part and parcel of the religious culture of the time, and have far more than a surface meaning. Now above all, scripture (the Old Testament) formed the basis of this culture. Thus titles applied to Jesus (Messiah or Christ, son of David, son of God, suffering servant, prophet), and expressions like vine, marriage, Zion, water, breath, are like chapter headings, with a rich content which has come to maturity over a long period in the history of Israel.

However, to speak of a Contents page is too mundane. What we have, rather, is a universe of symbols.

A universe of symbols

Earlier (p.94), I distinguished between two types of language: that of science, which gives information, and that of relationship, which uses symbols. Let us now put these two kinds of expression in context again, with the help of a simple example.

If I say to a child, 'That's a brave man', I'm using the language of science; the word 'brave' has a quite precise sense, defined by the dictionary, and I am applying it to this man. The word sums up what I know of him, but it does not enrich the knowledge I have of him. If I say, 'This man is a lion', I am using symbolic language; the child will not imagine that this man is an animal, with claws (using language which gives information), but he will transfer to the man all that the image of lion evokes, always supposing that he knows other lions than his cuddly toy! At this point we are touching on both the riches and the limits of symbolic language: it enriches our knowledge of the object to which we apply it, but it makes sense only to people who have had the same experience. If a child does not know what a lion is, he has to be taken to the cinema, or to the zoo: it is only when he has some experience of a lion that I can use the word as a symbol.

The Old Testament, a world of symbols

From what I've just said, we can draw two practical conclusions for reading the Bible.

When we read anything from the Old or New Testament, we have to ask whether it is providing information or acting as a symbol; in the latter case, we must then ask what connotations it had at that time. Otherwise we run the risk of making ridiculous mistakes. To take one example: for a present-day Christian, Son of God has a precise meaning, signifying great strength, whereas Son of Man conjures up weakness. Now we have seen that for Israel, Son of God was the equivalent of Son of David; it was an important title, but not a supernatural one. By contrast, in some instances Son of Man conjured up the heavenly figure of the book of Daniel, to whom God entrusted the judgment at the end of time. This figure therefore had divine, supernatural characteristics; it was much stronger than Son of God!

We may draw a second conclusion: when we read the Old Testament we should resist seeing Jesus in it as long as possible. Let me explain that with an example. Suppose we are studying Daniel 7. If, when we read the phrase 'Son of Man' there, we say 'That's Jesus', we have applied to Christ a meaningless title, or one with an inappropriate meaning (like saying that a man is a lion to a child who knows lions only as cuddly toys). So to begin with we must forget Jesus and look for the meaning of the expression Son of Man in the book of Daniel. When we see that the Son of Man is a collective figure, that he represents all believers brought into the presence of the glory of God because they have put that above their lives, we shall be able to apply it to Jesus: and in this way our knowledge of Christ will be remarkably enriched.

So the Old Testament is indispensable to our understanding of the New. That is important, but we are still talking on an intellectual level. We shall now see that on a more existential level, the Old Testament is the reflection of our own human life.

2. The Old Testament as a reflection of human life

We could say that God made his people live through great hopes and great human experiences. So reading the Old Testament is like reflecting in depth upon our own lives. We discover this, simply by reading it, and Jesus and Paul tell us the same thing.

Reading the Old Testament

This first journey through the Old Testament will have allowed you to discover a certain number of texts. After spending the time needed to get used to the vocabulary, the imagery, the historical situation, you will certainly have noticed, here or there, that the fundamental elements in your own life have in fact been evoked here. Perhaps that is more immediately evident in the wisdom writings: the innocent Job who suffers and wants to know why; Koheleth expressing the absurdity of the human condition; the freshness of the love of the betrothed couple in the

Song of Songs; the cries of suffering or wonderment in many of the psalms. In all this, it is almost our own life which is being presented to us, as though in a mirror, so that we can reflect on it. However, that is also true of the other texts: our thirst for liberation and our desire to be free men is expressed through the epic of the Exodus or the expectation of the new exodus; the cries of the prophets demanding justice and respect for the poor are added to our social concerns; reactions, whether violent or non-violent, to the persecution of Antiochus express our present-day alternatives and their ambiguities. You could certainly continue the list, but we must stop there.

At this first level, anybody can have this experience, whether or not they are believers. The Bible is one of the great works of humanity, and the characteristics of these great works is to express the essential quality of being human. The Bible does this in its own way, like Greek epics or Babylonian myths. Luke and Paul show us that this is still more true for the believer.

How Jesus taught – according to Luke

On Easter Day, two discouraged disciples were going back home to Emmaus. 'We had hoped that he would be the one to deliver Israel. . .' This remark reflects a bitter experience and dashed hopes. Jesus does not reproach them for it, but contents himself with noting that they have kept to the Old Testament hope. He goes through the scriptures with them again, and they find that their hearts are afire, so that they recognize the risen Lord in the breaking of the bread.

Like these disciples, we too sometimes get 'cut off'. The Old Testament is there to re-establish all our human connections and to bring us, if we have patience, towards the one whom it announces.

The history of Israel as a 'mock up'

Paul expresses this in theological terms. He declares that the events in the history of Israel are types of what we are (I Cor.10.6,11). The Greek word *tupos* (type) is usually translated 'model' or 'example'. However, the type is precisely the opposite of the model; it would be better translated 'mock up' or 'pattern' (of a garment).

In the case of a model or example, the important thing is the model and not the copy. With the mock-up or pattern it is the other way round. If an engineer constructs in his laboratory a mock-up of the dam he is to build, or if the couturier cuts out of newspaper the pattern of the garment that she wants to make, it is the dam or the garment which are important. The mock-up or pattern are a kind of anticipation of the reality which a human mind is imagining in advance.

The case of Israel is a special one. The events in its history have a value in themselves. However, for the believer, they are something more: they are an anticipation of his life. In some way God was thinking of us when he was talking with Israel.

It is important to understand this if we are to avoid a moralizing approach. One example should make this clear.

The temptation of Jesus in the wilderness

Our imagination sometimes works like this: Jesus was tempted and resisted; I must imitate him. So we have the pattern: Jesus (model) + us. That's not wrong, but it can lead us to a kind of moralizing (we have to be kind like Jesus), or worse, discourage us: if someone presents me with too good a model I may admire it and say to myself, 'That's not for me.'

Now Matthew and Luke show that Satan repeats for Jesus the fundamental temptations experienced by the people in the wilderness. Thus Jesus again takes up the history of Israel, but he makes it succeed because he responds as the people should have done (see 'You only had to. . .' on p.57).

These temptations experienced by the people in the wilderness, a 'mock up' of our own, are still ours today. So Jesus experienced our own temptations. This gives us the pattern: Israel, a mock-up of ourselves, + Jesus + ourselves.

Jesus is not primarily a model to copy; he is the one in whom our life has succeeded and in whom we now can and should live.

3. The time of the promise goes on

To a large extent, the Old Testament is promise. Remember, for example, the prophetic texts, the royal psalms or the apocalypses, where the good news is announced. One day, God will establish his kingdom; then the poor will be happy, because that will be the end of poverty: evil, injustice, suffering and even death will be overcome.

We only have to look around us (and within ourselves) to know that this has not yet been realized, that evil, suffering and sin still exist. The Jews looked for a Messiah who would establish this kingdom of God by himself, all alone, and in a flash. Christians recognized Jesus as this Messiah, but they discovered that he had only inaugurated the kingdom, leaving it to his disciples, given new life by his spirit, to work for it.

The coming of Christ did not suppress this expectation. On the contrary, it strengthened hopes. The promise contained in the Old Testament remains the programme for Christians to carry out, as it was for Jesus.

3. Word of God and words of men

We have already come up against this question (p.76). We ought to return to it now, because you will certainly be asking it as you come to the end of this study.

People usually approach the Bible with the conviction that it is the Word of God (whether they accept the conviction as believers, or reject it as non-believers); the Bible is the holy book of Jews and Christians, a sacred book.

Now throughout this study you may have had the impression that I was robbing the Bible of its sacred character. We have been studying it with analytical methods as though it were a secular text. We have watched the way it came into being, starting with the reflection of the people, prophets, wise men, priests. In the end, there is a risk that it may seem to us above all to be the word of men. 'God said to Abraham . . . to Moses . . .'; we probably feel that it would have been better to say, 'People said that God said to Abraham. . . They interpreted. . . They divinized their human words by turning them into the word of God. Who can guarantee that they were right?'

Perhaps we should revise our conception of the word of God. The analogy with the incarnation will help us here. That leads us to recognize the importance of the Holy Spirit and its role in the faith.

Jesus, the Word of God made man

Our amazement at the way in which this Bible, the Word of God, is so strangely human is exactly the same as that of the contemporaries of Jesus. After the resurrection, they became aware that they had lived in intimate association with the son of God, the word incarnate. However, they had only seen and heard a man, human words. The word of God does not come down from heaven in a visible way, as though by magic. Humbly, it makes itself one with us, and we have to know how to discern it with the eyes of faith.

'The word is very near you; it is in your mouth and in your heart, so that you can do it' (Deut.30.14). So it is in man's heart, in his actions, in his everyday behaviour, as in the great events of the world, that we have to decipher this word. At an ordinary human level, actions and objects say something: 'That was an eloquent action. . . That smile spoke volumes. . .' In the same way, we have to decipher the word of God through human words, attitudes and events.

The role of the Holy Spirit

There is a risk that we may describe as the 'word of God' what is only the expression of our human choice. What guarantees that the biblical authors did not do the same thing?

The believer who recognizes the Bible as the word of God recognizes it, by the same token, as being an inspired word. He sees here an action of the Holy Spirit. 'When the Spirit of truth comes, he will guide you into all the truth, for he will not speak on his own authority', says Jesus to the disciples (John 16.13). To dream of a word of God in a pure state, fallen down from heaven, is perhaps to want to do the work of the spirit! And of faith!

The role of faith

We want proof. We are like the Jews who asked Jesus for great signs in the heavens. And Jesus said to them, 'No sign shall be given to this generation except the sign of Jonah. For as Jonah became a sign to the men of Nineveh, so will the Son of man be to this generation' (Luke 11.29f.). Jonah preached without performing miracles or giving proofs; he simply preached, and the inhabitants saw in his words the word of God inviting them to be converted. Similarly, in Jesus' human words, in his human form, people were to perceive the mystery of God.

The consequence of this is important. If the Word of God had fallen in a pure state from heaven, we could do nothing but repeat it. If, however, it is the humble deciphering of human events by generations of believers, it continues to present itself to us in events of today. Reading the Bible perhaps invites us less to repeat what was discovered by our ancestors in the faith than to do what they did: to read the Word of God in our lives and in the life of the world.

4. Eucharist

Very often, when we have come to the end of a course of this kind, I have been asked, 'What did you have in mind when you suggested this course to us? What is the "ideology" of this book? Where is it meant to take us?'

Whether asked in a friendly way, or with some more sinister motive, this question is important. It shows that we never read the Bible objectively – any more than any other text. Nor is the course presented here completely innocent in this respect. I'm not going to give you my 'ideology' – ideology exercises a force without our being aware of it. My final concern is more modest. I shall give up the impersonal tone I've been using so far and go over to the first person. I would like to tell you what this study of the Bible has given me, and what I hope that it will give others.

Christian and intelligent?

I believe very strongly that God wants us to use our minds and that he does not ask us to sacrifice our intelligence when we begin to read the Bible. We are men and women of the twentieth century, moulded by science, in the arts as well as in the applied sciences, and it is as people of the twentieth century that we should become believers, without having to give up either our faith or science.

So a first benefit that studying the Bible has brought me is the discovery that one can be both Christian and intelligent. And that's quite something. Let me give you a rather crude example (you can think of others for yourself). Believers have often come under a great deal of fire – and still do – over the creation stories. As a Christian, someone might feel obliged to accept what these texts seem to affirm (direct creation by God, in six days, and so on); at the same time, however, because he or she is also a twentieth-century person, they will hear a little voice muttering inside, 'But I can't believe that!' A matter-of-fact study of the stories, as of many others, will show us that there is no clash between science or history and faith. We can belong completely to our age and still believe, without being pulled two ways the whole time.

Christian and free?

Too often the Christian seems rather alienated, hemmed in by beliefs and prohibitions as by a barbed wire fence. However, one conviction stands out from all the Bible: God wants men and women to be free and responsible.

But it is true that the way in which we approach the Bible is not completely open. A story may make the point as well as anything. I was studying a teaching problem with students from many different countries: in what order should the texts of the Old Testament be presented to people coming to them for the first time? Various possibilities were mentioned: to follow the pattern of 'sacred history' (creation – the fall – Abraham – Moses), or to follow the pattern now adopted in catechetics (Abraham – Moses – the creation stories), or again, to begin with the Exodus as we have done here. A nun from Latin America said to us: 'At home, the Bible is part of the teaching given in schools. So there are recognized textbooks and they follow the pattern of sacred history. We've formed a catechetical centre where we train teachers who want to begin with Abraham and deal with the creation stories later.' She added: 'So far the government hasn't noticed. But when it does notice, there will be trouble. . .' On reflection, that's obvious. The pattern of 'sacred history' is essentially conservative: it gives pride of place to an all-powerful God, absolute master, creator of mankind which has only to obey him. Granted, mankind rebelled through sin, but God remains master because he punishes and forgives. . . And we can understand how an authoritarian government will find such a pattern congenial: it can make an unconscious assimilation between this God and the masters of the country. By contrast, the other pattern – the one which God made his people follow – is subversive: it brings to light that God above all a God who liberates, who wants man, all men, to be free and responsible.

Thus the way in which we begin the Bible can have a great influence on our religious mentality, and also on our human attitude; it can also contribute to the formation of docile citizens or responsible human beings.

The humanity of God

I might put the same thing in a different way by talking, like the book of Wisdom, of the humanity of God and his humility. God is the one who is utterly different, the Lord of history, Creator of the universe, the transcendent God. That is what he is and that is what he remains. However, above all he seeks to be the God who is near, who goes with his people step by step, with an infinite respect for mankind, who does not violate their faith by miracles and never destroys it. He is a God who wants mankind to stand on its own feet, free, and he gives mankind the world to shape and history to make.

And this God is faithful. We have seen how the Bible expresses his involvement with Abraham. Once for all, God has thrown the weight of his faithfulness into the balance of history. Here is the ultimate and definitive security of mankind, which makes people perfectly free: whether we are saints or sinners, we know that we are unfailingly loved by God, who is faithful. We know how important it is, humanly speaking, to be loved if we are to act: we need someone to count on us, to have confidence in us. Here is the enormous and unshakable security of the believer: he knows that God loves him, that God has confidence in him, despite everything.

History, both the history of the world and the history of the church, can have its setbacks and failings. However, that should not lead us to despair: in silence, invisibly, God goes with men and puts his trust in them.

The eucharist

If I had to sum up the fundamental attitude which studying the Bible can instil in us, I would say, without hesitation, it was that of thanksgiving, of the eucharist.

A scholar gave a magnificent summary of this in the title which he gave to his commentary on the Book of Joshua: 'The gift of a conquest'. That says it all. The entry into Canaan was a conquest: if Joshua and the people had not fought, they would not have conquered this land. They were the ones who occupied it. But at the same time they recognized that it was a gift. When we studied a text from Deuteronomy (p.58), we saw how the fact of telling a story – the credo – changed the significance of the produce of the soil; at the beginning, the Israelite could put his hands on the fruit and vegetables which he had grown and say, 'This is my produce.' The story of the action of God for his people led him to recognize, with joy, and with open hands, that his produce, his life, were a gift of God. 'Blessed art thou, O Lord, who givest us this bread and this wine, the fruit of man's labour', declares a prayer from the Catholic liturgy, taking up a Jewish formula.

It seems to me that the Bible leads us to recognize that everything depends on man, that he has to shape himself, the world and history, but that at the same time he is the finest present that God gives. 'I praise you, God, for having made me the amazing wonder that I am' (Ps.139.14). 'The Lord had done marvels for me. . .' (Luke 1.49).

**Ebil-Il the steward, at worship
(Alabaster, Mari, the middle of the third
millennium.)**

114

If You Want to Know More . . .

Throughout this book I have made few references to other books or commentaries. That was deliberate: you can get a long way with just a good Bible and this guide. However, if you want to explore further, here are some useful works.

Reference books

A wealth of information about the content of the Bible can be found in two dictionaries: James Hastings, *Dictionary of the Bible*, T. & T. Clark, and the five-volume illustrated *Interpreter's Dictionary of the Bible*, Abingdon Press. Two convenient atlases are Lucas Grollenberg, *Shorter Atlas of the Bible*, Penguin Books, and the *Oxford Bible Atlas*, edited by H. G. May, Oxford University Press: each has an illustrated text as well as the maps. There are many commentary series, with a separate volume for each book or a small group of books: the Cambridge Bible Commentaries are simple and factual; in America the Layman's Bible Commentaries published by John Knox Press are very readable; the Old Testament Library, published by SCM Press and Westminster Press, is harder going, but the substantial volumes are very rewarding. Big one-volume commentaries also contain articles on general topics; there are three good ones to choose from: *The Jerome Biblical Commentary*, edited by R. E. Brown, J. A. Fitzmyer and R. E. Murphy, Geoffrey Chapman/Prentice-Hall; *The New Catholic Commentary on Holy Scripture*, edited by R. C. Fuller, Leonard Johnston and Conleth Kearns, Nelson; *Peake's Commentary on the Bible*, edited by M. Black and H. H. Rowley, Nelson. Texts relating to the world of the Old Testament can be found in: *Near Eastern Religious Texts relating to the Old Testament*, edited by Walter Beyerlin, in the Old Testament Library, and *Ancient Near Eastern Texts*, edited by J. B. Pritchard, Princeton University Press (there is a fascinating companion volume of *Ancient Near Eastern Pictures*).

General Works

Some valuable studies of the Old Testament as a whole are:

Bernhard W. Anderson, *The Living World of the Old Testament* (American title *Understanding the Old Testament*), Longmans/Prentice Hall.

G. W. Anderson, *The History and Religion of Israel*, Oxford University Press.

John Bright, *A History of Israel*, SCM Press/Westminster Press.

Alan T. Dale, *Winding Quest*, Oxford University Press.

John H. Hayes, *An Introduction to Old Testament Study*, SCM Press/Abingdon Press.

Henry McKeating, *Studying the Old Testament*, Epworth Press.

Roland de Vaux, *Ancient Israel*, Darton, Longman & Todd.

Robert Walton (ed.), *A Basic Introduction to the Old Testament* (American title *Bible Study Source Book – Old Testament*), SCM Press/John Knox Press.

Books on particular subjects

The following books deal with subjects that we have explored in this guide. They are listed in the order in which we came to them.

George W. Ramsey, *The Quest for the Historical Israel*, SCM Press/John Knox Press.

E. W. Heaton, *Solomon's New Men*, Thames & Hudson/Universe.

E. W. Heaton, *The Hebrew Kingdoms*, Oxford University Press.

Gerhard von Rad, *The Message of the Prophets*, SCM Press/Harper and Row.

Walter Zimmerli, *The Law and the Prophets*, Blackwell.

J. Lindblom, *Prophecy in Ancient Israel*, Blackwell/Fortress Press

P. R. Ackroyd, *Exile and Restoration*, SCM Press/Westminster Press.

P. R. Ackroyd, *Israel under Babylon and Persia*, Oxford University Press.

Martin Hengel, *Jews, Greeks and Barbarians*, SCM Press/Fortress Press

D. S. Russell, *Between the Testaments*, SCM Press/Fortress Press.

D. S. Russell, *The Jews from Alexander to Herod*, Oxford University Press.

One book will lead you on to another and there is no end to reading them; however, don't forget the most important thing – not to lose sight of where you started from!

Jewish Literature outside the Bible

In Bibles which follow the Protestant tradition, like the Revised Standard Version, the last book of the Old Testament to be written, Daniel, comes from the second century BC; in the Catholic tradition, presented by versions like the Jerusalem Bible, the last books of the Old Testament were written about a century before our era (except for the Book of Wisdom, which does not form part of the Jewish Bible). In a Catholic Bible, there is nothing between this book of Wisdom, written about 50 BC, and the first book of the New Testament to be written, I Thessalonians. Was this a century without literature? At all events, it is a particularly interesting century for Christians, since this was the century in which Jesus lived.

In fact, literary activity at that time was intense, and biblical scholars are now hard at work in this area.

The Law, written and oral

God gave his Law to Moses on Sinai. However, for the Jews, only one part of the Law was put into writing: the rest was handed down orally (see p.79).

The written Law is essentially the five books of the Law (the Pentateuch). The Prophets shed light on it; the Writings meditate on it. Together, all these books form the Bible.

Following after the Writings, a large number of books were written round about the Christian era. Some of them have been known for a long time; others have been discovered recently, like the writings from Nag Hammadi in Egypt, found in 1945, and the Qumran writings found in 1947.

The oral traditions are more difficult to follow, precisely because they are oral. They hand on traditions which run parallel to the written Law; they meditate on the scriptures, relate them to the present day, produce new traditions. . . And it is often very difficult to tell at what particular period this or that tradition came into being.

Jewish writings

Writings of an apocalyptic nature

Many of these works have been known for a long time. They include, for example, the books of Enoch, Jubilees, the Psalms of Solomon, the Testaments of the Twelve Patriarchs, the Assumption of Moses, the apocalypses of Elijah and Abraham, IV Esdras (which appears in the Latin Bible, the Vulgate), and so on. Not all these books are apocalypses in the strict sense, but they are all stamped by this trend. The trend is especially important for understanding the New Testament.

The Qumran writings

These manuscripts, discovered from 1947 onwards in caves near the Dead Sea, have made known to us the thinking of the Essenes, pious Jews who withdrew to the 'monastery' of Qumran at the time of the Maccabees and lived there until it was destroyed by the Romans in AD 70 (see p.85). The best guide to these writings is Geza Vermes, *The Dead Sea Scrolls in English*, Penguin Books 1970.

Other writings

We should at least note the work of the Jewish historian Flavius Josephus, who was born about AD 30 and died at the beginning of the second century. He rewrote the Bible in his *Jewish Antiquities*. In his many books, Philo of Alexandria, who lived from about 13 BC to AD 50, tried to express his Jewish faith in the context of Greek culture. He was writing at the time when the Gospels came into being.

Oral literature

People also talk about rabbinic literature. The rabbis are

the Pharisee scribes who at the time of Christ were already beginning to fix the way in which the Law was to be put into practice (see, for example, the rabbi Gamaliel in Acts 5.34). They did this by their knowledge of the Law and the commentaries which they produced on it. After the fall of Jerusalem in AD 70, these Pharisee scribes moved to Jabneh (near modern Tel Aviv), reorganized Judaism and gathered the traditions together. The oral literature is not entirely rabbinic, but it was collected together by these rabbis.

I shall mention the chief collections so that you can give a context to the names which you will have heard mentioned (for example, the Talmud). It will also show how intensely these Jewish believers worked in reflecting on the Law. This is interesting for those wanting to know more about Judaism; it is also interesting as we try to understand how the New Testament came into being. The first Christians were Jews, trained in the same methods of relating scripture to the present. The Gospels underwent a long period of oral formation and transmission before they were put down in writing, and in this way they are parallels to the rabbinic traditions.

I have chosen the title oral literature rather than rabbinic literature to stress this fact: the collections I shall be mentioning have come down to us in written form, but for the Jews they are essentially collections of oral material. To suggest a comparison: a composer writes the score of his symphony, but it is not produced to be read, but to be played and listened to; it is only put into writing as an aid to the memory.

Oral traditions

The rabbis handed on to their pupils what they themselves had received (cf. I Cor.15.1–3). These traditions are of two kinds: the Halakah gives interpretations of the Law aimed at helping people to act on it, practical rules for living (the root *halak* means way, road); the Haggadah is meant, rather, to be edifying (see p.81).

A systematic editing of these traditions began at the end of the first century AD. The first collection produced by this oral editing is called the Mishnah. Rabbis provided comments on this Mishnah in both Palestine and in Babylon; their commentaries came to form the Gemara.

The Talmud (instruction) is a collection of all these traditions: the Mishnah is the basic text, supplemented by the Gemara and other traditions which had not found a place in the oral collections (the Tosephta). The Jerusalem, or Palestinian, Talmud was only formed in the fourth century; the Babylonian Talmud, which is fuller, was finished towards the end of the fifth century.

Midrash

Researches into scripture, or scriptural commentaries made in the schools and synagogues, culminated in collections of midrashim (see p.81).

Targum

The Targum is the translation of the text of the Bible, read in Hebrew in the synagogue, into Aramaic. This translation was made orally, and was an adaptation which related the text to its new setting. So it is very interesting in showing us something of how scripture was interpreted at the time of Christ (see two brief examples on pp.38,52. For more details see R. C. Musaph-Andriesse, *From Torah to Kabbalah,* SCM Press 1981 and OUP, NY 1982).

Qumran manuscript. Temple scroll

117

The history and the literary history of Israel

This diagram is a summary, so don't begin here!
The dotted vertical lines divide up history into centuries, from 2000 BC to AD 100.

1. History: the upper part of the diagram

The rectangle running right through the diagram, above the figures indicating the centuries, represents Egypt: its history is divided into the various dynasties.

The rectangles above that appear one after the other in succession: they represent the peoples of Mesopotamia (the Sumerians, Akkadians, Assyrians, Persians, Babylonians), of Asia Minor (the Hittites), or of Europe (Greeks and Romans), who in turn became masters of the Middle East.

The rectangle in blacker lines represents Israel. It was divided into two when the United Kingdom of David and Solomon broke into two parts: the Northern Kingdom (or Israel, Samaria), and the Southern Kingdom (or Judah, Jerusalem).

2. Literary history: lower part of the diagram

This part of the diagram shows the particular period in which a book of the Bible was composed (sometimes this is pure hypothesis). The straight lines ———— indicate the composition of a book. The broken lines - - - - represent an oral tradition on the way to becoming an edited text.

The dots surrounding a straight line . . . ———— . . . indicate a probable period.

The vertical grill between 600 and 500 represents the time of exile in Babylon.

The two horizontal grills between 1000 and 700 represent the northern kingdom. For the Law, the letters JEDP represent the traditions edited at different periods. J = Yahwistic tradition (at Jerusalem in the time of Solomon); E = Elohistic tradition (in the northern kingdom, about 750); JE = the Jehovistic tradition (a fusion of the Yahwist and the Elohist in Jerusalem); D = the Deuteronomic tradition (a core formed in the north was taken up and completed in the south); P = the priestly tradition (during and after the exile in Babylon).

These four traditions, regrouped after the exile, constituted the Law (or the Pentateuch), divided into five books: Genesis, Exodus, Leviticus, Numbers, Deuteronomy.

Analytical Index

God. Some ways in which he makes himself known

Yahweh, 20, 73
Elohim, 19, 50, 73
Liberator and Creator, 31, 39, 47, 73, 98, 113

Jesus. Titles given to him

Elijah, 46
Immanuel, 43
Messiah, 65, 67, 86
Son of David – Son of God, 42, 86, 102
Son of Man, 91
Suffering servant, 67, 77
Wisdom of God, 92, 93

Holy Spirit, 66, 76, 77, 86

Figures from the Bible

Abraham, 37, 51, 52, 71
David, 34, 42
Elijah, 45, 46, 76
Jacob, 37, 52
Moses, 27, 32, 38, 42, 53, 71, 78
Nathan, 34, 42

Groups or peoples

Canaanites, 16, 19, 20, 34, 45, 47, 48, 58
Cyrus, 65
  Cyrus cylinder, 67
Diaspora, 75, 92
Essenes, 85
Hasidim 85 (see Hesed, 49)
Hasmoneans, 85
Lagids, 84
Maccabees, 85
Pharisees, 85
Sadducees, 85
Samaritans, 45, 75, 79
Seleucids, 85

Some themes

Amen, 49, 83
Beautitudes, 67, 97, 102
Blessing, 37, 70
Blood (life), 68
Circumcision, 64, 71
Covenant, 51, 60, 62, 71

Creation, 39, 72, 88, 98
Evil-suffering, 63, 82
Exodus, 24, 31, 49, 67, 71, 72, 92, 98
Fear of God, 51, 52, 82, 87, 97
Gospel, 67, 92
Human sacrifice, 51
Impurity, 69
Judaism, 66
King, 34, 36, 43, 45, 80, 86, 102
Law (written and oral), 79, 100, 106
Love, language of, 49
Marriage, symbol of the love of God, 47, 87
Obedience, 100
Original sin, 41
Patriarchs, 38
Poor, God's (Anawim), 97
Priesthood, 68, 69
Prophet, 43, 50, 53, 62, 89
Propitiation, 71
Resurrection, 88, 91
Retribution, 106
Ritual (cult), 20, 24, 66, 68
Sabbath, 64, 71, 73
Sacred, 68, 69
Sacrifice, 68, 69
Shema, 57, 100
Sin, language of, 105
Social justice, 47
Synagogue, 75
Torah, see Law
Universalism, 35, 36, 46, 61, 77, 81
Zion (daughter of), 61, 77

Literary questions

Apocalypses, 6, 89
Apocrypha, 86
Aramaic, 75
Canon, 86
Deutero-canonical, 6, 86
Deuteronomist (tradition) (D), 27, 56
Elohist (tradition) (E), 27, 50
History (historical fact), 9, 10, 32, 63
Jehovist (tradition) (JE), 27, 55, 60
Koine (common Greek language), 7, 84, 93
Languages (two types of), 94, 109
Languages of the Bible, 7
Literary genres, 25
Massoretes, Massoretic text (MT), 7
Methods of analysing a text, 11

Principal texts studied

Cherubim. Ivory panel from the palace
of Ahab at Samaria (ninth century BC)

This wall painting, measuring 2.50 metres by 1.75 metres, adorned the great hall of the palace of Mari (destroyed in 1760 BC) on the Euphrates. It is now in the Musée du Louvre, in Paris.

It has been called the Investiture Fresco, or, sometimes, the Paradise Fresco.

In the upper rectangle in the centre, the king, probably Zimri-lim, is receiving the staff and the ring, attributes of power, at the hand of the goddess Ishtar, goddess of war. She has her foot on a lion, which is her emblem. The goddess and the king are surrounded by deities.

Below, two goddesses are carrying jars from which four rivers flow.

On each side there are two trees, one very stylized, the other representing a palm tree. The first kind is guarded by three 'cherubim': a winged sphinx, a winged griffin and a bull with a man's head.

Many of the details depicted here recur in the stories of earthly paradises: the authors certainly drew on the same common source. In particular, we find again the two types of tree, the four rivers and the cherubim. However, we can see one important difference: in the Bible the centre is occupied not by the king, but by man, whom the one God makes master of creation.

Table of Contents

A Canaanite prince, seated upon a throne made up of two cherubim, is drinking from a cup and taking a lotus flower offered to him by the queen. A girl is playing a nine-stringed lyre. She is followed by officers, and two kings in chains. The winged disc of the sun is above them. (An ivory found at Megiddo)

The Books of the Bible

Abbreviations, and the pages in this book on which they are mentioned

Old Testament

(The Deutero-Canonical books are printed in italics)

Amos	Amos 47	Judith	Judith 88
Bar.	*Baruch 92*	I Kings	I Kings 42, 45, 46, 55, 59
I Chron.	I Chronicles 79	II Kings	II Kings 45, 46, 55, 59
II Chron.	II Chronicles 42, 79	Koh.	Koheleth 87
Dan.	Daniel 88, 90	Lam.	Lamentations 65
Deut.	Deuteronomy 45, 55, 56	Lev.	Leviticus 65, 85
Eccles.	Ecclesiastes (also called Koheleth; for references see below)	*I Macc.*	*I Maccabees 88*
		II Macc.	*II Maccabees 88*
Ecclus.	*Ecclesiasticus (also called Sirach;* for references see below)	Mal.	Malachi 76
		Micah	Micah 43
Esther	Esther 88	Nahum	Nahum 60
Ezra	Ezra 79	Neh.	Nehemiah 75, 79
Ex.	Exodus 26, 30, 38, 51, 53, 60	Num.	Numbers 53
Ezek.	Ezekiel 40, 66	Obad.	Obadiah 75
Gen.	Genesis 36, 51, 60, 70, 72	Prov.	Proverbs 82, 83
Hab.	Habakkuk 60	Ps.	Psalms 94
Hag.	Haggai 76	Ruth	Ruth 81
Hos.	Hosea 47, 48	I Sam.	I Samuel 35, 55, 59
Isa.	Isaiah	II Sam.	II Samuel 35, 55, 59
	(I Isaiah, chs. 1–39) 42	*Sir.*	*Sirach 87*
	(II Isaiah, chs. 40–55) 67	S. of S.	Song of Songs 87
	(III Isaiah, 56–66) 75, 76	Tob.	Tobit 87
Jer.	Jeremiah 62	*Wisd.*	*Wisdom 92*
Job	Job 82	Zech.	Zechariah
Joel	Joel 76		(I Zechariah, chs.1–8) 76
Jonah	Jonah 81		(II Zechariah, chs.9–14) 86
Josh.	Joshua 34, 55, 59	Zeph.	Zephaniah 60 ·
Judg.	Judges 34, 55, 59		

New Testament

Acts	The Acts of the Apostles	Luke	The Gospel of Luke
Apoc.	The Apocalypse: also called the Revelation of St John the Divine (see below)	Mark	The Gospel of Mark
		Matt.	The Gospel of Matthew
		I Peter	I Peter
Col.	Colossians	II Peter	II Peter
I Cor.	I Corinthians	Phil.	Philippians
II Cor.	II Corinthians	Phlm	Philemon
Eph.	Ephesians	Rev.	The Revelation of St John the Divine (also called Apocalypse)
Gal.	Galatians		
Heb.	Hebrews	Rom.	Romans
James	James	I Thess.	I Thessalonians
John	The Gospel of John	II Thess.	II Thessalonians
I John	The First Letter of John	I Tim.	I Timothy
II John	II John	II Tim.	II Timothy
III John	III John	Titus	Titus
Jude	Jude		

How to Read the
New Testament

A Guide to the Bible

'Do you understand what you're reading?' 'How can I, if there is no one to explain it to me?' This brief exchange, which Luke imagines in a conversation between Philip and the Ethiopian official (Acts 8.30), is a good indication of what I have set out to do in this book. It is a modest attempt to help others to read.

A travel guide

When you visit a monument with a guide – which may be either a person or a book – you expect the guide to be unobtrusive, to allow you to see the monument so that you take in all its essential features. This book is meant to be a guide of this kind to the New Testament, which will take you through it and be an unobtrusive help to understanding the texts.

Travel guides usually offer a number of options: 'If you only have a few hours to spare, see this and that. . .' If you have three days. . .' The same is true of this one. It is impossible to cover every aspect of the New Testament in so few pages. So I shall try to keep to essentials and give you a general idea, while at the same time pausing over important texts. If you can only spare a short time, you can't see everything, so make your own choice. It's not a matter of steeping yourself in every detail, but of getting to know your way round. During this visit you will make friends with Luke, John, Paul and others – and you can go back to see them another time.

Second part

It's always fascinating to begin a book with Volume 2: you can exercise your imagination, wonder what happened earlier. However, inevitably that's not the easiest way of understanding it. The New Testament is the second part of the Christian Bible; Volume 1 is the Old Testament, and it's better to start there.

You can begin with this book, *How to Read the New Testament*, if you wish, but many things will be clearer if you first look at *How to Read the Old Testament*. In any case, I shall refer to it often.

How to use this guide

When you visit a town, you may find buildings which have been constructed in stages. The cathedral, the castle, old houses have some parts which are Romanesque or Gothic, additions which were made in the Renaissance and the eighteenth century, and so on. Usually, you visit such buildings one after the other, and it is only afterwards that you get a general impression of the Romanesque atmosphere of the town, or the way in which it developed at the time of the Renaissance. A more technical approach is to go round the buildings once, looking only at the Romanesque parts, then moving on to the Renaissance sections, and so on.

This guide has been designed in such a way that you can visit the New Testament according to either plan. You can use it by yourself, or for study within a group. That's why it's been divided into eight chapters. A group meeting just once a month could go through the New Testament within a year.

The first section presents the work of a New Testament writer (Paul, Mark, John, for example). First comes a page of introduction to place the author and the work in its setting; then an overall view of the work; then suggestions for the study of certain specific texts; then (in the case of the four Gospels) the passion of Jesus; and finally the portrait of Jesus shown by that particular work. You can read through the whole of the section, and then return to any particular part in which you are interested. However, you will be advised to study the texts indicated by this sign 🐾 .These have been chosen because they are significant for the work in question. I have taken care to see that in this way you will be able to read the most important passages in the New Testament.

The second section of each chapter, which is indicated by a grey border around the page, traces right through the New Testament writings a theme about which the primitive community is concerned, such as preaching, miracles, parable, worship.

The two part form a whole, but they can also be studued separately. So the guide can be approached in two possible ways.

You can read it straight through, which is the easier approach. Alternatively, especially if you are in a group with an experienced guide, you can begin with a visit to the primitive community, in which case you will start by studying the second section of each chapter. Then, next time round, you will work through the first section.

You will understand these two different ways of approaching the book better when you've read the introduction as far as page 15. However, no matter which approach you choose, you should read all of the first two chapters as a start.

Which Bible?

This book can be used with any edition of the Bible. If you have a Bible, you can use this guide.

If you don't, then the two most useful translations are probably the Revised Standard Version (from which all the texts quoted in this guide are taken), or the Jerusalem Bible; the Standard Edition of the Jerusalem Bible also has introductions and notes to each book, but it is expensive. (If you have an old Bible, and don't want to go to the expense of buying a complete new one, you could buy a paperback edition of the New Testament and use your old Bible for the Old Testament.)

When it comes to studying the Gospels, you will find a Synopsis very useful (this is a book which puts the Gospels in parallel columns so that you can compare them). B. H. Throckmorton (ed.), *Gospel Parallels*, Nelson 1967, is probably the best.

Have a good journey!

It only remains for me to wish you a good journey through the New Testament, and to thank all those who have helped in the writing of this guide: the countless biblical scholars who are my friends, and from whom I have stolen so many ideas or pictures; all those who in the course of meetings or conferences have delighted me as we shared in reading these texts, including the groups in Chartres and Chateauroux who bravely agreed to act as guinea pigs by working with photocopies of the text of the guide.

THE JEWS SAID IT IS NOT LAWFUL FOR US TO KILL
ANYONE SO THAT THE WORD OF JESUS MIGHT BE
FULFILLED
SHOWING BY WHAT DEATH HE WAS
TO DIE THEN PILATE ENTERED THE PRAE-
TORIUM AND CALLED JESUS
AND SAID TO HIM YOU ARE THE KING OF THE
JEWS

...FOR THIS I WAS BORN
AND AM COME INTO THE WORLD TO BEAR
WITNESS TO THE TRUTH WHOEVER IS OF THE TRUTH
HEARS MY VOICE PILATE SAID TO HIM
WHAT IS TRUTH AND AFTER
HE HAD SAID THIS HE WENT TO THE JEWS
AGAIN AND SAID I FIND NO

This papyrus fragment, discovered in the sands of Egypt, belongs to the John Rylands Library in Manchester (hence the name which it has been given, the Rylands papyrus); it was published in 1935. The illustration above shows both sides of it; the text contained on it is John 18.31–33 and John 18.37–38. Alongside the reproduction of the papyrus, the same size as the original, I have put a literal translation of the verses so that you can have some idea of the words which the papyrus contains.

Scholars date it to some time before AD 150, because of the style of the writing. This is the earliest text of the New Testament that we have. Since John wrote his Gospel about AD 95–100, the papyrus shows that soon after its composition this Gospel had already spread to Egypt.

Getting Ready for our Journey

Before we set off to visit a foreign country, we usually learn something about its customs and way of life, the way in which the people there think and talk, so that we don't feel too lost and don't commit too many blunders. We may also look at a map, and bring ourselves up to date with the political, economic and social situation.

The New Testament is still something of a foreign land to us, even if we are very familiar with some passages. So our first stage will be to read the Acts of the Apostles, to learn about the world in which the first Christians lived.

Before that, however, we shall remind ourselves quickly of what the New Testament is, how it came into being. (It is worth your re-reading pp. 8–10 of *How to Read the Old Testament*, to remind yourselves of how the Bible came into being.) That will set the scene for this course, and also explain why I chose the particular stopping points that I did. You will also be able to see how there are two possible ways of using this guide (see p. 15).

This is what you will find in the following pages:

1. **The three stages in the formation of the New Testament**
   You can find these stages, along with a brief summary, in a diagram on pp. 10–11; pages 12–17 take it further and show how important the stages are.

2. **The literary genre of the Gospel** (pp. 18–19)
   Our good fortune in not having 'photographs' of Jesus.

3. **Literary genres in the Gospels** (pp. 20–21)
   A first introduction to the models and the styles that we shall be meeting.

preach

51
P
A preaches
U
L

63

writes his
letters

celebrate

CHILDHOOD OF JESUS'

PUBLIC LIFE 28 – 30

Jesus lives at
Nazareth as a
good Jew
practising
the spirituality
of the Pharisees

teach

'Council'
50

The disciples reread the
life of Jesus on the
basis of their life,
in the light of
the resurrection

Official Judaism rejects the Christians

JESUS OF NAZARETH (6 BC to AD 30)

Jesus was born in the reign of Herod, in all probability six years before the beginning of what we call the Christian era. He lived, in Nazareth, as a pious Jew, practising the Law in accordance with the spirit of the Pharisees, who were the most religious of the Jews.

About 27 or 28, his baptism by John the Baptist inaugurated the two or three years of his public life. He chose disciples and, with them, proclaimed the coming of the kingdom of God: by his words, and even more by his actions and his life. He never wrote anything. (That's not quite right. He did write something once, on the sand. . .)

He was condemned by the religious authorities and crucified by the Romans, almost certainly on 7 April 30.

THE COMMUNITIES (between about 30 and 70)

The resurrection of Jesus and the coming of the Spirit at Pentecost enabled the disciples to begin to discover the mystery of Jesus. These disciples remained Jews, but they formed an amazing group within Judaism: they were the witnesses to the risen Jesus.

(The grey area in this diagram is meant to represent the Judaism from which Christianity was born.)

The disciples sought to be faithful in two directions: to Jesus, and to a life which raised a great many questions.

It was in an attempt to answer these questions that they began to recollect what they remembered of Jesus. However, they did this in the light of the resurrection. These memories were focussed on three main points.

The disciples *preached*, to proclaim the risen Jesus: first to the Jews and then to the Gentiles. Here we have an announcement of the faith of the first Christians;

The disciples *celebrated* their Risen Lord, in the liturgy and above all in the eucharist. The eucharist determined the form of many memories of Jesus;

The disciples *taught* the newly baptized, and in order to do so recalled the actions and the words of Jesus.

Others soon joined the first disciples: Barnabas, the Seven (including Stephen and Philip), and above all, Paul. Paul was converted round about AD 36, and went on to bring the good news to Asia Minor, to Greece, and finally, to Rome. From that time Gentiles were able to enter the church without first becoming Jews: that was decided at the 'council' of Jerusalem in AD 50.

Formation of the New Testament

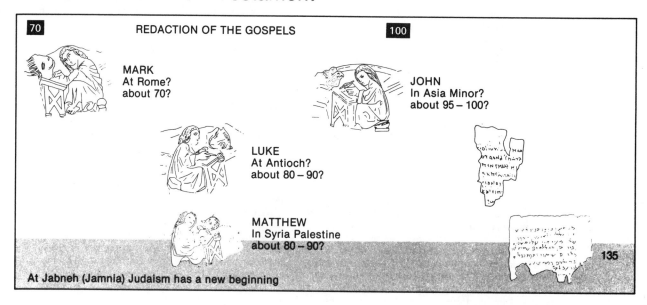

70 REDACTION OF THE GOSPELS **100**

MARK
At Rome?
about 70?

JOHN
In Asia Minor?
about 95 – 100?

LUKE
At Antioch?
about 80 – 90?

MATTHEW
In Syria Palestine
about 80 – 90?

135

At Jabneh (Jamnia) Judaism has a new beginning

Between 51 and 53 Paul wrote letters to various communities.

Throughout this period, official Judaism gradually began to reject the Christians.

In 70, the Romans destroyed Jerusalem. Pharisees who met at Jamnia (or Jabneh, the Hebrew spelling – the place is south of modern Tel Aviv) gave Judaism a new life, which has continued down to our own time.

THE REDACTION (or editing) OF WRITINGS (between about 70 and 100)

Four theologians bore witness to Jesus, bringing together traditions which had already been edited in various ways.

Round about AD 70 the Gospel according to St Mark put down in writing what was almost certainly the preaching of Peter in Rome. It seeks to show that Jesus is the Christ, the Son of God, especially through his actions and above all his miracles.

The Gospel according to St Luke was written about 80 or 90, for communities principally made up of former Gentiles. It shows how in Jesus God has visited his people and manifested his loving-kindness towards them.

Luke wrote a second volume, the Acts of the Apostles, in which he shows how the good news, carried by the apostles under the guidance of the Spirit, began to spread all over the world.

The Gospel according to St Matthew was probably produced about 80 or 90 also, in a community of former Jews who had become Christians. Matthew attacks the Pharisees of Jamnia and shows how Jesus fulfils the scriptures.

In their enquiry into the mystery of Jesus, Matthew and Luke go back to his childhood, which they present in the light of his life and resurrection.

The Gospel according to St John is a very profound meditation on Jesus as the Word of God. Written perhaps between 95 and 100, it shows how the crucified Jesus is still alive today and gives us his spirit. Through the signs performed by Jesus, we must believe if we are to see.

In Revelation, John – whether the same John, or another one – presents Jesus as the goal of history.

In the meantime, John, Peter, James, Jude and other disciples wrote letters to various communities.

In 135, after a second rebellion, the Romans decimated the Jews. For centuries the Jews were not allowed to enter Jerusalem. Christians had already left Jerusalem and were settled all round the Mediterranean basin.

In a very schematic way, the diagram on the previous pages shows the three main stages in the formation of the New Testament. It is so important that we shall keep returning to it. We shall do so by means of images and comparisons; that may be rather a dangerous way of going about things, but it will be more interesting, and you will know where to add a pinch of salt!

The most murderous woman. . .

One day I met the most murderous woman in the world. While visiting an archaeological site in Iraq, we were welcomed by the archaeologist's wife. It was only later that we learned that she was Agatha Christie, the author of so many famous detective stories. If only we had known at the time, we would have paid more attention to her; now, we were reduced to reconstructing our scant memories, the few words she had spoken, the way in which she was dressed, and so on.

We will all have had similar experiences.

So, too, did the first disciples. They followed Jesus simply because their master, John the Baptist, suggested that they should. They did not really know who he was. They listened to him attentively, as one might listen to a prophet. They even came to think that he might be *the* prophet, the Messiah. But it was only after Pentecost that they began to discover who this man, their friend, really was: the Son of God! Their memories of the few years which they had spent with him then took on a new importance, and they began to try to reconstruct them.

This became all the more important to them as the years went by. Towards the end of Jesus' life, they had begun to believe that the kingdom of God had dawned with him, and according to the beliefs of the time, that meant the end of the world. Yet months and years went by; they kept on waiting, but they had to get organized. Now every society needs rules to live by; and Jesus had left no writings.

Jesus never wrote anything

Jesus never wrote anything – except on one occasion, in the sand! He spoke, he lived; and that's all. It's important. Look at the Greek philosopher Socrates and his disciple, Plato. Socrates didn't write anything, either, and it was Plato who put the teachings of his master into writing. So we study Plato's works, although Socrates is the person in whom we're interested.

This is even more true in the case of Jesus. At the source of the good news, the gospel, we find the person of Jesus. Had he produced writings, we might have been tempted to regard him only as a master of wisdom. But because he lived, simply, to the full, as he did, we have to go back to his person.

And it is this person, with all his mystery, who made an impression on the disciples.

A photographic laboratory

The disciples were 'impressed' by the person of Jesus. The word 'impression' is also used in photography: when we take a picture of something, an impression is made on the film, the image is recorded on it, but we cannot see anything. For this image to appear, the film has to be put into a developing tank. (The French have an evocative word for this; they call it a 'revealer'.)

We might say that in the same way, the disciples had an impression made on them by the person of Jesus, by his way of living, by his words and his actions. However, at the time they were not aware of the fact, and after Pentecost everything remained dark. To bring to light the multiple image which they had retained of Jesus, they had to be subjected to a process of development, consisting in the life of different communities.

We know that the development of films in a laboratory is a tricky business: there will be more or less contrast in the photograph depending on the length of the original exposure or the materials used; the colours can be changed, different details can be highlighted. In the same way, the images of Jesus that we have differ, depending on the way in which they have been 'developed'; depending on the communities through which they passed, the questions which were raised.

Thus during the years after Pentecost we might compare Palestine, Asia Minor, Greece and so on to an immense photographic laboratory in which the various communities led the disciples to develop the many different images of their master. Some communities were made up of former Jews who had become Christians, some of former Gentiles, some of poor people and slaves, some of traders, craftsmen and other professional people.

Life as a process of development

Thus the life of the communities was the developing tank which made it possible for these images of Christ to appear. This came about above all as a result of three main activities.

1. Preaching

From the beginning, the disciples proclaimed their faith in the risen Jesus. They did so in brief phrases which summed up the essentials of the good news. Scholars use a Greek word, kerygma, to describe this preaching. Kerygma is the cry of the herald, of the local town crier. The disciples said, 'You crucified Jesus, but God has raised him, exalted him, made him Lord, and we are witnesses to that. He sends us his spirit. Believe in the good news and you will be saved.'

A collection was also made of the various beatitudes which Jesus could use to proclaim this good news: from now on the poor are no longer poor, since God has come to establish his kingdom. People told of the miracles of Jesus, which show his victory over evil, suffering, sickness and death.

They also took up parables, that form of teaching by stories which expresses well and simply the happiness which Jesus has brought, and the need to make a choice.

2. Celebration

The disciples re-enacted Jesus' last supper, which gave a significance to his death. To begin with, when only the first disciples were involved, there was no need to recall the last supper in detail; they knew what they were doing. Each one could still say how he understood it, and add details: we can imagine Peter telling how he had betrayed his master, John saying what he had felt at the foot of the cross. Soon, however, there were other disciples who had not known Jesus; they had to be told the significance of these actions of breaking bread and drinking wine from the cup. This is probably the way in which, very soon, a first passion narrative came into being.

However, when they told this story, the disciples were describing the suffering, the passion and the death not of a man now dead, but of someone who was still alive – and that made all the difference. We know that we do not talk about the illness of a friend or relation who may be in hospital, hovering between life and death, in the same way as we do later, when they are cured. In the celebration of the eucharist, Jesus makes himself present to his community, and it was in his living presence that his disciples told of his death. The passion narrative, like all the other stories about Jesus, is told in the light of the resurrection.

In this liturgical context people also brought to mind certain actions of Jesus which enabled the meal to be understood better: for example the feeding of large multitudes, where Jesus made a few loaves and fishes go round so many.

3. Teaching or catechesis

Now those who had newly been baptized had to live as disciples of Jesus. To discover how to live in community, to answer the many questions raised in everyday life, they kept returning to the life of Jesus, his words and his actions. They took up the parables and adapted them to their new situation: they had to watch, keep vigilant, become the good earth in which seed could grow... New teaching was looked for in the miracles: the tiny community had the feeling of being a frail boat tossed by storm and tempest; they could survive only because the risen Jesus stood up to the tempest in response to the prayer of his church, 'Lord, save us!' How were the authorities to act? They remembered that Jesus had said to them, 'You are the servants of others', and had left them only two rules, mercy and forgiveness.

Thus wherever Christian communities came into being, images of Jesus were developed in the disciples' memory. These images, these snapshots, were quickly formed into sequences. Before we see how this came about, we must recall one important event: the Jewish theologian Saul, or Paul, became a Christian.

Paul the theologian

The first disciples, Peter and John, were people without any great religious education. Paul was a rabbi. He spent his youth studying the scriptures. On the road to Damascus, the risen Christ seized hold of this Jewish theologian and made him a Christian theologian, one who reflected on the mystery of Jesus, on his role in God's plan. For fifteen years, from 36 to 50, he preached and founded communities; for the last fifteen years of his life he also wrote letters to his communities, which sometimes are real theological treatises. That helped other disciples to reinterpret their memories of Jesus.

Arranging slides

In the winter evenings, you may decide to bring out the slides which you took during your summer holidays and put them in order. Let's look at the various ways in which you might go about this.

The slides

During your holidays, whether you were at the seaside, in the mountains, or in the country, you will have taken pictures of things that appealed to you: landscapes, monuments, family scenes. These photographs were developed in a laboratory and have now become slides. To put them in order you will have to arrange them in some kind of sequence.

Sequences

At this point, you may pause. In what order do you want to keep them? You might arrange them according to place: pictures of mountains, of the sea, and so on; or by types – family photographs, whether they were taken in the mountains or by the sea; or you might simply want to keep them in the order in which you took them, to retrace the course of your holiday.

It is the same with the various images of Jesus developed in the various communities. They, too, were re-arranged in sequences. For example, miracles and parables were collected together; isolated sayings of Jesus, arranged one after another, became speeches. Or the Christians of Capernaum or Jerusalem remembered everything that Jesus said and did among them. When we open the Gospels, we have the impression that one day Jesus said to himself, 'What should I do today?' He looked at his diary: 'Miracles today.' And Matthew shows Jesus performing ten miracles one after the other. The next day it was a new programme, parables. Obviously things didn't happen like this; we can see that the Gospel writers incorporated into their work various sequences (parables, miracles, discourses) which had been constructed at an earlier stage. Again, at the beginning of Mark's Gospel, we find what has been called 'the day at Capernaum': Jesus calls the first four disciples by the lakeside, goes into Capernaum with them, preaches at the synagogue, drives out a demon, heals Peter's mother-in-law; in the evening the whole city gathers together and Jesus performs miracles; that night he goes into a desert place to pray, Peter goes to look for him and they go off again to preach. All these images of Jesus' activity in Capernaum have been brought together in a single sequence.

So you've collected together sequences of holiday photographs. Now some friends are coming round and you want to give a film show.

The show

You bring together all your different sequences. Perhaps you may add one or two pictures taken the previous year or slides bought at a shop (for example, of a monument which it was difficult to photograph). This show will be a good indication of what you thought of your holiday in retrospect. If parents and children each gave their own commentary on the same slides, the result would obviously differ but in either case it would show how one or the other felt about that particular time.

In the same way, at different times and in different communities, four disciples (whom tradition has called Matthew, Mark, Luke and John) set out to make their own presentation of Jesus. To do so they brought together various sequences which had already been constructed, added episodes about which they had gathered information, and made 'films': four films, each of which presents a particular way of seeing Jesus, the way in which the author and his community regarded him. So the Gospels tell us about Jesus, but they tell us just as much about the communities in which they were formed. An illustration may help you to understand this better.

Two books about Luther

Suppose we were to take two books written by Catholics about Luther, one in 1900 and one in 1980. The former, unfortunately, would go something like this: Luther, an unfrocked monk, seduced a nun and as a result of his pride subjected Europe to fire and the sword. . . The second would say: Like all of us, Luther had his weaknesses, but above all he was a very devout monk with a passion for God and for man's salvation; he had seen that the church had to reform itself, return to scripture – and by refusing to do so, the church forced him out. . . In these two books we shall learn something about Luther, but we shall above all discover the ecumenical attitudes of Catholics in 1900 and in our own day. In talking to us about Luther, these books also tell us just as much about the time in which they were written.

Similarly, the Gospels present Jesus to us, but they tell us just as much about their communities. To take just one example, when we hear the terrible words which Matthew's Jesus addresses to the Pharisees, we have to ask whether this is primarily the Jesus of the 30s opposing the Pharisees of his time or the risen Jesus, living in Matthew's community, about 80–90, opposing the Pharisees of Jamnia.

The way ahead

The diagram on pp. 10–11 and the explanations which I have given (don't forget that these are only comparisons) set out to identify the three main stages in the formation of the New Testament: Jesus – the communities – the redactors (who were editors – and more) who put together the New Testament books. How are we going to deal with them in this study? There are two possible approaches: research or exposition.

Think of an archaeologist excavating a site. In his work he begins at ground level, digs down, and gradually discovers various civilizations which have followed one another in this place: he goes back through history. If, however, he is giving a lecture, he will do things the other way round: on the basis of his discoveries he will trace the development of the various settlements from the earliest days down to modern times.

Here, too, I might have chosen the method of exposition: the first chapter could have presented what we can know of Jesus, and then, as a second stage, I could have tried to reconstruct the various sequences formed in the communities, ending by reading the Gospels and other texts.

Instead, however, I have chosen the order of research. What we have now are the Gospels and some letters – i.e. texts. What we read now is our starting point. At each stage, however, we shall try to discover what sequences existed earlier. To make it easier, each chapter will contain four pages (in a different typeface and with a grey border, so that you can find them quickly), presenting one of these sequences: miracles, parables, discourses, worship, and so on.

So there are two possible ways for you to use this book.

You can follow the order in which it has been presented; i.e., you can follow the order of research.

You can begin at the end (with what we know of Jesus), study the pages devoted to the sequences, and then those about the New Testament books themselves; i.e. you can follow the order of exposition.

The synoptic problem

A synopsis is a book which presents the Gospels in parallel columns, in such a way that you can read all similar texts at a single glance (Greek *synopsis*). The first three Gospels are similar enough for us to be able to put them in columns like this all the way through; that is why Matthew, Mark and Luke are called the synoptic Gospels (or just 'the synoptics', for short).

This similarity has raised the question whether these Gospels are not based on one or more *written* sources. For centuries scholars have produced one solution after another, sometimes extremely complicated and always hypothetical. To simplify things in the extreme (which inevitably means distorting them), one might say that it looks as though those who produced the Gospels as we now have them resorted to two 'quarries' of material. Matthew, Mark and Luke had access to one of these, which is referred to as the triple tradition; only Matthew and Luke had access to the other, which is often called the Q source (from *Quelle*, German for source). This source is seen as a collection of logia (from a Greek word *logion*, plural *logia*, which means words, sentences). This might be summed up in a diagram:

It is difficult to say whether Matthew and Luke had direct access to the first 'quarry', or whether they knew of it only through Mark. At all events, it is accepted that Matthew and Luke knew Mark's work, but are independent of each other.

Mark seems to be the inventor of the literary genre of the Gospel; in this way he provided a geographical and chronological framework for the story of Jesus. Matthew and Luke followed him.

Matthew and Luke made different use of what they discovered in the second 'quarry': Matthew ground it all up before incorporating it in his Gospel; Luke preferred to insert it into the framework he took over from Mark in two great blocks of material.

Both Matthew and Luke have texts which can be found only in their Gospels; Mark has very few of these.

On this double page, we shall be getting used to synoptic study by means of a very simple example. You can either read it now or skip it for the moment; we shall come back to it later.

A text: the healing of Peter's mother-in-law

This healing is reported in all three Gospels. This is how you will find the story in a synopsis.

Matt. 8	Mark 1	Luke 4
14 *And when*	29 *And immediately they left*	38 *And he arose and left*
	the synagogue	*the synagogue*
Jesus entered	*and entered*	*and entered*
Peter's house,	*the house of Simon and Andrew.*	*Simon's house.*
he saw his mother-in-law	30 *Now Simon's mother-in-law*	*Now Simon's mother-in-law*
lying sick	*lay sick*	*was ill*
with a fever;	*with a fever,*	*with a high fever,*
	and immediately they told	*and they besought*
	him of her.	*him for her.*
15 *and he touched her hand,*	31 *And he came and took her*	39 *And he stood over her*
	by the hand and lifted her up,	*and rebuked the fever,*
and the fever left her,	*and the fever left her;*	*and it left her;*
and she rose and served him.	*and she served them.*	*and immediately she rose and served them.*

The first thing we must do is to compare the texts. A simple way of doing that is to underline each word with a particular colour. There are naturally three primary colours: red, blue and yellow; mixing them produces all the rest. Red and blue make purple, red and yellow make orange, blue and yellow make green, red and blue and yellow make brown. Since there are three synoptic Gospels, simply give each of them one of the primary colours.

When a word is peculiar to Matthew, underline it in red; to Mark, in blue; to Luke, in yellow.

Underline a word common to Matthew and Mark in purple; to Matthew and Luke in orange; and to Mark and Luke in green; if it is common to all three, underline it in brown.

This work might seem very academic to you. But try it for yourself! It will help you to make discoveries, and you will have to read the texts very closely.

This brief study already enables us to note one or two things in the text as a whole. It is clear that Matthew is the shortest account and Mark the longest, but the three stories seem the same. You will have coloured few things in brown (common to all three): entered, house, mother-in-law, fever, left her, she served. There will be a good deal of red, blue and yellow, i.e. the words peculiar to each Gospel, and also green, words common to Mark and Luke. We might suppose that underlying what we have now is a common story which has been worked over by each evangelist.

The comments on each story will become clearer when we have looked at each of the Gospels in detail.

Mark is very specific; we can almost hear Peter talking. Do the words peculiar to him come from the earliest story? Have they been added by Mark, who is a skilful narrator? It's hard to tell.

However, Mark is also a theologian. 'Jesus and his disciples' is a characteristic way of talking about Jesus in this Gospel, hence his 'they', not 'he'. The expression 'lifted her up' almost certainly recalls the power of Jesus' resurrection: 'lift up' and 'raise, resurrect', is the same word in Greek. And Mark twice uses 'take by the hand' in a miracle story (5.41; 9.26–27).

Luke improves the text from a literary point of view. He stresses the power of Jesus: immediately.

Above all, Jesus rebukes, threatens the fever: this is the word used for driving out demons, and Luke uses it three times in a very few verses (4.35, 39, 41). We shall come back to this.

Matthew, as often in his miracle stories, keeps only two people: Jesus and the person concerned. He suppresses all secondary details, and this brings out the person of Jesus: he is the one who takes the initiative in coming to Peter's house, in seeing the sick woman.

She rises (again the same word as resurrection in Greek) and serves Jesus. We shall see that in this way she becomes a symbol of the church which serves its Lord.

Presenting the texts

In this diagram I have simply taken the titles of the texts that you would find in a synopsis, and I have limited myself to just a few chapters. That will enable you to see how the evangelists make different presentations of the same texts which have come down to them from the tradition. The arrows indicate the different positions of certain passages; we shall come back to them later.

A dash – in a column indicates that this Gospel does not have the episode which occurs in another. Thus Matthew and Mark do not narrate the coming of Jesus to the synagogue in Nazareth which is described in Luke 4.16–30.

A reference in brackets indicates that this Gospel has the same episode, but puts it in a different context. Thus the call of the four disciples put by Matt. 4.18–22 and Mark 1.16–20 before the day in Capernaum is put after it by Luke (5.1–11); the references in brackets opposite Luke 5.1–11 in the columns for Matthew and Mark recall where they included the episode.

For the moment, let us look only at the position of the story of the healing of Peter's mother-in-law.

Mark has constructed Jesus' day at Capernaum as a summary of Jesus' activity (see p. 14). Miracles form part of it, including the cure of Peter's mother-in-law.

Luke has taken up the sequence of the day at Capernaum, but he has included it in a much larger collection which extends from 4.16 to 4.44; thus we have not only a summary of the ministry of Jesus, but also a summary of the welcome which he receives, at first enthusiastic (4.16–22) and then hostile (4.23–30). In his programmatic sermon (4.16–21) Jesus announces that he brings liberation, but he does not

say what this is. By writing that Jesus *threatens* the fever, Luke transforms the healing story into an exorcism similar to the stories which precede it and follow it; thus these three exorcisms show us that Jesus has come to bring liberation from demonic powers.

Matthew puts this healing story in a collection of ten miracles which follow the great Sermon on the Mount. By this presentation he shows that Jesus is powerful in both word and deed.

2. The Literary Genre of the Gospel

We are so used to talking about 'Gospels' that we don't see how novel this kind of literature was when it first appeared.

The gospel and the Gospels

To begin with, people had only the 'gospel' (in the singular), the good news which Jesus proclaimed, the coming of the kingdom of God, the blessings offered to the poor. Paul also uses the word gospel in this sense.

Mark was probably the inventor of the literary genre of the Gospel, which is quite unlike any other type of literature. With him the gospel becomes a text, a story: the story of Jesus' activity. Until then Jesus had been the one who proclaimed the good news; now he became the one to be proclaimed: he himself was the good news.

However, Mark does not talk about Jesus in the past: it is interesting to note how rarely he uses the past tense (the Greek aorist, broadly speaking the equivalent of our simple past tense); he uses the present. This is not so much literary clumsiness as his theological conviction: the Jesus whom he portrays in his text is always present in his community; in particular, he is alive in the eucharist. For Mark, to remember Jesus is both to say that he is absent (his earthly story is in the past) and to say that he is present in the ongoing life of the community which believes in him and celebrates him. The Jesus of history continues to live in the form of the word, written and proclaimed, and in the form of the living Christ in whom the community believes. It is through the church's Christ of faith that we can get back to the Jesus of history.

The word 'gospel' (Greek *euangelion*, good news) was known to secular authors. It was used above all to announce a victory or great events in the life of the emperor. An inscription from 9 BC, found at Priene in Asia Minor, celebrates in this way the birth of Augustus (Luke may have been inspired by it in presenting the birth of Jesus: Luke 2.10–11):

Everyone may rightly consider this event as the origin of their life and existence. Providence has marvellously raised up and adorned human life by giving us Augustus . . . to make him the benefactor of mankind, our saviour, for us and for those who will come after us. But the birthday of the god (Augustus) was for the world the beginning of the joyful messages which have gone forth because of him . . .

No photographs of Jesus

At one time or another we have all dreamed of having photographs of Jesus, recordings of his words: we feel that if we had them, we would really know him. But all we have is texts composed by his disciples, 'paintings' or 'mosaics' representing him. However, surprising though it might seem, this is merely a matter of chance; if we had only photographs of Jesus, we wouldn't know anything about him. Suppose I see, in your home, a photograph of a man looking rather strangely at a woman. It's a photograph, so I know that it records a particular occasion (unless it's a trick photo); but what else can I say? Nothing! Was the man looking into space when the flash went off? Did he look away because he didn't want to see the woman (he's got a sad air about him)? Does he love her? You have to tell me. And you say, 'Oh, that's a picture taken at Michael's engagement party. Just look at his face, though! You wouldn't know how happy he was. And to think of all the years they've spent together. . .' While you're talking the photograph comes alive: the faces bring home to us a life of expectation and hope; I can imagine the day. . . And all that happens because you, who were there to witness their joy, can interpret the photograph to me. If I only had the photograph, I couldn't know anything about the couple. Thanks to your explanation, the couple becomes real to me and I can love them.

That is the good fortune we have with the Gospels. We think that they provide photographs of Jesus, but in fact they give us something much better: those who knew Jesus, his disciples, tell us who he was, how they gradually discovered his mystery; what changed their lives. A newspaper account of Jesus would not tell us much about him, and would give only a superficial impression. The witness of the disciples shows Jesus at a deeper level.

'Yes, but if we had a recording of his words, we would know precisely what he meant.' Is that really the case? We have all had the following kind of experience. A friend **says** something to us which we take in automatically, without paying too much attention to it. Some months afterwards, we say to ourselves, 'So that's what he really meant. . .' Now if you're repeating the phrase in question, do you try to reproduce exactly what this friend said at the time? I suspect that instead you will give an interpretation of it, showing what the person 'meant to' say, what you discovered at a much later stage. The phrase which you repeat will not be exact, but it will be much truer, since it will express what the person really meant to say.

Here again, it's our good fortune that we have the Gospels. They were not written immediately after the event, bringing us words with an enigmatic sense. They are the testimony of disciples who, some years afterwards, tell us what they have understood of the mystery of Jesus, and how their lives enabled them to discover his meaning.

Mosaics

To put it another way, we do not have photographs of Jesus, but rather paintings or mosaics. What we have are the words and actions of Jesus interpreted by authentic witnesses.

And the life of Jesus remains open. If he had left us a collection of rules, dictated sayings, we would only have had to reproduce them; we would be condemned to repetition. Since the disciples understood Jesus in the light of their lives, it follows that the life of our communities today is always the starting point from which we are better able to understand Jesus.

However, that is always on condition that we respect these witnesses. If we had four mosaics giving different representations of the same scene, it would not occur to us to say: 'These mosaics are so beautiful that I do not want to lose any of them; I shall demolish them and use the enormous pile of stones I get to make a single mosaic which combines all four of them . . .' That would be monstrous! The four Gospels are different, so we must study each one for itself, without dreaming of demolishing them and using the débris to construct a life of Jesus made up of the 'four Gospels in one'. If we compare them, and read them in a synopsis, we do so in order to have a better view of the details and the nuances peculiar to each of them, to have a better understanding of the features of Jesus which impressed the particular evangelist.

Faith and the Spirit

'That's all very well,' you might say, 'but all the same, I would feel much happier if I had photographs and recordings of Jesus. I can see the importance of the kind of testimony that you've been describing, but how can I be sure that the disciples were not mistaken in interpreting their memories?'

We would like to have proof, and that is only natural, because we are dealing with events on which the believer stakes his life. However, on the one hand we can be certain (and we shall return to this point at the end of our study) that the historian who studies the Gospels, whether or not he is a believer, will find enough solid evidence to demonstrate their historicity, and will often wish that he had as much evidence for other figures from antiquity. On the other hand, we might ask whether by looking for proof, the believer is not in fact seeking to do the work of the Holy Spirit and of faith.

We know that we can find proof for physical things, that such and such an object exists, but there is no proof for personal relationships. What proof do I have that I love and that I am loved? I must have confidence; I must have faith. Following Jesus Christ is always a matter of having confidence, having faith. We believe that when these disciples interpreted the words and the actions of Jesus, they were inspired by the Spirit: 'I will send you the Spirit,' Jesus said to them on the night of the Last Supper, 'and he will recall to you all that I have told you, and he will guide you into all the truth' (John 16.13).

Tracing paper

When we have a complicated diagram to reproduce (an industrial design, the anatomy of the human body), we may sometimes build up a series of sheets of tracing paper. The first will contain a framework (perhaps the human skeleton), and on top of that we shall put other drawings made to the same scale on tracing paper, representing the muscles, the various organs, and so on; in this way we can look at each drawing separately or, if we wish, we can put them together and see them superimposed one on top of another.

We can do the same sort of thing with the Gospels. On the portrait of Jesus of Nazareth which they had kept in their memories the disciples superimposed the features of the risen Jesus, as they had begun to discover them after Easter, the glorious countenance of the living Lord who was still in their communities. When we read the Gospels in rather too naive a way, everything might seem clear: Jesus presents himself as Son of God; Peter and the centurion proclaim him; and we are amazed that the Jews never recognized him as such. Everything is clear to us because we are looking at all the drawings together. However, for his contemporaries Jesus was above all one who raised a question and issued a summons. Faith, the light of Easter and the illumination of the Spirit were needed for people to see something of the riches of his mystery.

So as to be able to see this better, in this guide we shall sometimes look at all the drawings together, and sometimes try to distinguish the details of just one of them.

3. Literary Genres in the Gospels

When we are describing a car accident, we do not do so in the same way to both our friends and an insurance company: in each case the 'literary genre' is different. In the latter instance we fit our account into a 'mould': the identity of the people involved, witnesses, conditions and so on; in the former case we have more freedom. And in the former case the 'style' can be different: our account to our insurance company will be a very matter-of-fact affair; we can talk to our friends as though we were describing a national catastrophe.

This distinction between 'mould' and 'style' is completely empirical, but it can help us as we go on to read the Gospels.

Prefabricated moulds

There are, then, a certain number of models or moulds which we may use when we want to get a particular effect. We shall look at them briefly here, and then return to the main ones during our study.

The miracle story usually has five points:

- An introduction which presents the case;
- a request for intervention which shows the faith of the person who asks or the faith of those around him;
- the intervention of the person from whom the miracle is sought;
- the result;
- the reaction of the spectators: fear, admiration

We shall see, for example (p. 66), that Mark describes both the cure of a person possessed and the stilling of the storm in the same way and with the same words.

Parables were used at the time to give teaching that could be easily understood, or even to lead the audience to pass judgment on themselves without being aware of the fact.

The stories of the calling of the disciples by Jesus are usually brief (a glance, sometimes – the call – the response) and are modelled on the stories of callings in the Old Testament: thus Jesus calls with the same sovereignty as God!

One type of discourse, at least, is well known, namely the farewell discourse: an important person knows that he is about to die and gives instructions to his disciples.

The controversy or discussion between scholars was a genre in which the rabbis were trained. We often find the following pattern:
- An action or saying of Jesus provokes amazement, often feigned, on the part of the audience.
- The debate begins: 'Don't you believe. . .?', 'Haven't you read in scripture. . .?'
- At the end, the real point at issue emerges. It is necessary to make a choice, and often the parties differ.

Encapsulated maxims are produced when a saying thought to be important is put into a story which serves as a framework for it. This story, whether miracle, controversy or anecdote, is there only to set off the saying.

Floating sayings, as the scholars like to call them, are sayings of Jesus which people have remembered, though they have forgotten the context in which these sayings were first pronounced. They are given whatever context is possible, in a discourse or a story.

Different 'styles'

Here 'style' denotes a mode of expression intended to produce a certain effect. The important thing is the impression that the speaker wants to produce: to achieve it, he may use certain procedures or certain images which may astonish us. Let's look at some of these styles.

The style of the epiphany or theophany (in Greek, *theos* means God and *phainein* or *epiphainein* means to manifest) sets out to demonstrate the presence of God. People were inspired above all by the theophany on Sinai at which, according to the book of Exodus, there was lightning and fire and the mountain shook, showing that God was there. This brought about fear in the people present.

When people use these images or others similar to them, they do so to show that God is present; we need not necessarily think that the event described happened just like that. When we say 'It makes me sick to see this wretchedness', the expression 'makes me sick' is a way of expressing our compassion; we don't go to a doctor to get a diagnosis or some medicine. In the same way, the tongues of flame at Pentecost, the angel at the Annunciation or at the empty tomb, may perhaps also be images to express the presence of God. And when figures like Mary, the women, those who are listening to Jesus, 'are afraid', we are warned that they feel themselves to be in the presence of God.

The style of apocalyptic is even more disconcerting. We have already come across it with Daniel (*How to Read the Old Testament*, p. 90). Created at an agonizing point in history, in a time of persecution, apocalyptic kept an air of suffering. It endeavours to express a certainty at the heart of this anguish: God is the Lord of history and he will intervene in the end, when evil reaches its climax. The stars fall, the earth quakes, the heavens are rent asunder . . . these are all images meant to show us inner feelings like those we have when we say, 'I felt that everything was going to pieces, that the roof was coming in on me. . .'

The 'narrativization' of ideas is a barbaric expression which simply describes the way that people tell a story instead of expressing an idea in an abstract way. A rather sad story will make this clear. Some years ago a monk living in Palestine went down towards Akabah in a jeep; south of the Dead Sea he ran over a Bedouin and killed him. The court established that the Bedouin was in the wrong, but since he had been killed, according to tradition his tribe had to be paid 'the price of blood'. The parish priest of Kerak was put in charge of the negotiations. He described the accident in his own way to the chiefs of the tribe; the monk paid the price and they parted good friends. When they left, the monk protested to the parish priest of Kerak, 'What did you tell them? You know that it didn't happen like that!' 'Of course it didn't,' said the priest. 'Then why did you say that it did?' 'Listen,' said the priest. 'Was the Bedouin in the wrong?' 'Yes.' 'Well, that's what I told them.' We Westerners would have developed an abstract idea to show that the Bedouin was in the wrong; the priest demonstrated this in a story which he made up. The chiefs present also knew that things hadn't happened like that, but they understood the idea the story was trying to convey. Does that seem strange to us? We're doing the same thing when we tell a friend, 'I've been waiting here for hours.' He doesn't take the phrase literally; he simply understands it to say, 'You're late.'

We must remember this as we read some stories, and ask ourselves: are they historical, or are they meant to help us to understand a particular idea?

The stories of Jesus' birth and childhood belong to another 'style' which we have come across in the Old Testament, that of midrash (see *How to Read the Old Testament*, p. 81). People were engaged in 'research' (that's the meaning of the word midrash) into scripture to see how it concerned them in their day; they attempted to bring it up to date. They were able to discover in it rules for action, or edifying stories. One particular kind of midrash (the *pesher*) tries to show how events or people in the reader's day fulfil the texts of scripture. We shall see that the Christians used this kind of interpretation, but stood it on its head: they did not start from scripture, but from the person of Jesus, and tried to see his place in scripture, in the divine plan.

What should we remember?

That may all seem very complicated to you. Don't worry, because it will be much clearer when we are working with texts and discovering examples.

For the moment, the important thing is to draw your attention to one point: sometimes words mean something different from what they appear to say. In fact we are well aware of this, because we use language in a similar way all the time. If a stranger hears us say, 'the cat's got your tongue', 'my heart's in my mouth', 'he's buttering her up', 'she's got a cast-iron stomach', he might well wonder what strange set-up he had discovered. All these phrases and many others are true, not in what they say but in the meaning that they seek to convey. And we understand them instinctively because they are part of our culture.

The problem with the Bible is that it doesn't belong to our culture.

However, the more you use the Bible the easier you will find it to see what is the imagery and what is the meaning which the imagery conveys.

A tool box

You will find a tool box in *How to Read the Old Testament*, p. 14. This shows you how to strip down a text, i.e., it introduces you to questions which you can ask as you study a text. Read it carefully: it will help you all through this course.

④ Second journey. Paul, Silas and Timothy. Paul visits his communities. At Troas, he embarks for Europe and spends two years in Corinth (50 – 52).

⑤ Third journey. Paul and companions. Paul departs from Antioch, to which he has returned via Caesarea and Jerusalem. He stays two years in Ephesus (53 – 58). After a journey round Greece he returns to Jerusalem where he is arrested and then imprisoned in Caesarea.

③ First journey. Barnabas and Paul. From Antioch they go to Asia Minor via Cyprus. God opens the door of faith to the Gentiles (Acts 14.27). (45 – 48).

② ANTIOCH New missionary centre. There the disciples are called Christians.

① JERUSALEM Starting point. Preaching in Judaea. Peter goes to Joppa. Philip on the Gaza road and in Samaria.

⑥ JOURNEY IN CAPTIVITY After two years in prison in Caesarea (58 – 60), Paul appeals to Caesar. He is taken by ship to Rome where he spends two years in prison (61 – 63).

Rome •
Philippi
Beroea •
Thessalonica
Troas
Pisidian Antioch
Iconium
Tarsus
Corinth
Athens
Ephesus
Miletus
Laodicea
Colossae
Lystra
Derbe
Antioch
MALTA
CRETE
Cyprus
Damascus
Caesarea
Joppa
Pella
Jerusalem
Jamnia
Gaza
Alexandria

0 50 100 150 miles
0 100 200 300 km

A Roman travelling chariot
Bas-relief found in Carinthia (Austria)

22

The Roman empire
in the First Century

1 The World of the First Christians

Now we are off on our exploration of the New Testament. At this first stage we shall try to get to know the world of the first Christians. So that we don't get lost, we shall take as our guidebook the Acts of the Apostles. (We shall study its theology later.)

Read the Acts of the Apostles straight through, as though it were the account of a journey. You will come across many new terms, institutions, groups and customs which are unknown to you: try to discover what they signify, with the help of the notes in your Bible, a biblical atlas or a commentary (some books are listed on pp. 122–4). In the following pages we shall go back to them in a rather more systematic way.

To help you read Acts, here is a plan of its contents and some points to note.

A plan of Acts

Acts 1–5   The community in Jerusalem

Acts 6.1–15.35   Missionary activity
　　The Hellenists: Stephen and Philip (6–8)
　　The calling of Paul at Damascus (9.1–31)
　　Peter (9.32–11.18)
　　The church at Antioch (11.19–15.4)
　　Paul's first mission (13–14)
　　The 'Council' of Jerusalem (15)

Acts 15.36–28.31   Paul the missionary
　　Second mission in 50–52 (15.36–18.23)
　　Third mission in 52–58 (18.24–20.38)
　　Prisoner at Caesarea in 58–60 (21–26)
　　Taken as a prisoner to Rome in 61–63 (27–28).

Some features of Acts

Places. Palestine in the Roman empire. What are the great cities? What was the population of Jerusalem, Rome, Antioch, Tarsus?

The Roman empire. Look out for allusions to institutions (emperor, prefect, justice), to the means of communication, to the religious and social situation (Roman citizens, slaves) and to the economic situation (jobs, famine, the move of the couple Aquila and Priscilla).

Judaism. The institutions (Temple, Sanhedrin, synagogue), the religious groups (Pharisees, Sadducees). For a long time the Christians continued to remain a sect within Judaism.

The main characters. There are a great many in this lively book! If you have a working Bible, you might underline them in different colours. There are the divine figures: God and the risen Jesus (who is apparently absent, yet is present everywhere) and the Holy Spirit, and also the Word, which sometimes appears as a person (watch the vocabulary: speak, preach, voice). There are the disciples: who are they? What do they do? (Note the role of the laity, of women.) There are the opponents, Jews and Gentiles.

The life of the Christian community. For the moment we need only look at the features of this life in passing; we shall be studying them later in more depth. Preaching: look at the large number of speeches (by whom and to whom? Jews, Gentiles, disciples?). Liturgical life: breaking of the bread (eucharist), baptism, prayer (in what places?). Teaching of the newly baptized. Sharing concerns and sharing possessions.

Jerusalem as depicted on the Madaba mosaic (from near Mount Nebo in Jordan, sixth century AD)

23

The Roman Empire

In this first stage of our journey we are simply going to set the scene for the story of Jesus and the first Christians. To keep close to the text, I have chosen the Acts of the Apostles as our guidebook. If you have done the work suggested on p. 23 you will already have gathered a good deal of information, supplemented by the aids which you've used.

If you don't have time for that, you can content yourself with a 'guided tour': here you will find the main features you need to know, brought conveniently together. Wherever possible, however, we shall begin with some passages from Acts which you should read first.

Palestine was only a tiny province in the vast Roman empire. The Romans called the Mediterranean, around which their power was spread in the course of a few centuries, *mare nostrum*, our sea. In 63 BC the Roman general Pompey conquered Syria and Palestine; this was the beginning of a military occupation, the climax of which was the capture of Jerusalem by Titus in AD 70 and its destruction in 135. The well-known period of the *pax Romana*, Roman peace, dates from the reign of Augustus (30 BC to AD 14).

✠ Before going any further you should read some texts from Acts which will give you an idea of patterns of life in the Roman empire: 10.12; 13.6–7; 14.12; 16.16–40; 17.6, 16; 18.1–4, 12, 26–28; 19.9, 24; 21.31; 22.25–28; 23.23, 35; 24.22–23; 25.12; 27.1–44; 28.16; Luke 3.1–3. When you read these texts, note the institutions, the titles and the situations in them.

An empire on the way to becoming a society

Rome was at that time organizing its immense empire, rich and unrivalled. After three centuries of conquest, it was trying to unify its subject peoples. Several elements came to its aid.

Latin remained the *language* spoken in the west of the empire (Italy, Gaul, Spain). However, in the east, Greek, the common language (or *Koine*, the Greek word for common), had supplanted the majority of other dialects and was understood throughout the empire. In Syria and Palestine people continued to speak Aramaic, and Hebrew remained the language of the liturgy.

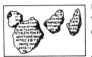

The Gallio inscription, found at Delphi, allows us to date Paul's first mission to Corinth (Acts 18.12)

The empire was divided into *administrative districts* which were more or less closely attached to Rome. Some were governed by a proconsul (like Sergius Paulus or Gallio), and others by a legate (Quirinius); some were entrusted to a prefect or procurator (Pontius Pilate, Felix, Festus); some retained a semblance of autonomy, like Palestine, with Herod the Great and his sons (see the diagram on p. 125).

There was *effective communication*. Roman roads (with their staging posts and their inns), reserved for imperial couriers, the army and a privileged few, made it possible to travel quickly to any destination in the empire. Numerous ships transported goods and passengers on rivers and above all on the Mediterranean, in so far as it was 'open', i.e. navigable (from March to November, see 27.9). There were 276 people on Paul's ship (27.37).

Justice was the same for all citizens. Any of them could appeal to Caesar, in which case all other justice would be put aside and he would be brought to the emperor's tribunal (25.12; 26.32).

Taxes, too, were levied on all inhabitants. There were direct taxes on property and on each individual (cf. Matt. 22.17); indirect taxes, like tolls and city rates, were collected by tax farmers, who paid the total sum and then sought to recover it (and make a profit) through collecting agents, publicans.

The *movement of populations* was common at the time. We have a good instance of this in the married couple Aquila and Priscilla: they came from Asia Minor in the first place, and settled in Rome, from which they were driven out in 49–50 by the edict of the emperor Claudius. Next they settled in Corinth; Paul lodged with them (18.2); three years later he found them back in Ephesus (18.26)!

An empire in the process of forming cities

It is difficult to calculate the population of the empire and of the great cities. The former has been estimated at about fifty million. For the great cities, figures have been produced like one or two million for Rome or Alexandria, half a million for Antioch, Tarsus, Corinth or Ephesus. Jerusalem had a population of only 50,000 (though this tripled or quadrupled at the time of the great festivals).

Not all the inhabitants had the same status. Some of the free men were Roman citizens; they had this much-envied title either by right (in Italy) or by birth (for example, the descendants of Roman colonists), or they bought it at great expense (like Lysias, 22.28). They had protection, and were exempted from certain taxes (16.37–39; 22.25). The other free men were the *peregrini*, that is to say, foreigners in Roman cities; they enjoyed fewer rights. The fate of the extremely numerous slaves (two out of three inhabitants in certain large cities) varied greatly depending on their master's feelings or their situation: this was very harsh in the country, and sometimes more bearable in cities, above all for specialist slaves like craftsmen, cooks, doctors and the like. They could be freed, either by their master, or by purchasing their freedom.

In search of deeper spirituality

In the conquered provinces, people felt that the national gods had failed because they had not been capable of defending their people against Rome. 'Atheism' spread everywhere; people no longer really believed in the gods, even if they practised an official religion which remained a cultural bond. They looked elsewhere for a meaning in life: to philosophical reflection, wisdom (17.16), or to the mystery religions, where they believed that initiation brought salvation.

Small associations of all kinds developed, not only for religious reasons but also to escape the depersonalization brought about by Roman society.

Jews and Christians in the empire

The focal point of Judaism was Jerusalem, centre of the official religion based on the Temple, and extending over the 'land of Israel', Judaea, as it was called at that time (it was only called Palestine, or the land of the Philistines, after 135). There were only about half a million Jews in this area, which was about the size of Belgium or Wales.

In addition, there was the Judaism of the Diaspora, the Dispersion. For a long time Jews had settled outside Judaea; some remained in Babylon after the exile, others were established in Alexandria, where they formed about a fifth of the population. Paul encountered flourishing Jewish communities in all the cities through which he passed (e.g. 13.14; 14.1; 16.13; 17.2; 18.4). It has been estimated that eight to ten per cent of the population of the empire was Jewish, perhaps seven or eight million. Proselytism, the desire to make conversions, was rife (19.13; cf. Matt. 23.15).

The Jews enjoyed a special status in the empire: they were exempt from military service, could observe the sabbath, and could pay an annual tax to the Temple. Thus officially they came under two jurisdictions: that of the emperor, and that of the Sanhedrin in Jerusalem.

To begin with, Christianity was simply a sect which arose within Judaism and enjoyed the same privileges. When it broke away from Judaism it became, under Roman law, an 'illicit religion', a superstition, and could henceforth be persecuted.

NB that some heights on this map are indicated + or − because a good deal of the land is below sea level.

Palestine

Economy

The physical map on p. 25 will enable you to locate the fertile plains (Jezreel, Sharon and the Shephelah), the hill-country of Galilee and Samaria/Judaea, where the stony soil is cultivated, sometimes by constructing terraces, and the Jordan valley with the oasis of fertility centred on Jericho.

The rains, which are quite heavy, fall only between October and March, and water has to be carefully conserved in cisterns.

Agriculture is the chief resource. Wheat, the basic food crop, and barley are cultivated virtually everywhere. Sowing begins after the first rains: barley is harvested before Easter and wheat between Easter and Pentecost.

The olive tree produces abundant oil which is exported to Egypt and Syria; figs are also exported, as far as Rome.

Vines are cultivated above all in Judaea. Wine-presses are built in the vineyards, as is a tower from which a watch is kept to guard against robbers and foxes.

As well as common fruit and vegetables like lentils, chick-peas and salad vegetables, we can also find more exotic produce which even made its way to the Emperor's table: pomegranates and dates from Jericho or Galilee, truffles from Judaea, roses (which were used for the manufacture of a perfumed essence), and above all Judaean balm, which was worth its weight in gold and was the object of a wholesale trade.

At that time, then, the country was very wooded . . . until the goats came along!

Livestock was reared everywhere. Sheep and goats produced meat, milk, leather and wool. The Temple, with its countless sacrifices, consumed a vast number of cattle. Robust little donkeys were also reared; they were extremely useful for agricultural work and for transport. For heavier goods the camel was used. The horse was a rich man's animal.

Roman coinage celebrating the conquest of Judaea. One side depicts Titus. On the other, Titus is standing underneath a palm tree; at the foot of the palm, *Judaea captiva*, Judaea captive, is weeping.

Industry prospered in several sectors. There was fishing in the rivers and above all in Lake Tiberias, which marketed smoked or dried fish all over the country.

Building did well. From 20 BC to AD 64 a good deal was done to adorn the Temple, and up to 18,000 men were employed in the work. Herod Antipas built Tiberias and fortified Sepphoris and Julias. Agrippa built a wall north of Jerusalem, and Pontius Pilate built a new aqueduct.

Craftsmen met the needs of everyday life: they made clothes (weaving, spinning, dyeing and fulling), vessels (pottery) and jewels.

The Temple was the great 'industrial complex'. Priests and Levites conducted business there; stone-cutters were continually at work; thousands of sheep and cattle were sacrificed there every year; skins (the property of the priests) were tanned, treated and exported. Precious woods and perfume were used there. The influx of pilgrims provided the basis for a good trade in food and also in souvenirs, since pilgrims had to spend a proportion of their annual income, a 'second tithe', in Jerusalem, in addition to the tithe they were obliged to deliver locally in kind.

Domestic trade consisted mainly of barter. Foreign trade was very varied. Imports were chiefly luxury goods: cedar from Lebanon; incense, aromatics, gold, iron and copper from Arabia; spices and fabrics from India. Exports were food (fruit, oil, wine, fish), perfume, skins and bitumen from the Dead Sea. The export trade was largely in the hands of great merchants.

All this meant that Palestine could have been a land 'flowing with milk and honey', had it not been for taxation and the unjust distribution of wealth.

Rich and poor

A minority led what was often a sumptuous life. They included the sovereign and his court, the priestly aristocracy of Jerusalem, the great merchants, the chief tax collectors and the great landowners (mostly from Galilee).

The middle class was made up of craftsmen and country priests; the small farmers, often in debt, were closer to being peasants.

Those who suffered the greatest deprivation were the workers and day-labourers, the unemployed, who often had no alternative to begging, and of course the slaves.

The sick (skin diseases, so-called 'leprosy', seem to have been common) and the infirm lived on alms; almsgiving was an important religious duty.

The robbers and thieves, of whom there were a large number, fall into a special category.

Social groups

I shall now introduce you to the various social, religious and political groups. In fact it is impossible to distinguish these groups clearly, since in many cases they overlap.

Alongside the rich, the middle class and the poor, we can isolate a number of special groups.

Read Acts 4.1–17; 5.17–42. Note the groups mentioned: what do they represent?

The clergy

The priestly aristocracy of Jerusalem were worlds apart from the rest of the clergy.

At the top of the hierarchy was the high priest. He was chief authority in the Law and the Temple, and president of the Sanhedrin; he was the only one with power once a year to enter the Holy of Holies, and he was the undisputed leader of the people. At one time he was nominated for life, but the Jewish kings and then the Romans appointed and deposed high priests to suit their ends; the high priest in office therefore sought to please the civil authorities. Besides, the post was enormously profitable: a share of the offerings, the profit on the sale of animals. And since the high priests were drawn from only four families, they had great political and economic power.

The various Temple authorities also made up part of this aristocracy and often came from the same families. All these priests were Sadducees.

There were about 7,000 country priests. They were very close to the common people and shared their life, their work and their poverty. Divided into twenty-four sections or classes, they functioned in the Temple in turn, for one week of the year and at the three pilgrim festivals. Lots were drawn as to who should offer incense, and since a

person could not enter the ballot again until everyone else had had an opportunity, to be successful was the chance of a lifetime (Luke 1.5–9). Some of the more learned were scribes. Many were Pharisees.

The Levites, a kind of inferior clergy who had lost all power, were the Cinderellas among the clergy. There were almost ten thousand of them, also divided into twenty-four sections, and once a year they performed subordinate functions in the Temple: they prepared sacrifices, collected the tithes, provided music and acted as Temple police.

The elders

The elders were a kind of lay aristocracy; the dividing line between them and others is rather blurred. Here again, there was a great difference between the village chiefs and the small group of rich merchants or farmers with seats in the Jerusalem Sanhedrin. They hung on to their power and consequently maintained close links with both the Roman occupying forces and the high priests. They seem to have been Sadducees.

The scribes or doctors of the Law

These were essentially specialists in the Law; they were given official recognition as such at the end of a long course of study, round about the age of forty. They had great influence as official interpreters of the scriptures, providing not only rules for everyday life but also legal judgments for the courts. Some of them were priests, but the majority were lay people and Pharisees. With their mastery in thinking of the people, they often shared the people's poverty. The most famous of them in this period were Hillel and Shammai (before the Christian era), Gamaliel, Paul's teacher (5.34; 22.3), Johanan ben Zakkai, the chief of the school of Jamnia after 70 (see p. 31) and Akiba, who was executed by the Romans in 135.

The scribes surrounded the Law with quite a 'hedge' of prescriptions. They might seem to us to be a yoke of bondage. In effect, however, they served as a means of liberation: by extending to all people the rules of purity which in primitive times were reserved for the priests, they allowed everyone to be close to God.

The publicans

These collectors were not the rich tax farmers, but their auxiliaries. They were Jews who collected taxes on behalf of the Roman occupation forces; for this reason, and because they had a tendency to increase taxation for the benefit of their own pockets, they had a bad reputation and were regarded as public sinners.

THE CLERGY

High Priest

Temple Commander

| *Worship* | *Temple guard* | *Temple finances* |
| Heads of 24 weekly sections | 7 supervisors | 3 treasurers |

| Heads of 156 daily sections | 4 chief Levites about 7200 priests divided into 24 sections about 9600 Levites divided into 24 sections | |

| musicians and singers | Temple guards |

Religious groups

These groups are usually called sects, but clearly in this context the word does not have any pejorative sense. The three main groups came into being in the time of the Maccabees (see *How to Read the Old Testament*, p. 85).

Read 4.1–17; 5.17–42; 18.24–48; 22.2; 23.6–9. Which sects appear? What is their teaching?

The Pharisees

They have had a bad press: that is a pity, and quite unfair. The Pharisees were holy men. They had separated (that is the meaning of the word) from the Hasmonaeans, whom they thought to have broken faith, and they had separated from sin. Above all they were concerned for the holiness of God and meditated faithfully on his Law. Because they knew that it is difficult to live constantly in the presence of the Holy God, they surrounded themselves with a whole network of practices. However, they were not hypocrites: when the Pharisee in Jesus' parable (Luke 18.9–13) says that he fasts twice a week and gives a tenth of his goods to the poor, that is what he does!

The Pharisees are authentic witnesses to the true faith, and Jesus, who was educated by them and taught how to pray to God, felt close to them. Their one fault was to think that they could rely on their holiness in approaching God, that their merits had won them a place in heaven. Perhaps Jesus was so firmly opposed to them because he was disappointed to see them pervert their holiness in this way, and also because they had such an influence on the humble people who admired them. Their influence was due more to their holiness than to their number: there were only about six thousand of them. Some Pharisees had a very open attitude to Jesus and his disciples (John 3: Luke 7.36; 13.31; Acts 5.34; 15.5; 23.9). They proved to be the saviours of Judaism after AD 70.

The Sadducees

These were aristocrats, and above all priestly aristocrats. Their teaching is not well known. They seem to have recognized only the Pentateuch as the Law (and not the Prophets); they did not believe in either the resurrection or angels (23.8). Political opportunists, they collaborated willingly with the Roman occupation forces in order to stay in power. They were very harsh to Jesus and to developing Christianity. They did not have enough religious vitality to survive the disaster of AD 70 and thereafter disappeared from history.

The Essenes

These were a kind of monastic order living as a community on the shore of the Dead Sea. More is known of their teaching since the discovery, in 1947, of the Qumran manuscripts. Under the leadership of a priest whom they called the Teacher of Righteousness, they parted company with the other Jews, whom they thought to be too lukewarm. They lived a life of prayer and meditation on the scriptures, preparing actively for the coming of the kingdom of God. Their monastery was destroyed by the Romans in AD 70.

The baptist movements

Between 150 BC and AD 300 there were many baptist movements, in Palestine and outside it. Their chief characteristics were the importance attached to baptism as an initiation rite or a token of forgiveness, and a hostile attitude to the Temple and to sacrifice. One group rejected any sacrifice which involved blood. The movement led by John the Baptist belongs in this trend, but there is nothing sectarian about it: it was open to all and did not reject any elements of traditional faith. It seems that this movement survived John's death, as there is evidence of a group of his disciples in Ephesus in about 54 (19.1–7).

The 'people of the land'

This is the scornful term used by the Pharisees to describe common people who knew nothing of the Law and were therefore incapable of observing its manifold regulations. This made them impure (cf. John 7.49; Acts 4.13).

The Samaritans

These did not, strictly speaking, form a sect. They were of very mixed origin (see *How to Read the Old Testament*, pp. 45,79), and were separated from official Judaism. They had the Pentateuch in common with the Jews, but built their own temple on Mount Gerizim. Relations between them and the Jews were very tense (cf. Luke 9.52; John 4.9; 8.48). Jesus' attitude towards Samaritans scandalized his contemporaries (John 4.5–40; Luke 10.13; 17.10–17). The Christian mission was first developed in their direction (Acts 1.8; 8.5–25; 9.31; 15.3).

A reconstruction of the altar of burnt offering in the Temple at Jerusalem

Gentile adherents to Judaism

For Judaism, the world was divided into two groups: Jews (who were circumcised), and Gentiles – or the nations (who were not). However, the latter could attach themselves to the former.

The proselytes (the term derives from a Greek verb meaning to draw near) were Gentiles who accepted the whole of the Jewish Law, not only beliefs but also circumcision and so on (2.11; 6.5, 13–43; cf. Matt. 23.15).

The God-fearers accepted Jewish belief but not circumcision, so they remained Gentiles (10.2, 22; 13.16, 26, 43, 50; 16.14; 17.4, 17; 18.7)

Political groups

Confronted with Roman occupation, the Jews became divided into collaborators and members of the resistance.

The rich and the senior clergy collaborated willingly in order to preserve their power. We know little about the Herodians, but these are clearly the supporters of Herod Antipas: they were hostile to Jesus (Matt. 22.16; Mark 3.6; 12.13).

By contrast, 'zeal' for the Law provoked the most religious of the Jews to offer resistance, non-violent on the part of the Pharisees, and violent on the part of those who from 66 onwards were called Zealots (some Zealots were called *sicarii*, after the name of their short sword, the *sica*, which could easily be hidden in clothing). They were mainly responsible for the revolt which culminated in the disaster of AD 70. Before that, there were several abortive rebellions led by people who claimed to be 'Messiah' (5.36; 21.38).

It is important to remember this impassioned situation in order to understand the different attitudes which people adopted to Jesus as messiah (e.g. John 6.15).

1 Holy of Holies
2 Holy place
3 Altar
4 Sanhedrin
5 Beautiful Gate

Courtyards
A of the priests
B of Israel
C of the women
D of the Gentiles

0   50   100   150   200 m

The institutions

Read Acts 3.1–2; 6.1–15; 9.1–2; 13.13–15, 44–52; 16.11–15.

The Temple

Herod restored the Temple to all its former splendour. It stood in the centre of a courtyard measuring about 300 metres by 500 metres. It was the holy place, where God made himself present, though approaches to him had to be strictly regulated. Only the high priest could enter the Holy of Holies once a year, on Yom Kippur, the Day of Atonement. It was an empty room, sealed off by the curtain of the Temple, which at one time contained the ark of the covenant. Around the altar was a first courtyard reserved for the priests. Next came the courtyard of Israel (the males) and the courtyard of the women, which was separated from the courtyard of the Gentiles by a balustrade which no Gentile might cross on penalty of death.

Sacrifices were offered on the great altar, twenty-five metres long and seven and a half metres high. Here, morning and evening. a lamb was consumed as a 'perpetual sacrifice', along with numerous private sacrifices.

At festival times, there were far more sacrifices; priests and Levites bustled about and the crowds surged in.

The paschal lamb had to be sacrificed there before being eaten at the family meal. After the final destruction of the Temple in AD 70, the Jewish Passover was celebrated without a lamb.

The Temple was not only the centre of religion but the political centre (the Sanhedrin met here); because of all the activity it generated it was also the economic centre.

The synagogue and Jewish worship

The word synagogue primarily denotes the congregation of believers. Like our word church, it has come to denote the building in which the community meets. Even more than the Temple, which was a long way off for many people, who could only go there (theoretically) at festival time, the synagogue was the place where the beliefs and religious practices of the people were shaped.

Services, which took place three times a day, had an element of teaching: there was a reading of the Law which was elucidated through the reading of a prophetic text, and then a sermon. Any believer could preach (cf. Luke 4.16f.), but in practice preaching was restricted to scribes and Pharisees, who thus shaped the common faith in accordance with their doctrine. Apart from the recitation of psalms, prayer consisted essentially in the three great benedictions, which provided the framework for the recitation of the Shema, a summary of the faith of Israel (you can find one of these prayers and some information about it on pp. 108–9). It ended with the Eighteen Benedictions, for the wonders of God towards his people.

The festivals

The three great pilgrim festivals were particularly important; they brought the people together around the Temple and strengthened communal faith.

The festival of **Passover** celebrated the liberation of the people at the time of the Exodus (see *How to Read the Old Testament*, pp. 24ff.). About 200,000 pilgrims came to Jerusalem for this occasion. On the afternoon of 14 Nisan, lambs were killed in the Temple, which were then eaten by families after sunset. The festival lasted for eight days. Excitement was so great at Passover time that the Roman authorities feared riots, and the procurator, who usually lived in Caesarea, also came up to Jerusalem.

Pentecost, fifty days later, was originally the harvest festival or the Feast of Weeks (Ex. 23.16; 34.22). At the beginning of the Christian era it had become the celebration of the giving of the Law on Sinai, the festival of the covenant and the renewal of the covenant (in much the same way as the Christian may 'renew' his or her baptismal vows at the Paschal vigil).

The **Feast of Tabernacles** was the most spectacular. To recall the time in the wilderness, each family built a hut out of branches on the edge of the city (the equivalent of a modern balcony or spare room). Some rituals were very popular, like the procession of priests to the fountain of Siloam, accompanied by people carrying palms (cf. John 7.37ff., and perhaps the 'branches' spread before Jesus on his entry into Jerusalem), together with the lighting of the four candlesticks which illuminated the whole city (cf. John 8.12).

Yom Kippur, or the day of Atonement, was a penitential festival. This was the only time in the year when the high priest entered the Holy of Holies to offer the blood of sacrificial victims in expiation (see the Letter to the Hebrews, p. 54). Rosh ha-Shanah, or the New Year Festival, was the preparation for it. The Feast of Hanukkah, or Dedication, celebrated the purification of the Temple by Judas Maccabaeus in 164 BC (see John 10.22). Purim, or the Feast of Lots, commemorated the salvation gained for the people by Esther; this festival has become the equivalent of a carnival.

The sabbath

Along with circumcision, keeping the sabbath has become the most sacred Jewish practice. Its strict rest, apart from exceptional activities which are laid down in minute detail, was meant to enable people to stop work and to praise God. It could become an insupportable burden (cf. Mark 2.27).

The Sanhedrin

The Great Sanhedrin in Jerusalem (the word comes from a Greek term meaning to sit together) was made up of seventy-one members: elders, high priests (Sadducees) and some scribes (Pharisees). The high priest presided over it. The Sanhedrin was probably inaugurated about a century before Christ; it had sessions in the Temple, twice a week. It had political power: it enacted laws, had its own police, and could pass the death sentence, though in the time of Christ it no longer had the power to carry this sentence out. It was the supreme religious court which fixed doctrine, established the liturgical calendar and regulated religious life. In AD 70 it ceased to exist as a political power; it moved to Jamnia, where it continued to function as a religious power. All over the place there were lesser sanhedrins made up of twenty-three members (cf. Matt. 10.17).

Restoration of the synagogue at Capernaum (about AD 200)

Jamnia – Judaism after AD 70

The Jews rebelled against the Romans in 66. At the end of a bloody war Titus, son of the emperor Vespasian, whom he succeeded, captured Jerusalem in 70. The Temple was destroyed. Thousands of Jews were killed or sold as slaves. Was this to be the end of Judaism?

Some Pharisees, including Johanan ben Zakkai, re-assembled before the final downfall of Jerusalem, at Jamnia (present-day Jabneh, south of Tel Aviv). They succeeded in giving their religion a new lease of life, and modern Judaism is the heir to their efforts. Since the other groups (the Sadducees and the Essenes) had disappeared in the troubles, from now on Judaism was to be Pharisaic. However, for the moment, it had to defend itself on two fronts.

Within Judaism, an end had to be made to the divisions between Jews. One liturgical calendar was established, and synagogue worship was unified; above all, a 'canon of scripture' was established. This was a list of books which were to serve as a rule (Greek *kanon*) of faith. Only those books written in Hebrew were retained, though the Jews of Alexandria recognized others which were written or circulated in Greek (this difference has passed on to our day in the difference between Catholic and Protestant Bibles; see *How to Read the Old Testament*, p. 86).

Externally, Judaism was confronted with Christianity, which was well rooted in Palestine (the Christians left Jerusalem before 70 to settle at Pella, east of the Jordan, and in Galilee), and also in Asia Minor, Greece and Egypt. . . Measures were taken at Jamnia to prohibit Christians from taking part in Jewish prayer; a petition was introduced into the Jewish prayer called the Eighteen Benedictions against 'heretics, apostates and the proud', i.e. Christians. The break was made. Christianity became a Jewish sect rejected by Judaism.

The Christians and Jamnia

The Council of Jamnia is never mentioned in the New Testament. However, some details are best explained by the influence of this revival of Judaism, above all in the Gospel of Matthew, which gathers together the traditions of communities living in Syria-Palestine, i.e. those most closely in contact with the Pharisees of Jamnia. Matthew brings out the similarities and the conflicts.

The conflicts are the most obvious. In Matthew, Jesus is very hard on the Pharisees (Matt. 23); he contrasts Christian prayer with theirs (6.5–6), and the 'yoke' which he proposes is easy compared with the numerous practices which the Pharisees require (11.29–30); the crowds recognize that his authority is not like that of the scribes (7.29). However, in reading Matthew we must always ask who is speaking, the Jesus of the 30s or the risen Lord of the 80s and 90s attacking the Pharisees of Jamnia.

Matthew is also concerned to show his deep agreement with the best of this Pharisaism. The Sermon on the Mount is presented as a great catechism, parallel to the teaching of Jamnia and based on the same three pillars of Judaism: justice, traditional good works and worship. On two occasions in Matthew, and in that Gospel only, Jesus quotes Hos. 6.6 (Matt. 9.13; 12.7); this was in fact a text dear to the heart of Johanan ben Zakkai, the founder of Jamnia. We are told one day one of his disciples was bewailing the destruction of the Temple; it was no longer possible to offer sacrifices to gain forgiveness for sins. 'Do not be troubled, my son,' replied Johanan, 'We have an expiation which is worth just as much: acts of mercy. For according to scripture, I want love, not sacrifices.'

Bas-relief from the triumphal arch of Titus in Rome, depicting the seven-branched candlestick from the Jerusalem Temple

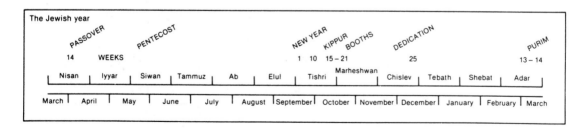

The Jewish year											
PASSOVER	PENTECOST					NEW YEAR / KIPPUR / BOOTHS			DEDICATION		PURIM
14	WEEKS					1 10 15 – 21			25		13 – 14
Nisan	Iyyar	Siwan	Tammuz	Ab	Elul	Tishri	Marheshwan	Chislev	Tebath	Shebat	Adar
March	April	May	June	July	August	September	October	November	December	January	February	March

The First Christians

During our journey we shall see who the first Christians were and how they lived. Here we can gather together some details provided by our reading of Acts.

Here are some important texts: 1.13–15; 2.41, 42–46; 3.1; 4.23–31, 32–37; 6.1–15; 9.1–2; 14.27; 15.1–12; 18.24–28; 20.17–38; 21.8–10... Try to describe the life of these first Christians.

A rejected Jewish sect

To begin with, and for a long time afterwards, the disciples of Jesus seemed to be no more than a sect within Judaism. They only took the name 'Christians' some years after the resurrection, in Antioch (11.26). Peter and John went to pray in the Temple, Paul preached in the synagogues and went to the Temple to fulfil a vow (21.26). The first followers of Jesus may have had different doctrines from their Jewish contemporaries, but their practices were the same.

Jewish rejection of Christianity began when the Hellenists – Greek-speaking Diaspora Jews who had settled in Jerusalem – questioned these practices (in particular the veneration of the Temple and its sacrifices), and the gulf widened when Gentiles were accepted into the church (at the 'Council' of Jerusalem).

Community life

This church, the assembly of those who had heard the call of God, gathered together in the name of Jesus, Christ and Lord, and was inspired by the Spirit.

According to Luke, it had three main characteristics:
(i) The disciples were constant in passing on the teaching of the apostles. In this catechesis given to the newly baptized, the scriptures were interpreted in the light of the risen Christ; the words and actions of Jesus were recalled and a rule of life was discovered in them. In this way, little by little, the content of the Gospels was brought together.
(ii) The disciples were constant in brotherly communion, a sharing of concerns which was expressed in the sharing of possessions: none of them was in need, because none laid claim to his own personal possessions; they held everything in common.
(iii) The disciples were constant in the breaking of bread, i.e. the eucharist, and in prayer. They prayed in the Temple, in their own homes, or elsewhere (21.5).

The Spirit and the ministers of the church

The Risen Christ had given his Spirit to the community to inspire it. He also gave the community ministers to be at the service of the believers. The various ministries came into being gradually and gradually became distinct.

The Twelve stand apart. As the foundations of the church they were never replaced as such.

In Jerusalem they established elders (or presbyters, the Greek word from which our 'priest' derives), and Paul did the same in his communities. Paul also appointed other authorities, overseers (Greek *episkopos*, which led to our words bishop, episcopacy). The Hellenists were appointed for service or *diakonia*; they were later made the precursors of deacons (though they themselves were not so much deacons as authorities in the church). We can also see the emergence of teachers, prophets and prophetesses (21.9).

However, you must not think that the hierarchy as it was recognized from the second century onwards had yet come into being: that was still in the process of formation.

A missionary community

The disciples felt responsible for passing on what they had discovered to everyone. 'We cannot keep silent,' Peter declared to the Sanhedrin (4.20). Driven by the Spirit, the community in Antioch sent Barnabas and Paul on a missionary journey (13.1–3), and in his enthusiasm for the faith Apollos began to catechize even before he was fully trained (18.24–28).

A community which is one and yet diverse

This one church is also the church of Jerusalem, the church established at Antioch, at Ephesus, and so on. The character of each community was moulded by its experience, its historical and economic situation, and its past; a community made up of Jews who had become Christians did not feel the same way as one which had grown up in a Gentile setting. As we shall see when we study the Gospels, the portraits of Jesus Christ were in turn coloured by the life of these communities.

They make us ask, what portrait of the risen Christ does our particular community reveal in the world today?

2 Easter

Christ the Sun. The earliest known Christian mosaic (Vatican, middle of the third century)

We began our journey through the Old Testament with the Exodus: this event, along with all the reflection to which it gave rise, was in fact the basis of Israelite faith. In the same way, before we read the books of the New Testament, we shall pause at the event which is the foundation of Christian faith, the resurrection of Christ.

This stopping point is important not only for doctrine but also for our learning.

It should allow us to check that Christian faith is based on this event, a mystery so rich that the disciples had to use a variety of images in their attempts to express it.

It will also help us to prepare for the later stages of this book; in fact it will cause us to go quickly through the main stages of the formation of the New Testament. The diagram on pp. 10–11 gave a brief summary of them; here, we shall see in detail how these accounts came to be written.

The stamp test

A magazine once suggested a test to its readers: 'Take a postage stamp and write what you believe on the back of it.' Even if you choose a large stamp and write very small, there is not much room, and you are forced to keep to essentials! What would the first Christians have written on their stamps? That is roughly what we are going to try to discover. In other words, we are going to see what was the good news, the essential message that they proclaimed when they were presenting their faith to a new audience.

Scholars call this essential message, proclamation, news, the kerygma, a Greek word which denotes the cry of a herald or the proclamation that the town crier used to make in former times.

Our course

We shall move on in three stages:

1. The disciples proclaim their faith: the kerygma. On the basis of some speeches from Acts we shall try to see what was the cry, the kerygma, which the disciples used to proclaim their faith to non-believers.

2. The disciples celebrate their faith: creed and hymns. By studying a creed and a hymn quoted by Paul, we shall see that when Christians assembled, they proclaimed or sang the same essential faith.

3. The disciples tell of their faith: narratives. We shall then be able to touch on the latest texts, the Gospel accounts of the appearances of the risen Jesus and his ascension. We shall see that they do not say any more than the kerygma, the creeds and the hymns, but that they say it in a different way, in the form of history.

Before you begin this part of the study, here is a little exercise which you can try (if you want to):

- When you hear the word 'resurrection', what words or images, what comparisons (e.g. spring, light) come to mind? Try to reply without thinking too hard.
- When you think of the resurrection of Christ (in meditation, prayer), what texts of scripture do you spontaneously go to?
- What is important to you in life?

Now go on to the studies I've suggested, without thinking any more about your answers: we shall come back to them later.

The Disciples Proclaim their Faith: the Kerygma

When reading the book of Acts, you will certainly have noticed that it contains a great many speeches: eight by Peter, nine by Paul and seven by various other people. As we read some of them, we are going to try to discover what was the essential message that the Christians had to proclaim.

Peter's speeches – or Luke's?

Still, one question arises. Whose voice are we hearing? Is it that of Peter or Paul, or is it that of Luke? It's clear that the author of Acts has rewritten these speeches. They are not just notes taken by a listener, or summaries. Luke, like other historians of his time, followed the practice of composing real miniature speeches, with a beginning, a development and a peroration.

However, all scholars recognize that Luke did not invent all these speeches; he took up earlier material. For example, we can see how certain titles given to Jesus (e.g. *pais*, the Greek word for child or servant) were no longer in use in the time of Luke; to speak of Christ as a man attested by God with mighty works and wonders and signs which God did through him is an indication of reflection on the mystery of Jesus which is still in its infancy.

So we can use these speeches to see how the first Christians proclaimed their faith.

Some speeches in Acts are addressed to disciples, for example Paul's farewell to the leaders of the church in Ephesus (Acts 20.17–35), but the majority of them are addressed to Jews or Gentiles, to persuade them to be converted. It is here that we shall try to discover the essential message proclaimed by the Christians, the kerygma.

♥ The kerygma in the speeches in Acts

Let's read some speeches addressed to Jews. Peter makes five speeches: Acts 2.14–41 (the day of Pentecost); 3.12–26 (after the healing of the lame man); 4.9–12; 5.29–32 (before the Sanhedrin); 10.34–43 (before the Roman officer Cornelius), and Paul makes one: 13.16–41 (in the synagogue at Pisidian Antioch). We may add to these the dialogue between Cleopas and Jesus on the road to Emmaus (Luke 24.19–27).

When you read these speeches you will find that there are always three elements:

The event of Jesus... The speaker recalls facts from the life of Jesus. Note which facts are selected, which are not mentioned, and which are stressed.

...interpreted by the scriptures... In many Bibles the quotations from the scriptures are either indented or printed in italics; you should be able to see at a glance how many there are in some speeches. Their aim is to place the life of Jesus in the context of God's plan, in order to make sense of it. Note, too, the names or titles given to Jesus; they usually come from scripture.

...challenges us. These speeches are never the simple explanation of a teacher who is imparting new knowledge to his pupils. The preacher is concerned for his proclamation and is aware that what he is saying forces his audience to make a choice.

If you are working in a group, here is an easy way to study the speeches. Draw eight vertical columns on a blackboard or a sheet of paper: one large enough for you to put down what you discover, in abbreviated form, and seven others, with enough space to note references from other speeches. Each member of the group should then take a speech and read it carefully; then the group should meet and one person should write down in the large column what they have discovered (for example, the miracles of Jesus or his teaching); the others will note down in the relevant column the verse from the speech they have read in which the subject is mentioned.

On p. 44 you will find how the diagram should look when it is completed. However, do not look at it now; it is much more instructive to make it for yourselves.

When you have done the work, think about the diagram. Which features of the life of Jesus do you find in all the speeches? Which do not appear in any of them? Which appear only in some? Try to sum up the kerygma, the proclamation of the faith of the first Christians. Compare it with what you wrote on your postage stamp.

Images to express Easter

Even a quick study of the speeches in Acts shows that Easter is at the heart of Christian faith.

But how did the disciples talk about this event, this mystery? We have become accustomed to using only the word resurrection in connection with it. Did they do the same? What complementary images did they use to present its different aspects? We can see from various summaries.

Reread some verses from the speeches in Acts: 2.23–24, 32–33; 3.13, 15; 5.30–31; 10.40.

Here are some summaries taken from other books:

If you confess with your lips that Jesus is Lord and believe in your heart that God raised him from the dead, you will be saved (Rom. 10.9).

Christ died and lived again (Rom. 14.9).

God has highly exalted him and bestowed on him the name which is above every name (Phil. 2.9).

Christ, the firstborn from the dead (Col. 1.18).

Christ, put to death in the flesh but made alive in the spirit (I Peter 3.18).

Why do you seek the living among the dead? (Luke 24.5).

They had certain points of dispute with him about their own superstition and about one Jesus, who was dead, but whom Paul asserted to be alive (Acts 25.19).

What imagery is used? In fact our word resurrection translates two Greek words: to be raised up (from the dead, from the 'hole'), and to be woken up (from the sleep of death). They are just two images; there are many others.

The various images can be grouped together along two main lines. Some indicate above all that we rediscover the life lost in death; afterwards things are as they were before. Others say that there will be more, that things will be better than before. Try to sort these out.

Some of the imagery will certainly remind you of texts or figures from the Old Testament: which are they? How does that help you?

Note the figures who intervene.

Finally, you might like to go back to the imagery that you thought of spontaneously (see p. 33). Does it belong with the two main lines that I mentioned earlier? Or only one of them? If so, which?

Two images

Christians have felt that the whole of the mystery of Easter cannot be expressed in a single image, so they have used a great many. To simplify things, we can put these into two main groups.

Before and after, or a return to life

Those who die are thought of as falling into a great hole (Sheol, or the nether regions); or perhaps they fall asleep. The resurrection is the fact of raising them up or arousing them. After death they come back to the life that they had before. 'Lazarus, arise,' writes St John.

The advantage of this kind of imagery is clear: it has a context in history, it gives a clear indication of continuity: things are as they were before. Those who knew the person before can recognize him again.

The disadvantage is that it says nothing about the nature of the life which is rediscovered: one can just as well say Lazarus was raised (to die again!) as one can say that Jesus was raised.

Below and above, or an entry into glory

Since people instinctively locate God above, in heaven, the one who has died is said to have been brought near to God. He is exalted, glorified; he ascends into heaven. This imagery has certainly been sustained by reflection on the symbol of the Son of man, the symbol of those who remained faithful to God to the point of martyrdom. Daniel introduces this symbol by showing the Son of man brought on the clouds into the presence of God (Dan. 7, see *How to Read the Old Testament*, p. 91).

The advantage of this kind of imagery is that it states clearly that we are not just talking about a restoration to life as it was before; there is more to it than that. We may say that Lazarus was raised, but not that he was exalted or glorified.

The problem, if this image is used in isolation, is that one might imagine that some element of man (his spirit, his soul) ascends to heaven, and that it is not the whole man, body and spirit, that is glorified.

The risen Christ exalted

The disciples felt that they had to use both kinds of imagery: Jesus was risen, so the one who was now alive was the same being whom they had known earlier: his friends recognized him. But he was also exalted, glorified, he had ascended into heaven; so this was not just a matter of rediscovering life as it was before: Jesus was introduced to a new life, the life of God.

The Disciples Celebrate their Faith: Creed and Hymns

Every group wants to make itself known by proclaiming, in brief slogans, the essentials of its beliefs. The disciples proclaimed their faith: the kerygma.

At the same time, however, every group needs to remind itself of its basic principles whenever it meets, whether these may form a party political programme, club rules, or whatever. Similarly, when they met together, the disciples celebrated their faith. They expressed it in their creed, sang it in hymns, or meditated upon it in what they were taught.

Try to distinguish between the events which belong in history (those which anyone can verify) and those which can be seen only by the eyes of faith. Is the phrase 'the third day' a piece of historical information or an affirmation of faith?

What imagery is used to express the mystery of Easter (see p. 35 again)?

Compare this creed with the creed we use today. What differences can you see?

A creed. I Cor. 15.1–11

We have the good fortune to possess one of these very ancient creeds; Paul quotes it in his letter to the Corinthians. Begin by reading the text.

Some things about this passage are worth noting. Note, first, a change of style: in the middle of a narrative account we come up against a number of short phrases (and scholars note that this is not Paul's usual style). Besides, Paul tells us explicitly that this is not his own work. He is not using his own words, but reciting someone else's. He indicates this by taking up terms used at that time by the rabbis: the disciple *receives* something from his teachers and then in turn *hands it on* to his own disciples.

Paul was almost certainly writing to the Corinthians round about Easter 57. He reminds them of what he told them when he founded their community, in 51. So twenty years or so after Easter, this creed had already been formulated.

He says that he received it himself. When? Was it perhaps from Ananias at the time of his baptism in Damascus, round about 36 (see Acts 9.10ff.)?

In Greek, the form of the verb indicates above all the aspect of particular actions: the present indicates something that lasts, the aorist (roughly speaking, our simple past tense) indicates what happened once at a given moment; the perfect (roughly speaking, our composite past tense) shows the present result of a past action: an event took place once, but its consequences are still felt. Now we may note that all the verbs in this creed are in the aorist except for one, 'He is risen': thus the resurrection is an event which took place once, in history, but has a lasting result. Christ is alive for ever.

Read this creed again carefully.
Note which events happened at one time.

The third day according to the scriptures

There is general agreement that the starting point of this phrase is to be found in Hosea 6.1–2. The Israelites, shattered by the prophet's preaching, improvised a penitential liturgy. Read this text. Two days, three days, in this context indicates in a little while.

However, by the time of Christ this phrase had taken on a theological significance. This is how the Targum (see *How to Read the Old Testament*, p. 81), interprets this verse from Hosea:

He will revive us on the day of consolations which must come; on the day when he makes the dead live again, he will raise us up and we shall live before him.

And a rabbinic commentary on Gen. 22.4 declares:

The third day, that is to say the day on which life is restored to the dead, as it is written in Hosea: on the third day he will raise us up and we shall live before him.

So in the time of Christ, when people talked about the third day according to the scriptures, they were not giving an indication of time (the day after tomorrow); they were making a theological statement. It denotes what we call the day of general resurrection at the end of time.

In talking of the resurrection on the third day according to the scriptures, the disciples were not giving a date (it is not known when the event took place; all the texts say is that on Sunday morning the women discovered that the tomb was empty); they were proclaiming their faith. The day of general resurrection (the third day) had already arrived with the resurrection of Jesus (Matt. 27.52–53 tells us so in strip cartoon fashion); our own resurrection lies behind us, and has already been realized in Jesus.

A hymn. Philippians 2.6–11

In the Letters, the Gospels or Revelation we can find hymns composed by the first communities. Paul reminds the Philippians of one when he invites them to practise humility by following the example of Christ.

Read this text in your Bible.

How is the Easter event expressed? Is the imagery of resurrection used? What kind of imagery *is* used? (The name given to Jesus is that of Lord.) So this mystery can be expressed otherwise than in the language of resurrection.

Who are the main characters and what is their role?

The interpretation by scripture was not made explicitly, but it is present in this hymn. In fact the hymn is based on a contrast. Jesus did not act like Adam, who wanted to snatch at equality with God (see Gen. 3.5): on the contrary, he acted like the servant in Isa. 53 (see *How to Read the Old Testament*, p. 67). Compare v. 7, he emptied himself, with Isa. 53.12; v. 9, God highly exalted him, with Isa. 52.13. How do these two texts allow us to locate the destiny of Jesus within God's plan? How, by virtue of these two texts, is our destiny bound up with that of Christ?

Meditation on a psalm. Ephesians 4.7–10

Paul wants to show that God gives to the church what it needs to fulfil its mission, namely, to construct the body of Christ: he makes a gift to believers of the various ministeries: apostles, prophets, evangelists, catechists, those who build up the community. In this connection Paul bases his words on Ps. 68.19 as it was interpreted at the time (according to the Targum). First let us compare this verse in

The Hebrew Text	The Targum
Thou didst ascend the heights leading captives into captivity	*Thou didst raise up to heaven Moses, the prophet, leading captives into captivity (that is, thou didst teach the words of the Law);*
and receiving tribute from men, even from the rebellious in order to have a dwelling place, O Lord God.	*thou didst give them to the children of men, and even to the rebellious if they turned to thee, the rest of the holy presence of the Lord God.*

He made himself visible

On several occasions the verb 'he appeared' occurs in the creed contained in I Cor. 15, and we are used to talking about the appearances of the risen Jesus. This word is ambiguous: it might suggest a ghost or, by contrast, some kind of presence that could be photographed.

The form of the Greek verb used here has a rather different connotation; it means 'he made himself visible'. That is, it stresses the fact that Jesus took the initiative in manifesting himself to whom he wished. The Jewish philosopher Philo, a contemporary of Paul, demonstrates this well: speaking of Abraham's vision of God, he writes: It was not Abraham who saw God; God made himself visible to Abraham.

The use of this Greek form in the Bible is significant. In the Old Testament it is used for theophanies or appearances of God (e.g. Gen. 12.7; 17.1; Judg. 13.21) where there is more stress on the mission that is entrusted than on what might have been 'seen'. This is one way of saying that the invisible made itself felt.

In the New Testament, Matthew, Mark and Luke use the word in the account of the Transfiguration: Moses and Elijah make themselves visible (perhaps inwardly) to the disciples. Luke uses it quite often: an angel makes himself visible to the shepherds (1.11) or to Jesus in the agony in Gethsemane (22.43); tongues of flame appear at Pentecost (Acts 2.3); Jesus appears to Paul on the Damascus road (though his companions see nothing! 9.17) or in a dream (16.9), and so on. An ancient hymn speaks of Jesus making himself visible to the angels (I Tim. 3.16).

All this suggests that we should be careful: when they used this word the disciples did not claim that Jesus showed himself to them in visible fashion, in a way that could be filmed. They stressed the initiative of Jesus and left open the possibility that these appearances were primarily inward experiences.

For the Targum it is no longer God who ascends to heaven to establish himself in his dwelling place; Moses ascends Sinai and there receives the Law, to give it to men.

Paul meditates on this psalm. In it, he no longer sees Moses but Jesus, the new Moses, who ascends to heaven after having come down to earth and even to hell. Thus the whole mystery of Easter is presented by this image of descent and glorification.

(We shall see that Luke uses the same psalm to interpret Pentecost. See p. 84.)

The Disciples Tell of their Faith: Narratives

We have listened to the disciples proclaiming their faith to non-believers (the kerygma) and celebrating it in their communities (the creed, hymns); the centre of this faith is always the fact that God has raised up, glorified, given power to this Jesus who was crucified.

They also expressed the same faith in another literary genre, that of narrative. Here they did not make their affirmations in brief formulas, but told stories and made people see. This literary genre corresponds to the needs of a community which had already been formed and which wanted to know more about the meaning of an event; it was a community that had also had liturgical experience. We shall come back to this, but the fact must be stressed very strongly as we begin our next readings. The narratives do not say more about the event itself than the brief statements of the kerygma; they simply say it differently and develop its meaning.

The four Gospels have handed down to us narratives of this kind. They can be classified into three groups, each meeting a need in the community:

The community celebrates its faith in the very place where the event took place: narratives about the empty tomb (Matthew, Mark, Luke, John).

It shows that the apostles' experience of the risen Jesus made them official witnesses: accounts of appearances to the eleven (Matthew, Luke, John).

It appeals to experience had in the liturgy or within the church: appearances to the disciples on the Emmaus road (Luke) or to Mary Magdalene (John).

We shall look quickly at these three kinds of narrative.

(a) Narratives of celebration by pilgrimage. The empty tomb

When believers make a pilgrimage to the Holy Land, they like to have a celebration at the very sites of the events which took place there: for example, at the Holy Sepulchre they recall the event, meditate and pray.

Scholars, on the basis of their study of the texts, have conjectured that the accounts of the empty tomb arose in this way: the first Christians made a pilgrimage to the tomb of Jesus, an empty tomb, and celebrated their faith there.

This gave rise to a first narrative which each evangelist took up in his own way to express his theology.

We shall just read Mark's account.

🐾 The empty tomb. Mark 16.1–8

Read this text. Note the indications of time, the places, the main characters, the actions (look back at the 'tool box' in *How to Read the Old Testament*, p. 14). Try to note these different points in two columns, putting conflicting items opposite each other.

What transformation has taken place between the beginning and the end of the account?

The indications of time suggest a transition from darkness to light (morning, sun, light), from old to new, from sacred to religious, Jewish time (the sabbath – and not Saturday – was over) to cosmic, secular time (the first day of the week).

In terms of place, the closed tomb, guarding its dead, is contrasted with a tomb open on life; here Jerusalem, for Mark the symbol of those who are shut up in their own ideas and kill those who differ from them, is contrasted with the Galilee of the Gentiles, gateway to the world.

Of the main characters, one is absent: Jesus. The young man suggests the new way in which Jesus is now present: he is in white (opposed to the darkness of the tomb), seated on the right, like the glorified Christ, and it is he who transforms the women's quest. They come to the tomb to anoint the body of Jesus, that is to say, to preserve a corpse, but he is no longer there. They come to touch a dead body, but they receive a message. They and the apostles 'will see' the risen Lord when they have proclaimed him as far as Galilee, that is, to the end of the world and the end of history (see p. 62).

(b) Stories of appearances to create official witnesses

Matthew, Luke and John end their Gospels with the accounts of one or more appearances of Christ. In this section we shall look at the appearances to the eleven apostles. We shall keep for the next section appearances to other disciples, which are of a different kind.

The Gospel of Mark probably ended with the flight of the women from the tomb; 16.9–20, which was added afterwards, is simply a summary of Matthew and Luke (look at the way in which it is presented in your Bible).

The stories of the appearances to the eleven seek to show that Jesus himself made them his witnesses. We are not going to read all the stories nor study them in depth (though we shall come back to some of them later). What we need to do here is to check that these stories take up, in their imagery, the affirmation made in the kerygma (look again at p. 19 on 'making ideas into narratives').

Adoration of the glorified Christ. Matt. 28.16–20

Begin by reading this text. Remember the two groups of imagery used to present the Easter event: which is taken up here?

Let's look at the text again. The eleven leave, as in a procession, for the mountain where Jesus, the new Moses, had given them his new law (Matt. 5.1). They prostrate themselves before him: this is the word which in the Greek Orthodox liturgy still denotes the gesture of adoration. 'Come to them' is surprising, since the disciples are lying at his feet. However, in the Bible, He who Comes is sometimes a divine title. By quoting the phrase from Daniel 7 (see *How to Read the Old Testament*, p. 91), Jesus presents himself as the Son of Man who comes into the presence of God on the clouds of heaven. So he is already exalted and glorified. Because of this he can send his disciples on their mission into the world.

So this text takes up in narrative form one of the ways in which Christians tried to present Easter in the kerygma: here is the pattern of exaltation, from below upwards. The only feature belonging to the other pattern (resurrection) is the mention of doubt (v. 17); however, it does not fit very well and could have been added afterwards.

Coin of Agrippa II. On one side, Vespasian crowned; on the other, a goddess carrying an ear of corn and a cornucopia.

The recognition of the risen Lord. Luke 24.36–53

Read vv. 36–43: on what pattern is this account constructed? Then vv. 50–53: what is the pattern here?

It is clear that Luke is using the imagery of resurrection. Jesus takes the initiative in making himself visible. There might be doubts that this is a collective illusion, so Jesus shows that he is as he was before: he has a body and he can eat. All this could be said of Lazarus (except, of course, that Jesus is present in the midst of them without having entered).

Luke then develops one of his favourite themes: Jesus can only be known truly through the interpretation of the scriptures, and the scriptures cannot be understood unless the Risen Lord reads them to us himself (vv. 44–49).

Then Luke describes the ascension (on the evening of Easter Day!); this is a way of saying in narrative form that Jesus is exalted, glorified. When we study Luke-Acts we shall see that Luke has another account of the ascension, which is put at least forty days after Easter. The fact that the same author can give two accounts of the same event, placing them at two different points, warns us that he is not concerned with chronology and history, but with theology.

The two sides of a coin

A coin has two sides, but it is difficult to see both of them at once; to do that, you have to cut the coin laterally in half. Similarly, one cannot see two profiles of a face at once: in some of his pictures Picasso projected a human face so that one could see every aspect simultaneously.

This is rather what Luke has done. He is well aware that there are two main ways of expressing Easter: to say that Jesus is risen or to say that he is exalted. These are the two inseparable sides of the same mystery. Because both seemed to him to be essential, he chose to put them side by side: Jesus is risen – he ascended into heaven. Perhaps we have been too quick to suppose that these were two successive events in history (as if one were to believe that there were two coins) when in fact it is a matter of two aspects of the same mystery.

(c) Christian experience. Appearances to disciples

The stories of the appearing of Jesus to Mary Magdalene in John and to the disciples on the Emmaus road in Luke are of a special kind. They do not set out to show that Jesus is risen or exalted or that he provided official witnesses. They simply seek to help us share in the joy of the disciples' rediscovery of their Lord and their renewal of a loving relationship with him; they are meant to teach us that we today can have the same experience.

We are simply going to read the story of the Emmaus road (Luke 24.13–35) and to compare it with another of Luke's accounts, the baptism of an Ethiopian official (Acts 8.26–40). To make things easier you will find the translation of these two texts side by side on the next page.

If you have time, begin by studying it with the help of your 'tool box'; you will see that the questions under the heading 'the text' work very well and help you to understand the texts.

Luke is trying to reply to a question: How do we meet the Lord Jesus today? He shows the role of three essential elements: knowledge of the earthly life of Jesus – scripture – sacraments. Read the texts and look for these three elements and the role they play.

Cleopas and his companion are very familiar with the life of Jesus: they are talking about it to each other (literally, they are engaged in a homily), they recall it, and their speech is as complete and precise as the speeches of Peter. However, for them things no longer make sense. If the life of Jesus is to make sense, it must be interpreted by the scriptures (what we call the Old Testament); however, this interpretation can be made only by the risen Jesus. After that he can be recognized in the sacrament. And the fact that Jesus disappeared the very moment that they recognized him warns us that from now on it is in the eucharist that we encounter the living Christ. By using a past continuous tense in v. 30 instead of the simple past, Luke probably wants to suggest that Jesus continues to give bread all through the history of the church.

The Ethiopian official is in a different situation. A convert to Judaism (a proselyte), he knew the scriptures, but they did not make sense to him. For them to be made comprehensible they had to be illuminated by the life of Jesus. And here again, only the risen Lord could bring this about, through his witnesses. In fact it is clear that Luke presents Philip as he presents Jesus: each of them appears and disappears mysteriously, and interprets the scriptures (compare Luke 24.27 and Acts 8.35). From now on in the church it is no longer Jesus himself who acts; or rather, he still acts but does so through the medium of his ministers to the degree that they are inspired by the Spirit (Acts 8.26, 29, 39). And the official, too, has the experience of a personal encounter with Jesus in the sacrament of baptism. (I have put v. 37 in brackets because it is not in all the manuscripts; this is probably a formula from the baptismal liturgy which crept into the text afterwards.)

As you read the text, note too the play on words which cannot be reproduced in English: three verbs with the same root are intertwined (you can identify them by the superior figures which mark them): ginoskein[1], to know/understand, epiginoskein[2], to recognize, and anaginoskein[3], to read.

Above all, look at the change in the situation between the beginning and the end. At the beginning, the eyes of the two disciples are kept from recognizing him (v. 16): so it is not that Jesus has changed or disguised himself as a beggar; his disciples have changed. They are so wrapped up in their disappointed hope that they have made themselves incapable of recognizing that this hope has been realized in Jesus, though in a different way from their expectations. Similarly, in the Gospel of John, Mary Magdalene thinks in such a way of Jesus – the Jesus of whom she dreams – that she prevents herself from recognizing him when he introduces himself to her. At the breaking of the bread their eyes were opened: this change of heart which allows them to recognize their Risen Lord does not come from man; their eyes are opened as Jesus opens up the scriptures to them.

When Peter goes to the tomb (v. 24), he does not see Jesus; however, at the end it is said that Jesus has made himself visible to Peter (v. 33). Similarly, the disciples do not recognize Jesus on the road: they recognize him in the breaking of bread (v. 31) and they declare that he made himself known to them (v. 35). Jesus always takes the initiative.

Mosaic from Ostia (Italy)

Luke 24.13–35 The disciples on the Emmaus Road

[13]That very day two of them were going to a village named Emmaus, about seven miles from Jerusalem, [14]and talking with each other about all these things that had happened. [15]While they were talking and discussing together, Jesus himself drew near and went with them. [16]But their eyes were kept from recognizing [2] him.

[17]And he said to them, 'What is this conversation which you are holding with each other as you walk?' And they stood still, looking sad. [18]Then one of them, named Cleopas, answered him, 'Are you the only visitor to Jerusalem who does not know[1] the things that have happened here in these days?' [19]And he said to them, 'What things?' And they said to him, 'Concerning Jesus of Nazareth, who was a prophet mighty in deed and word before God and all the people, [20]and how our chief priests and rulers delivered him up to be condemned to death, and crucified him. [21]But we had hoped that he was the one to redeem Israel. Yes, and besides all this, it is now the third day since this happened. [22]Moreover, some women of our company amazed us. They were at the tomb early in the morning [23]and did not find his body; and they came back saying that they had even seen a vision of angels, who said that he was alive. [24]Some of those who were with us went to the tomb, and found it just as the woman had said; but him they did not see.'

[25]And he said to them, 'O foolish men, and slow of heart to believe all that the prophets have spoken! [26]Was it not necessary that the Christ should suffer these things and enter into his glory?' [27]And beginning with Moses and all the prophets, he interpreted to them in all the scriptures the things concerning himself.

[28]So they drew near to the village to which they were going. He appeared to be going further, [29]but they constrained him, saying, 'Stay with us, for it is toward evening and the day is now far spent.' So he went in to stay with them. [30]When he was at table with them, he took the bread and blessed, and broke it, and gave it to them. [41]And their eyes were opened and they recognized [2] him; and he vanished out of their sight. [32]They said to each other, 'Did not our hearts burn within us while he talked to us on the road, while he opened to us the scriptures?' [33]And they rose that same hour and returned to Jerusalem; and they found the eleven gathered together and those who were with them, [34]who said, 'The Lord has risen indeed, and has appeared (made himself visible) to Simon.' [35]Then they told what had happened on the road, and how he was known to them in the breaking of the bread.

Acts 8.26–40 The Ethiopian official

[26]But an angel of the Lord said to Philip, 'Rise and go toward the south, to the road that goes down from Jerusalem to Gaza.' This is a desert road. [27]And he rose and went.

And behold, an Ethiopian, a eunuch, a minister of Candace the queen of the Ethiopians, in charge of all her treasure, had come to Jerusalem to worship [28]and was returning; seated in his chariot, he was reading [3] the prophet Isaiah. [29]And the Spirit said to Philip, 'Go up and join this chariot.' [30]So Philip ran up to him, and heard him reading [3] Isaiah the prophet, and asked, 'Do you understand[1] what you are reading [3]?' [31]And he said, 'How can I, unless someone guides me?' And he invited Philip to come up and sit with him. [32]Now the passage of the scripture which he was reading[3] was this:

As a sheep led to the slaughter
or a lamb before its shearer is dumb,
so he opens not his mouth.
[33]In his humiliation justice was denied him.
Who can describe his generation?
For his life is taken up from the earth.

[34]And the eunuch said to Philip, 'About whom, pray, does the prophet say this, about himself or about someone else?' [35]Then Philip opened his mouth, and beginning with this scripture he told him the good news of Jesus.

[36]And as they went along the road they came to some water, and the eunuch said, 'See, here is water! What is to prevent my being baptized?' [[37]And Philip said, 'If you believe with all your heart, you may.' And he replied, 'I believe that Jesus Christ is the Son of God.'] [38]And he commanded the chariot to stop, and they both went down into the water, Philip and the eunuch, and he baptized him. [39]And when they came up out of the water, the Spirit of the Lord caught up Philip; and the eunuch saw him no more, and went on his way rejoicing. [40]But Philip was found at Azotus, and passing on he preached the gospel to all the towns till he came to Caesarea.

And Now. . .?

We began this stage with two main aims in view: to check that the resurrection of Christ is the centre of Christian faith and to discover more fully how the writings of the New Testament took shape.

However, it is probable that on the way another focal point has emerged: how did the resurrection of Christ take place? How will ours take place? Obviously these are important questions, but they go beyond the scope of this course; all I can do is to give you some indications of where you may find help, by referring you to other books (see p. 123).

▚ It would be a good thing if, either by yourself, or better in a group, you tried to sum things up.

How did the first Christians talk about Easter? Why is it important that they used several different images?

How is this faith expressed in the various literary genres: proclamation to non-believers, celebration, stories? Do the stories in fact say more about the mystery than the kerygma, or not?

▚ I also suggested that you might try a little exercise (p. 33). It's worth going back to that now.

We use imagery to talk about the resurrection. What? Does it above all (or exclusively) express the resurrection aspect, a return to life as it was before? Does it also express the extra element which the imagery of exaltation and glorification seeks to evoke?

We have favourite texts from scripture, and that is fine. But we have seen that each text gives us only one aspect of the event. What aspect is expressed by our favourite texts? Should we consider adding to them?

You may have been surprised by the question 'What is important to you in life?' But if belief in the resurrection is basic, it cannot be disconnected with what is important for us. Go back to your answers: what connection does your faith in the resurrection have with them?

Some strong points

First, let's bring together some firm conclusions that have emerged in the course of our work.

No one ever says that they saw Jesus in process of being raised (unlike a great many paintings which, from this perspective, are dangerous). The disciples say that they saw the risen Jesus. They stressed one aspect or another depending on the circumstances, and sometimes two different ones at the same time. They recognized Jesus, so he was the person they had known before his death; however, this was not just a return to life but an entry into definitive life: he is exalted, glorified, he has ascended to heaven, is seated at the right hand of God, made Lord.

This event can only be perceived in faith. We do not see the Risen Lord when we want to, as we might see a friend today; he makes himself visible when he wants, where he wants and to whom he wants. So the witnesses had a very real experience (which they expressed, for example, by saying that Jesus was capable of eating, see Luke 24), even if they were the only ones to do so. Thus Paul's companions saw that something had happened to him, but they did not see the Christ. The use of this expression 'made himself visible' may point to an experience which was real but completely inward.

Our faith rests finally on the affirmation that God works in us. The Gospel of Mark did not have any account of an appearance of Jesus. The young man (i.e. God) asserts that Jesus is risen: that is to be enough to bring about faith.

The scriptures (for us, the Old Testament) are basic to any belief in and understanding of this mystery. We have seen this in connection with the stories of the Emmaus road and the Ethiopian official; we could have read it also in the episode where John shows Peter and the other disciples coming to the tomb (John 20.3–9): the other disciple also went in, and he saw and believed; for as yet they did not know the scripture, that he must rise from the dead (vv. 8f.); if they had understood the scripture, they would not in fact have needed to see the empty tomb (with their physical eyes) in order to believe; they would have believed and seen the Risen Lord (with the eyes of faith: John 20.29).

The scriptures make sense of the earthly life of Jesus, and this life makes sense of the scriptures.

However, only the Risen Lord, either by himself (Luke 24.27, 45) or through his disciples (Acts 8.35), can make sense of the scriptures.

The episodes of the Emmaus road and Ethiopian official, like many others, show us that the believer of 82 or 1982 is not at a disadvantage in comparison to the first disciples: they too can have and must have the same experience of meeting the Risen Lord, since he is always also present in reality in the unknown brother whom one meets on the way, and in the sacraments, above all the eucharist.

That may present us with a question: is the experience of the Christian today fundamentally different from that of Thomas and the other apostles? Obviously, this question can be answered in different ways. Here is one of them. This experience is basically the same: if a non-believer, utterly ignorant of Christianity, went into a place where Christians were worshipping, he would see from their attitude that something was happening; if he asked them what it was, they would reply, 'The Lord Jesus is present among us, he invites us to his table, we eat with him, we listen to him and speak to him. . .' and this reply is remarkably like the accounts in the Gospels.

However, there is one difference: in these accounts it is said that the disciples recognize Jesus. They had known him in his earthly life, and so they could verify that their experience of the Risen Lord now corresponded to the experience of the earthly Jesus which they had had before. And for us that is impossible. To verify the authenticity of our experience we have to compare it with that of the apostles. Certainly the experience itself is not fundamentally different, but the reference to the past which authenticates it is different: for the apostles it was the life of Jesus; for us it is the experience of the apostles.

An observation

We have seen that the first Christians used two main kinds of imagery to evoke the mystery of Easter: that of resurrection and that of exaltation. We have seen the advantages and disadvantages of each type when it is taken by itself (see p. 35).

We might ask – though this is only a hypothesis – whether some of our difficulties do not derive from the fact that we have separated these two types of imagery.

In the case of Jesus, we have virtually limited ourselves to the language of resurrection. And that has led us to ask questions about how it took place: what kind of body did he have? could he eat? The language of exaltation should remind us that while indeed he is a real man, and therefore has a body, he is exalted, and therefore different. Now, to take up a phrase of Paul's, he has a spiritual body.

For ourselves, often without being aware of it, we keep only the imagery of exaltation: when we die, our bodies will turn to dust but some part of us, our soul, will go up to heaven; so we see no need to get our bodies back again. The language of resurrection should remind us that we can exist only as corporeal beings.

A certainty

It is useless and impossible to imagine how the resurrection took place. The only certainty the believer can have is to hold on to two things: Jesus is risen and glorified and we shall be with him. When we read Paul as the next stage, we shall be able to look at the words which he used or invented with the help of the preposition *with*: suffer with, die with, rise with, be glorified with, live with. . . We shall be for ever with him.

The event of Jesus...	Acts 2.14–41 Pentecost	3.12–26 Lame man	4.9–12 Before	5.29–32 Sanhedrin	10.34–43 Cornelius	13.16–41 Paul	Luke 24.19–27	Other texts from Luke
Earthly ministry								
preaching of John the Baptist						24–25		Luke 3.15–16
Jesus of Nazareth	22		10		38		19	
his baptism by John					37–38			*He stirs up the people, teaching*
teaching					(36)		19	*throughout all Judaea, from Galilee*
miracles	22				38			*even to this place,* Luke 23.5
Death								
condemned by Jewish leaders	23, 36	13,15,17	10	30	39	27	20	Luke 23.2, 4, 5, 20, 22, 23, 25, 51; Acts 7.52
executed by Gentiles	23, 36	13, 14				28		
through God's plan	23, 36	18	28			27	25–27	Luke 18.31 *Everything . . . will be accomplished*
innocent		13				28		Luke 23.4, 14, 15, 32
buried						29		
Easter								
God raised him up	24, 32					33		
God raised him		15	10	30	40	30, 37	34	
We are witnesses	32	15		32	39, 41	31	48	Acts 1.8–22; Luke 24.48; Acts 1.3–4
exalted to God's right hand	33	13.21		31				Luke 24.51; Acts 1.9–11
he gives the Spirit	33							

...interpreted by the scriptures...

Titles								
Before: Child, servant		13.26	27, 30					
Holy, righteous	(27)	14						
After: Lord of life, saviour		15		31				
judge of living and dead					36			
Before and after: Lord	36					36		
Christ	31, 36	18, 20						

Scripture. In general								
Scripture announces his day		24			(43)	(27–40)		
his suffering		18					26–27, 46	
his last coming	20	20						
The Jews chief heirs	39	25				26–33		**Quotations in other texts**
through them, Gentile salvation	39	25						

Particular texts								
Ps. 16.10 *Your holy one to see corruption*	25–31					35–37		
Ps. 2.7 *You are my son*	30					33, 20		Acts 9.20; Heb. 1.5; 5.5; Mark 1.11; Luke 3.22
Ps. 110.1 *Sit at my right hand*	34							Matt. 12.36; Heb. 1.13; Mark 14.62; Acts 7.55; Rom. 8.34; Eph. 1.20; Col. 3.1; I Peter 3.22; Heb. 1.3; 8.1; 10.12; 12.2
Ps. 118.22 *Stone rejected/exalted*			11	31				Mark 12.10; I Peter 2.7
Isa. 55.3 *Realities promised to David*						34		
Joel 3 *Gift of Spirit*	17, 21, 39							
Deut. 18 *Prophet like Moses*		22						Acts 7.37; John 6.14
Hag. 1.5						41		

...challenges us

salvation by faith					43	38		
salvation only in name of Jesus	(21, 39)		12		43			
be converted	38	19		31				
baptism for sin	38	19, 26		31	43	38		
gift of the Spirit	38							

ΠΑΥΛΟΣ ΑΠΟΣΤΟΛΟΣ ΧΡΥ ΙΗΥ ΔΙΑ ΘΕΛΗΜΑΤΟΣ
ΘΥ ΚΑΙ ΤΕΙΜΟΘΕΟΣ Ο ΑΔΕΛΦΟΣ ΤΟΙΣ ΕΝ ΚΟΛΑΣΣΑΙΣ
ΑΓΙΟΙΣ ΚΑΙ ΠΙΣΤΟΙΣ ΑΔΕΛΦΟΙΣ ΕΝ ΧΡΩ ΧΑΡΙΣ ΥΜΙΝ
ΚΑΙ ΕΙΡΗΝΗ ΑΠΟ ΘΥ ΠΑΤΡΟΣ ΗΜΩΝ ΕΥΧΑΡΙΣΤΟΥΜΕΝ

3 Paul and his Letters

The beginning of the Letter to the Colossians. A papyrus from about 230.

Paul has the reputation of being a difficult author. That's true. But he is so engaging! All through his letters he reveals himself for what he is, a saint with countless failings. He talks about himself all the time; he is emotional, and needs to have faithful friends by him. When he was a Jew he was an integralist; now that he has become a Christian he remains in character and his colleagues and congregations learn this to their cost: Peter ('I opposed him to his face because he stood condemned', Gal. 2.11); Barnabas, who wanted to take his young cousin John Mark on the mission, against Paul's wishes ('There arose a sharp contention, so that they separated from each other,' writes Luke in Acts 15.39); the Corinthians whom Paul proposes to visit again, so as to thrash them into behaving themselves (I Cor. 4.21; see 11.16). At the same time he is someone who is utterly caught up in his mission; all that counts for him is love for his Lord and the service of his communities, his dear children for whom he feels as emotionally and as physically as a mother.

Many passages in his letters seem obscure to us (they already did so to the author of II Peter 3.16!). We shall not spend time on them here; you can go back to them later. Above all we shall try to discover the main outlines of his theology and read some of those marvellous passages in which we discover Christian faith in the first flush of youth, when we can see, also through Paul, what the grace of God can achieve in the heart of man.

Paul's life can be divided into two almost equal parts: for thirty years he was a Pharisee (he was perhaps born about AD 5 and had his experience on the Damascus road about 36); then for thirty years, as a Christian (he died as a martyr in Rome, probably in AD 67), he was the tireless missionary who founded communities throughout the Mediterranean basin and wrote to his Christians.

Paul the Pharisee

Born in Tarsus, the capital of Cilicia in Asia Minor, a university city with perhaps more than 300,000 inhabitants, Paul was at the crossroads of two civilizations.

As a Jew, a Pharisee, he studied in Jerusalem under one of the greatest rabbis of the time, Gamaliel (see Acts 22.3; 5.37). He was back in Tarsus during the time of Jesus' activity, of which he seems to have been unaware. Perhaps in his parents' home, he had learned to weave the rough material, made of goats' hair, which in French, cilice, takes its name from the province of Cilicia. He was almost certainly a rabbi, and therefore married.

At the same time, however, he received from his parents the status of Roman citizen, and on occasion he would use his privileges with pride (Acts 22.25–28). He probably went to the university, and used its learned approach to literature; at times he also quotes poetry (Acts 17.28). His double name, Saul(Jewish)/Paul(Greek) indicates that he belonged to two civilizations.

As a sincere Pharisee, Paul had only one passion: to serve God by scrupulous observance of the Law. He could even say that the Law was his life. When he returned to Jerusalem in about 36, he was appalled at the preaching of Peter and others. Because he was a theologian, he probably saw better than Peter that the message of the apostles ran the risk of overturning Judaism: they put this Jesus, rightly condemned by the authorities as a blasphemer, on the same level as God. An intransigent Pharisee when it came to the purity of faith, Paul decided to fight against this new sect. He approved the death of Stephen and left for Damascus to pursue disciples of Stephen who had taken refuge there.

A coin from Tarsus

On the Damascus road

The glorified Lord who appeared to Paul was the one who had died an accursed death on the cross: the whole of Paul's theology is contained in this reversal. Jesus had been condemned by the Law of whom the religious authorities were the guardians; he was accursed of God, who had done nothing to deliver him, as it is written: 'Cursed (by God) is the man who is hanged on the tree' (Deut. 21.23; cf. Gal. 3.13). Now God had glorified this 'accursed' man! That meant that God had taken his side. So the Law which had condemned him was itself condemned by God. The Law had come to an end. For Paul, his very life was falling apart... So we can understand how he remained in Damascus for three days, blind, prostrate, trying to make sense of things. And in that tormenting, vast abyss, Jesus took his place. From that time on Paul was to say, 'My life is Christ.'

All his theology can be found here in embryo, like an intuition which it took him all his life to explore. I shall try to bring out some of its main features here.

Justification by faith. As a Pharisee, Paul believed himself to be justified by his faithful observance of the Law; he thought that everything he did, his efforts, his 'works', as he called them, made him righteous before God. Now he discovered that only Christ could make him righteous. So it was not a matter of achieving his salvation but of receiving it freely, from God's hands, in faith. By believing in God, by holding fast to Christ with all one's being, by having complete confidence in him, one was saved, made righteous. Of course that did not mean that it was enough to believe and then to act in any old way. Those who believe, those who love, try to live accordingly; however, what they then do is not done in order to compel the love of another; it is because they know that they are loved.

The grace of God became a key word in Paul's theology. He discovered that he was loved by God, freely and mercifully. God does not love us because we are good, but in order that we may become good. The source of Paul's joy and security and that of the believer is that they do not rely on what they do or what they are (which can often be demoralizing), but on the love of God, who is faithful.

Jesus Christ crucified. The accursed man hanging on the cross is glorified. Paul tries to understand what this means. If God glorifies him, it is because this death forms part of his plan. So Paul has to reread the scriptures. In particular, the Servant Songs in Second Isaiah give him an answer (see *How to Read the Old Testament*, p. 67). Jesus has not been condemned because of his own sins;

'he was wounded for our transgressions, he was bruised for our iniquities, and with his stripes we are healed' (Isa. 53.4–5). From now on, the cross, always illuminated by the resurrection, will be at the heart of Paul's theology.

It is there, at the feet of the crucified Jesus, that he discovers himself to be a sinner. However, he is a pardoned sinner. Brooding on his sins can only lead to sterile remorse; we see our sins on the faces of others, in the evil that we have done to them. Paul sees this in the tortured figure on the cross. What he sees there above all, however, is forgiveness. From now on, becoming aware of our sin is thanksgiving to God who purifies us from it through Jesus Christ.

The church as the body of Christ. Why are you persecuting me? asks Jesus of the man who is persecuting the Christians. Paul can see the intimate union between Jesus and his disciples: they make up a single body, the church. From now on, this is to be the foundation for Paul's morality: through faith and baptism the Christian puts on Christ, becomes his body, and lives accordingly.

Apostle of Jesus Christ. 'We cannot refrain from speaking,' said the apostles. When someone finds that they are loved with such a love, and it becomes the very meaning of their life, they must want this fact to be known to other people. For Paul, to preach Jesus Christ became a vital necessity (I Cor. 9.16), and to proclaim him to all men, Jews and non-Jews, was a labour of love.

Entry into a tradition. Paul had all the gifts for becoming the leader of a sect: he was intelligent, passionate, chosen directly by God. Yet he was baptized at the hands of Ananias, who does not seem to have been outstanding either for his knowledge or for his courage (Acts 9.13). His call at Damascus, exceptional though it may have been, brought him, humbly, into the tradition of the church. And it was at the moment when he received baptism into this church that his eyes were opened.

It would be wrong to believe that on the Damascus road Paul received a ready-made theology which henceforward he had only to draw on. The Lord had 'made him his own' (Phil. 3.12) or, to take up the imagery I developed earlier (p. 12), had made an impression on him. For this image of the Risen Christ to be revealed fully to Paul, however, he needed the experience of everyday life in contact with different communities, whose questions would force him to deepen his knowledge of Christ. We shall discover that this took place in four main stages. Before we go through them, let's read his letter to the Philippians, in which he opens his heart to us.

Letter to the Philippians

Paul's letters are usually occasional writings; that is, he is replying to questions from a community or dealing with certain doctrinal or moral lapses. His letter to the Philippians, which is perhaps composite, consisting of three different letters, is different. It seems to have been written simply because Paul is very fond of his Philippians, the only church from which he was willing to receive financial help: he had enough confidence in their disinterested love to know that he would not be tied by this help. In the letter, he opens his heart to them, and tells them of his joy and his sufferings (he was in a Roman prison and was feeling sick and discouraged); he shows them his passionate love for Jesus and the meaning which Jesus has given to his life. He is probably writing from Ephesus round about 57.

❤ Philippians 3

You should begin with this chapter.

Paul is the target for attacks from Jews or rather, from Judaizing Christians, that is, Christians who are reverting to Jewish practices in the belief that there they can find security before God (3.1–3; 18–19). For the difficult expressions, see the notes in your Bible or a commentary.

Paul has reason to be confident in himself (3.4–6); how does he see this (3.7–13)? How could we put verse 9 into contemporary language?

Note the significance of both the Christian's passivity (Christ does all things) and his activity (what he must do): how are these two aspects expressed?

Note, too, the expressions which indicate unity with Christ. What does faith mean to Paul?

❤ The letter as a whole

This letter does not present any great difficulties. A good way of studying it would be to read the text straight through, underlining in different colours the following words (or equivalent expressions): Jesus (note the prepositions associated with his name: for, with, in), gospel – joy – suffering.

This letter glows with a feeling of tenderness towards the Lord Jesus who has made Paul his own (3.12), and whom on this one occasion he calls Jesus my Saviour (3.8). The primitive hymn which we have already read (p. 37) sums up the whole mystery of Jesus.

Christian life is the work of God (1.6; 2.13) and it is a life in Christ. This knowledge (3.8) is an indissoluble communion with the suffering and death of Christ (note the expressions which show this for Paul, for Epaphroditus and for the Christians) and his risen life. The Christian life is the work of Christ; Christ is the one who does everything in the believer. Our works are to no effect (3.4ff.).

However, this Christian life should be shown outwardly in actions: prayer (4.6), the glorification of God in our body (1.20; 3.21), unity between Christians (2.1–4), and by a kind of state that can be summed up in the word joy (note the causes of this joy).

Finally, the joy of the Christian consists in proclaiming the gospel, in words but also in his life, and by putting himself at the service of others. For communion with Jesus creates communion among brothers and sisters: note Paul's passionate love for his fellow Christians.

Four stages

We can divide Paul's letters into four groups, which mark so many stages in his thought.

I and II Thessalonians (51)
Paul takes up the main themes of the kerygma; he lives in the hope of the imminent coming of Christ.

I and II Corinthians, Galatians, Philippians, Romans (56–58)
There is one central question here: how can we become righteous and be saved? We are not justified by what we do (works, observing the law) but by faith in Christ. Paul sees the role of Christ above all in his church.

Colossians, Ephesians, Philemon (61–63)
Because he wrote these letters from prison in Rome, they are often called the Captivity Epistles, or Paul's Letters from Prison. Here Paul discovers the place of Christ in history and in the universe.

Titus, I and II Timothy
These Pastoral Letters were written either by Paul before 67 or by a disciple who took up his spiritual legacy after his death. They have one concern: to organize the churches and to keep pure the deposit of faith.

I and II Thessalonians

These letters, which were sent from Corinth in 50–51, are the earliest writings in the New Testament. They introduce us to a very young church founded in a Gentile setting, a minuscule community in a vast city of perhaps 300,000 inhabitants. In it we discover enthusiasm and a brand-new faith, a somewhat disordered hope, and passionate love, all aroused by the preaching of Jesus Christ.

Here Paul touches on the question of eschatology, or reflection on the end of time. He still thinks that the definitive coming of Christ is very near. Some Thessalonians therefore ask what good it is to go on working. Like other Christians, Paul takes time to accept that the delay before this coming – the time of the church – may be a long one (it is still going on!). It is worth singling out some points from these texts, which are sometimes difficult (see the notes in your Bible). Hope does not make the believer immobile: he has to live as though he had eternity before him, while being aware that the Lord is near. It is no use asking how the end will come: it is enough to know that after our death we shall be for ever with the Lord (I Thess. 4.17). To evoke the coming of Christ Paul draws on imagery which will have been well known to the Thessalonians: the *parousia* (a Greek word meaning entrance) of the emperor as he makes a triumphant entry into his city.

In these letters we also find some first preliminary reflections on the ministry of the apostle. This consists essentially in preaching the word. It calls for assurance and faithfulness; these can be recognized from two signs, authenticity and disinterestedness. Paul takes up these two themes at length in II Corinthians.

❤ The Christian life

We could spend some time on the way in which Paul presents the Christian life. It consists in becoming involved in the plan which God had formed from eternity and which he realized in Jesus Christ: in Jesus we are sanctified by the Spirit in order to form the church.

Here are some points that you might study.

God has a loving purpose. Note the terms which express this calling (Greek *klesis*), this choice or election. What kind of God is involved in this call?

God puts his plan into practice through Jesus Christ. Men are challenged, invited to become involved in it, when the word of God is proclaimed to them. Note the expressions which indicate the dynamism, the power of this word which acts in the believer. What is the content of this word? Compare it with the kerygma. The proclamation of this word compels those who hear it to make a choice: they either reject it (in which case, what is the consequence?), or they accept it.

Acceptance of the word is faith, hope and love. These three virtues have already been brought together: in what way are they qualified (verbs and adjectives)?

Faith is acceptance of the Word (I Thess. 2.13; II Thess. 2.13). What role is played by the Spirit? And by man? Try to describe this faith. It is often accompanied by verbs indicating a journey: it is not a question of 'having' faith, but of making the journey, of progressing in faith. And morality, Christian action, is a consequence of this.

Hope is expectation: of what? Note its two characteristics: patience (constancy) and vigilance. How does it fare when faced with the sleep of death?

Christian life is love or life in Christ. Note the expressions which indicate this union with Christ – whether present or future.

It is the Spirit which consecrates and sanctifies. Note the passages in which the Spirit is mentioned. What is his role?

The church (Greek *ek-klesia*) is the community of those who have responded to the call (*klesis*). It is not a group of like-minded people, but a group of people who are chosen by God and who respond to his call. How is that expressed? What consequences might it have for our communities today?

All this is the work of the grace of God and calls forth thanksgiving from the believer. How is that expressed? How is prayer presented?

Thus Christian life is a personal relationship with each of the persons of the Trinity: what is the relationship of each person with the believer, and vice versa?

The Great Letters: Corinthians, Galatians, Romans

Paul spent three years in Ephesus in the period between 53 and 58; from there he wrote several letters to the Corinthians, the Galatians and almost certainly to the Philippians. From Corinth, where he spent the winter of 57–58, he wrote to the Romans.

One question haunted him at the time. What does it mean to say that we are 'saved by Jesus Christ'? He gained a deeper understanding of the role of Christ in the history of salvation, within the community of believers where he is present through the word, the sacraments, and life lived sacrificially.

Christ in the history of salvation

As a Jew, Paul thought that he could find salvation by observing the Law. Now although the Law was holy, since it had been given by God, it had been condemned in Jesus Christ. In order to try to understand what this meant, Paul reread the history of salvation in his own way.

Well before Moses, God had made a unilateral covenant with Abraham: he was the only one to make promises, without imposing any conditions on mankind (read Gen. 15; see *How to Read the Old Testament*, p. 60). If God is righteous, that is to say, faithful, he must give happiness to Abraham and his descendants no matter how they may behave.

Now the people behaved badly. At that time God gave them the Law of Sinai, a bilateral covenant: he committed himself to bringing happiness to his people on condition that they obeyed his commandments (read Ex. 19–20; see *How to Read the Old Testament*, pp. 51, 60). The Law was given by God because the people had sinned. It was a kind of strait-jacket: since the people had proved incapable of obeying God in love, they had to obey him because of the Law. God acts like a father with his son; there is no contract between them, and the father has trust in his son, who obeys him in love. However, if this love should cease, the father will discipline his son with an iron hand, will impose rules on him until he arrives at a better frame of mind. So the Law was given to keep people in the love of God. It is holy, because it comes from God. However, in fact it increases sin because it tells us what we must do without giving us the strength to perform it, to such a degree that with the Law, people are fully aware of their own sinning. So God finds himself in a dilemma: to be righteous and faithful to his covenant with Abraham, he must bless his people; to be righteous according to the covenant made on Sinai, he must abandon the people to the death which they deserve because of their conduct.

God then had this loving idea. Since death stands at the end of the road marked by the Law, he himself will undergo this death in the person of his son; the death of Christ is also that of all sinners in him; thus God is faithful to the agreement made on Sinai. However, he turns this death into a gateway to life: in the risen Christ all men can achieve life and happiness. God is faithful to his promise to Abraham.

So the important thing is for men to be in Christ: united to him by faith and baptism, the believer shares with him in making this transition from death to life; he finds salvation, not in the works that he can do, but in Jesus.

So for the believer the Law is at an end: the only thing that counts is to be created anew in Jesus Christ and to be inspired by his spirit.

Plan of Paul's letters

Paul writes in the manner of his time (for an example, see p. 50).

Address. Letters began: So and So to So and So, Greetings. Paul names both himself and his fellow workers; he names his correspondents and sends them greetings.

Read all the addresses straight through. What is the Christian pattern of greeting?

Prayer. A short prayer was offered to the gods.

Read all the thanksgivings straight through; for what does Paul bless God?

The body of the letter. Paul's letters usually have two parts.

Teaching: Paul develops an important point of teaching, or one that is not properly understood by his Christians.

Exhortation (or *paraenesis*, as some Bibles call it): Paul draws practical consequences from the teaching of which he had just reminded his readers. Morality, or the Christian way of behaving, is based on this teaching.

Salutations. Paul ends by giving news of his fellow workers and greeting the Christians to whom he is writing. He concludes with a short form of blessing.

I CORINTHIANS

Corinth was a busy port, a cosmopolitan city of about 600,000 inhabitants, two-thirds of whom were slaves. It had quite a reputation: 'To live like the Corinthians' meant to have very loose morals. It was there, with the small Christian community, made up of poor people who had enthusiastically come to Christ, that Paul 'invented' Christian ethics. The letter which he wrote to them tried to show how faith in Christ and baptism put a completely different complexion on the various situations of everyday life. We shall return to this point at more length on pp. 55–56.

You should read at least some texts from the letter: the hymn of love (13); the earliest account that we have of the Last Supper (11.17–34) and the early creed that we have already studied (15.1–11, see p. 36); belief in the resurrection of Christ and in our own resurrection (15).

II CORINTHIANS

Relations between Paul and his community were often turbulent; his authority, and consequently the true faith, had been put in question. In this letter Paul defends him-

---

Here is a letter written by a young Egyptian, serving in a Roman legion, to his father on arrival in Italy (a papyrus from the second century AD).

(Salutation and prayer) *Appion to Epimachus, his father and lord, heartfelt greetings. Above all, I hope that you are well and that all continues to go well with you, and also with my sister, her daughter and my brother.*

I thank the Lord Serapis for having saved me when I was in danger on the sea.

(Content) *As soon as I arrived at Misenum, I received from Caesar my travel allowance: three gold pieces. That was good. I beg you, my lord father, write me a short letter, first about your health, secondly about the health of my brothers, and thirdly so that I can revere your hand, since you brought me up well. That is why I hope for rapid promotion, if the gods are gracious.*

(Final salutation) *Many greetings to Capito, my brothers, Serenilla and my friends. I am sending you my portrait by Euthemon. My military name is Antonius Maximus, a centurion of the Athenonike. I hope that you are well. Serenus, son of Agathos Daimon, greets you, as does Turbo, son of Gallonios.*

The address can be read on the back: *To Philadelphia, for Epimachus from his son Appion. To be sent by the first Apamean cohort of Juluis Antonius, to the secretary, from Appion, to be delivered to Epimachus, his father.*

---

self, and the greater part of it is devoted to the apostolic ministry as Paul sees it (1.11–7.16). He feels the tremendous responsibility that he bears: as he presents the word of God, he knows that he is offering his audience the choice to be for or against Christ (2.14–4.44). The passage in which Paul demonstrates that thanks to Jesus the Christian reads the scriptures in a new way and at last understands their true meaning may seem to you to be rather complicated, but in it you will discover at least one very fine affirmation: the Christian who accepts Christ is transfigured by the glory of God which shone on the face of Jesus, and he is illuminated by it in order to give light to his brothers (3.5–4.6).

In Jesus, who died because of the sin with which he identified himself (5.21), God has reconciled us to himself; in Christ, henceforth we are a new creation.

If you want to see the sufferings which Paul endured and at the same time the grace with which he was blessed, read 11.16–12.10.

Finally, in 13.14 you will recognize a blessing which can still be heard in churches today: it is the first clear attestation of belief in the Trinity.

GALATIANS

These rather foolish Galatians are the first cousins of the Gauls; like the Gauls, they were impulsive, engaging and freedom-loving. They gave Paul's preaching an enthusiastic welcome and committed themselves to Christ. However, other preachers came, and they began to 'Judaize', that is, they added Jewish practices to their Christian faith. Although they were former pagans, they submitted to the yoke of the Jewish Law. No doubt they were well-meaning, but Paul sensed danger: if you have to add anything (in this case, Jewish practices) to Christian faith, it is a sign that faith in Jesus is not enough to save us. Paul launches a passionate counter-attack, drawing on all his theology, and it is rather complicated! Finally, however, he asks his Christians only one question: 'Do you remember what you became through your commitment to Jesus Christ? Are you faithful to your baptismal promises?'

After a very lively introduction, Paul defends the gospel that he preaches, in three stages.

Where does his gospel come from? He received it directly from Christ, on the Damascus road (1.11–2.21).

What is the content of his gospel? Rereading the history of the people of God, he shows that the Law was merely an escort to lead us to Christ. Now that we have come to him, we no longer need it (3–4). As you read these passages you will find some very fine statements: on faith in Christ (2.16, 20), on Abraham (3.6–14), on the equality of all men in Christ Jesus (3.26–29), and on the spirit of sonship (4.6–7).

Where does his gospel lead to? To freedom (5–6). For a Christian there are no more commandments; only this inner law, the Holy Spirit, which is in the heart of every believer and tells him what he must do. 'In Christ you are a new creation; live as free men' (5)!

The letter to the Galatians is a polemical letter. It has a great many obscure passages, but Paul's passion gives it an extraordinary feel. Read it without bothering too much about the difficult phrases; they will make more sense later – perhaps!

Some months later, Paul took up the same ideas in a longer piece of writing which remains one of the high points of his thought: the letter to the Romans.

ROMANS

There have been many different analyses of the letter to the Romans. This one may help.

In the doctrinal part (1–11), Paul develops the same idea in four different ways.

As a statistician, he makes an observation: all men, whether or not they are Jews, are sinners; they all need to be saved by Jesus Christ (1.18–5.11).

As a believer, he begins his reflections by noting what we became at baptism: baptism united us with Jesus, who died and rose again and is the new Adam, the second first man. In him we are a new creation (5.12–7.6). (For original sin see How to Read the Old Testament, p. 41).

As a psychologist, he shows us that man is torn inwardly between the good which he wants to do but cannot, and the evil which he does not want to do and yet does (7.7–25). The spirit unifies the believer again by reconciling him with God, whom he can call 'Abba, Father', with others and with the whole universe (8).

Finally, as a historian he rereads the history of Israel: he shows the tragedy of Israel's refusal to recognize the Christ; he proclaims that Israel will be saved when all the people do recognize Christ as Messiah (9–11).

In the moral section (12–15), he draws the consequences of this faith for everyday life (see p. 54).

You should read at least Rom. 6–8, pausing over certain passages.

❦ Baptism. Rom. 6.1–7.6

Paul wants to reply to an objection which might arise from

what has gone before: he shows that the Christian need no longer sin. As usual, he bases this ethical statement on doctrine.

Look for some of the important words which colour this text (unfortunately they are now translated in any old way in our Bibles): baptize (in Greek, the word means dip into); serve, servant (or slave, 6.6, 19; read I Thess. 1.9; for the transition from servitude to service see How to Read the Old Testament, p. 31); offer oneself – in the Greek Bible, this word often expresses the offering of oneself to God in worship, e.g. Deut. 10.8; 17.12; 18.5, 7; 21.5, and in Rom. 6.13 (twice); 6.16, 19; 12.1; obey, 6.12, 16 (three times), 19; this verb sometimes defines the Christian: Rom. 10.16; I Peter 1.2, 14, 22.

Note the contrasts: formerly/now; new/old (6.4; 7.6); death/life; wages/free gift (do we 'deserve' heaven?).

Note the comparisons between the destiny of Christ and that of the believer; in particular see the expressions which mark the similarity: as, with, like. . . By whom is Christ raised (see 6.14; 8.11; Col. 2.12)?

Look again at the tenses of the verbs. What is in the past? What is in the future?

Given all these observations, what meaning is attached to baptism in this passage?

If you have time, you might like to look at other images of baptism in Paul:
bathe, be washed: I Cor. 6.11; Eph. 5.26; Titus 3.5.
be buried with Christ: Gal. 3.27; Col. 3.9.
be sealed, as a mark of ownership: II Cor. 1.21f.; Eph. 1.13; 4.30.
illumination: Eph. 5.14.

❦ Life in the Spirit. Romans 8

Romans 7 showed us man divided: even if some passages are obscure (with their reference to earthly paradise and to the Law) we can easily recognize ourselves in this tragic description. Is there any hope? (Be careful about the word 'flesh' in Paul: it does not denote sexuality, as we might say 'the sins of the flesh', but the whole of man as he rejects God; the old man, or the sinful ego.)

Romans 8 shows how the Spirit unifies the believer again. Note how it brings him into communion with God, with himself, with others, indeed with the universe.

You should study the hymn to the love of God which ends this part (Rom. 8.31–39).

Note the context of a trial that we find here. On whom can we rely in order to win? On ourselves? On God?

What is the ultimate assurance of the believer?

The Letters from Prison: Colossians, Ephesians, Philemon

Between 58 and 63, Paul spent four years in prison, first in Caesarea and then in Rome. He had time to meditate. An opportunity to think more deeply about the mystery of Christ was presented to him by the Colossians, who were tempted to locate Christ among the various heavenly powers whom some believed to exist between God and men. Paul succeeded in bringing together his thought by placing Christ at the heart of the universe and of the church. He expresses this in his letter to the Colossians (and also in his letter to the Ephesians, which in some respects is similar and may even have been written by a disciple) and his note to Philemon.

The note to Philemon is the most personal of Paul's letters; in it he comes fully to life. Here we can guess at the nature of life in a church which has grown up in the Gentile world. People have been amazed that Paul does not call for the abolition of slavery. However, he does something better than that: by establishing the equality and even the brotherhood of all men, masters and slaves, he overthrows this institution from within.

In his letter to the Colossians, thanks above all to what he discovered in scripture about the Wisdom of God (see *How to Read the Old Testament*, pp. 92–93), Paul succeeds in placing Christ in relationship to God – he is the Son in whom the fullness of the deity dwells – and in relationship to the world – he is the one by whom and for whom all things were made. This gives our human life new meaning: since nothing escapes the influence of Christ, when we construct the earthly city we are also, mysteriously, building the kingdom of God. From now on we should live as though we were already risen with Christ (3.1–4).

🐦 The Lord of the world. Col. 1.15–20

Here two strophes are hinged on a central verse: 16d–17a sum up the first strophe, 17b–18a the second.

Begin by looking for corresponding expressions: the prepositions used (in, by, for), the titles given to Christ. Some come from the Old Testament. What do they mean? (For 'image', see *How to Read the Old Testament*, p. 93.)

The first strophe presents the place and role of Christ in the universe: what are they? The second presents the place and role of Christ in mankind reconciled with God, in the church: what are they?

The letter to the Ephesians offers a harmonious synthesis of Paul's thought. It does not present any great difficulties. As you read it, you will find some very fine passages. Let me single out some of them: the majestic hymn on God's plan of bringing all things together in his Son (1.3–14); the reconciliation of all beings in Jesus Christ (2); a fine prayer that we should be rooted in the love of Christ (3.14–21); the organization of the church (4.1–16, a text that we have already studied, p. 37); an old hymn quoted in 5.14: the church as bride of Christ, and marriage (5.21–33).

Two images of the church

Paul uses two complementary images to present the church; both are necessary.

The church is the body of which Christ is the head, receiving from him its vital impulses. The advantage of this image is that it shows the unity between the church and Christ.

The church is the bride of Christ. The advantage of this image is that it shows that Christ and the church remain two entities: the church is not holy as Christ is, but its love is constantly called forth by his own.

The Pastoral Epistles: Timothy, Titus

Whether they were written by Paul, or by a disciple after his death, these letters clearly show his preoccupations at the end of his life: to keep intact the faith in Jesus Christ received from the apostles. Here the church already seems to have a structure, with different ministries, notably the episcopate and the diaconate. They also allow us to share in the praise of the early church, thanks to the hymns which they quote: I Tim. 2.5–6; 3.16; 6.15–16; II Tim. 2.8–13.

Hebrews and the Catholic Epistles

JAMES

It was Saturday evening in a country church: a woman from the parish read the epistle, splendidly, a passage from James on riches. Our breath was taken away by the relevance of these words. 'Do you believe?' asks the author (writing between AD 60 and 80). 'That remains to be seen. Show me the practical consequences of your faith, and first of all your regard and your love for the poor. Otherwise, your faith is not true. . .'

HEBREWS

This is not a letter so much as the sermon which a pupil of Paul's addresses, round about AD 70, to some disoriented Christians. They are Jews who committed themselves to Christ enthusiastically; now, however, they have become disillusioned and miss the fine ceremonies of Judaism. They have suffered for their faith as Christians, and now new difficulties are imminent. The author tells them off: 'You suffer too much in comparison with what you believe; give up the "milk and water" of the children's catechism; you must deepen your faith. Are you bewildered by what is happening now, by your difficulties? Fix your gaze on the leader of the faith, Christ our high priest.'

In a constant mixture of teaching and exhortation, the author meditates on Pss. 2 and 110 and refers to the ceremony of Yom Kippur, the Day of Atonement, which was well known to his readers. This was the only day in the year when the high priest could go into the holiest part of the Temple, where God dwelt; he took blood there to obtain forgiveness for sins.

This is an image: if we are truly to be able to enter God's presence, it is necessary that Christ, the high priest, should have appeared there with his own blood, i.e. the offering of his life. The Jewish priest had to perform the same ritual all over again every year, but Christ entered once for all into the presence of God, thus definitively giving us access to him. Now, with our eyes fixed on Christ, we must go towards the promised land in faith and hope, without flagging.

You should read at least some passages: 5.1–10 on the humanity of Christ; 7.20–28 on Jesus the only priest; 9–10, the new covenant; 11, the journey in faith.

I PETER

This letter almost certainly comes from Rome and was written round about AD 64. It is not read often, which is a pity, because apart from some pieces of out-of-date teaching, it fits our present situation very well. Peter is addressing the exiles of the dispersion (Greek Diaspora); these do not form a racial or national group, but are a great brotherhood spread over the world (5.9), united in the same faith and the same pattern of moral and social conduct, which has to stand out clearly from that of their contemporaries.

The doctrinal part (1.1–2.10) develops some great themes of scripture which make it possible to live like this: the Exodus; the Suffering Servant of Isaiah who offers himself for the salvation of all; the stone rejected by the builders which God has made the foundation stone; the image of Jesus rejected by his people but exalted by God, on whom Christians, as living stones, build up a spiritual edifice.

The second part of this baptismal catechism draws some practical conclusions from this: they can be summed up in the need to conduct oneself well among non-believers (see p. 54). And Peter gives a magnificent definition of witness (3.15).

This new people of God has come into being in dispersion; it is called from amidst the nations, where it lives without ever ceasing to belong to them. A people in exodus, its purpose is to proclaim by its praise and its conduct the mighty acts of the one who has called it from darkness to his wonderful light (2.9).

JUDE

This letter is sometimes disconcerting, and makes use of some contemporary Jewish texts. It was written in 80 or 90 to put Christians on their guard against false teachings.

II PETER

Although this letter is attributed to Peter, it was written at the beginning of the second century. It calls on Christians to remain faithful to their vocation, despite false preaching, even if the coming of Christ is delayed. At least look at its interpretation of the Transfiguration (1.16–18) and its definition of the inspiration of scripture (1.20–21).

Paul's Christ

At each stage I shall try to present Paul's Christ, Mark's Christ, Luke's Christ and so on.

That's a risk, since such brief portraits are inevitably subjective. But at least they will help us to see that the New Testament does not give us a single picture of Christ: his personality is too rich to be capable of representation in a single picture, and everyone develops his own perspective from what he is and what he has experienced. Every Christian, every community today, offers the world a different face of Christ. All these different aspects enable us to get nearer to the one who remains invisible to us.

In Paul's life there is a before and an after: Damascus is a threshhold. Before, Paul was a Pharisee and, because of his faith, was against Jesus, whose disciples he persecuted. Afterwards, he was utterly devoted to the one who had seized hold of him on the road. Peter, John and the first disciples slowly discovered the personality of their master, and it was only after Easter and Pentecost that they began to feel that their friend was Son of God. They resemble those Christians of today, baptized from birth, who have to discover from within the nature of the faith which they have received. Paul is akin to the converts whose life is turned upside down, in a moment.

Unlike the evangelists, Paul did not write a book in which we can find his thought in final form: he wrote letters, very much governed by circumstances, and in them we can see the development of his discovery of Christ.

The one who was accursed is glorified

The one whom Paul thought to be accursed by God, since he had been condemned by the religious authorities and by the Law, now appeared to him in the glory of God: as we have seen, this is the source of Paul's thinking. He puts this appearance on the same level as the appearances of the Risen Lord to his disciples; because of it, he is an apostle in just the same way as they are (see the various forms of address in which he declares himself to be 'called to be an apostle', and I Cor. 15.9; 9.1; Gal. 1.1).

Paul certainly did not know Jesus during his earthly life; right from the start, he encountered him as the risen and glorified Lord.

The Lord who comes

Paul presents his experience on the Damascus road as a 'revelation' (Gal. 1.16). The first stage of his Christian life was marked by the astonished enthusiasm of the convert who has been seized by Christ. He was so fully aware of the life of Christ in him and the new world to which he had been introduced by baptism that he had only one desire, that the day of the Lord, the Parousia, should come quickly and put an end to history. Paul began his ministry living, and making his fellow Christians live, in imminent expectation of the Lord who was to come.

The crucified one who brings salvation

However, the parousia delayed. People had to hang on. Above all, Paul made a fuller discovery of Greek thought and its concern for human wisdom (I Cor. 1–2). Without doubt his failure at Athens left a mark on him (Acts 17). He puts more and more stress on the theology of the cross, which to begin with he had left rather in the shade: I decided to know nothing among you but Jesus Christ and him crucified (II Cor. 2.2). Paul becomes more acutely aware of the weakness of the Law: the justice which comes from the Law and from all that we do is of no account; we are saved by grace, by unconditional commitment to Christ by faith and baptism. The new Adam is the second 'first man' of a new world.

All through his letters to the Corinthians, the Philippians, the Galatians, the Romans, he shows in concrete terms what must be the nature of everyday life with Christ, *in Christ*, the significance of being saved by the cross.

The Lord of the world and of history

Paul's reflection through his four years in prison, his meditation on the scriptures, and in particular the wisdom texts, and the crisis with the Colossians, led him to accord Christ his true place in the universe. Christ is not just the saviour of his community, he is the Lord of history, the image of the invisible God, the firstborn of all creation, the creator of the universe, by whom and for whom all things were made. He is the one in whom God seeks to bring all together. He is Lord to the glory of the Father.

Christian Action or Christian Morality

The Christian way of life, what we call morality, does not appear in the New Testament in the form of commandments and prohibitions. Throughout the Epistles and the Gospels we can see a common teaching: united to Jesus by faith and baptism, we become a new being; from now on, therefore, we must live like new beings. We must imitate the Father, whose children we have become, and his Son, and allow ourselves to be guided by the Spirit. It is by living our everyday existence in this way that we offer spiritual worship to God.

A baptismal catechism

At a very early stage baptism seems to have been accompanied by a catechism, instructions which developed the consequences of baptism for everyday life. In fact we find the same pattern, taking up the same themes, in different writings, but all in the context of baptism. Here's one example.

If you have time, read I Peter 2.1–10. The author presents baptism as a new birth (v. 2); the newly born, built on Christ as a living stone, become a community. From now on they can offer their spiritual worship to Christ (v. 5). The author then develops some aspects of this worship, which consists in behaving well in the midst of pagans (v. 11); he describes how people should behave before the authorities (2.13–17), how servants should behave to their masters (2.18–25), wives to their husbands and husbands to their wives (3.1–7), and how Christians should behave in the community (3.8–12).

James sums up the same teaching: new birth (James 1.17–18); the consequences for daily life (1.26–27).

Paul reminds the Colossians that baptism is dying and living with Christ (Col. 2.20; 3.1) and he continues: live accordingly (3.5). He first says this in general terms (3.5–17), and then takes up this teaching to apply it to each category of the faithful (3.18–4.1).

After reminding the Ephesians of their baptism (5.14), the author talks about how they should live (5.15) and develops the same themes (5.21–6.9).

If you don't have much time, you could read just I Peter 2.1–5 and Rom. 12.1–2. In Rom. 6, Paul has recalled his teaching on baptism, and then, in Rom. 7–8, has shown how the Christian lives inspired by the Spirit. In Rom. 12 he develops the practical consequences: the true worship that we must offer to God is the offering of our very persons, daily life lived in a certain way in a certain spirit. The rest of ch. 12 traces out the main lines of authentic Christian behaviour.

Norms for Christian action

For a Christian, the Law no longer holds. He must be guided only by the Spirit; he must live as one who is united with Christ and who imitates the Father.

The Spirit as the 'law' of the Christian. Jeremiah had announced that God would remake his covenant and put the law in the heart of every believer (Jer. 31.31–34), and Ezekiel had given its name to this 'law': the Spirit (Ezek. 36.26–27). Paul takes up this teaching and develops it, in particular in his letter to the Galatians: Christ has freed you, so allow yourselves to be led by the Spirit (see Gal. 5, especially 5.1, 13, 18, 22–25).

Life in Christ. Christian morality consists in living our lives as the new beings we have become once faith and baptism have united us with Christ. Become what you are is a good summary of the thought which Paul takes up in so many ways. You can see this from a great many texts. To keep things simple, we shall limit ourselves to I Corinthians.

One might say that in writing to his Corinthians, Paul invented Christian morality. These Gentiles had committed themselves to Christ with enthusiasm. However, one cannot change overnight from one kind of life (for Corinth read Soho or 42nd Street, New York, to get some idea of the atmosphere) to life in Christ. So Paul tried to work out with the Corinthians how this new life should change their behaviour. He did not say to them, 'You must . . . that's forbidden. . .' He asked them, 'What did you become through your faith? What is its consequence?' So his letter is a succession of specific instances.

As you read some texts, see what the particular issue is and what Paul appeals to as the basis of his morality.

Petty squabbles (I Cor. 1.10–4.21). The Christians adopt rival leaders (1.11–12). To what does Paul refer in an attempt to restore unity? See 1.13; 3.16–17.

A disreputable Christian who is living with his stepmother (5). How does Paul deal with this? See 5.7–8.

Christians who go to law (6.1–11). How does Paul deal with this? See 6.11.

Christians who set themselves above morality (6.12–20)! What does Paul refer to, to remind them of the Christian understanding of the body? See 6.15, 19–20.

Is the Christian condemned to the ghetto (8–10)? Underlying this strange problem of meat sacrificed to idols is a very topical question: what is the status of the Christian in the world? In Paul's day, meat offered to idols in the temples and not consumed was sold in the market; every Christian ran the risk of buying some. If he was to be certain of not doing this, was he to give up meat, or have a Christian butcher? Are Christians condemned to living in a ghetto, to creating their own Christian institutions (from trade unions to schools)? For Paul, the only principle was love (8.1–3). All that God has created is good, provided that one accepts it with thanksgiving (I Tim. 4.4–5). So Christians are free to eat meat and to resort to civic institutions. However, love counts above their rights: if by doing this one risks causing offence, it is better to refrain (I Cor. 8.9–13).

Like the Father. Since faith and baptism unite us to Jesus, and the Spirit makes us sons of God (Rom. 8.15–16), the only rule is to be holy as the Father is holy. Matthew stresses this in the great catechism which he puts on the lips of Jesus in the Sermon on the Mount.

You might read the Sermon on the Mount (Matthew 5–7), underlining all the mentions of the Father. What significance does this give to all these 'laws'?

Read the parable of the merciless servant (Matt. 18.23–25). How should the disciple behave in imitating the Father (God)? He should forgive because he knows himself to be forgiven: that is the basic attitude of the Christian.

Under grace

You are no longer under the Law but under grace, Paul says yet again (Rom. 6.14). 'Should you not have had pity on your fellow servant, as I had pity on you?' asks the master (Matt. 18.33). This was the foundation of morality for the first Christians.

It is not a matter of *doing* something, of earning one's salvation, but of *receiving* it in thanksgiving (see p. 46 again: 'Justified by faith'). Because we know that we are loved freely, by grace; because we know that we are forgiven, we feel the need to love God in return and to love others, to pardon them, to hand on to them what we ourselves have received. We do not practise morality because we are Christian but because we are human; we do not perform works in order to obtain salvation, but because it has been freely given to us. What we do, our 'works', are not like a bunch of flowers which a child gives to its mother in order to be allowed to go to play with a friend, but like the bunch of flowers the child gives on Mothering Sunday, because it knows that it is loved and wants to express the fact. The Christian aspect of morality does not lie primarily in what we do but in the sense that we give it: the wife who irons her husband's shirt does not do it better or less well than the laundry worker, but for her the shirt is her husband's.

Amazed at being so loved, at being freely pardoned, the Christian, in Jesus, inspired by the Spirit, wants to be like his heavenly Father and to hand on to all the joy which Christians receive from him.

4 The Gospel according to Mark

Mark and the lion. Keystone of the rood-loft at Chartres (thirteenth century)

Mark is generally given the honour of having invented the new literary genre of the Gospel. Jesus proclaimed the gospel, that is, the good news that, through him, the kingdom of God had come. Mark wrote a book presenting the good news about Jesus. The one who proclaimed, Jesus, became the subject of the proclamation: it was now his words and his actions which were proclaimed as the good news, the gospel. And the title given to this kind of book from the second century onwards is significant: the Gospel *according to* Mark, the Gospel *according to* Luke, and so on. Jesus proclaimed a single gospel; the evangelists present the life of Jesus as they saw it, in accordance with what they had discovered; they give their testimony.

Of course Mark did not make it all up himself. Words and actions of Jesus had been brought together before him, first orally and then in writing. Several collections already existed: a collection of sayings (or logia), an account of the passion from the arrest of Jesus to his burial, and doubtless other sequences (see p. 15). As the first to write a book which brought them all together, Mark imposed a geographical and chronological framework on the life of Jesus, a framework which Matthew and Luke were to take up after him (but not John). This framework is useful but, as we shall see, it is more theological than historical: Mark does not claim to represent events as they actually happened. He offers a certain view of the ministry of Jesus as seen by him and the community whose spokesman he was.

Mark's community

It is generally accepted that the first Gospel was written in Rome, about AD 70, and takes up the preaching of Peter. Round about 110, the bishop Papias was already writing: 'Mark was an interpreter of Peter and wrote down

carefully what he remembered – though not in order – what was said or done by the Lord. He had in fact neither heard the Lord nor followed him, but later on, as I said, he followed Peter. The latter formulated his teachings as was needed, though without making an ordered composition of the oracles of the Lord.'

The indications that we can note in his work fit this tradition very well. His community was made up of former Gentiles: Mark is obliged to translate Aramaic words and to explain certain Jewish customs. We can understand the importance attached to the evangelization of Gentiles, and it is no chance that the finest confession of faith occurs on the lips of the Roman centurion at the foot of the cross.

This community was threatened with persecutions. The faith which Mark presents is not a quiet faith: it comes up against opposition and is forced to take risks. That fits in very well with what we know of the church of Rome under Nero. Peter suffered martyrdom in AD 64.

So this is a community 'dispersed among the Gentiles', as Peter wrote in his letter.

The author

The author of the Gospel was almost certainly the young John Mark mentioned in Acts (12.12). He left on a missionary journey with his uncle Barnabas and Paul, but he left them when they embarked for Asia Minor and preferred to return home to his mother (Acts 13.5, 13)! Paul refused to take him on his second mission; this will have been the cause of his parting from Barnabas (Acts 15.36f.). However, they were later reconciled, since we find Mark at Paul's side again during his imprisonment by the Romans (Col. 4.10), and Peter indicates in his letter that Mark, his son, is with him in Rome (I Peter 5.13).

A millstone closing the entrance to a tomb

57

The Gospel as a Whole

All too often we know only separate bits of the Gospels. So first of all, you are invited to take a guided tour (for Mark, this will take about an hour). You will certainly be amazed at how interesting you will find it.

If you have time, take the Gospel of Mark and read it purely for pleasure. At the end, take stock of your impressions: see what has delighted you, what has astonished you, what you have discovered. If one particular feature has caught your eye (the titles given to Jesus, the way people look at him), you can read the Gospel again and take special notice of this theme.

If you have less time, and want to take a guided tour straight away, here are some points of interest.

Geography

Mark has given a very simple framework to the life of Jesus. After his baptism in the Jordan (1.1–13), Jesus preaches in Galilee (1.14–9.50), goes up to Jerusalem (10), preaches and dies in Jerusalem (11.1–16.8); the angel of the resurrection announces that the disciples are to gather together again in Galilee.

However, the Gospels are not Ordnance Survey maps; their geography is primarily theological. If you compare the maps in the margin, you will see to what extent they differ among themselves.

In Mark, Galilee is opposed to Jerusalem.

Galilee of the nations, or Galilee of the Gentiles, as it was called at that time, had experienced many invasions, and in the eyes of the religious authorities belief there was not very pure. Nothing good could come out of Galilee, far less a prophet (cf. John 1.46; 7.52). However, Isaiah (8.23) had announced that one day God would manifest himself there to the Gentiles, so Galilee was also a symbol of hope and opportunity. Now it was there that Jesus was born, lived and preached, and the crowds gave him an enthusiastic welcome. This region was opened up; from there Jesus went to the Gentiles in Tyre and Sidon (7.24, 31).

By contrast, Jerusalem seems to be a city shut in on itself, a refuge for the godfearing, certain of their truth and not allowing any contradiction. From the beginning of the ministry of Jesus, in Galilee onwards, the fiercest attacks on him came from Jerusalem (3.22).

The two shores of the lake

Jewish shore — Gentile shore

Sidon
Tyre
Caesarea Philippi
Capernaum
Nazareth
Gadara
The way of obedience
Jericho
Jerusalem

Lake Tiberias is no longer neutral: the west bank is Jewish and the east bank is Gentile. Constantly, and despite the storm, Jesus draws his disciples towards the Gentile shore, in this way preparing them for a mission which they will find it difficult to understand.

The mystery of Jesus

From his very first words, Mark lets his readers into the secret: the Gospel of Jesus, Christ, Son of God. Two titles appear beside his name, Jesus, which identifies him as a man: Christ/Messiah and Son of God. John the Baptist claims to be the forerunner of the Messiah, and the Father proclaims to Jesus that he is his Son (1.1–13). So the reader knows what is going on. However, from this point on he is invited to share with the disciples their slow discovery of the mystery of Jesus. This takes place in two stages.

In the first stage (1.14–8.26), Jesus proclaims the imminent coming of the kingdom of God, and gives signs of its coming, miracles. However, he refuses to say who he is and forbids the demons to divulge it: there is a secret, what has been called the 'messianic secret'. The only title which Jesus applies to himself is the mysterious title Son of man.

The second part (8.27–16.8) begins with Peter's proclamation, 'You are the Messiah.' We have the impression that Jesus breathes a sigh of relief; one step has been taken: his disciples have seen one part of his mystery. At the same time, however, he is disturbed: there is a risk that they, too, will get the wrong idea about the Messiah, will see in him the liberator who will establish the kingdom of Israel by force of arms. He forbids Peter to communicate his discovery, and at the same time leads his disciples towards the second stage: the Son of man will suffer and be put to death!

In a series of controversies at Jerusalem (11–13), Jesus introduces another title, Son of David. That, too, is dangerous, and only heightens the opposition from the religious authorities. Here we are at the heart of the drama. These authorities were looking for the Messiah, and one would expect that they were most qualified to recognize him when he appeared. However, they had a very precise idea of him, *their* idea. Now Jesus presented himself as the Messiah, but he did not correspond to their ideal. Opposition between these two conceptions became so strong that someone had to die: either the authorities had to die to the notions they had previously entertained and accept this disconcerting Messiah, or they would persevere with their ideas and Jesus had to die. Because he knows that he is already condemned, and that there is therefore no danger that he will be taken to be a temporal Messiah, in the dramatic scene of the judgment before the Sanhedrin Jesus clearly declares himself to be Christ. And he is condemned to death.

However, at the foot of the cross a Gentile takes over and finally recognizes Jesus as Son of God. Jesus, condemned by the Sanhedrin, and the centurion, over the corpse of a crucified man, tell us the journey that has to be made for the confession of Christian faith to be true.

And by means of this drama, Mark continues to make us ask questions. Jesus is disconcerting! Are you ready to die to the idea you have of him, in order to accept him as he is?

🦊 During your reading you might underline in different colours the titles given to Jesus, the people who recognize him, etc.

A human drama

Jesus did not leave anyone indifferent. As soon as he appeared, groups formed and there were questioners, friendly or hostile. Right at the beginning, Jesus chose disciples, particularly the Twelve, to be with him. This was the first group, which was often under strain because of the disciples' failure to understand. The family of Jesus rarely appears, and when it does, it tends to be hostile. There is always a crowd; Jesus loves the people and makes his disciples serve them. However, this crowd is fickle. Jesus' enemies come from Jerusalem; they appear right at the beginning and are unrelenting.

🦊 You could assign a colour to each group and by marking your Bible, see how they come up against one another and clash, and also how people can change sides.

As you go through the Gospel, you can distinguish six stages.

1.14–3.6. Each of the groups establishes its position.

3.7–6.6. The break between Jesus on the one hand and his enemies and kinsfolk on the other is complete. Taken out of the crowd, the disciples are given private teaching (parables and miracles).

6.6–8.26. A rift develops between Jesus and his disciples: they do not understand his mission or their own. Jesus sends them out on a mission and shows them that his table is open to all (the feeding of the multitudes); he makes them serve the crowd and draws them towards the Gentile side of the lake. They remain deaf and blind; this is represented by two miracles.

8.27–10.52. The disciples do not understand the course of suffering on which Jesus is leading them (see 10.32).

11.1–13.37. In Jerusalem, Jesus confronts his adversaries (the parable of the vineyard); the story of the withered fig tree symbolizes their situation.

14.1–16.8. Jesus prepares his disciples for the drama, but in vain. He dies alone. However, the angel of the resurrection puts the disciples on their way; only when they get to 'Galilee', i.e. to the end of the world and the end of history, to which Jesus has gone before them, will they 'see' the Risen Lord. The conclusion (16.9–20, as your Bible will indicate) was added later.

Some features of Mark

Mark is written in a popular style; he deliberately substitutes 'and' or 'immediately' for other conjunctions, and some of his phrases aren't quite right. For example, he writes: 'The blind man beginning to see said, "I see people, it is as if they were trees which I see walking" ' (8.24). He uses words which were considered vulgar at the time (2.11 might be translated 'pick up your sack'), and is not afraid of repetitions.

Mark is a marvellous storyteller. He does not have many speeches. His narratives are always specific and lively, sprinkled with touches from real life. The verbs are often in the present tense, which makes his accounts so vivid, but he also mixes tenses. The use of the word 'for' on numerous occasions appeals to a logic which disconcerts us ('. . . for she was twelve years old', at the end of the story of the raising of Jairus' daughter, 5.42).

He makes an emotional impact, less by his appeal to our feelings than by his blunt account of the facts: this is particularly evident in the account of the passion.

Mark's Gospel has been called the Gospel of before Easter; it shows us Jesus through the eyes of Peter as he follows his master on the roads of Palestine. But Mark is also a profound theologian, and he retells the life of Jesus in the light of Easter.

Some Texts from Mark

We have now read Mark straight through. Next, we shall be reading some texts from the Gospel in more detail. You won't be able to study them all, so choose!

❦ Title. 1.1

Mark proclaims Christian faith in a terse phrase. He also announces the stages through which the disciples had to go (and still have to go) to arrive at it. This title, like the prologue to the Gospel of John and the infancy narratives in Matthew and Luke, shows the theological profundity which Christians had achieved forty years after Easter.

Beginning. The ministry of Jesus ushers in something new in history, a new creation ('beginning' is the first word of Genesis). This is a beginning which opens up all the period of our history. There is a task to be performed!

Gospel. This word, 'good news', takes us back to the announcement made by Second Isaiah (see *How to Read the Old Testament*, p. 67). Compare this gospel of Mark with that of Jesus (Mark 1.14–15); the difference I pointed out on p. 57 leaps out at us: Jesus proclaimed the good news of the coming of the kingdom of God; Mark proclaims the good news about Jesus. The one who proclaims has become the subject of the proclamation! From now on the arrival of the kingdom of God is embodied in the person of Jesus.

Jesus. This simple name evokes the human aspect of the 'carpenter, the son of Mary and brother of James, Joses, Jude and Simon', whose sisters are also known (Mark 6.3). He is a man, but also someone quite different.

Christ. Jesus is the Messiah announced by scripture, the one whom God was to anoint in order to invest him with his mission and establish his kingdom. We have seen how Mark's Jesus rejects this title and forbids anyone to attribute it to him ('the messianic secret'); Peter proclaims it at Caesarea Philippi, but Jesus compels him to keep quiet, and foretells his sufferings (8.29–30). He only accepted the title when he was condemned (14.61–62).

Son of God. In the time of Jesus this title was virtually equivalent to Son of David. After Easter it gradually took on the stronger significance which we now attach to it. The Gentile at the foot of the cross was charged with proclaiming it.

❦ The baptism of Jesus. 1.9–11

The baptism is indicated by one word (Matthew and Luke mention it in a subordinate clause and John doesn't mention it at all). The essential feature is the theophany (or manifestation of God) in action and in word.

The heavens opening is a theme from apocalyptic. The heavens are 'closed' because there are no longer any prophets; the spirit does not come down to guide the people any more; history has therefore come to an impasse. However, people waited for the end of time, when the heavens would open (see the box below). By using a term which should be translated 'rent' here, Mark is clearly seeing the event as a response to the anguished appeal of Isa. 63–64; read that text, and especially 63.10–13, 19. How does it illuminate this scene?

The symbolism of the dove remains obscure. Hosea 11.11 and IV Esdras (a Jewish writing which appeared for a while in the Latin Bible) compare the people to a dove. That would signify that the coming of the Spirit on Jesus is to constitute the new people of God.

The voice brings together several texts. 'My son' comes from Ps. 2, 'beloved' from Gen. 22.2, 12, 16 (the sacrifice of Isaac); this is the only time when the phrase 'beloved son' occurs in the Old Testament. To be well pleased with: Isa. 62.4; 42.1 (quoted by Matt. 12.17). What meaning does the saying take on in the light of this?

What we have here seems to be a private experience of Jesus: it is his investiture as Messiah, perhaps the Messiah destined for sacrifice, as Isaac was.

'The heavens shall be opened, and from the temple of glory shall come upon him sanctification, with the Father's voice as from Abraham to Isaac. And the glory of the Most High shall be uttered over him, and the spirit of understanding and sanctification shall rest upon him' (Testament of Levi 18.6–8).

'And a man shall arise from my seed, like the sun of righteousness, walking with the sons of men in meekness and righteousness; and no sin shall be found in him. And the heavens shall be opened unto him, to pour out the spirit, the blessing of the Holy Father. And he shall pour out the spirit of grace upon you, and you will be to him sons in truth' (Testament of Judah 24.1–6).

The Testament of Levi and the Testament of Judah belongs to a collection of apocalypses known under the name of the Testaments of the Twelve Patriarchs. They are certainly pre-Christian, but they may have been retouched by Christians.

Five controversies. 2.1–3.6

This group of five discussions between Jesus and his adversaries introduces us to the literary genre of controversy (see p. 20). We shall study two of them.

The healing of a paralysed man. 2.1–12

Look at the main characters: what are they doing? What are they saying? Note the contrasts: lying, sitting, standing.

This is a strange story: The paralysed man does not expect to hear that particular saying (v. 5). The story is formed by the combination of a miracle story and a controversy: try to distinguish them both.

The miracle (3.5a and 11–12). Look for the different elements (see p. 20). Jesus turns a bed-ridden invalid, who needs assistance, into a man on his feet who can look after himself. How can that signify the coming of the kingdom of God? What is the crowd's reaction? In Greek, the verb 'arise' is the same as that used for resurrection: for a Christian, to put others on their feet can be experienced as a way of realizing the resurrection of Jesus today.

The controversy (5b–10). The scribes are seated, in their official position (see pp. 58–59). They are already thinking to themselves what they will later shout aloud at the time of Jesus' trial: this man is blaspheming! For a Jew, the phrase 'Your sins are forgiven' must mean that they are forgiven by God; however, at the very least Jesus shows that God's forgiveness is bound up with his action in Jesus. He presents himself as the Son of man to be found in Daniel 7, to whom God has entrusted all power and, according to Jewish tradition, judgment over men.

The combination. How do these two healings, of body and soul, help to illuminate each other? What do they teach us about the salvation brought by Jesus? Is this not the word spoken by him (v. 2)?

The call of Levi. 2.13–17

Mark notes that Jesus taught the crowds. However, here again, this teaching is given above all through actions.

The starting point of the controversy is the story of a call, of a kind that can often be found in the Gospel. This kind of story usually has three elements: Jesus' glance – the words 'Follow me' – and an obedient response.

Levi is a tax collector, and therefore considered to be a sinner. To celebrate his call, he gives a party: this is the starting point of the controversy, since Jesus is sitting at table with sinners.

Fasting and the Bridegroom. 2.18–22

As often, this controversy has been supplemented by two short parables, for the purposes of teaching. Mark presents Jesus as the Bridegroom, the divine partner in the covenant (see *How to Read the Old Testament*, pp. 47, 61). Fasting gives place to the wine of the wedding feast.

The Lord of the sabbath. 2.23–28

In this classic controversy, Jesus puts forward a revolutionary principle by referring to scripture: the sabbath, and therefore every institution, whether religious or human, is at the service of men.

Healing on a sabbath. 3.1–6

1. Again he entered the synagogue
   and a man was there who had a withered hand.
2. And they watched him, to see whether he would heal him on the sabbath,
   that they might accuse him.
3. And he said to the man who had the withered hand,
   'Come here.'
4. And he said to them, 'Is it lawful on the sabbath
   to do good or to do harm,
   to save life or to kill?'
   But they were silent.
5. And he looked around them with anger,
   grieved at their hardness of heart,
   and said to the man, 'Stretch out your hand.'
   He stretched it out, and his hand was restored.
6. The Pharisees went out, and immediately held counsel with the Herodians against him, how to destroy him.

Look for the main characters: Jesus and his adversaries; the sick man only serves as an occasion for the controversy. Note the parallels brought out by the way in which the text has been printed. The synagogue is the place of the Law; the religious authorities are at home there. At the beginning, Jesus enters; at the end, they go out.

This head-on clash is over the significance of the Law: Jesus' opponents are caught up in their ideals (the disciples are reproached for this hardness of heart: 6.52; 8.17). For Jesus, the most important thing is not the practice of a law, but man. In this confrontation, who comes out on top? However, 'how to destroy him' creates a sense of suspense which is only resolved by the passion (for 'accuse' see 15.3–4). By raising up Jesus (evoking the 'resurrection'), God shows that he is Lord over the Law.

What significance might this text have today?

🐾 The blind man of Jericho. 10.46–52

Who are the main characters? What do they do? What do they say? Note the transformation brought about between the beginning and the end: a blind man – sitting – at the side – of the road/he saw – he followed him – on – the road. What is this transformation (is it the same 'road'?), and how is it brought about?

Look for the usual features of a miracle story (see p. 20); the plea for intervention (vv. 47–50) here is of disproportionate length; there is no final reaction. This story must have been used as more than a simple miracle story.

See the passage which leads up to it: in 10.32–34 the disciples are going up to Jerusalem: what road are they taking? Can the disciples see it? In 10.35–45 are not James and John blind? Note the link between this story and the one which follows (the same question appears in verses 36 and 51).

Look at what happens next. In 11.11ff. they arrive in Jerusalem: Jesus is hailed as Son of David (v. 10). But can the crowd see the significance of this title, which will be discussed in Mark 11–13?

What meaning does this story seem to have by itself? In the context of Mark's Gospel?

Here we arrive at a turning point in the Gospel of Mark. Jesus knows where his journey to Jerusalem is taking him. He warns the disciples three times (8.31–33; 9.30–32; 10.32–34). However, they are frightened and blind. The inability of James and John to understand is obvious: they have the wrong idea of the Messiah. According to Mark, this miracle is an attempt by Jesus to open the eyes of his disciples. Bartimaeus becomes the model of the true believer. He 'sees', not only with his physical eyes; he follows Jesus on this 'road' which is more theological than geographical, the ascent to the cross. When he asks, 'Let me see', Jesus does not reply 'See', as he does in Luke (18.42), but 'Go'. The blind man's faith enables him to follow Jesus.

Here he has done something for which the rich man did not have the courage (10.17–31). He has left everything. While he was still blind (physically), he threw off his mantle, all that he had, sprang up, and came to Jesus (v. 50).

For the people, Jesus was only the man from Nazareth (v. 47): for the blind man he is the Son of David, not the figure dreamed of still by James and John, but as Jesus will himself present him: the suffering Messiah.

🐾 The empty tomb. 16.1–8

This is the conclusion of the Gospel; verses 9–20 were added later.

Try to put into two columns the contrasts which are either implicit or explicit. The time: the sabbath (religious time) is past/the first day of the week (secular time); darkness/light, morning. . . The places: closed/open; here (Jerusalem)/Galilee. . . The actions: anoint a corpse/hear a message. . . The main characters: corpse, in the dark, lying, naked/young man in white, sitting on the right, clothed. What do these contrasts suggest to you? What transformation has taken place between the beginning and the end? How is it achieved?

Mark's Gospel ends with this story. So to believe in the resurrection of Jesus it is not necessary to have 'seen' it: it is enough to believe in God who affirms it.

The women come to anoint a corpse; they go away with a message. They wanted to seal up Jesus in death; they have to announce that he is alive. Jesus is no longer a body that can be touched; he has become a word that must be proclaimed. One of the ways in which he remains mysteriously present in history is in preaching. Now he is seated at the right hand of God, as is suggested by the attitude of the young man. And it is only when the disciples arrive in Galilee (to which he has preceded them), i.e. to the end of the world and the conclusion of history (see the geography, p. 58), that they will 'see' him. Matthew will tell us that the resurrection of Jesus is the end of time: everything has been accomplished! Mark stresses the other aspect: everything has still be done!

If you have put the contrasts in two columns, you will have seen that everything that belongs to the old world (darkness, the corpse, the sabbath and Jewish time, the tomb with its dead sealed inside) is now past. A new world has begun: it is the beginning of a new creation (cf. Mark 1.1).

Other texts studied elsewhere

The Passion according to Mark

An account of the passion of Jesus from his arrest to his burial must have existed from a very early stage. The four Gospels take it up, but each gives it a particular tone.

Mark is addressing non-believers or those whose faith is weak, and he wants to lead them to join the Gentile at the foot of the cross in proclaiming that Jesus is truly the Son of God.

By narrating the facts without embellishing them, he is trying almost to upset us. With him we can see better how disconcerting the realization of God's plan is for men. The cross is scandalous. However, it is there that the Son of God reveals himself.

The silence of Jesus during his passion is impressive. Jesus knows that people are 'hardened' when it comes to penetrating his mystery, that there is a risk that they will understand him wrongly. Throughout his ministry, too, he always refuses to say who he is. Now that he is condemned, there is no longer any danger of interpreting his titles as a concern for power, so he agrees to lift the veil somewhat. From his arrest on, despite the questions pressed on him, Jesus opens his mouth only three times: before the High Priest he declares that he is Messiah/Christ and Son of Man; before Pilate he acknowledges that he is king of the Jews; on the cross, he takes up the complaint of the Suffering Servant in Isaiah, bringing upon himself all the suffering and anguish of the world, 'My God, why have you forsaken me?'

In Mark, Jesus' solitude stands out in all its harshness: he goes forward alone, abandoned by all, denied by Peter, into the dark night of the cross. It is by accepting the call to follow him so far that his disciples can proclaim him Son of God.

The conflict between Jesus and the high priests comes to a head with the conspiracy against Jesus (14.1–2): from this point on, Jesus is doomed. He knows it. During a meal with Simon (14.3–9), a woman pours perfume over his head: Jesus sees this as the celebration of his burial. So he goes to meet his passion in full awareness.

The story of his farewell meal (14.22–25) is framed by the intimation of Judas' betrayal (14.17–21) and Peter's denial (14.26–31). So Jesus knows what is to come; he

is the one who directs his passion (14.10–16). At the last supper, he offers his body and his blood in total destitution, knowing that he can expect neither recognition nor fidelity from men. The account of the institution, which comes very close to that of Mark, takes up the liturgical text of celebrations in the Palestinian churches.

In Gethsemane, Jesus is in anguish, prostrate (14.32–42). Fully man, he is afraid of death. The name which he uses in his cry to God, 'Abba, Father', sheds momentary light on this tragic scene. When he is arrested, all forsake him (14.43–52), even the young man who tries to follow him but flees, naked. This word, which brings the story to an end, sets its tone. Jesus drives himself, naked, into his passion. And the disciple who plunged naked into the pool at the time of his baptism would know that this was the course he too was to follow.

At the trial before the Jews (14.53–64), Jesus for the only time in Mark proclaims who he is: Messiah, the glorified Son of man. However, everyone seems to go wild at this affirmation: the guards mock him (14.65), Peter denies him (14.66–72). Jesus keeps silent.

At the Roman trial (15.1–15) Jesus claims to be king of the Jews and the high priests call for his death. . . Their king is crowned with thorns (15.16–20)!

The scene on Calvary (15.21–41) takes up the theme of the two trials: the title King of the Jews is recalled between two mentions of the crucifixion (vv. 25, 27), and the high priests mock his claim to be the Christ. However, it is by dying abandoned by all, apparently even by the Father, by taking upon himself all human suffering as the Suffering Servant, that Jesus reveals how he is both Christ and King. The Gentile calls on us to recognize him as Son of God. And by marking out his narrative with the hours of Christian prayer (terce, sext, none, vv. 25, 33, 34), Mark invites us to celebrate him in faith.

In Mark the account of the burial is peaceful (15.42–47). The last honours are paid to Jesus. And the night of the burial becomes a night of expectation.

The Christ of Perpignan (fourteenth century)

Mark's Jesus

A man

Mark presents us with the everyday Jesus, a man like ourselves. We get the impression that we are discovering him, from day to day, through Peter's eyes. During the two years of their life together, Peter had watched Jesus on the roads of Palestine, had welcomed him into his home at Capernaum, had watched him eat and sleep, talk and pray. He had seen him angry at the synagogue or in the Temple, irritated towards a leper or towards his disciples, full of pity when confronted with the crowd, amazed that people in Nazareth would not believe in him. He had watched the harassed life of Jesus as a wandering preacher, which at times did not even allow him a chance to eat; he had seen Jesus asleep, exhausted at the height of a great storm.

Peter had been impressed by the way Jesus looked, his anger, his questioning, his love; he had been intrigued by the mystery of Jesus, as on the first night that Jesus spent at his home or when he saw him get up before dawn to go to pray alone in a desert place (1.35).

Mark does not hesitate to report certain features which must have stunned his audience, accustomed to seeing Jesus as the Son of God: Jesus did not know everything; he did not know what his disciples were talking about and had to ask them (9.16, 33); he did not know when the end of time would come (14.33); he was afraid of death (14.33) and died in despair (15.34). He was so disconcerting that even his parents did not believe in him: 'He's lost his head' (3.21).

A 'man with' – a man by himself

Mark's Jesus is above all Jesus-with-his-disciples. His first act is to call them, and then to choose twelve to be with him. His opponents try to break up this team by attacking Jesus in the disciples' presence and the disciples in his (2.18–27). Jesus prepares these disciples for their future ministry by making them serve the crowd, a service which comes before rest or food (6.31f.), and by directing them towards the Gentiles.

Against this background, the solitude of Jesus appears all the more dramatic. He is alone, because he cannot make his companions realize his mystery; they are hardened (6.52; 8.17), doubt, abandon him the moment he is arrested, and deny him.

The teacher

Straight after his baptism, Jesus preaches that 'The kingdom of God is at hand.' For Mark, Jesus is the one who teaches the crowd (about twenty times). When he sees the crowds who have followed him into the desert and have nothing to eat, Jesus takes pity on them, and begins to teach them, guessing that this is their most important hunger (6.34).

Now the paradoxical fact is that there are very few discourses in Mark. Did he perhaps want to convey that Jesus taught above all by the way in which he acted? Proportionately, the miracles occupy a major part of Mark's Gospel: they show by actions that the kingdom of God is at hand, that Jesus is stronger than evil (3.27).

The crucified Messiah

Jesus refuses to have himself proclaimed Messiah or Christ, and he imposes silence on those who discover who he is, whether these are people whom he has healed or the demons: this is what is referred to as the 'messianic secret'. Many people expected that the Messiah would re-establish the earthly kingdom of Israel. Jesus does not want them to get the wrong idea of the Messiah: he is the Messiah, but not in that sense. He gives himself this title only when it is no longer possible to make a mistake, when he has been condemned to death. It is by suffering and death that he will establish a spiritual kingdom. And he tries to lead his disciples along this road (8.34–38).

The Son of Man

The most frequent title Jesus uses in Mark is Son of Man (fourteen times). Perhaps Jesus was fond of it because it unveiled his mystery while at the same time concealing it. In itself, the expression in fact means simply 'man'; however, when there is a reference to the vision in Daniel 7 (see *How to Read the Old Testament*, p. 91), it takes on the strong sense of the heavenly being to whom God entrusts judgment.

The Son of God

This title is rare, but it appears as the climax of the faith to which Mark seeks to bring his reader. He uses the title in his introduction (1.1), and the centurion proclaims it at the foot of the cross (15.39), echoing the voice of the Father at the baptism and the transfiguration.

The Miracles and the Kingdom of God

The time is fulfilled and the kingdom of God is at hand: repent and believe in the gospel' (Mark 1.15). This cry of Jesus immediately after his baptism is a good indication of the tone of his preaching; with his ministry, the kingdom of God is on its way.

The kingdom of God

At a time when monarchy was the universal political system, it was natural that Israel should use the image of 'king' to evoke the power of its God. For Israel, God is the sole king, and the earthly king is only his representative. This faith developed when the people experienced the failure of the earthly kingdom. During the exile in Babylon, Second Isaiah announced that God would finally show himself as king (see *How to Read the Old Testament*, p. 67).

Messianic beliefs over the course of centuries deepened this expectation. It was thought that God would establish his kingdom by the agency of his messiah. The messiah most often had the features of the son of David, shepherd of Israel (II Sam. 7; Ezek. 34; Zech. 9–14; Ps. 2, see *How to Read the Old Testament*, pp. 42, 66, 86, 103). The apocalypses, with the figure of the son of man in Daniel 7, brought another component: this kingdom is universal and is for the end of time.

Two main functions were attributed to the king, and thus, *a fortiori*, to God the King.

He was to ensure the liberty of his people: he was a warrior chief who destroyed their enemies. At the time of Christ this led some Jewish groups to cherish the hope that by establishing his kingdom God would free Israel from Roman domination (cf. Luke 24.21). It is notable that Jesus never takes up this aspect.

The true king was also to ensure the reign of justice among the people; he was above all the king of the poor, the oppressed, those who had no voice. And Second Isaiah proclaimed this gospel, this good news: 'God will reign! Blessed are the poor, the sick, the oppressed, since henceforth their misery is at an end.' This is also the good news proclaimed by Jesus. He proclaims it by both his actions and his words. In the next section we shall be hearing his words, above all the beatitudes. Here we are going to look at his actions: the miracles.

Jesus proclaims the kingdom of God

You might begin by looking at the good news (Luke 3.18) proclaimed by John the Baptist (Mark 1.2–8; Matt. 3.1–12; Luke 3.1–18) and the way in which the evangelists sum up the preaching of Jesus (Mark 1.14–15; Matt. 4.17; Luke 4.16–21).

John the Baptist's question

John announced the Messiah who would establish the kingdom of God, purify his people, destroy the sinners. And he thought he could recognize him in Jesus. Now Jesus welcomed sinners, refused to judge and allowed his precursor to be put in prison, facing certain death. We can understand John's doubt and his question. Read Luke 7.18–23 (= Matt. 11.2–6).

What does Jesus do before replying (v. 21)? Look also at Luke 7.11–17, which Luke has put just in front of the passage.

Which prophetic oracles does Jesus take up in his reply (see the notes or references in your Bible)?

What significance does that give to Jesus' miracles and to the beatitudes: 'Blessed are the poor'?

That is particularly important in understanding the miracles. For us they are primarily extraordinary facts, and we ask, 'What actually happened? Are they historical?' For Jesus, as for his contemporaries, the miracles are signs: they say something and speak of someone. To shift the question in this way is essential. Let's take a trivial example. A science teacher gives a flower to a pupil: the question is obviously 'What is it?' A boy gives this flower to the same girl: the question then is, 'What does this mean?' In the one instance the interest is in the flower as an entity; in the other, it is in its message, and what it is as an entity becomes purely secondary. That is important, and we shall be coming back to it.

If you have time, you might also look at the expression 'kingdom of God' in the Gospels, or read Matt. 13 and see what the parables are talking about.

We shall be studying one miracle story, the stilling of the storm. That will help you to see how this kind of story is constructed and what it means.

A miracle story: the stilling of the storm

Matt. 8.18–27	Mark 4.35–41	Luke 8.22–25
[18] Now when Jesus saw great crowds around him, he gave orders to go over to the other side.	[35] On that day, when evening had come, he said to them 'Let us go across to the other side.'	[22] One day he got into a boat with his disciples, and he said to them, 'Let us go across to the other side of the lake.'
[19] And a scribe came up and said to him, 'Teacher, I will follow you wherever you go.' [20] And Jesus said to him, 'Foxes have holes, and birds of the air have nests; but the Son of man has nowhere to lay his head.' [21] Another of his disciples said to him, 'Lord, let me first go and bury my father.' [22] Jesus said to him, 'Follow me, and leave the dead to bury their dead.'		(Luke 9.57–58) (Luke 9.59–60)
[23] And when he got into the boat, his disciples followed him.	[36] And leaving the crowd, they took him with them, just as he was, in the boat.	So they set out.
[24] And behold, there arose a great upheaval on the sea so that the boat was being swamped by the waves;	[37] And a great storm of wind arose and the waves beat into the boat, so that the boat was already filling.	[23] And as they sailed, he fell asleep. And a storm of wind came down on the lake and they were filling with water, and were in danger.
but he was asleep.	[38] But he was in the stern, asleep on the cushion; and they woke him and said to him,	
[25] And they went and woke him, saying, 'Save, Lord, we are perishing.'	'Teacher, do you not care if we perish?'	[24] And they went and woke him, saying, 'Master, master, we are perishing!'
[26] And he said to them, 'Why are you afraid, O men of little faith?' Then he rose and rebuked the winds, and the sea, and there was a great calm.	[39] And he awoke and rebuked the wind, and said to the sea, 'Peace, be still' And the wind ceased, and there was a great calm. [40] He said to them, 'Why are you afraid? Have you no faith?'	And he awoke and rebuked the wind and the raging waves; and they ceased, and there was a calm. [25] He said to them, 'Where is your faith?'
[27] And the men marvelled saying, 'What sort of man is this, that even winds and sea obey him?'	[41] And they were filled with awe, and said to one another, 'Who then is this, that even wind and sea obey him?'	And they were afraid, and they marvelled, saying to one another, 'Who then is this, that he commands even wind and water, and they obey him?'

Read these texts carefully and compare them: underline words in different colours (see p. 16). See where one Gospel has more or less than another; note how Mark shifts v. 40; watch the different use of words.

A miracle story usually fitted into a prefabricated 'mould': look for the five points indicated on p. 20. Does Mark's v. 40 fit into this mould?

Read each of the accounts. To put them in context, go back to the synopsis on p. 17.

Mark. Can you find the features picked out on p. 59? Why does Jesus rebuke the storm as though it were a demon? The word for fear used here appears only four times in the New Testament: in John 14.27 as a verb, in II Tim. 1.7 as a noun and in Rev. 21.8 as an adjective. What kind of fear is this? Towards which shore of the lake are they going (look at the geography on p. 58)? What episode follows this story in all three Gospels? Does that explain the fear of the disciples and the rebellion of the demon?

Why does Mark recount this miracle? What is the meaning with v. 40? Without v. 40?

Luke. Which is he interested in, the ship or the disciples (look at the end of v. 23)? Which episode has he put immediately afterwards? The word Luke uses for Master is peculiar to him (5.5; 8.45; 9.33, 49; 17.13). What is its significance?

Matthew. In which direction do the words which he has added shift the sense (follow, vv. 19, 22, 23; disciples, v. 21)? In whom is he interested (see the end of v. 24)? The word upheaval is used once in the Gospels as one of the signs of the end of time (Mark 13.8; Matt. 24.7; Luke 21.11). Matthew uses it again (noun or verb) in 21.10; 27.51, 54; 28.2, 4: what sense does this give to the narrative (see p. 71)? *Kyrie, sozon,* 'Lord, save,' is a liturgical invocation. Matthew has put v. 26 at the centre of his account: the reproach is addressed to disciples who already believe, but not enough. 'The men' (v. 27) in Matthew usually denotes unbelievers (4.19; 5.13; 10.17; 10.32). On the basis of all this, what significance would you attach to this account?

The significance of the miracle

The miracle, as I said earlier, is a sign. But for whom? Let me take a trivial instance: by the roadside I see a triangular metal plate with an X on it; if I didn't know the highway code I might ask, 'What is it?'. If I do know the highway code, the sign says to me, 'Caution, crossroads.' Similarly, reactions of non-believer and believer to an event will differ, and the story which each tells of it will not be the same.

For the non-believer, the extraordinary fact poses a question: 'Who is this man who is capable of. . .?'

For the believer – and only for him – the event is a miracle, that is to say, a message, a fact in which he discovers a word of God addressed to him.

Now it seems that in the primitive community, before the redaction of the Gospel, the story of the stilling of the storm was used in both ways.

Let's take Mark's account. If we read it without v. 40, we have a text which exactly fits the mould of the miracle story. It is addressed to the disciples before Easter who had not yet discovered the mystery of Jesus, and it could be presented to non-believers; it leads them to ask: 'Who is he. . .?'

With v. 40, the account becomes a catechism put forward to believers: they know who Jesus is. So why this fear? Where is their faith?

This use in catechesis could lead to the development of fully-fledged teaching. Thus Matthew is addressed to disciples, to people who follow Jesus in the ship (there is only one). This ship, shaken by an upheaval – the unleashing of evil powers characteristic of the end of time – is in peril of sinking. In the midst of this ship-church, the disciples pray, *Kyrie, sozon.* Jesus reproaches them for their fear, this apostolic fear of sailing out into Gentile territory, and for their little faith: they already have faith, but not enough. And non-believers all down history have asked how this ship-church can stay afloat when evil is unleashed. We can draw several conclusions from this.

The miracle is a sign. What interests the evangelists' contemporaries is not the fact itself – they are a good audience, and at that time they had no difficulty in accepting the possibility of miracle – but its significance: what does it mean? In *whose name* are you doing that? In the name of the prince of the demons, as Jesus' adversaries claim (Matt. 12.24)? 'It is by the spirit that I act,' replies Jesus, 'and that is a sign that the kingdom of God has come upon you' (Matt. 12.28).

So the important question is not to ask 'What happened?' (you can do that, but it's of secondary importance, and if you can't find an answer, it doesn't really matter), but rather to look for the meaning.

The evangelists often developed this meaning with the believers in mind: that is what we must discover above all.

Miracles and modern man

The miracles bother us. At one time people believed because of them; now people believe despite them. However, perhaps that is only because we get the wrong idea about them. Let me go back over one or two points.

A miracle is a sign. The road sign by the side of the road is real (it is made of metal) and has a shape (circular, triangular); the actual signs may differ, but that's not important: the essential thing is the message they convey, indicating a curve, or a crossroads. Similarly, miracles have a historical reality: they are facts so extraordinary that people notice them. But the essential thing is their message. What is it?

A miracle is a sign only for believers. A present exchanged between friends is a present only because they are already friends; an object given to us in the street by an unknown person is not a sign but a question. If we are to recognize a particular fact as a miracle, we must already have faith. The medical bureau at Lourdes, made up of believing and non-believing doctors alike, only affirms that a particular cure cannot be explained by science. The believer can then, if he or she likes, see the cure as a miracle. For that, the event has to fit into a certain context; it has to correspond with other facts, with statements. Lourdes is primarily a place of prayer, and it is in this context that cures can take on meaning. The miracles of Jesus are always bound up with his teaching.

For the non-believer, a miracle is a question, and never a 'proof'. If I don't know the highway code, the strange object by the side of the road raises a question for me. However, it's no use my examining it: I have to go and ask someone who knows what it means. That tells me its significance, and that is what I accept.

Similarly, an unexplained fact can make a non-believer ask the question, 'What is it?' The believer can then give his interpretation: 'That's a sign from my God.' The unbeliever will accept this interpretation by becoming a believer, or he will reject it and look for another explanation. The miracle is not a proof; people are not converted by miracles – it simply raises a question, but does so because of the meaning handed down by believers.

A miracle is a sign relative to its time. Facts can be extraordinary to one period and no longer so to another. The medical bureau at Lourdes declares that a particular cure cannot be explained by the present state of science. It may be explained one day. That doesn't matter much. If a miracle were a proof, it would be dishonest of God to take advantage of our ignorance to grab us, like a missionary proving God by switching on a tape recorder. If it's a sign, the supporting evidence is not so important; we are concerned with doctrine and not with a portent. Perhaps some of Jesus' miracles might seem explicable to us today.

However, to attempt to discover 'what happened' is to take a wrong turning. To take one example. A native who is an animist tells me, 'The gods are angry; they are spitting fire on the mountain.' He gives me his interpretation as a believer. But what is actually happening? If I did not know the country at all I would know that something was going on, but I would be incapable of saying whether it was a volcanic eruption, a forest fire or a storm. At the time of Jesus, miracles were common among Jews, and the famous Greek sanctuaries associated with miracles, like Pergamon and Epidaurus, with their votive offerings and their hospitals, were as important as Lourdes. Jesus would not have been a religious man of his time if he had not done miracles.

The essential thing is not to check the historicity of a particular miracle but to see what, today, might be a miracle for our contemporaries.

And the sphere of the extraordinary has shifted. It is perhaps less in the physical realm – science has taught us that we can (or will be able to) explain everything – than in the spiritual realm: for instance, a miracle could be an act of forgiveness. In a harsh and violent world, in the struggle for life, the free gesture – even more the gesture of forgiveness – becomes extraordinary and can lead the non-believer to ask, 'Why are you doing that?'

The miracle stories in the Bible should lead us less to ask what happened and more to ask, 'How, today, can I be a miracle, a sign posing a question to those among whom I live?'

Between a married couple, everything becomes a sign of love. Going through the Bible should lead the believer to discover that the whole world is miracle, a sign of the tenderness of God.

Matthew and the angel. Keystone of the rood-loft at Chartres (thirteenth century)

5 The Gospel according to Matthew

When we change from Mark to Matthew, we get the impression that we are moving into different country, just as we might go through a mountain pass and find another valley spreading out before us. With Mark we may sometimes have the illusion of discovering Jesus of Nazareth through Peter's eyes. With Matthew, we are never quite sure whether we are beside Lake Tiberias in the year 30 or at the celebration of the liturgy in a Christian church of the 80s. Or rather, Matthew puts us in two places at the same time: he deliberately places upon the Jesus of history the tracing paper of the Lord living in the church (see p. 19). Thus the countenance of Jesus of Nazareth is revealed to us through the glorious features of the risen Lord celebrated by the church.

The 'church's Gospel'

That is the title given to this Gospel, which has left its stamp on Western Christianity more than any other. It is the only one to use the word church (16.18; 18.17); it is concerned with the church's organization, with the brotherly life and the catechesis which it presents in the striking form of five great well-constructed discourses.

It introduces us to the heart of a church which celebrates its Lord in the liturgy: it puts the tracing paper of Christians worshipping the Risen Lord, chanting *Kyrie*, *sozon* (the equivalent of *eleison*), at the height of the storm, over the disciples of Jesus. It is also a church which runs the risk of stifling itself and having only 'little faith' (8.26).

Matthew's church

The situation of the communities among which Matthew was preaching largely influenced his witness. Three main aspects appear as we read the text.

The communities seem to have been composed above all of Christians who had come from Judaism. They knew the scriptures well: more than 130 passages have been noted in which Matthew refers to the Old Testament. For them, the Law remains the rule of life: 'I have not come to abolish the Law but to fulfil it,' to bring it to its culmination, to perfection, declares Jesus (5.17). They are very familiar with the way in which the rabbis interpret scriptures, and some of their questions (about fasting, almsgiving and divorce) are typically Jewish. It is no coincidence that Jesus is presented as the new Moses.

These communities are in conflict with official Judaism as it was reborn at Jamnia (see p. 31). Christians had already been driven out of their synagogues as Matthew writes. And the very harsh attacks made by Jesus on the Pharisees (Matt. 23) are perhaps less those of the Jesus of the 30s than those of the risen Lord, living in his community in the 80s, against the Pharisees of Jamnia.

These communities are open to Gentiles. By Christian conviction, reflecting on the missionary impetus of the first years of the church, these Jews who had become Christians rediscovered in the words of Jesus his concern to send his disciples all over the world.

The author

A second-century tradition which cannot be checked says that Matthew, the customs officer of Capernaum, who became one of the Twelve (9.9), wrote down the words of Jesus in *Aramaic*.

The present author of the Gospel, an unknown figure, was perhaps inspired by him. He wrote, *in Greek*, round about 80 or 90, in the communities of Syria and Palestine, perhaps at Antioch.

Moses and the Law. Dura-Europos synagogue (Syria, before AD 256)

69

The Gospel as a Whole

It would be a good thing to start, as with Mark (p. 58), by reading the Gospel of Matthew straight through. Here are some landmarks for your guided tour.

Matthew's geography

Matthew follows Mark's scheme, but differs from him in not stressing the opposition between Galilee and Jerusalem. Galilee is the important area. It takes on two particular aspects.

During the ministry of Jesus it emerges as a Jewish area, the borders of which he scarcely crosses; while Jesus goes towards Tyre and Sidon, Matthew notes that the Canaanite woman has come out of her territory (15.21). Jesus preaches only to Jews, and forbids his disciples to approach Gentiles and Samaritans (10.5–6).

After the resurrection, Galilee becomes the gateway to the world, as Isaiah proclaimed (Matt. 4.14–16). It is there – and not in Jerusalem – that the glorified Jesus appears to his disciples and sends them out to preach all over the world (28.16–20).

The most Jewish of the Gospels

He refers constantly to the scriptures: more than 130 times, 43 of which are explicit quotations; 11 are introduced by the formula 'This happened that the saying of the Lord by the prophet might be fulfilled. . .' A true rabbi, he sometimes brings together several passages in a subtle way to produce a quotation which suits him; thus he combines Zech. 11.12 and Jer. 18.2 to explain the death of Judas (27.9), or Zech. 9.9 and Isa. 62.11 to give messianic significance to Jesus' entry into Jerusalem (21.1–19).

His manner of expression is Jewish. He talks of the kingdom of heaven rather than of the kingdom of God, because Jews do not pronounce the divine name. He loves repetitions, particularly inclusions, the repetition of the same expression at the beginning and the end of a passage (5.3, 10; 6.25–34). He uses parallelism (16.25; 7.24–27). He is fond of numerical groupings, whether these are symbolic or simply meant as aids to the memory: seven petitions in the Lord's Prayer, seven parables, seven loaves and seven baskets, three temptations, three good works (6.1f.), three tithes (23.23), etc.

Sidon
Tyre
Caesarea Philippi
Capernaum
Nazareth
Second return to Galilee 4.14
Jerusalem
Jericho
Jesus as a child reenacts the Exodus

Infancy:
To Egypt on the route of the Exodus

The kingdom of God and the church

Jesus inaugurates the kingdom of God (see p. 65). The church is not identical with this kingdom, but it is the privileged place where it is manifested in the world. The kingdom of God and the beginnings of its realization in the world form the central theme of Matthew.

How does he develop it? Some characteristic features will enable us to see this.

The infancy narratives (1–2) are in fact the theological prologue to the Gospel.

An identical closing formula (7.28; 11.1; 13.53; 19.1; 26.1) marks out five great discourses constructed by Matthew. They alternate with six narrative sections in the Gospel, accounts of the actions and sayings of Jesus. What is the link between the narrative sections and the discourses? An inclusion, a repetition of the same phrase at the beginning and the end of the first grouping (4.23; 9.35), gives some indication there: in a discourse Jesus presents a theme which he then puts into action. We might assume that this sequence also holds good for the other groupings.

Two passages at the beginning (3–4) and in the middle of the Gospel (16.13–17.27) are also similar, and serve as a transition. An identical formula, which we find only here, introduces two successive phases of the ministry of Jesus: 'From that time Jesus began to preach, saying . . . the kingdom of heaven is at hand' (4.17), or, 'to show his disciples that he must suffer' (16.21). In both cases there is a proclamation of a title of Jesus: Son (the heavenly voice) or Messiah (Peter); in both cases Jesus is tempted by Satan or by Peter described as Satan.

In the light of these observations we might imagine that Matthew develops his theme of the kingdom and the church in this way.

To begin with, Jesus proclaims to everyone the arrival of the kingdom, which he inaugurates with his actions. He prepares his disciples to continue his work by sending them on a mission. In fact, he is the one who goes off to preach! His disciples will only really be ready for their mission after Easter.

Jesus then devotes himself to the training of his disciples. Peter proclaims Jesus as Messiah, but also tempts him. Jesus gives a rule of life to his church. Then he announces the coming of the kingdom, inaugurates it by his death and resurrection, and sends his disciples to preach it in the world.

Prologue. Presentation of the mystery of Jesus (1–2)

Part one. Jesus preaches the kingdom of God to all men and prepares for the church (3–16)

Transition. The Father proclaims his Son, who is tempted by Satan (3–4)

1. The kingdom of God is at hand (5–9)
    Jesus manifests it through
        his words: the Sermon on the Mount (5–7)
        his actions: ten miracles (8–9)
2. Jesus sends his disciples to preach, and he himself departs to proclaim the kingdom (10–12)
    Discourse commissioning the disciples (10)
    Jesus on his mission (11–12)
3. The decisive choice demanded by the proclamation of the kingdom (13.1–16.12)
    Discourse consisting of seven parables (13.1–52)
    Towards Peter's confession (13.53–16.12)

Part two. Jesus prepares the church for its role in the kingdom of God (17–28)

Transition. The church confesses and tempts its Lord (16.13–17.27)

4. The kingdom of God passes from the Jewish people to the church (18–23)
    Discourse: the 'community rule' (18)
    From Galilee to Jerusalem (19–23)
5. The definitive inauguration of the kingdom of God at Easter (24–28)
    Apocalyptic discourse: the definitive coming of the kingdom of God in Jesus (24–25)
    The death and exaltation of Jesus inaugurating the definitive coming of the kingdom (26–28)
    The church sets out to preach in the world.

The end of time

Mark ends his Gospel by saying: everything has still to be done; the Risen Christ will not be seen until the end of history. Matthew declares: With Jesus, everything has been achieved; the end of time has arrived; victory is won; it remains only to occupy the territory! We should pause for one significant detail.

In his apocalyptic discourse Jesus gave a sign of the end of time: there would be 'upheavals' (Mark 13.8; Luke 21.11; Matt. 24.7). This is not a reference to a historical phenomenon (an earthquake) but a symbolic image.

Matthew, and only Matthew, uses the noun or the verb six times elsewhere. At the 'upheaval' of the cross, the dead are raised (27.51) and, confronted with the sight of this 'upheaval' (27.54), Gentiles acknowledge Jesus as Son of God. On Easter morning there is an 'upheaval' and the enemy, 'caught-by-the-upheaval', are as though they were dead (28.2, 4). So the death-and-glorification of Jesus is the sign for the end of time.

The city is in an 'upheaval' when Jesus enters Jerusalem; this is an image of his glorious entry into heaven (21.10).

So one of the signs given to make it possible to recognize the coming of the end of time takes effect at the time of the passion and resurrection. The kingdom of God is definitively inaugurated by this event. But the church, a frail ship battered by the upheaval (8.29: this is the word usually translated as storm, see p. 87), must experience this crisis all through its history.

Some features of Matthew

Matthew is a teacher. He rearranges the words of Jesus into five great speeches, doubtless in order to present him as the new Moses. He stresses the need to understand the word and not just to hear it (13.19–23). He abbreviates the miracle stories, often keeping only two figures, Jesus and the person concerned; the stories lose their vividness but make a greater impact as teaching.

He is a scribe versed in Jewish methods of interpreting the scriptures, knowing how to draw from his treasure things new and old (13.52).

His Christian faith makes him see Jesus of Nazareth as the glorified Lord. At the very beginning, and frequently after that, he proclaims Jesus to be Son of God, whose majesty and authority are transparent.

The whole of the Gospel unfolds in a liturgical atmosphere: the disciples who worship their Lord in the community appear through the disciples who follow Jesus on the roads of Palestine.

This Gospel, which is centred on the kingdom of heaven and its outcome in the church, has been called the Gospel of the church, and it has left a profound mark on Western Christianity.

Some Texts from Matthew

🦊 The temptations of Jesus. 4.1–11

Let us pause over one feature of the Gospel: how Jesus' life and our own make sense thanks to the scriptures.

It is quite probable that Jesus began his ministry with a 'retreat' and that he was tempted during it (read Mark 1.12–13). However, he was tempted all through his life, by his opponents and by Peter (e.g. Matt. 16.23; 27.42; John 6.15). Christians tried to work out the significance of these temptations. One tradition, taken up by Matthew and Luke, seeks to express it.

Read the text of Matthew. What does desert, forty, temptation suggest? See how each of these temptations is constructed.

The devil puts Jesus in one of the situations experienced by the Israelites in the desert (v. 4 = Ex. 16.14; v. 7 = Ex. 17.1–7; v. 10 = Ex. 23.20–30; 34.11–14). So Jesus was repeating the journey made by his people. They had failed to reach their destiny on entering the promised land because they had been unable to cope with these temptations.

Jesus responds with a quotation from Deuteronomy (see *How to Read the Old Testament*, pp. 57, 111). So Jesus undergoes these temptations and responds to them as the people should have done in order to succeed. The history of his people, taken up by Jesus, succeeds through him: from now on it is possible to enter the promised land, and Jesus proclaims, 'The kingdom of God is at hand' (4.17).

So the temptations of Jesus are his own, but at the same time he is taking on the temptations of his people. (By placing here the genealogy from Jesus back to Adam, Luke is doubtless affirming that Jesus is taking on again the temptations of all humanity.)

Paul takes up these same temptations of the people (I Cor. 10.1–11) to show that they are our own. That happened to them as a type of ourselves (vv. 6, 11). The type is not an example or a model, but a mock-up or a pattern (for a dress, for example). This mock-up represents in advance the object that is to be made; it is this object. The temptations of the people of Israel are a mock-up of our own, and these are the ones which Jesus experienced. We do not have so much to imitate Jesus (that might simply be moralism) as to live out our own existence (and our temptations) in him, because he has taken them on and has already overcome them.

🦊 The Sermon on the Mount. 5–7

Here we shall be reading Matthew: we shall compare his text with that of Luke later (p. 77). If you want, you can go on to study the Beatitudes now (p. 78).

Begin by reading through this Sermon carefully. There is a plan on the opposite page to help you.

Who is speaking? To whom? Who: Jesus of course, but how is he presented? What mountain is this? What Old Testament figure is he replacing? To whom: Jesus is teaching the crowds and the disciples. This is not the first proclamation, aimed at conversion (the kerygma), but a kind of catechism for those who have already discovered the pearl of great price and are ready to give up everything in order to possess it. The presence of the disciples indicates that this is possible: some have already made the choice to follow Jesus.

Note the refrains and the expressions which recur. 'You have heard. . .' 'Your Father who sees in secret. . .' Underline the word Father: it occurs twenty-one times in Matthew, twice in Mark and five times in Luke. It also occurs three times in John. There are sixteen occurrences in the Sermon: in which part? What significance does that give to Jesus' teaching?

One feature of the Sermon is impossible to reproduce in English. The Sermon alternates between the second person singular and the second person plural (to show this, the plural use of 'you' is marked with an asterisk* in the table opposite). The plurals (and similarly those phrases which begin 'whoever' or its equivalent) give general rules which apply to everyone everywhere: the singular use gives individual instances; they are meant to help people discover their own way of practising the general law in their particular situation (Jesus himself did not in fact observe the precept given in Matt. 5.39; see John 18.23). In each passage try to work out the general law, to see ways in which it is applied, and to look for examples which would apply today.

You can work out how Jesus fulfils the Law of Moses: he does not destroy it, but, following the line of the prophets, pushes it to extremes. He internalizes it: it is no longer a matter of outward attitudes but of love. He makes it personal: it is a question of living under the Father's gaze, and that is possible from now on because Jesus is the Son and invites us to enter into this filial relationship which he enjoys with the Father.

	Luke	Matthew	Mark
Opening 5.3–16			
5.3–12 The Beatitudes. The good news (originally 3,6,11–12)	**6.20–26**(24–26)		
5.13–16 Christians, the salt and the light of the world	14.34–35		9.50
	8.16; 11.33		4.21
I The new justice is superior to the old 5.17–48			
or, what is the significance for everyday behaviour of having experienced the good news?			
The principle			
5.17 Not to abolish the Law and the Prophets, but to fulfil	21.32–33; 16.17		
5.18–19 Anyone who breaks a single commandment		24.34–35	13.30–31
Five specific applications: 'You* have been told . . . I tell you*', 5.21–48			
5.21–24 'Do not kill' – not to be angry with one's brother			11.25
5.25–26 Hasten to be reconciled with your adversary	12.57–59		
5.27–28 'Do not commit adultery' – Do not even desire another woman in your* heart			
5.29–30 If your eye is an occasion for sin, pluck it out		18.9,8	9.47,43
5.31–32 Anyone who repudiates his wife	16.18	19.7–9	10.4–12
5.33–37 'Do not perjure yourself' – Do not swear oaths at all			
5.38–42 'An eye for an eye' – Turn the other cheek	**6.29–30**		
5.43–48 'Love your neighbour and hate your enemy' – Love your* enemies	**6.27–28,32–36**		
II The inward character of the new justice 6.1–18			
or, in what spirit are we to perform the traditional good works when we are children of the Father?			
The principle			
6.1 Only be concerned with the Father when you do good works			
The three traditional good works in Judaism			
6.2–4 Almsgiving in secret. 'Your Father who sees in secret'			
6.5–6 Prayer in secret. 'Your Father who sees in secret. . .'			
6.7–15 'Our Father. . .'	11.2–4		
6.16–18 Fasting in secret. 'Your Father who sees in secret. . .'			
6.19–21,22–23 The true treasure. The eye, the light of the body	12.33f.; 11.34f.		
6.24–34 Choosing between God and money. Trust in the Father	16.13; 12.22–31		
III Three admonitions 7.1–27			
or, who is a disciple? How to be one			
	(38a)	15.14;	
7.1–5 Don't judge. The log and the speck	**6.37–42**		4.24
	(39–40)	10.24	
7.6 Don't desecrate holy things			
7.7–11 The efficacy of prayer	11.9–13		
7.12 The golden rule: Do not do to others	**6.31**		
7.13–14 The narrow gate which leads to life	13.23–24		
7.15–20 The false prophets: they can be recognized by their fruits	**6.43–45**(45)	12.33–35	
7.21–27 The true disciples: Don't say 'Lord', but do the will of the Father	**6.46**		
7.22–23 It is not enough to drive out the demons in his name	13.26–27		
Build your house on the rock	**6.47–49**		
The effect on the crowd 7.28–29	7.1; 4.32		4.22
'He teaches as a man who has authority'			

NB The additions made by Matthew are in *italics*. The references to the speech in Luke **6.20–40** are in **bold**.

❦ Recognizing and following Jesus. 16.13–28

These three episodes form a turning point in the Gospel of Matthew (see p. 71).

Compare the response of Peter in Matt. 16.16; Mark 8.29; Luke 9.20; John 6.69. What, then, might have been this response? How does Matthew explain it by putting over it the 'tracing paper' of Christian faith? The importance of Peter's role in the first community was recognized by all Christians. Was this role handed on to successors? Here the Christian traditions differ.

❦ The community rule. 18

Jesus gives two groups of rules which he illustrates by two parables (18.10–14,23–25). What rules (what canon law?) did Jesus in fact leave to his church?

18.20 is very strong. A rabbi who died in 135 declared: 'When two people are sitting talking about the Law, the Shekinah (God's holy presence) is in their midst.' So Matthew puts Jesus in place of the Law and of God!

❦ The infancy narratives. 1–2

These narratives, like those in Luke, are not folklore, but theology, like Mark 1.1 or the hymn in John 1.1–18. Sometimes a film gives the main themes as a background to the credits, and then by a flashback puts the last images of the film at the beginning. Matthew does the same thing here, and puts at the beginning the main figures in the Gospel, telling us who Jesus is, the new Moses, and what his mission is to be.

Read these two chapters carefully: in the light of reading the Gospel as a whole (p. 70), try to see how Matthew immediately anticipates the features of the life of Jesus.

After the genealogy we have a sequence of five episodes, made up of two groups which are enclosed one within the other, each having a quotation from scripture:
1. The announcement to Joseph (1.18–25). Isa. 7.14.
a. *The magi* (2.1–12). Micah 5.1 + II Sam. 5.2.
2. The flight into Egypt (2.13–25). Hos. 11.1.
b. *The killing of the children* (2.16–18). Jer. 31.15.
3. The return to Nazareth (2.19–23). Isa. 42.6; possibly 49.6.

The first group (1, 2, 3), centred on the angel of God and Joseph, uses the same pattern: situation, message of the angel and mission, scripture, fulfilment of the mission. The second group (a, b) contrasts the two kings, Herod and Jesus.

The genealogy tells us who Jesus is: Christ, son of David, the beginning of the new creation (compare 1.1 with Gen. 5.1).

The announcement to Joseph tells us how Jesus is son of David despite the virgin birth. Being a just man, Joseph does not want to pass this miraculous child off as his own; however, God asks Joseph to give the child his name and his social position by making him part of a line.

The episode of the magi is a piece of scriptural research, a midrash *pesher* (see p. 21). Beginning from memories of Herod's bloody acts, Matthew constructs a story based on Isa. 60; 62 and the star in Num. 24.17 (which was seen as a portrayal of the Messiah at that time, see the box below). He did this to show how Jesus would be rejected by the Jewish authorities and the civil power, but recognized by the Gentiles.

The flight into Egypt shows in symbolic fashion how in Jesus the people achieve a successful exodus. The way to the kingdom of God is at last open.

Numbers 24.17

in the Hebrew text	in the Palestinian Targum
A star	*When the mighty king*
issuing from Jacob	*from the house of Jacob*
shall become ruler	*shall reign*
and a sceptre shall arise	*and when the Messiah, the powerful sceptre*
issuing out of Israel	*of Israel shall be anointed. . .*

So Matthew's star is real; it is the Messiah, Jesus, who has just arisen, and to his light the Gentiles, represented by the Magi, come.

Other texts studied elsewhere

The Passion according to Matthew

**The Last Supper
Lambert Rucky**

Matthew writes for Christians who already have faith and want to deepen it. He tries to unveil the significance of the death of Christ.

He is writing for Christians of Jewish origin: he shows how in Jesus God keeps the promise which he made to his people, and how Jesus fulfils the scriptures. Through its leaders, this Jewish people has rejected Jesus, so now the promise passes to a new people, the church. However, the church must stay on the watch: it, too, can refuse to follow Jesus.

In his presentation of events, Matthew seeks above all to show the power and the authority of Jesus.

Jesus is Son of God; he knows what will happen to him. He accepts this; indeed, events take place as they do because he foresees them.

Jesus is Lord over the whole world. The Father has entrusted his own power to Jesus, who could make use of it to escape death. However, that death marks the end of time and ushers in the arrival of the new world, the kingdom of God in which we now have to live.

The account of the conspiracy (26.1–5) seeks to answer two possible difficulties. How could the Son of God have been put to death? By placing the account on the lips of Jesus, Matthew shows that he is the one who directs events, and the leaders carry them out ('Then. . .', v. 3). How could the religious leaders, whose task it was to recognize the Messiah, condemn him? It was because they were those evil ones who, according to Ps. 2, came together against the Messiah (*How to Read the Old Testament*, p. 103). It is clear that from now on this messiah will be enthroned over the whole world as Lord. And Jesus sees his anointing in the house of Simon (26.6–13) as the celebration of his burial.

The account of the farewell meal held by Jesus (26.26–29) is framed by the announcement of Judas' betrayal and Peter's denial; so Jesus is well aware of the hands into which he will be putting his body and his blood. However, in this way he fulfils the scriptures (v. 31).

Up to that point, Jesus has celebrated his passion with the majesty of the celebrant at the altar. The account of the agony in the garden (26.36–46) shows him to be fully

man: three times Matthew adds the expression, with them, with me (vv. 36, 38, 40). Like everyone who suffers, Jesus feels the need of the presence of his friends. Even that is denied him; they are asleep. However, in reciting the Our Father to help himself to accept the Father's will, he rediscovers all his strength; at the time of the arrest (26.47–56), he teaches once again and refuses to use the power which the Father has given him.

At his trial before the Jews (26.57–68), Jesus proclaims that henceforth, from now on (v. 64), he will be instituted by the Father into the power of the exalted Son of Man, the enthroned Messiah. The accounts of Peter's denial (26.69–75) and the death of Judas (27.3–10) remind us tragically that we can refuse to recognize his humiliated Lord. Above all, Matthew shows that here the oracle of Zechariah is being fulfilled; the people at that time rejected God, and to make mock of him paid him the derisory price of a slave (*How to Read the Old Testament*, p. 86). In Jesus, then, it is God himself who is being sold.

In the scene of the Roman trial (21.11–26), Matthew adds the intervention of Pilate's wife: even the Romans recognize that Jesus is righteous. Pilate washes his hands of him and the people take responsibility for his death: 'His blood be on us'. From now on, in order to be saved, everyone, Jews and Gentiles alike, will have to enter into the covenant sealed with the blood of Jesus.

For Matthew, the death of Jesus (27.32–54) marks the end of the old world and the beginning of the new world. In this way it fulfils the scriptures, which Matthew quotes abundantly.

Jesus dies apparently abandoned by all, even by God. But his death is resurrection: the earthquake, the upheaval, is an image of the end of time; at that moment the saints rise and enter the heavenly Jerusalem and the Gentiles recognize that Jesus is Son of God.

The high priests seal the tomb and set a watch (27.55–61): the power of the Risen Jesus only appears the greater. They themselves remember the forecast of the resurrection. Apparently all is over. Matthew warns us that it is only just beginning, and that the dawn of the resurrection is breaking in the night of the tomb.

Matthew's Jesus

The Lord living in his community

With Mark we discovered primarily the man Jesus; Matthew presents us from the start with the glorified Lord, celebrated in his community. The disciples prostrate themselves in adoration before the Risen Jesus (28.17), as do the Magi (2.2,11), the leper, the centurion, the disciples in the storm, though they should prostrate themselves only before God (4.10).

The fact is that by virtue of his resurrection, Jesus is truly God with us: the name Emmanuel, proclaimed at his birth (1.23), is given to him only on Easter Day; it is even the last saying in the Gospel: 'I am (the equivalent of God in the Old Testament) with you' (28.20).

He is the well-beloved Son of God. Mark does not use this title very much, and makes us see how difficult the disciples found it to recognize him. In Matthew, Jesus presents himself in this way (11.27; 26.63–64) and the disciples proclaim him to be Son of God on several occasions (e.g. 14.33; 16.16).

Matthew's Jesus is also solemn, hieratic. Matthew leaves out Jesus' emotion and his not-knowing (compare Matt. 13.58 with Mark 6.5) and stresses his power (4.23; 8.24; 15.30). Once, however, this Lord shows himself to be very human by looking for some affection from his friends in his agony.

Jesus is the saviour of his community. The miracles show him to be the suffering servant of Isaiah who takes our infirmities upon him (8.17). By schematizing the miracle stories, by effacing the human features of Jesus and presenting Peter's mother-in-law (8.15) or the disciples in the storm (8.25) in the guise of the Christians of his time, Matthew shows that the Lord Jesus is continuing his saving work in the community in Matthew's own day.

Jesus is the Lord of his community. Moses had given the Law to the people; Jesus is the new Moses who gives the new law, in the Sermon on the Mount and on the mountain where he appears at Easter. The concern of this law is that men should be perfect as the Father is perfect. Restoring the ancient Law to its original purity, Jesus looks for mercy and not sacrifice (9.13; 12.7), and again it is mercy and forgiveness that he leaves as a rule for his church (18.21–35). He wants his disciples to have an intelligent faith, to understand, and asks this of them several times (e.g. 13.19,23,51; 15.10).

Jesus is the model for his community. 'It is fitting for us to fulfil all righteousness', he says to John (3.15), and in a text which appears only in his Gospel, he presents the life of Jesus as the only way of arriving at knowledge of the Father (11.27–30).

The Messiah of Israel

For Matthew, Jesus is the Messiah looked for by Israel and announced by scripture. As a true rabbi, Matthew skilfully quotes the scriptures to show that Jesus fulfils them. He frequently gives Jesus official titles like Messiah (Christ), Son of David, King of Israel. Rejecting him or accepting him decides whether a person belongs to the true Israel: the Gentile magi worship him, but Jerusalem rejects him; priests and scribes condemn him, while the Roman centurion and his men proclaim him Son of God. The kingdom, too, will be taken away from the former to be given to others (parable of the murderers in the vineyard, 21–41). The Messiah of Israel becomes the world's Messiah.

The Son of Man

In the tradition of the apocalypses (see Dan. 7), people looked to the coming of the Son of Man at the end of time to give judgment. For Matthew, Jesus is this Son of Man; he declares himself to be Son of Man before the Sanhedrin and proclaims that from now on people will see him (26.64). Easter is truly the parousia of the Son of Man coming on the clouds (26.64) to his prostrate disciples (28.18), having received all power (28.18; cf. Dan. 7.14). Matthew is the only one to speak of this parousia or arrival (24.3,27,37,39) of the Son of Man. In fact for him it denotes the moment when the kingdom of God takes its place in our history. That happens at the time of the resurrection; this parousia also takes place every time one meets the Son of Man mysteriously present in the little ones with whom he identifies himself (25.31–46).

Jesus sends his community

Enthroned as Son of Man, sovereign judge and lord of all the world, Jesus has won the final victory. Now the territory has to be occupied, so he sends his disciples to establish his victory throughout the world. He had prepared them for this mission (10), but at that time he was the one who went out to preach. The real mission begins on Easter Day (28.18–20).

Catechesis. The Discourses

When the audiences had heard the preaching (the kerygma) of the disciples and had themselves become disciples of Jesus Christ through faith and baptism, it still remained to complete their teaching. 'They devoted themselves to the apostles' teaching', writes Luke (Acts 2.42). When we studied Christian action (pages 55–56), we discovered this catechesis through the Epistles. Now we shall look at it through the discourses of Jesus in the Gospels.

Jesus preached; that's quite obvious. Did he talk at length, like the discourses in the Gospels? That's possible. At all events, however, these discourses are for the most part the result of the work of the communities which brought together the words of Jesus to make them into a kind of catechism.

The most obvious instance of this is the Sermon on the Mount in Matthew, and the corresponding Sermon on the Plain in Luke. We have already studied Matthew's text (p. 73). Here we shall compare the two texts.

Place and importance

In Matthew, the sermon is a programmatic discourse of Jesus, the first one which he gives: it contains 107 verses. In Luke there are only 30 verses, and the programmatic discourse is given earlier, in the synagogue at Nazareth (Luke 4.16–30). Mark does not have one at all!

Towards an earlier text

Without claiming to be able to go back to the words of Jesus, we can try to see whether Matthew and Luke were inspired by a text which they found in their source and how they have modified it or enriched it.

Go back to the diagram on p. 73. If you look at the Luke column you will see that the whole of the discourse in Luke 6.20–40 reappears, sometimes in a different order, in that of Matthew, apart from 6.24–26 and four other verses: 38a, 39, 40, 45.

After a very careful study, the French scholar J. Dupont has produced the following hypothesis. Matthew reproduces his source, but adds to it a certain number of teachings (which have been put in italics in the diagram). Luke reproduces the same source, which had already been enlarged by four verses; however, he prunes it, putting certain pieces of teaching elsewhere.

Whatever the exact position may be, this first form of the discourse was already a collection of isolated sayings of Jesus which had been made by the community; some could be the summary of one of his sermons, others a condensation of a long piece of teaching given in the form of questions and answers. By collecting them together in this way, the disciples wanted to present the whole of Christianity (as a kind of catechism) in comparison to the teaching of Judaism which might already have been put forward by the Pharisees of Jamnia (see p. 31).

Matthew's sermon

Matthew takes up this catechism faithfully. He stresses the practical consequences, and gives instances of possible applications.

In the light of the study made earlier (p. 72), try to distinguish the main outlines of this catechism on the conduct of the perfect disciple.

Luke's discourse

Luke's discourse is much shorter and keeps the character of a gospel, the proclamation of good news (for the Beatitudes see pp. 78–79). Hearing it makes us feel the demands of a different way of life, and Luke focusses his catechism on this love.

Compare Luke 6.36 and Matt. 5.48: what is the difference? What significance does it give to Christian life?

Compare Luke 6.33–35 and Matt. 5.47; what is the difference? Luke is virtually the only one, along with I Peter, to use the term 'do good' or 'good conduct' (I Peter 2.14,15,20; 3.6,17; 4.19; see pp. 54–55). What vision of the Christian life does Luke give us?

Compare the refrain in Luke 6.32,33,34 and Matt. 5.46. What difference is there? The word translated 'acknowledgment' or 'recognition' (with a risk of suggesting the idea of a quid pro quo, if not some recompense) is grace. What we receive as a quid pro quo for our love is not a reward, but grace.

Read the discourse again in the light of these observations. Try to identify the main outlines of this catechism about the behaviour of the one who knows himself or herself to be loved freely by God.

The beatitudes

The Sermon on the Mount in Matthew and the Sermon on the Plain in Luke open with the proclamation of the beatitudes. Jesus' message is thus essentially an announcement of good cheer. But for whom, and how?

Sad to say, we must recognize that as a result of a tragic misinterpretation, the beatitudes have often been used as an opiate to soothe the suffering or the rebellion of the poor. They seemed to say, 'You poor are fortunate because you are loved by God, so – stay poor! Accept your lot and one day, in heaven, you will be happy.' Now we shall be seeing that Jesus proclaimed exactly the opposite: 'You poor are fortunate since from now on you will no longer be poor, because the kingdom of God is on its way.'

Begin by comparing these beatitudes: which ones do Matthew and Luke have in common? To whom are they addressed (they – you)? What kind of poverty is it in Luke? In Matthew? Distinguish the two series of beatitudes: the first eight in Matthew (same style, same expression, kingdom of God, at the beginning and the end) and the ninth (a change of style and of those to whom it is addressed).

The beatitudes before Matthew and Luke

Jesus doubtless proclaimed beatitudes at different times. The community made a first collection which a scholar, J. Dupont, has reconstructed with some degree of probability (see the bottom of the opposite page). What might their significance be at this stage? (We shall only be studying the first series.)

To discover this, we have to put the beatitudes back into Jesus' teaching about the kingdom of God. Read again what I said about it on p. 65. Compare the beatitudes common to Matthew and Luke and Jesus' reply to the messengers from John the Baptist. In his reply Jesus quotes the prophets, so he is aware of realizing their proclamations in his actions. Read some texts again: Isa. 49.9; 52.7; 60.6; 61.1; 35.5–6. During the exile, or just afterwards, prophets announced that God would reign, that he would finally manifest himself as the good King that he was. What signs does he give? Are not these the signs which Jesus performs? So Jesus is affirming that the kingdom of God is at hand in his person and that from now on there will no longer be any poor; that is why they are said to be happy.

An objection: if this is the meaning of Jesus' proclamation, he was wrong, because there are always poor and there is always injustice. To raise this question, though, is to note that unfortunately we Christians have not done our work. People were in fact waiting for a Messiah who would establish the kingdom of God single-handed. Jesus came as Messiah, but he inaugurated this kingdom only by entrusting to his disciples the task of realizing it. The first Christians understood this very well: they held their possessions in common, Luke writes, and there were no longer any poor among them (Acts 4.34). One cannot proclaim the beatitudes without doing everything possible to remove poverty in all its forms, sickness and injustice.

The primary meaning of the beatitudes, then, is theological; they speak of God, the God of the poor, who is going to establish his kingdom of justice and love by his Messiah and his disciples. In the Gospels they have become christological: in different ways Matthew and Luke lay stress on the one by whom this kingdom arrives, Christ.

The beatitudes according to Luke

To whom are the beatitudes addressed? The second person plural is directed to the disciples. Jesus tells these Christians who are poor that their wretched situation is only to be expected: it is the result of their faithfulness towards him. However, at their death, God will rectify the situation.

The beatitudes according to Matthew

Matthew does not just address Christians, but everyone. He is the only one to spiritualize these beatitudes and make them attitudes of mind. Jesus asks those who, like the first disciples mentioned in Acts, try to see that there will no longer be any poor, 'With what feelings are you acting?' Paul understood this very well when he wrote, 'though I sell all my goods to feed the poor and have not love, I am worth nothing' (I Cor. 13.3). We have to fight until there are no longer any poor, but we have to do so with a humble heart. Only those who feel like this can help the poor without smothering them with pity. This attitude has its source in Jesus, who is meek and humble in heart (Matt. 11.29). Only when we know that we ourselves have been given abundant grace can we pass on this good news to the poor, to help them emerge from their poverty.

Matthew 5.3–12	Luke 6.20b–23	Luke 6.24–26

3 *Blessed are the poor in spirit,*
   for theirs is the kingdom of heaven.
	20b *Blessed are you poor,*
	   for yours is the kingdom of God.
		24 *But woe to you who are rich,*
		   for you have received your
		   consolation.

4 *Blessed are those who mourn,* *for they shall be comforted*	*(see 21b)*	*(see 25b)*
5 *Blessed are the meek,* *for they shall inherit the earth.*		

6 *Blessed are those who hunger and*
   thirst for righteousness,
   for they shall be satisfied
	21 *Blessed are you who hunger now,*
	
	   for you shall be satisfied.
	   Blessed are you who weep now,
	   for you shall laugh.
		25 *Woe to you that are full now,*
		
		   for you shall hunger.
		   Woe to you that laugh now,
		   for you shall mourn and weep.

7 *Blessed are the merciful,* *for they shall obtain mercy.*		
8 *Blessed are the pure in heart,* *for they shall see God.*		
9 *Blessed are the peacemakers,* *for they shall be called sons of God.*		

10 *Blessed are those who are persecuted*
   for righteousness' sake,
   for theirs is the kingdom of heaven.		

11 *Blessed are you when men*
   revile you
 and persecute you
 and utter all kinds of evil against you
 falsely
 on my account.
	22 *Blessed are you when men*
	   hate you
	   and when they exclude you
	   and revile you
	   and cast out your name as evil
	   on account of the Son of man!
		26 *Woe to you*
		
		   when all men speak well of you,

12 *Rejoice and be glad,*
   for your reward is great in heaven
 	
 for so men persecuted
 the prophets who were before you.
	23 *Rejoice in that day, and leap for*
	   joy,
	   for behold, your reward is great in
	   heaven
	   for so their fathers
	   did to the prophets.
		for so their fathers
		   did to the false prophets.

An earlier version of the text has been reconstructed with a high degree of probability.

Blessed are the poor, for the kingdom of heaven is theirs.
Blessed are those who mourn, for they shall be comforted.
Blessed are those who hunger (and thirst), for they shall be satisfied.
Blessed are you when men hate you and exclude you and insult you
and give you an evil name because of the Son of man;
rejoice and be glad, for your reward is great in heaven,
for so men persecuted the prophets (which were) before you.

The good news of the kingdom of God

The essence of the good news, the gospel that Jesus proclaimed, was that the reign, the kingdom of God, was at hand. Through his actions (the miracles, and also his specific attitude towards the poor, the insignificant and the scorned) and his words (the discourses of which the beatitudes bring out the main theme), Jesus shows that this kingdom is at hand. Above all he is the one who proclaims and inaugurates this kingdom.

Now we can see that in the community and in the Gospels, people proclaimed the good news about Jesus. The one who had made the proclamation became the subject of this proclamation. There is a shift of interest, but the meaning remains the same. 'The dead are raised' was one of the staggering signs of the advent of the kingdom. To proclaim that Jesus is risen is to affirm that *in him* the kingdom has come. This man, transfigured by the Spirit, is the symbol of man who has entered the kingdom.

However, in the light of this the disciples understand better that it is also *through Jesus* that the kingdom arrives. To proclaim the risen Jesus is another even clearer way of announcing that the kingdom of God is here.

The beatitudes: a political programme

If Jesus merely inaugurated this kingdom, we can understand that the beatitudes and all the teachings which are developed from them remain for all Christians a programme of action in their specific political, social, economic and family life.

They remind us that the motive behind our action must be the service of others, primarily the poor, so that there are no longer poor among us. The motive can never be money or power.

They also allow the Christian to give a deeper meaning to his human work: a doctor who fights against sickness, a worker who makes life more humane for others by the products that he makes, a teacher who helps young people to discover themselves, anyone who works so that others around him can live happy lives, standing on their own feet, have

the right to suppose that in a modest but effective way they are bringing about the kingdom of God.

Why does Jesus ask so much?

You will have been struck while reading the beatitudes, the Sermon on the Mount, the discourses of Jesus, by the terrible demands that he makes. You must give everything immediately! How is that possible?

You will also have noted Matthew's stress on the heavenly Father. We are to be as perfect as he is. That stress changes everything. Morality, Christian action, is not a law code which has to be applied: it is a loving demand. When we know ourselves loved with such love, we cannot but want to be like the one who loves us. So this demand is infinite, like the love of God. But when it is a loving demand, everything becomes possible.

What Jesus offers is not renunciation but happiness. The word 'blessed' in the beatitudes means 'happy'. The parables of the treasure and the pearl (Matt. 13.44–46) say this clearly: Jesus is addressing people who already have the experience of that love, who have already discovered the marvels of this kingdom and who are therefore ready to give everything in order to gain it. The law of the gospel can be absolute because it invites us to more-than-living, to happiness.

And the witness of those who have already made this choice is an essential element. When Jesus preaches on the mount, he is surrounded by his disciples (Matt. 5.1): those who hear this call of Jesus see that it is possible to respond to it since some men have already made their choice. And it is no coincidence that the beatitudes end with two comparisons: 'You are the salt of the earth. . . You are the light of the world' (Matt. 5.13–16). That is the best-ever definition of the church. The church is not a container for those who are saved ('no salvation outside the church'); it is a signal, a light on a mountain, revealing a meaning to life, serving as a beacon for the way 'to those who walk in darkness' (Isa. 60), a light which does not come from itself but which draws on its source by which it is illuminated.

Luke and the ox. Keystone of the rood-loft at Chartres (thirteenth century)

6 The Work of Luke: The Gospel and Acts

Luke is original in having written a work in two volumes: the Gospel and the Acts of the Apostles. They should be read together. We have already gone through Acts, rather superficially, using it as a tourist guide; we shall go back to it here, along with the Gospel, to discover the plan of Luke's work.

Taking up the comparison on p. 19, one might say that Luke, like the other evangelists, put over the life of Jesus the tracing paper of the life of the church; in Acts, however, he wanted to give us this overlay by itself.

A believing historian

Modestly, Luke does not write a Gospel but 'an account of events', so that the disciple can confirm his faith: he says as much in a prologue characteristic of the historians of his day (1.1–4).

However, the historian Luke is a believer: what he narrates is for him good news which he wants to share. He constantly tells his reader, 'You can't read this in a detached way; you must choose for or against, and you must do so today. . .' His account therefore never has the cool tones of a description; it is always at the same time an exhortation. The disciple is at the heart of his preoccupations; he is the one who is being addressed and is being persuaded to enter the marvellous world which Luke has discovered.

Luke's community

We do not know anything precisely about the community in which Luke was writing, but we can easily imagine the kind of church in which his message took shape: these were communities which had grown up on Gentile territory; Greek, like the churches of Antioch or Philippi. As we read the work we can pick out several of their features.

These Christians are former Gentiles. Luke, himself a Greek, adapts to their mentality. He stresses the reality of the resurrection (which the Greeks will have found difficulty in accepting), but uses a vocabulary which says more to them: 'Jesus is alive'. He uses the term 'saviour' to explain the title Christ/Messiah, which will have been obscure to his readers. Emperors were called 'Lord', so Luke is careful to say that Jesus is the only Lord. He avoids the word 'transfiguration' (Greek *metamorphosis*), because there were several accounts of the metamorphoses of Greek gods.

These Christians know that they are accepted into God's covenant with Israel by grace and not by birth. They are keen to reread the scriptures, to find in them the loving plan of God.

They have had experience of the Spirit: their churches came into being outside the Jerusalem circle, and were formed through the word of God and the Spirit. They know that faith in Jesus has brought them into a tradition, that of the apostles, which Luke investigates with care, but they know how to live it out in the freedom of the Spirit which drives them towards their fellow Gentiles. Unlike Matthew's communities, those of Luke find no difficulty in universalism.

The author

Traditionally, since the second century Luke has been seen as the 'beloved physician' (Col. 4.14) who accompanied Paul from Troas to Philippi, where he probably lived between 50 and 58. He rejoined Paul at Miletus, followed him to Caesarea and then to Rome (according to the passages in Acts written in the first person). Perhaps he came from Antioch, of Gentile (or Hellenistic) ancestry? An educated man, he handles with some skill the Greek commonly spoken at the time (the *koine*).

A stone discovered at Caesarea bearing the name of Pontius Pilate

The Gospel and Acts as a Whole

As with Mark and Matthew, it would be a good thing to begin by reading the Gospel and Acts straight through, as though it were a novel. It will take time, but you will see that it pays off.

Here are some points to guide you in your reading.

Luke's geography

The Gospel. In the first volume, Jerusalem has a central place. The Gospel begins and ends in the Temple (1.5f.; 24.52–53). The childhood of Jesus, from Nazareth to Bethlehem and back to Nazareth, comes to a climax in the arrival of Jesus at his Father's house, the Temple (2.41f.), and the Risen Lord shows himself only in Jerusalem (this forces Luke to change the saying of the angels at the tomb, 24.6).

Jesus begins his preaching in Galilee, but does so in order to be able to return to Jerusalem: the second part is organized as an ascent to Jerusalem (9.51–19.28). The paschal mystery has to unfold in the holy city, because 'it is not fitting that a prophet should perish outside Jerusalem' (13.33). In fact Jesus fulfils the divine plan announced by scripture with the holy city at its centre. However, Jerusalem rejects Jesus.

Acts. The second volume also shows how the Word spreads from Jerusalem, into Judaea and Samaria, and then to the ends of the earth, whose capital at that time was Rome.

Three periods in the history of salvation

The other evangelists think of two periods in the history of salvation: that of the promise and that of Jesus with his church. By writing two volumes, Luke can distinguish the times in a better way: that of the promise, that of Jesus, and that of the church.

1. The time of the promise

This is the time of the Old Testament. For Luke, it comes to an end only with the 'Today' in the sermon at Nazareth (4.21). John the Baptist is charged with preparing the people of the promise to welcome the prophet, but he himself remains within this time of preparation (7.28). Jesus also forms part of it; he comes to receive John's baptism in the midst of the people (3.21). These people

have returned to the desert to reenact the exodus which failed the first time (the story of the temptations); Jesus is even mankind as a whole, the new Adam, at last taking his place in a true relationship with God (the genealogy, which goes back to Adam). From now on the gateway to the kingdom of God is open to the people of the promise and to all men: God's 'Today' can resound in our astonished ears (4.21).

Luke often refers to the scriptures, but in a different way from Matthew. He does not try to cite precise texts; for him scripture is as it were a subterranean water-table which gives life and meaning to events. And Jesus draws on it copiously before opening the minds of his disciples to understand the scriptures on Easter Day (24.45). That explains the numerous occasions on which Jesus uses the word 'must': it is not a question of blind obedience to a programme prepared in advance, but rather of shaping his life in such a way as to put it back into continuity with God's plan (see p. 113).

2. The time of Jesus: the Gospel

Luke uses material which he receives from the tradition: the Gospel of Mark (or an earlier version of its text) and the logia source which he shares with Matthew (look back at p. 15). However, he arranges these skilfully by adding to them traditions peculiar to himself in order to present us with the divine plan as he sees it.

Leaving aside the birth narratives, to which we shall return, and the time of preparation, the itinerary of Jesus consists of three main stages:

In Galilee, Jesus proclaims his paschal mystery (4.14–9.50). The sermon at Nazareth (4.14f.) is the programmatic speech for it. By bringing together two visits, one in which Jesus is well received and the other, much later, in which he is rejected, Luke shows how this proclamation is to be received. In this part he follows Mark closely except for the discourse on the plain (see p. 77) and the section between 7.1 and 8.2, where he presents Jesus as the new Elijah, the prophet who is the friend of sinners.

Jesus goes up to Jerusalem towards his paschal mystery (9.51–19.28). This is the most original part of the Gospel: the ascent to Jerusalem by Isaiah's servant.

In Jerusalem, Jesus fulfils the paschal mystery (19.29–24.53). On Easter day Jesus shows himself alive to his disciples and ascends to heaven.

3. The time of the church: Acts

Luke uses various pieces of material, some very early, which he brings together or rewrites: themes from the preaching of Peter, Paul and Stephen (see p. 34), archives from the communities in Jerusalem or Antioch, reminiscences of the activity of Peter and Paul, no doubt his travel diary when he himself accompanied Paul (the passages in Acts written in the first person).

The plan of the book is presented clearly by Jesus: the disciples are to be his witnesses in Jerusalem, Judaea and Samaria and to the ends of the world (1.8). The main figures in this development are Peter, then the Hellenists, and finally Paul, but above all the Spirit and the Word of God.

The plan of the book might be outlined as follows:

I. From the beginning of the church to the Council of Jerusalem. 1.1–15.35

   The community at Jerusalem. 1.1–5.42
   The church is opened up to Gentiles. 6.1–15.35
   Luke presents successively the missionary activity of the Hellenists (8.1–9.31), of Peter (9.32–11.18 and 12.1–23), and of the church at Antioch (11.19–14.28). This culminates in the Council of Jerusalem (15.1–11), followed later by a meeting held by James (15.12–35).

II. From Jerusalem to Rome: Paul. 15.36–28.31

   In the course of his missionary tours Paul founds communities in Asia Minor and Europe. Taken to Rome as a prisoner, he preaches the gospel there with confidence.

Theological prologue. Luke 1–2

What we call the birth narratives or the infancy narratives are in fact a theological prologue to the whole work, both the Gospel and Acts. As with Matt. 1–2 (cf. p. 75), this is a kind of background to the 'credits', as in a film, where Luke presents the most important themes in advance. It might be interesting to look at the main ones in the order in which they appear.

(i)   Jerusalem and the Temple: prayer (1.5f.).
(ii) Jesus, Son of David, Son of God, welcomed in faith by Mary, the daughter of Zion. The role of the Spirit (1.26–38).
(iii) The role of women, the Spirit, prayer, the humbling of the rich and the proud and the raising up of the lowly (1.39–56).
(iv) The name John, which means 'God is gracious', and the visit of God to his people (1.57–80).

(v)   The good news to the poor (the shepherds): a saviour, Christ the Lord. God's today. The glory which shines out from this child on all men. And the result: joy for the world. This is the essential feature of the plan of Acts as suggested here, along with the role of the missionaries who go into the world: Peter, Paul and ourselves (2.1–21).
(vi) Again the Temple and the Holy Spirit, prayer, light for the Gentiles. There is a dispute over the significance of Jesus, in the face of which a choice has to be made (2.22–39).
(vii) As the culmination of the childhood of Jesus: the Temple and the first of Jesus' sayings to mention the Father. The first ascent to Jerusalem which evokes thoughts of the last: a disappearance for three days, being sought by the women; the Father, 'I must be about my Father's business', that 'the Christ must suffer to enter his glory'.

Some features of Luke

Luke's is the most 'modern' of the Gospels. His Greek education has given the author a concern for clarity. He handles the common Greek language (or *koine*) spoken at that time with a degree of elegance. However, he is also capable of imitating the language of the Greek Bible, very much coloured by Semitic turns of phrase, for example in the infancy narratives.

He deliberately interrupts his account with brief pauses or summaries, in which he sums up either features which he wants the reader to remember or the progress of the action. Thus three summaries present the activity of the community in Jerusalem (Acts 2.42); the growth of the Word of God is mentioned in Acts 6.7; 12.24; 13.49; 19.20; the expression 'we are going up to Jerusalem' maps out the central section of the Gospel.

As a good historian, he is concerned to locate events in history (2.1–3; 3.1–2); however, he has a poor knowledge of Palestine. He does not know about the construction of houses there or about the climate, and often he is content with very vague chronological notes: 'One day'. His interest is primarily theological.

Simply reading the Gospel, one is struck with the delicate way in which he treats Jesus, the poor, women, fishermen. Dante rightly called him 'the evangelist of God's tenderness'.

Some Texts from Luke

✤ Jesus' programme. Luke 4.14–44

With Matthew, it is the Sermon on the Mount followed by the miracles which makes up Jesus' programmatic discourse. For Luke, this function is fulfilled by the discourse at Nazareth.

Begin by reading this text carefully. What are the places: Galilee, Judaea, but also the synagogue (the place of Jewish religion), outside the city? Who are the main figures?

Look for the key words: Spirit, good news, poor, today, Elijah, go his way (or ascend), Word. . .

Put the Isaiah quotation back in its historical context (see *How to Read the Old Testament*, p. 77). In this context, what do words like poor and freedom imply? Where does Luke end the Isaiah quotation? Why?

Look for the 'inclusion' which marks off this section (inclusion is a procedure which consists in repeating the same things at the beginning and end of a passage to show that it is a unit). Teach or proclaim in the synagogues (vv. 15, 19, 44); all, crowd (vv. 15, 42); announce the good news (vv. 18, 43); sent (vv. 18, 43). How do the three miracle stories with the verb rebuke (vv. 35, 39, 41) become a concrete realization of this programme (see p. 17)?

Note how the account doesn't quite hang together. Why this abrupt change of attitude in v. 22? In Luke, has Jesus already performed miracles at Capernaum (v. 23)? Look at the arrangement indicated on p. 17.

After this study, go back to the text as a whole.

Who is Jesus? Look at his titles (vv. 18, 34, 41; the new Elijah), the authority of his words (vv. 32, 36), glorified (v. 15; elsewhere God is the only one to be glorified).

What is his mission (vv. 18–19)? The liberation is made specific by the three miracles (see Acts 10.38). At whom is this mission directed: the Jews (his own country, synagogue), the Gentiles (the example of Elijah and Elisha)? What will be his welcome by the Jews?

What awareness does Jesus have of this mission? Look at the verb 'go up' or 'go his way' (vv. 30, 42).

What connection can you see with the beatitudes?

✤ The church's programme. Acts 1.12–2.47

Peter's speech (already studied on p. 34), inserted into the account of Pentecost, forms the programmatic discourse for the infant church. Here we shall look at the whole section.

Begin by looking for the inclusion which marks off this section: they, all (the group of 120), continue, prayer (1.14; 2.42); meet, united, together (the same expression, which is rare in Greek: 1.15; 2.44, 47). In this way we move from a group of 120 to a group of '120 to whom God adds 3,000' (2.41, 47). The text shows what the church needs to preach and to grow.

Note the words which recur in Acts 2 (sometimes translated by different words in our Bibles): tongue (vv. 3, 4, 11); dialect (vv. 6, 8); voice (v. 6, translated noise, rumour, v. 14); speak (vv. 4, 5, 7, 11, 31).

Look for the main characters involved. In particular see the role of God, Jesus, the Spirit, the disciples.

Pentecost appears as the fulfilment of the mystery of Christ, a sign that he is exalted – and as the beginning of the mystery of the church. How would you express it?

The Jewish feast of Pentecost at that time celebrated the giving of the Law on Sinai. Can you see connections between the event as it was described at the time (see the box below) and Luke's account? This Jewish feast was a festival of the new covenant (reread Jer. 31.31f.; Ezek. 36.26), and Ps. 68 was read on it (see p. 37). The Spirit is the gift which the exalted Jesus gives to his church.

The voice of God once came from Sinai; now it comes from the church, the voice of God in the world.

Jews meditated on Ex. 20.18: At Sinai the people saw the voices and the thunderings. The Jewish philosopher Philo, a contemporary of Jesus, wrote: Since God does not have a mouth, he decided that by a miracle an invisible sound should be produced in the air, a breath which, articulated into words which turned the air into fire with the form of flames, made a voice resound in such a way that those who were furthest away could hear it as clearly as those who were nearest. . . A voice resounded from the midst of the fire which came down from heaven and became articulate in the native language of the hearers' (*De Decalogo* 9, 11). And Rabbi Johanan, active between AD 90 and 130, declared that the voice of God divided itself into seventy languages. Since for Jews there were seventy Gentile nations in the world, this was a way of saying that the Law was addressed to all men.

The glory of the Son of God. Luke 9.28–36

The account of the transfiguration is also given in Matt. 17.1–9 and Mark 9.2–10, and by John 12.28; II Peter 1.16–18. This text is important and calls for deep study. Here I can only give you a few comments to follow up.

In the life of Jesus. The event is situated towards the end of Jesus' ministry in Galilee: the crowds who had followed him now left him; the Jewish leaders increased their pressure. Jesus was aware that he was causing too much of a disturbance; if he continued, he risked death. And clearly he accepted this fate as a risk which went along with perseverance in his mission. He went up to Jerusalem under no illusions about the fate which awaited him, and he proclaimed it to his disciples.

In this context the transfiguration would seem to be a response from God to the faithfulness of Jesus and the anguish of his disciples. In what was no doubt an inner spiritual experience to which the three disciples were made privy, the Father shows Jesus the conclusion of his going up: beyond death he will find the glory promised at the end of time to the Son of man (see Daniel 10).

In times of doubt when we no longer know what to do, we may return to those moments of light we may have experienced when our vocation, our mission in life, seemed clear, and this will help us to be faithful to that light. Similarly, in this luminous experience, Jesus and the disciples could find the strength to enter on the agony and the passion. And it is no coincidence that these two scenes, the transfiguration and the agony in the garden, have points in common.

After Easter, the disciples knew that Jesus was caught up in the glory of God at his resurrection. So in the accounts as we have them, Jesus and his disciples go up towards death in the light of Easter, perceived in advance. This aspect is kept above all by Matthew and Mark.

Luke has taken up this story in a more personal way. Jesus goes up the mountain to pray (v. 28); it is during his prayer (v. 29), all through the night (v. 32), that he has this experience. By reaching down in this way to the sources of his being, Jesus sees the glory in which he has been invested since his birth, and in an inward conversation with the two great mystics of the Old Testament, Moses and Elijah, he can serenely envisage his exodus (v. 31): his death and exaltation.

By showing the disciples entering the cloud (v. 34) and stressing prayer, Jesus reminds us that we, too, can know something of such an experience; in prayer we can share in this glory of the crucified Lord and live our daily life in the light of this faith.

The servant goes up to Jerusalem. Luke 9.51–62

The central part of the Gospel (9.51–19.28) is arranged as an ascent to Jerusalem. The introduction indicates the significance it has for Jesus and what it implies for the disciples.

Jesus resolutely takes the road to Jerusalem, or literally, he sets his face to go up to Jerusalem. By making this allusion to Isa. 50.7, Luke shows Jesus to be the suffering servant going in full awareness to be taken up, that is, to his death-exaltation (see p. 111).

He is the new Elijah (v. 61, which alludes to I Kings 19.19), utterly dedicated to his mission, carried along by the Spirit, but not the Elijah of one Jewish tradition who pours out the wrath of God on his enemies (v. 55).

Jesus warns his disciples that to follow him requires total dedication, in which the demands of the mission go above everything else (vv. 57–62; Matthew put these verses at the beginning of his account of the stilling of the storm: see p. 66).

Ten lepers. Luke 17.11–19

You could read this text, simply looking in it for the great themes of Luke's work, especially those that he develops in the 'ascent to Jerusalem'.

The verb 'go up' appears at the beginning and the end: as he was going up; arise, get up (vv. 11, 19; see also vv. 9, 51, 53, 57; 10.1; 13.22, 33). What does this tell us about the way in which Jesus envisages his life and that of the disciple?

Jesus, Master, have mercy on us. The faith of the ten lepers is wonderful. They address Jesus by his first name, as does the thief on the cross (23.42); he too is to obtain salvation. Master: Luke is the only one to address Jesus by this title, which suggests power (5.5; 8.24; 9.33, 49). 'Have mercy' appeals to that which is most profound in God, his tenderness and his pity.

How is the leper described? Successively as one of the ten, a Samaritan, a stranger (v. 18). Here we can detect Luke's universalism: the Samaritans (cf. Acts 8) and the Gentiles hear the message better than the Jews.

Jesus Son of God: the leper prostrates himself when he gives thanks (Greek, 'making eucharist'); usually this was a gesture made only towards God.

From now on salvation is open to all, Jews and Gentiles, solely by faith in Jesus.

The theological prologue. Luke 1–2

These chapters, which form the prologue to the whole of Luke's work, both the Gospel and Acts, are very rich. Here are some suggestions for reading them.

Look at the plan. Write the titles of the episodes in two columns; in this way you will get a parallel between the childhood of John the Baptist and that of Jesus, both linked by the visitation.

Study the prayers: the Magnificat, the Benedictus, the Nunc Dimittis. As you look at the references in your Bible, see how Christian prayer draws on the Old Testament, to which it gives new meaning.

Look for the main themes which Luke develops in his work (see p. 83).

Now you can study the account of the annunciation (see p. 112).

▶ The birth of Jesus. Luke 2.1–20

The event (vv. 1–7). Stripped of all the folk lore with which we have decked it out, the birth is marvellous, like all births, but matter-of-fact. Because the main room was not the place in which to give birth, used as it was by all the family, a peasant mother would retire into the only place where it was quiet and warm: the stable.

The invisible aspect of the event (vv. 8–20). Angels and shepherds take it in turns to announce the birth, while the glory of God shines over it all (vv. 9, 14, 20).

The angel announces the good news (evangelizes). This word, which occurs more than a dozen times in Acts, sums up the activity of the Christian missionaries (5.42; 8.4, 12, 25). Compare v. 12 with Acts 2.36; 5.42; 11.20; 13.33–36; Phil. 3.20.

The shepherds. Using the literal translation in the next column, underline the words which recur and where they do so: what the shepherds do, what the two groups who hear them (v. 18 all those who, v. 19 Mary) do, and their attitude.

Say. This verb, which is very common in Acts, denotes the preaching of the Christian missionaries. The shepherds do not come to adore, but to preach a sermon!

Make known. Almost always, this verb expresses the revelation which God or Jesus has made to the disciples and which in turn they hand on to everyone: e.g. John 15.15; I Cor. 15.1; II Cor. 8.1; Eph. 1.9; 3.3, 5; 6.19.

So Luke took the Christian missionaries as his model for the shepherds. They therefore become the model for what every Christian should do in the world.

Two groups of hearers form: here are two attitudes which Jesus and then his disciples will encounter. All (all those who hear the message of Jesus or of the church down the ages) wondered: in Luke this attitude denotes an attitude of welcome which is only transitory, without roots (see 4.22; 8.13). By contrast Mary prefigures those who hear the Word and let it come to fruition in their hearts.

Note the shift in meaning of the term word (*rhema* in Greek): the shepherds heard a word pronounced (v. 17), they come to see a word which has come to pass: a baby (v. 15). The Word has been made flesh!

15. When the angels went away from them into heaven,
the shepherds said one to another,
'Let us go over to Bethlehem and see
this word (rhema) which has come to pass,
which the Lord has made known to us.'
16. And they went with haste,
and found Mary and Joseph,
and the babe lying in a manger.
17. And when they saw it
they made known the word (rhema)
which had been told them concerning this child.
18. And all who heard it were amazed
at what the shepherds had told them.
19. But Mary kept all these words (rhema),
pondering them in her heart.

Other texts studied elsewhere

The Passion according to Luke

To enter into Luke's account you must not just read it, but meditate on it as the two disciples were doing on the Emmaus road, when the words and the presence of Jesus as he explained the scriptures to them made their hearts burn within them. On this *via dolorosa*, Jesus is going with us, even if our eyes are still prevented from recognizing him.

Luke's whole account is stamped with delicacy and tenderness for his Lord Jesus. He cannot bring himself to report some details which were too distressing: he does not say that Jesus was scourged; Judas does not kiss Jesus, but simply 'draws near' to do so.

However, Luke is aware of the magnitude of the terrible struggle which takes place between Jesus and the powers of evil. The passion is the last decisive combat. Jesus comes out of it as victor through his patience, a word which is not a very good rendering of the Greek *hypomone* (that word suggests the attitude of the believer enduring blows in his trial because he is sustained by God, see Luke 8.16).

The whole of the passion is internalized. The decisive struggle takes place in Gethsemane: it is in this inner struggle, an agony, that the blood of Jesus flows. Comforted by God, as Elijah once was (I Kings 19.5f.), Jesus emerges victor, and now at peace, held in his Father's arms, he can forget his own suffering, to be entirely at the disposal of others. He welcomes Judas gently, heals the servant's ear, gives Peter heart again by his glance (22.61), speaks to the women who lament his fate, forgives his executioners and those who condemn him. Pilate proclaims him to be innocent three times, as do the women, the people, the thief on the cross, the centurion.

Jesus can die at peace. The cry which he utters on the cross is no longer the scream of human suffering confronted with death; it is the evening prayer known to every Jew: 'Into your hands I commend my spirit'. However, Jesus prefaces it with the term which marks his unparalleled intimacy with God: 'Father'.

In this way Luke invites us to enter with Jesus into his passion: with Peter to recognize our weakness and to feel upon us the forgiving gaze of our Lord; to carry his cross behind him, like Simon of Cyrene; and with him to abandon ourselves to the Father's arms.

The Last Supper (22.14–38) is above all the farewell meal in which Jesus expresses his trust in God and gives his last commands to his disciples. It is also the prophetic action by which he expresses the significance of his martyr death: the inauguration of the new covenant.

The agony followed by the arrest (22.39–53) is the decisive moment when Jesus emerges victor over the power of evil. The new Elijah, fortified by God, he goes forward into the night of his passion, at peace, entirely submissive to his Father's will.

The Jewish trial (22.54–71) opens with the account of Peter's denial. In this way Luke tells us, 'If you cannot follow the passion as a saint, you can always follow it as a forgiven sinner. The gaze of Jesus can always bring about a new being in you.'

Luke makes the high priest repeat his question. In this way Jesus proclaims clearly that he is Christ and Son of God.

During the Roman trial (23.1–25) Pilate declares three times that Jesus is innocent. The account of the appearance before Herod doubtless indicates that one cannot simply have a curious interest in Jesus.

At Calvary (23.26–49), Jesus declares his innocence to the women who are lamenting him, and consoles them. He asks the Father to forgive his executioners. He opens up paradise to the thief confident enough to call him by his first name, and dies in peace in the Father's arms.

The burial (23.50–57) is prepared for affectionately by the women. However, with all these spices they are wanting to keep him dead. They do not yet know that the light of the sabbath is already dawning (v. 54), and better still, the light of the resurrection.

You should read one after another the various disciples' passions which Luke has constructed on the same pattern. The passion of Stephen makes present that of Christ (Acts 4.23–31); Stephen is condemned for the same reasons; he dies forgiving his enemies, his eyes fixed on the Risen Jesus (Acts 6.8–15, 54–60). Paul goes up to Jerusalem, like his master, to bear witness there (Acts 20.22; 21.11).

Twelfth-century
Christ. Chapelle
St-Michel, Le Puy

87

Luke's Jesus

Luke did not know Jesus personally. So the Jesus whom he discovered is not primarily the itinerant prophet of Galilee but the glorified Lord showing himself to Paul on the Damascus road, the Lord whose face he discerned in a community like that of Philippi, where the loving power of Jesus was so strong that it enabled great ladies like Lydia and dockers in the port to live side by side in the same communion. Luke also finds features of this Jesus in the memories of the witnesses whom he questions.

The Lord Jesus. Luke is the only evangelist to call Jesus 'Lord' when he is talking about him. The glory of Easter is reflected back on his earthly life. This glory surrounds Jesus from his birth onwards (2.9, 32). The transfiguration is less an anticipation of the future glory of Easter (Matthew – Mark) than an emergence of the glory which he possesses from his conception, because he is born of the Spirit (9.32). The glory which he is to show as Son of Man is his own (9.26, compare Matt. 16.27; Mark 8.26). All men glorify him (4.15), though God is the only one who should be glorified.

Jesus is king (that is perhaps clearer to Greek readers); Luke is the only evangelist to say so, and he does it six times (1.32–33; 19.12f., 28f.; 22.28f., 67f.; 23.40f.).

Luke knows that Jesus acted as Lord and Christ only as a result of his resurrection (Acts 2.36); however, that is possible because he is Lord and Christ in his very being, as the infancy narratives affirm. The title Son of God is not a simple recognition of his role (equivalent to Son of David), but an affirmation of his nature (1.35; 22.70).

The Spirit of Jesus. This expression appears only twice in the New Testament (Acts 16.7; Phil. 1.19; spirit of Christ in Rom. 9.2; I Peter 1.11). The Spirit of God has so entered into Jesus that people can talk of *his* Spirit. Jesus is conceived by its power (1.35); it shows itself at his baptism (3.22), leads Jesus into the desert (4.1); Jesus is endowed with the Spirit to be made the bearer of the good news (4.14, 18). It is in the spirit that Jesus trembles for joy (10.21).

Through his glorification Jesus receives the Spirit from the Father, to give it to us (Acts 2.38) if we ask him (Luke 11.13; compare Matt. 7.11). Acts emerges as the Gospel of the Spirit which gives life to the community after Pentecost, as it gave life to Jesus and to the first witnesses of his life (Luke 1.15, 41, 67; 2.25–26).

Jesus is *the prophet* charged with revealing God (7.16, 39; 24.19; Acts 3.22–23), and his death is that of a prophet (13.33; Acts 7.52). Luke deliberately presents him as the new Elijah (see *How to Read the Old Testament*, p. 46).

The aspect of God which he reveals is above all that of the tenderness of the Father for all men. The main passage in which Luke presents Jesus as prophet (7.11–50) ends with the forgiveness of the woman who was a sinner. This love which arouses the Father's compassion (15.20) is shown by Jesus himself (7.13), and the disciple must show it too (10.33).

The coming of Jesus is God's visit. In Luke, the proclamation of judgment as by a prophet becomes the good news of salvation, a year of grace (4.19; cf. 1.68, 78; 7.16; 19.44). By his attitude Jesus makes this love of the Father visible: he is the friend of publicans and sinners (7.34). He is the saviour, the deliverer from Satan who holds men's hearts in thrall, and from evil which tortures their bodies. Jesus is the friend of sinners, because they need God in the same way as the sick person needs the physician (5.31), but even more because God needs them to show his forgiveness (15). Luke has a great attachment to women, often scorned at that time (Mary, Elizabeth, Anne, Mary Magdalene, Martha and Mary, the women who accompany him); some go on to play an important role in the church (Acts 1.14; 12.12; 16.14; 21.9).

Man before God. Jesus is not only Lord and Christ, but also fully man. He lives what he proclaims so perfectly that he is the model of the perfect man, transfigured by the Spirit, living in his Father's arms: his first word, like his last, speaks of the Father (2.49; 23.46). He constantly lives in the Father's presence and his prayer is a demonstration of it: it is while he prays that he receives his great revelations (baptism and the transfiguration); he spends his nights in prayer (5.16; 6.12; 9.28), and his disciples are so impressed that they want to be introduced to the secret of this relationship with God (the Our Father, 11.1).

Thus the very person of Jesus is at the centre of the Gospel. Confronted with him, men must choose. For this being who is so full of tenderness is also terribly demanding: men must make their choice for him today, simply because he is who he is. This total faith which obtains salvation is the source of the joy which irradiates the Gospel and transfigures the disciple.

The Parables

The parable is essentially a comparison developed in the form of a story. Its primary purpose is not so much to teach as to make its audience reflect on their behaviour, to make them pass judgment on themselves and so lead them to change this behaviour. Because we are bad at judging ourselves, the parable leads us to judge ourselves without being aware of the fact. For example, David sinned by seducing the wife of his officer Uriah and making sure that Uriah died in battle. The prophet Nathan had to make him aware of his sin. That was rather a delicate matter! So Nathan told David a feasible story (it had to be feasible, for David to accept it) about a rich land-owner who stole a poor man's only ewe lamb. David cried out, 'That man deserves to die,' thus passing judgment on himself without being aware of it. Nathan could conclude, 'You are that man' (II Sam. 12.1–15).

The parable, then, is a simple comparison. The details of the story are there only to add verisimilitude. So we need to try to sum up a parable in two phrases. 'Just as. . ., so. . .' Just as this man sinned in taking the poor man's ewe-lamb, so you David. . .'

It is important to distinguish parables carefully from another literary genre which resembles them closely: allegory.

Allegory also takes the form of a story, but is aimed at teaching. It is a story constructed expressly to help us understand something, and the details correspond to particular entities. So Jesus says, 'I am the vine, you are the branches. . .'

It is important to make a careful distinction between these two genres and to resist the temptation to interpret the parables as though they were allegories, although this is often done. Thus the parable of the Good Samaritan invites us to a particular kind of behaviour: 'Just as he was a neighbour to the wounded man without being concerned with his religion or his opinions, so you should make every person your neighbour.' The Fathers made the parable into an allegory – very fine, but far from the actual text: the wounded man was humanity attacked by the devil, the Samaritan was Jesus, the inn was the church, and so on.

However, we must not rule out the possibility that Jesus might have slipped allegorical features into a parable. Features which to us might seem trivial spontaneously evoked themes of scripture for Jews; thus, because of Isa. 5, the vine suggested Israel.

Rereading the parables

Jesus told his parables to Jews. In the community, they were now addressed to Christians. This change of audience often led to a change of meaning, which was expressed in a new conclusion.

In the light of Easter, people had a tendency to move from a theological interpretation to a christological interpretation: the parables of Jesus speak of God and his kingdom; the disciples were interested in Jesus, who inaugurated this kingdom.

There was a tendency to bring together parables which originally had a separate existence: the meaning of one of them would have repercussions for the meaning of another.

Sometimes the context given by the evangelists to parables would influence their meaning. This was also the case with the larger collections. Mark and Luke both put the chapter of parables at the beginning of Jesus' preaching in Galilee: they are primarily a simple way of presenting the kingdom of God. Matthew has put them towards the end of this preaching, at the moment when the crowds were already leaving Jesus. They seem primarily to be his last warning towards them: if you reject my message, it will be harvest: time for sorting out! (see p. 17).

Some practical rules

Reduce the parable to a simple composition (Just as. . . so. . .) making sure that it makes sense historically.

Leave aside all historical details that are not taken up again in the conclusion.

Distrust apparent conclusions which do not make sense historically.

The audience: to whom is the parable addressed by Jesus? To whom is it addressed by the disciples? Has the change in audience led to a change in meaning?

Does a change in the context of the parable change its meaning?

Single out possible allegorical features: have they served to give the parable a new interpretation?

Who is the parable talking about? God? Jesus?

The labourers in the vineyard. Matt. 20.1–16

Read this parable and the context in which it is set (19.27–30). With the help of the rules given on p. 89, try to distinguish the various conclusions with which it has been provided: why has it been reread, and in what way?

Read the rest of this page, but only when you have done that.

This text is a good example of the rereading of a parable. Let's look at the three successive conclusions which Matthew provides.

'For many are called, but few are chosen' (v. 16b). This phrase, with its 'for', is clearly a conclusion. It suggests the following comparison: 'Just as the master called many workers, and only a few came, so. . .' Now that does not match the story, since all those who were called actually came! So that's only a pseudo-conclusion. Some translations of the Bible leave it out, because it does not appear in all the manuscripts: it might have been borrowed from Matt. 22.14, where it fits better.

'So the last shall be first and the first last' (v. 16a). Does this conclusion fit the story well? The first workers protest, not because they are paid after the others, but because they are paid the same amount. So this, too, is a pseudo-conclusion.

'. . . because I am good' (v. 15). Here there is no interest in the first and the last; the intermediate categories are there only to add verisimilitude to the story. This phrase leads to the comparison: 'Just as the master is not unjust in giving as much to the last as to the first, because his standard for wages is not the work done but his own goodness, so God is not unjust in opening his kingdom to all, even sinners, because he does not reckon up our merits but does so of his own good will.'

Try to see which successive situations match these various conclusions.

Jesus spoke to Jews and, more precisely, to the religious élite, the Pharisees, who were scandalized at seeing him welcome sinners. They had taken a good deal of trouble to practise the Law, and some found it unjust that they were not to receive a greater reward because of their merits (see the rabbinic parable in the box opposite). Jesus replied to them: rewards are not measured by human merits but by God's goodness.

In the community, the audience for the parable changed: it was no longer addressed to Jews, but to the disciples. The primary sense, which was still valid for Christians, was retained (one need only think of the reactions which are still provoked: 'In that case it's not worth putting oneself out to earn heaven!'). However, by allegorizing one detail in the text it was turned into a piece of teaching. At this period the Gentiles had entered the church before the Jews, who had all rejected it as a people. History became a warning to them. If you reject the message, the Gentiles will enter the kingdom before you.

This threat was heightened by the addition of v. 16b, which takes up 22.14: You have all been called to enter the kingdom, says Jesus, but in fact very few people accept.

Matthew has put the parable after Peter's question (19.27); in this way it seems to be an illustration of Jesus' reply: the Twelve precede the Jewish leaders, though they were called after them.

The Fathers, and preachers after them, have made the parable into an allegory by adding secondary details. Irenaeus saw it as the call which God made to the five ages of humanity: to Adam, Noah, Abraham, Moses and all men through Jesus Christ. For Origen and Gregory, God calls us ceaselessly, at the five ages of life: birth, childhood, adolescence, maturity and old age. That is true, but it's a long way from the parable!

Rabbi Za'era, who lived about AD 300, tells a parable to explain the scandal of the death of a young rabbi.

What does the death of Rabbi Bun remind us of? It reminds us of a king who employed many workers in his service. One of them showed more zeal in his work than the others. Seeing that, what did the king do? He took this worker aside and walked up and down with him. That evening, the workers came to be paid, and the king paid a full day's wage to the one with whom he had walked. Seeing this, the other workers complained, and said, 'We are tired from working all day; that man, who only worked for two hours, has received the same wages as we have.' 'But,' retorted the king, 'he did more in two hours than you did all day.'

Thus Rabbi Bun only studied the law up to the age of twenty-eight; but he knew it better than one who had studied it devotedly to the age of a hundred.

On this page, we shall now go through two parables to illustrate what we saw on p. 89. You can begin by studying them by yourself. If you have a synopsis, use it.

🦋 The parable of the feast and the parable of the wedding garment. Matt. 22.1–14; Luke 14.15–24

When we leave secondary details on one side, the parable, which is common to Matthew and Luke, is simple. The Pharisees feel that they have a right to the kingdom because of their merit in practising the Law; the sinners have no rights, so why does Jesus welcome them? Jesus recognizes that the feast was prepared for the righteous, but because they reject the last decisive call he issues, the 'righteous' should not be surprised to see their place given to others.

Luke makes the parable into an exhortation to Christians. Verses 18–20 develop the main reasons (principally concern for temporal matters) which prevent Christians in his community from responding totally to the call of God. Look at the context: 14.1–14. The connection between vv. 21b and 12–14 is illuminating: people are not interested in the merits of those newly invited, but primarily in God's concern not to see his plan brought to nothing.

Matthew has rearranged two parables.

He has added some allegorical features to the parable of the wedding feast, which allow it to be read as the history of Israel: here is a king (as God is king of Israel) who holds a wedding feast, a symbol of the messianic age. The sending of servants and the way in which they are maltreated suggests the fate of the prophets and the burning of the city, the ruin brought on Jerusalem in 70.

The parable of the wedding garment makes sense in isolation, but when attached to the previous parable it seems to make no sense: how can one criticize a tramp for his dress when he has been compelled to come? Here it becomes a warning to Christians: God has brought them into the church without any merit on their part; however, this is not an automatic assurance of being allowed into the feast. They, too, are liable to the divine judgment; the church is the time when the good and the bad (cf. v. 10) are still mixed while waiting for the final sifting (see the parable of the wheat and the tares, Matt. 13.24–30).

🦋 The parable of the murderers in the vineyard. Matt. 21.33–44; Mark 12.1–11; Luke 20.9–18

This parable, which is taken up by all three synoptic Gospels, is important; it expresses more clearly than the rest how Jesus felt about himself: directed towards Jerusalem at the time when the conflict between him and the Jewish authorities was coming to a climax, it is the last warning that Jesus gave them.

You should study all three texts carefully in a synopsis. The diagram below will enable you to see how the meaning has developed between the time of Jesus and that of the evangelists, as the parable was handed on through the community. It would be a worthwhile exercise to write down the conclusions to this parable in three columns: Matt. vv. 42–45; Mark vv. 10–12; Luke vv. 16b–19.

Jesus	The community	The evangelists
is interested in the outcome of the kingdom.	is interested in the fate of Jesus.	are interested in the outcome of the kingdom
Parable of judgment, announcing punishment.	Allegory of the destiny of Christ.	and the destiny of Christ.
The history of salvation reaches its goal after numerous prophets have been sent.		
	adds a quotation (or two): Ps. 118: announces Easter: Isa. 28.16: a choice has to be made.	**Mark** ends with the Easter alleluia. **Luke** quotes the announcement of Easter; adds Isa. 28: a choice has to be made.
If Israel (the husbandmen) rejects the son, the kingdom (the vineyard) will be given to others.		**Matt.** takes up the Easter Alleluia; returns to the primitive sense the kingdom given to others (v. 41), i.e. the church (v. 43); ends with the need to choose (v. 44).

Parables of the kingdom. Matt. 13

Most of the parables are about the kingdom of God and how people should behave in the face of its imminent coming. Matthew 13 gathers a number of these together. You could read them with the help of the table below.

Jesus addresses them to the crowd and explains some of them to his disciples. These seven parables are a good summary of the different aspects of the kingdom. Jesus proclaims that this kingdom is inaugurated by his preaching; it will develop, but only if his hearers are good ground (the sower). To those who are amazed at the very modest beginnings of this kingdom, Jesus retorts: against all odds and despite everything, the seed of the kingdom will become a great tree; it is leaven which will make all humanity rise (parables of the mustard seed and the leaven). The kingdom is so marvellous that as soon as one discovers it one is tempted to leave everything for it (the treasure and the pearl). Throughout the time of its growth, which is also the time of the church, good and bad are mixed: it is still a time of waiting and of mercy, but at the end of time, God will sort things out (the wheat and the tares, the net).

This allows us to distinguish three realities.

- The kingdom of God is an eschatological reality, belonging to the end of time, in which only the righteous will share. However, from now on it has been inaugurated and is at work in the world.
- The kingdom of Christ or of the Son of man will extend from the resurrection to the end: it covers the whole world. Saints and sinners are still mixed in it. At the end of time Christ will hand it back to the Father (I Cor. 15.24).
- The church is not identical either with the kingdom of God (which will be realized only at the end of time) or with the kingdom of Christ (which extends to all men, whether or not they are believers). The church is the particular place in the kingdom of God where it exercises its action fully (or should do so). This is normally the place from which Christ radiates his power and extends his kingdom in the world.

The purpose of the parables

If Jesus uses this simple language, well known to his audience, he clearly does so in order to be understood. How can he affirm the opposite (Matt. 13.13–15; Mark 4.12; Luke 8.10)? We must see that for Jesus, as for Isaiah whom he quotes, this is an interpretation: in fact this preaching was not heard and understood, and in fact his audience was not converted. This interpretation, whether it comes from Jesus or from the community, is an attempt to put the refusal in the context of God's plan (see *How to Read the Old Testament*, p. 63, 'God will punish you,' where we have a very similar interpretation).

Parables about behaviour in Luke

More than the other evangelists, Luke uses the parables to show how disciples should behave. They should mistrust money and concern for material things which are likely to stifle their spiritual life (Lazarus, 16, 19–31; the rich man, 12.16–21; the feast, 14.16–24). They must pray assiduously (the importunate friend, 11.5–8; the widow and the judge, 18.1–8; the Pharisee and the publican, 18.9–14). They must be neighbours to everyone without taking account of nationality or religion (the Good Samaritan, 10.30–37). In a word, they must model their conduct on that of the Father who loves freely and delights in forgiving (the lost sheep, the lost coin, the father and his two sons, 15; the two debtors, 7.41–43).

The sower	To the crowd: the kingdom is inaugurated, and will surely come if accepted.
	To the disciples: the aim of the parables for the crowd.
	interpretation of the parable (by the community?)
The wheat and the tares	To the crowd: Good and bad are mixed now, but at the end of time God will separate them.
	To the disciples: the aim of the parables for the crowd.
	interpretation of the parable (by the community?).
The net	To the crowd: the same sense as the parable of the wheat and the tares.
	To the disciples: Jesus does not need to interpret it, since they have understood.

7 The Work of John: The Gospel and the Letters

John and the eagle. Keystone of the rood-loft of Chartres (thirteenth-century)

The Gospel of John is a strange book. The words in it are very simple, everyday words, yet specialists have still not succeeded in plumbing their depths. Children are at ease with it and mystics make it their bedside book. Like the synoptic Gospels, it narrates the life of Jesus, but it does so in a very different way from them.

The spiritual Gospel

The Gospel of John has been called the spiritual Gospel. It is in fact the witness of a man and a community whom the Spirit has brought nearer to all truth (16.13) as a result of long meditations. So we shall first look at some influences which affected that community. The only thing really necessary for it is the presence of the Risen Lord as experienced in worship. The celebration of the sacraments – baptism and the eucharist – often crops up in this Gospel. It is there in the last resort that the words and actions of the earthly Jesus make sense.

John's community

This is generally thought to have been at Ephesus. There it was subjected to various influences.

Greek philosophy. Just as we may be stamped by thinkers of whom we are perhaps unaware, but whose ideas form part of the air we breathe, so the Greeks 'breathed' Hellenism, that culture dependent on philosophers like Socrates, Epictetus and the Stoics.

In Alexandria, Philo tried to make a synthesis between this Greek philosophy and his Jewish faith. John's community lived in this kind of atmosphere, as is clear from some of his themes, or from the fact that he calls Jesus the Logos, the Word.

Gnosticism. This current is difficult to define, because it can take many forms. Its basic element is that those represented by the trend, the Gnostics, think that they can acquire salvation by knowledge (*gnosis* in Greek), which is reserved for those who have been initiated. The Gospel of Thomas, discovered in Egypt in 1946, gives us an example of it. John had to fight against Gnostic tendencies in his community, and it is certainly no coincidence that he presents Christ primarily as the one who reveals God's secrets.

Judaism. John draws primarily upon Jewish faith. He has assimilated the great themes of the prophets and the wise men. The Exodus, the paschal lamb, manna, water, the vine, all contribute towards his presentation of Christ. Jesus is the shepherd, the light, and above all 'I am' (equivalent to Yahweh), images or titles reserved for God.

The Essenes are known better since the discovery of the Qumran manuscripts in 1947. It is worth noting the points of contact between John's doctrine and theirs; the Spirit which guides men into the truth, dualism or opposition between two realities like light and darkness, truth and the lie. However, this shows above all that John and the Essenes draw on the same Old Testament texts.

The author

It is probable that the source of the Gospel is to be found in the personality of the apostle John. However, his work went through several stages before its final redaction about 95 or 100. We might think in terms of a 'Johannine school', a group of disciples meditating on the apostles teachings and making them more profound.

Papyrus from before 150 (see p.8)

93

The Gospel as a Whole

Begin by reading the Gospel of John straight through; you may possibly find these notes helpful.

John's geography

The geography of the synoptic Gospels is simple and, above all, theological. That of John is primarily – geographical! The author knows the country well, and when he differs from the others on a historical point (the chronology of the passion, for example) people nowadays have a tendency to trust him. Archaeology has revealed the exactness of some details like the existence of the pool with five porticoes, north of the Temple.

In the synoptics, Jesus preached in Galilee and then went up to Jerusalem for the Passover: his public life could amount to no more than a few months. For John, it lasts more than two years: Jesus in fact goes up to Jerusalem for at least three Passovers: 2.13; (5.1;?) 6.4; 11.55. John describes regular journeys from Galilee to Judaea where Jesus must have spent a long time, especially in Jerusalem (1.19–51; 2.13–3.36; 5.1–47; 7.14–20.31).

Some themes

We shall begin by looking for a few major themes which may allow us to find the key to the composition of the Gospel as a whole.

The word *hour* recurs often, but on nine occasions it seems to have a special sense: Jesus or John declare that this hour has not yet come (2.4; 7.30; 8.20). By contrast, on Palm Sunday, Jesus is anguished because the hour has come (12.23,27). Chapter 13 begins solemnly: 'Jesus, knowing that the hour had come for him to pass from this world to the Father . . .' (13.1); Christ affirms this to his disciples (16.32), and says so again in his prayer to the Father (17.1).

Thus throughout a section of the Gospel Jesus goes towards his hour, and this comes on the evening of the Last Supper. This hour is that of his return to the Father. That points us towards another theme.

The contrast between above and below. There is a universe above, that of God, which is Spirit, love, freedom, light, and the 'world' below, which is flesh, slavery, hate, darkness.

Reconstruction of the pool with five porticoes in Jerusalem

Jesus has always belonged to the universe above. The Word of God, he has come down into the world to reveal God to us, and to give us true knowledge (or *gnosis*). His passover is the hour of his return to the Father.

The whole of his life is framed by two great hymns: the hymn to the Word descending from heaven to become man (1.1–18), and the priestly prayer of the Word incarnate returning towards his Father (17). However, if the Word came down alone, in his exaltation he takes with him all those who believe in him (14.3).

Belief. At the end, John expresses his purpose clearly. 'These signs have been written that you might believe that Jesus is the Christ, and that believing you might have life in his name' (20.30–31). So John wants to evoke faith: this consists in recognizing Jesus as Messiah and Son of God. This faith, which is a living bond, is another name for love. To believe is to have life from the Son; to refuse to believe is to choose death.

Life, death, love. These three key words (or equivalent expressions) are distributed in a significant way through the Gospel: three-quarters of the use of the theme 'life' are in John 1–6, those of the theme 'death' in 7–12 and those of the theme 'love' in 13–20.

These several features allow us to think, if not of a plan, at least of a progression.

The 'Jews' and the 'world' in John

We need to pay great attention to the meaning of the word 'Jew' in John. Sometimes it has its ordinary meaning, denoting the inhabitants of the country; sometimes it has a quite specific sense, and denotes those who have not accepted the message of Christ. In this sense, John, who is a Jew by race, is not a 'Jew' but a Gentile, who refuses to accept that Jesus could be described as a Jew. Confusion between these two senses has unfortunately helped considerably to favour the antisemitism which John certainly rejects.

Similarly, the word 'world' denotes the humanity which God so loved that he gave his Son (3.6), but often it is a synonym for the enemies of Christ (12.31; 15.18ff.) that the Father has given him to do.

The signs and the hour

The Gospel is divided into two main parts, the book of signs (1–12) and the hour of Jesus (13–20).

John has been fascinated by this 'hour of Jesus', which he presents as a unity: the death of Jesus is at the same time his exaltation. Christ is raised up on the cross as on a throne of glory; from there he pours the Spirit upon the world. This is the manifestation of love.

However, this mystery is too rich, and it passed too quickly. According to John, Jesus is well aware that his disciples are in danger of missing its meaning. In addition, for two years in advance he develops this meaning sacramentally, by signs: his miracles, but also, in a more general sense, his works (words and actions), which show forth the Work.

These works evoke two different reactions from those who witness them: some believe and thus move towards life; others reject them and choose death.

1. The book of signs (1–12)

A. *The signs announce the life that God gives (1–6)*
The disciples give their testimony: the community (1.1–18), John the Baptist (1.19–44), the first disciples (1.35–51).

A series of episodes announces this gift of life: the sign of Cana manifests the glory of Jesus (2.1–12); by driving the merchants out of the Temple, Jesus gives a sign: the true temple is his body (2.13–25); he explains to Nicodemus that faith is birth (3.1–21); and John, the bridegroom's friend, gives his last testimony (3.22–36).

With the Samaritan woman, Jesus begins from the symbol of the water of life (4.1–42).

Then there is a whole section on the Word which gives life (4.43–5.47).

The bread of life is developed at length (6). The conclusion of this text prepares for the two following sections: some disciples refuse to believe and so join up with the opponents whom Jesus will be confronting in the next section. Peter proclaims the faith of the group which remains faithful (the equivalent of the confession at Caesarea Philippi in the synoptic Gospels); this faithful group will now fade into the background, leaving Jesus alone to face his enemies; it reappears above all in the last part.

B. *Jesus and those who seek his death (7–12)*
In this section Jesus is alone, facing his opponents, and John shows us what is at stake in the struggle: they want his death; by rejecting him, they are choosing their own death.

We can see this through the great confrontations at the time of the Feast of Tabernacles, when Jesus declares that he is the light and the source of the Spirit (7.1–8.2). The healing of the man born blind shows the division which has been brought about (9).

Then Jesus affirms that he is the shepherd who gives his life for his sheep (10.1–21), the Son of God (10.22–42), the resurrection and the life (Lazarus, 11.1–45).

The last episodes take us to the threshhold of the hour (11.46–12.50).

The community can then bring this first part to an end: the nature of true faith (12.37–50).

2. Jesus' hour (13–20)

John presents the Last Supper above all as the farewell discourse in which Christ says good-bye to his disciples and leaves them his instructions: their brotherly love will from now on be the way in which Jesus remains present in the world.

The trial is a good demonstration of the dramatic *quid pro quo*. Jesus is condemned to death; in fact it is he who is judging the world. And his death becomes the source of life; from his open side flows the spring of water announced by Ezek. 47.2; Zech. 13.1: the symbol of baptism and the Spirit.

Some features of John

John is fond of great unified constructions; we do not find any rapid accounts of miracles as we do in the synoptics, but broad narratives of seven chosen miracles (four of which are peculiar to John), often accompanied by discourses, which become the occasions for teaching.

His thought progresses in a spiral. We find that the thought in each construction is self-contained, but when we take it with the next section, we are led to look at it on a deeper level.

John deliberately begins from concrete realities: water, bread, birth; but he shows how these can bring us to a higher level. For him these everyday realities are symbolic: they enable us to catch a glimpse of the world of God, or better, they create a bond with him (that is the meaning of the word 'symbol', which etymologically signifies that which unites).

Some Texts from John

⚜ The purpose of the work

The signs are written here that you may believe that Jesus is the Christ, the Son of God, and that believing you may have life in his name (John 20.31).
I write this to you who believe in the name of the Son of God, that you may know that you have eternal life (I John 5.13).
Compare these two conclusions. Underline the themes they have in common. What is the purpose envisaged by each of these works? I John has been called the book of Christian experience. What do you think of it?

⚜ Believers

Rather than treat a theme, say faith, in an abstract way, John prefers to show a man or a woman who believes and who thus becomes the type, the model, of the believer. Without going into too many details, you might read a certain number of texts to make up for yourselves a series of portraits of believers.

Faith born out of witness. 1.35–51
See how each person is taken by the hand by someone else in order to be led to Christ.

Knowledge or rebirth? 3.1–21
Nicodemus is a scholar, a rabbi, who can discuss with Jesus on equal terms. What does faith mean to him?

Belief in the Messiah, the saviour of the world. 4.1–42
As you read the account of Jesus' meeting with the Samaritan woman, see how Jesus begins from specific details: the water and the woman's love life. How do they help us to discover his mystery?

Belief in the word of Jesus. 4.43–54
Note the progression between the two occurrences of the verb believe: in v. 50, the centurion believes what Jesus says, and so he is to see the miracle (which is still in the natural realm); in v. 53 he sees the miracle and believes. Note this sequence carefully: seeing (with physical eyes) and believing – believing in order to see (with inner eyes). It often occurs in John.

Those who are truly blind. 9.1–41
There is a contrast here between a blind man who sees the essential thing and people with sight who are blind to it. Try to retrace the steps by which Jesus progressively leads the blind man to discover who he is.

Seeing in order to believe. 20.1–10
Look at the 'other disciple's' pattern of faith: *He saw and believed because they had not yet understood the scripture.* In other words, when the Risen Christ has opened their minds (or ours) to the scriptures, there is no longer any need to see in order to believe. Scripture is enough to show us who Jesus is.

Believing in order to see. 20.24–29
Thomas is presented here as the type of the doubting man. To what faith does Jesus want to lead us (look at Peter's response in 6.69)?

The sign of the bread. 6.1–71

This section, one of the longest in John, is important. Placed at the end of Jesus' preaching in Galilee, it sums up the essential features of his ministry. Chapter 5 showed the unbelief of the Jews of Jerusalem. Chapter 6 shows the unbelief of the crowds in Galilee. Apart from the tiny group of the Twelve (and even one of them will betray him, v. 71), all Israel refuses to believe.

The miracle of the bread (6.1–15) is a parallel to five other accounts which appear in the synoptics. Like them, John sees Jesus' action in giving thanks and distributing the bread as an anticipation of the Last Supper. However, he makes it above all the messianic banquet: this is the feast which the Messiah holds and which was expected at the end of time. John stresses Jesus' initiative (he is the one who does everything, and distributes the bread); the crowd recognizes him as the Prophet and wants to make him king.

The walking on the waters (6.16–21) stresses the person of Jesus. This is a royal progress of 'I am' (God) in all his glory. By showing the divine power of Jesus, the narrative seeks to prepare the disciples for accepting the message of the bread of life.

After the crowd searches for him and the dialogue about the work (6.22–29), Jesus speaks of the bread of life.

♥ The bread of life

Underline the words which keep occurring and the place of the words in the text (our Bibles translate two different Greek words by 'eat'; in vv.54, 56, 57, 58b, the verb used is in fact our 'munch', which is very realistic). See if some expressions make an inclusion.

Note the objections in vv.30,40–41,52: in this way John is deliberately starting an argument.

You will have noticed that the important words in the text all reappear in the quotation in v.31. This discourse is perhaps a homily (furthermore, Jesus is preaching in the synagogue, v.59), built according to the rules of Jewish preaching. The starting-point is a quotation from scripture, generally from the Pentateuch; each of its words is then taken up and applied to the present, to show how they apply to the audience. Usually a second quotation, from the prophets, appeared in the course of the commentary (v.45 here paraphrases Isa.54.13). There is deliberate use of the contrast, 'Not . . . but . . . for', as at vv.32–33; 46–47.

After the quotation in v.31 and the contrast in v.32, an inclusion marks off the first section: vv.35, 48. From v.49, which takes up v.31a, we have a second section. Verse 58 serves as a conclusion to the whole passage.

What bread is Jesus speaking of in 35–48? Note the frequency of the word 'believe' and its equivalent, 'come to'. The theme of the word of God on which one feeds, which one eats in faith, is well known; see, for example, 'Man does not live by bread alone but by every word which comes from the mouth of God' (Deut.8.3), or Wisdom 16.26; Ezek.3.1ff.

What bread is Jesus speaking of in 49–58? Compare 'My flesh for the life of the world' and 'My body given for you' (Luke 22.19).

There has been much argument over the history of the formation of this text. One might think that Jesus was presenting himself only as the Word incarnate that his hearers might 'eat', i.e. receive by faith. After Easter, the disciples understood that on the evening of the Last Supper Jesus also gave himself in another way: his very being (flesh and blood) given for us becomes food. John will then have reread the whole of the discourse in a eucharistic perspective.

How does that help you to see the link between word, eucharist, faith and life?

♥ John's 'Acts of the Apostles'. 13–17

To put it briefly, we might say that John has placed on the lips of Christ, in the discourse after the Last Supper, the essentials of what Luke tells us about the life of the church in Acts. This whole section is in fact composed of two discourses which overlap slightly.

When you read these texts, see what is said about God/ the Father and about Jesus, who he has come from the Father and returns to him; he comes to his disciples after his resurrection in a new spiritual presence; he leads them to the Father. And see what is said about the Spirit.

Try to discover the situation and the questions of a specific community – John's community and your own.

First discourse. 13.31–14.31

First look for the joins: the inclusion from 13.33 to 14.28: 'I am going . . . I will come'; from 14.1 to 14.27.

Underline words which recur: believe, and expressions connected with it: know, perform works, produce fruit; love, and the expressions associated with it: observe the commandments, the word, dwell. 14.1–14 is centred on faith, 14.15–24 on love. Watch the numerous prepositions: in, with and so on.

How does this passage express the essential elements of the mystery of the ascension (the glorification of Jesus) and Pentecost (the new presence of Jesus through the Spirit)?

Second discourse. 15–17

You might see how this discourse develops the same themes, and pause over certain texts.

The vine (15.1–17). How is the doctrine of the church as body of Christ expressed under the form of an allegory?

The Spirit and the community over against the world (15.18–16.15). Look at the roles of the Spirit, making known the Father and Jesus, defending the faith of the believer, and showing him that Christ is victor.

The community charged with bringing Christ to birth in the world (16.16–33). To shed some light on vv.21–22, reread Isa.27.17,20; 66.7,14, and a text to which we shall be returning later: Rev.12.4–6. The passion is presented as the suffering of the community bringing Christ into the world all through its history.

The prayer of Christ through his passion, his resurrection, and his life in the church (17).

♆ The prologue. 1.1–18

This magnificent hymn is difficult. In very simple words, it condenses a long theological reflection.

As a first approach, you might try to look for its structure and see how its thought is rooted in the scriptures.

For the structure, begin by looking for words which recur and passages which correspond. This hymn seems to have been constructed concentrically, according to a procedure common at the time, which we find quite often in the Bible.

1–5	The Word with God	16–18
6–8	John the Baptist	15
9–11	comings of the Word	14
	12–13	

So at the centre (vv.12–13) we find the divine sonship offered to believers. The other matching strophes are not simple repetitions. Verses 9–11 seem to present the comings of the Word into the world and among his Jewish people (his own); v.14 celebrates the incarnation. Verses 1–5 locate the Word in eternity and in his creative action; vv.16–18 stress the revelation accomplished through Jesus Christ.

For the biblical roots of the thought of the prologue, see a commentary or the notes or references in your Bible. Here are just a few points.

In the beginning. The opening of the Gospel is the same as that of Genesis. The coming of Jesus is a new beginning for the world (see, similarly, Mark 1.11).

Denoting Christ as Logos (Word) puts him in the biblical tradition: God creates through his Word (Gen.1; Isa.40.26; Ps.33.6) or through his Wisdom (Wisdom 7.22), to whom he gave being before all things and who lives beside him (Prov.8.23–36; Wisd.7.22–30). This Wisdom, that is to say, God as he is wise, has come to dwell among men (Sirach 24.1–22), and is sometimes identified with the Law, the presence of God among his people (see *How to Read the Old Testament*, pp.83,87,92). However, to call Christ Logos also puts him in the context of Stoic thought, for which this Logos is the principle which maintains the cohesion of the world.

He dwelt: literally, he set up his tent among us (cf. Sirach 24.7–8). The Greek word *skene* (tent) seems to contain an allusion to the Shekinah, the real presence of God among his people. Jesus is the true Temple from which the glory of God radiates towards us.

The First Letter of John

The community is undergoing difficulties: there are divisions (4.3), Christians do not love one another (2.9; 4.20), think themselves to be sinless (1.10), or are tempted by Gnosticism; they claim to be able to attain God by knowledge alone, without being concerned with the way they live (2.4); others have left the community and denied Christ (2.19,22).

To respond to this situation, John appeals to a twofold experience:

His experience as a witness (1.1–4). Read these verses. He does not say that he has seen or heard the Word, but that what he has seen of the Word (human words and actions) has allowed him in faith to go to the heart of the mystery of this man, to recognize in him the Son of God.

The experience of Christians (5.13). He appeals to what Christians have received in their baptismal catechesis and to what they experience in their everyday life. In faith they are to discover that they have been inseminated by the Word of God (2.14; 3.19), that they have been imbued with this Word as though with an oil, thanks to the Spirit (2.20,27).

The basic theme which keeps recurring, as though in a symphony, is that 'You are in communion with God'. However, this mystic has his feet on the ground: this communion with God must manifest itself in the fruits which it produces.

It is difficult to find a plan to the letter, but do we need to find one in a meditation? It is more important to see how the letter matches our own personal experience.

In your reading you might pay particular attention to some features.

The main characters: the Father, Jesus, the Spirit, the author and his community, the believers, those who go astray. How are they presented? What is their role? With what themes are they associated?

The main themes. Note the words and expressions which recur; try to regroup those which go together and to note what contributions these relationships make to the basic vocabulary, for example; love, know, communion, abide in, sin, devil, world, spirit of evil, antichrist, light/darkness, life/death, justice, etc.

The Passion according to John

John meditated on the passion a long time after the events, in the light of the Spirit and the life of the church, and particularly the celebration of the sacraments.

In his account, which is very close to that of the synoptics, he chooses the episodes which have the most significance. He presents this passion as the triumphal progress of Jesus towards the Father. Jesus knows that he is going to die; he knows what kind of a death it will be, and he goes to it freely: 'No one takes my life from me, but I lay it down of my own accord' (cf. 10.18). All the details of the passion not only fulfil the scriptures, but also fulfil the announcements of them made by Jesus.

John underlines the majesty of the Son of God who suffers. When he is arrested, Jesus does not refer, as he does in Matthew, to the legions of angels who could save him: it is enough for him to say, 'It is I', or 'I am', for his enemies to fall back. And it is as king that Jesus is crucified: Pilate recognizes this at his judgment seat (19.13), and the inscription on the cross proclaims Jesus king in several languages (19.19–20).

John does not separate death and exaltation. The lifting up of Jesus on the cross is also his ascension into the glory of God, whence he sends the Spirit upon the world (19.30). 'I, when I am lifted up from the earth, will draw all men to me' (12.32). The cross becomes the throne of glory from which Jesus founds the church: from his open side spring water and blood, the two sacraments of baptism and the eucharist.

The arrest in the garden (18.1–12). John does not describe Jesus' agony (but he has taken up its essentials in the episode of Palm Sunday, 12.23,27) nor the flight of the disciples. He simply shows the majesty of Jesus. The 'I am', repeated twice (vv.5,8), was God's own name in scripture.

The Jewish trial (18.13–27). John does not describe the appearance before the Sanhedrin, and he is the only one to report the interrogation before Annas. Jesus presents himself as one who reveals God in his full light: the verb 'I said' occurs five times, and 'I taught' comes once. There is a tragic contrast: while Jesus is giving his last testimony, Peter is denying him. And despite himself, Caiaphas tells us the significance of the passion: Jesus is dying for all the people (v.14).

The Roman trial (18.28–19.16). This is the principal scene in John's passion. The comings and goings of Pilate, from Jesus who is inside to the Jews outside, break up the event into seven matching scenes, with the crowning of Jesus with thorns at their centre. This is the great legal action between Jesus and the Jews. Jesus is accused, but in fact he is the judge. Jesus is king, but he is a sovereign who reigns over those who hear his word. At the centre is the crowning of Jesus with thorns, stripped of all details (spitting, genuflections), which highlights the title king. And the scene ends with an apotheosis: Pilate makes Jesus sit at his tribunal to proclaim him king (v.13).

Calvary (19.17–37). It is again as king that Jesus is crucified: the inscription bears this out. And the Jews again reject him. The seamless garment which Jesus wears is not torn (Greek *schizo*, hence our word schism). John sees this as a symbol of the unity of the church: Jesus dies to gather into one the children of God who are scattered abroad (11.52).

John is the only one to attach any importance to Mary at the foot of the cross. By calling her 'woman' and giving her the disciple as her son, John seems to suggest the special role of Mary in the church.

Jesus hands over the Spirit (v.30). By using this strange phrase, which is odder in Greek than in many English translations, Jesus portrays Jesus as sending out his Spirit into the world.

The final scene, which appears only in John, shows the significance of the death of Christ for us. He is the paschal lamb of the new covenant. Even more, he is God himself being pierced, as Zechariah 12.10f. foretold (see *How to Read the Old Testament*, p.86). Jesus is the true temple in which the deity dwells, this temple whence Ezek.47.1–12 sees flowing from the right side the water which is the symbol of the spirit. And the water and the blood become symbols, in the church, for the two sacraments of baptism and eucharist.

The burial (19.38–42). Jesus is buried by two nobles, Joseph, the timorous disciple (v.38), and Nicodemus, who had come to see Jesus by night. They lay him in a garden – John is the only one to say this, twice – in a place from which life burgeons.

Descent from the Cross. Museum of the Louvre

John's Jesus

'That which was from the beginning, which we have heard, which we have seen with our eyes, which we have looked upon and touched with our hands, concerning the word of life . . .' (I John 1.1). This confidence is a good summary of John's experience. In Paul's life there was a time before and a time after: Jesus changed from being an impostor to being Paul's Lord. John did not experience the same break. Over a number of years he had been the friend of a man, a prophet, in whom he gradually came to recognize Christ. After the night of the passion, he discovered to his amazement that his friend was the Son of God, indeed is the Son of God. Here is the paradox of John's Jesus: he is a very human figure whom one can see and touch; but in him, with the eyes of faith, illuminated by the Spirit, one can perceive the amazing mystery of the Word, the Son of God.

A man

John's Jesus is very human: he has our body and our psychology. Tired, he quenches his thirst by a well, and asks for a drink from an unknown woman (4.5ff.); he has a home where people can spend the evening with him (1.38; 3.2); he has a friend, Lazarus, and women friends, Martha and Mary (11–12); he knows distress and weeps for his friend Lazarus (11.33,35); he goes to a wedding (2.1ff.); he is capable of getting angry and overthrows the heavy tables of the merchants (2.15).

A marvellous psychologist, he knows the human heart (2.25). Infinitely respectful of others, he can remind the Samaritan woman of her turbulent sex life without making her feel under judgment, much less condemned, and the same goes for the woman taken in adultery. He is someone capable of revealing to people, even though they are sinners, what is best in themselves.

A man of God

Here is an interesting personality test to try out! Whatever people ask him, Jesus has only one answer: the Father. Where have you come from? The Father. Where are you going? The Father. What are you doing? The work of the Father, his will. What are you saying? Nothing of my own, but what I learned from the Father. Even more than abstract arguments about the Trinity, this text introduces us to the heart of the divine mystery. Jesus is always completely free, completely himself, but at the same time he is totally related to the Father, with the Father (1.1).

The one who reveals God

As one who was always with God, God's Word and Wisdom, Jesus knows his secrets and has come to make them known. Above all, John's Christ is the one who reveals the Father to us.

He does so through his words; and does so perhaps above all through his signs, his miracles, his actions, his way of life: 'Philip, he who sees me sees the Father' (14.9). He reveals him again by giving us the Spirit which flows from his open side (7.38; 19.30,34), the Spirit whose task it is to lead us into all truth (16.13).

The Son of Man

It is amazing, in so mystical a work, to be plunged into the heart of a trial. Legal terms appear constantly: witness, judgment, accuser, convince, paraclete (defender, advocate). This is because Jesus is the Son of Man, the figure from Daniel who was expected to pass judgment at the end of time. Jesus declares to Nicodemus that he is the only one to have come down (3.11–13); he does not want to be the judge who condemns, but only the Son who saves; however, because he is the light, he forces those who speak with him to reveal themselves, to choose: he provokes judgment. Yet he is alongside the believer as his advocate.

This trial will continue until the end of the world, and Jesus will also send another paraclete (14.16), the Spirit, who will defend him in the believer's heart.

The Son of God

Finally, Jesus can reveal God because he himself is Son of God. The formula 'I am', rare in the synoptics, appears frequently on the lips of John's Jesus, and is even used as an absolute on four occasions (8.24,28,58; 13.19). It corresponds to the name Yahweh, God's own name (Ex.3.6,14).

The life of the believer

Jesus came in our flesh simply to serve believers; he is the shepherd who gives his life for his friends; he is light; he is the resurrection and the life.

Worship – Life Lived in the Eucharist

For today's Christian, the word worship is likely to suggest ceremonial. For the first Christians, as for Jews, above all it suggested everyday life. To offer worship or to serve God was simply to live one's daily life, giving it a particular significance. And this significance was expressed in certain actions which were strictly cultic. To take an example: married couples do not work differently from single people, but usually the whole of their life is coloured by their love; the actions by which they show this love are the expression of their whole life, and they contribute towards giving meaning to this life. Similarly, acts of worship, cultic acts, express life lived in the eucharist and make life itself a eucharist.

Read Rom.12.1–2; I Peter 2.5 again (and what I said on p.55): the sacrifice of Christians is their very persons, their existence lived out as obedience of faith (Rom.1.5; 16.26; Phil.2.17; I Peter 1.2,14,22). For 'obedience' see *How to Read the Old Testament*, p.100.

Spiritual worship in the Old Testament

The true worship which the prophets call for is righteousness and justice towards one's neighbour (Amos 5.21; Isa.58); it is love and not sacrifices (Hos.6.6, quoted by Jesus according to Matt. 9.13; 12.7). Reread the magnificent summary in Micah 6.8 (*How to Read the Old Testament*, p.43).

Blessings in Judaism

Blessings form the very fabric of the life of Jews.

The day is interspersed with synagogue prayers: in the morning, at mid-day and in the evening; long prayers of thanksgiving accompanied by readings and psalms.

Every action is sanctified by one of the hundred benedictions, short phrases built on the same model: 'Blessed art thou, king of the universe, who . . .' Thus, on rising, 'thou who givest souls to their mortal body'; on washing, 'thou who sanctifiest us by thy commandments and hast ordained that we should wash our hands'; on dressing, 'who clothest those who are naked'; in going to the toilet, 'who hast formed man with wisdom and hast created channels . . .'

Thus the whole of daily life, even its most basic aspects, is lived as a thanksgiving. This is exactly the point that Paul takes up in reply to Christians who reject certain foods or even marriage: 'For everything created by God is good, and nothing is to be rejected if it is received with thanksgiving; for then it is consecrated by the word of God and prayer' (I Tim.4.4–5).

Meals, especially festive meals, are religious acts. The father of the family or the one who presides says the blessing, takes bread and distributes it. Saying the blessing is not a matter of blessing the bread, but of putting it back into the vital current which comes from God: God is life, and by blessing one draws on this life. The bread thus charged with divine life is shared and distributed to those at the meal who by eating it are themselves drawn into this current of divine life.

The response to this benediction, this blessing, the gift of God's life, is eucharist, man's thanksgiving: he recognizes in joy and wonderment that every gift, beginning with that of life, comes to him from God.

Christian worship

Born within Judaism, Christianity took over this attitude and these practices. It simply gave them a new colouring, because Christians know that everything comes to us from Jesus and that every eucharist goes to the Father through him.

When we read the book of Revelation, we shall see that Christian liturgy takes over Jewish worship (p.108). The Psalms, too, are re-read in the light of Christ: see the fine liturgy described in Rev.4.23–31.

We shall see how Christians also wrote their own prayers, and we shall study the Lord's Prayer.

For the moment, we shall be dwelling on the centre and the climax of the Christian eucharist: the last supper of Jesus. The accounts are too rich to be studied in one page, so we shall keep to one particular aspect. By looking at the two interpretations given by the Gospels, we shall see better how daily life and worship are united; Jesus is present through the offering of his person and the community of Christians who love him.

✠ The institution of the eucharist

The context

One of the first narratives to be composed was that of the passion. It ran from the arrest of Jesus to his burial, and thus described the *outward* course of the passion. Very soon, the disciples felt that they should preface it with two other narratives which would make it possible to grasp the *inner* meaning of the events. The account of the agony in the garden shows how Jesus, fully man, sorrowfully accepts his imminent death and restores meaning to it: he makes an offering out of failure. The account of the last supper shows how Jesus celebrates his passion in advance. The last supper, the agony, the way of the cross: these are three presentations of the passion, each one of which says everything, but does so from a different point of view.

The texts

The synopsis opposite gives the four accounts of the last supper that we have. John is absent, but he too speaks of the eucharist.

Read Mark 14.23–25. Does the account seem to you to be straightforward? Look at the end of v.23 and v.24; does the content of the cup ('this', v.24) denote the same thing as 'the fruit of the vine' (v.25)? Read the text leaving out v.24b ('This . . . for many'): what kind of meal is this? Read the text with v.24b: what kind of a meal is this?

Read Luke 22.15–18 + 21–38, then 22.19–20. Can you see two kinds of meal?

The memory of Jesus' last supper has been interpreted in two ways: as a farewell meal in which Jesus gives his last commands to his disciples, or a liturgical meal in which Jesus, by a prophetic action, holds a liturgical celebration of his death. Here is an example. Two sons are back one evening at the home of their old father; he takes the opportunity of the meal to share his belongings between them; the sons leave, and the father dies soon afterwards. It is possible that each of them might describe the meal in a different way: one would remember above all that it was his last meal with his father; he talked to them and told them to stay together, to love each other; the other, more realistic, simply recalls the sharing of the inheritance.

A Christian symbol: the bread and the fish (Catacomb of Callixtus, Rome, second century AD)

A farewell meal

The farewell discourse is a literary genre which is well known in the Old Testament and Jewish literature (see e.g. Gen.49; I Kings 2; Tobit 4; 14). Someone who knows that his death is near gathers together his children or his disciples: he exhorts them to be virtuous, above all to show brotherly love; he often puts forward his own past life as a model and makes prophecies about the future. Sometimes this takes place at a meal.

Reread Luke 22.15–18 + 21–38; Mark 14.25; Matt.26.29; John 13–17. Here the last supper was recalled as Jesus' farewell meal; he gives his commands: 'By this sign men shall know that you are my disciples: Love one another . . .'; he prophesies his future: he affirms his trust in God. After his death he is certain to enter the kingdom of God; and he announces the future for his community: that his disciples shall stay united until the final coming of this kingdom. The way in which Jesus remains present in the world is through the community formed of those who share his bread and live accordingly.

A liturgical meal or a prophetic action

The prophets have already introduced us to actions which not only give a message but realize in advance what they express (*How to Read the Old Testament*, p.43).

The action of Jesus in breaking bread, giving it, and pouring wine, realizes in advance the gift of his body and his blood. And because this action is a meal, that is, something that one can have again, with food that one can eat, by re-enacting this meal we can assimilate the very person of Jesus, given over to death and risen again.

Matthew, Mark and Luke put the meal in the setting of the Jewish paschal meal (celebrated in that year on the eve of Good Friday), but they saw its meaning differently.

Matthew-Mark. Read Ex.24.4–8. The death of Jesus appears above all as the realization of the cultic sacrifice which implemented the covenant.

Luke-Paul. Read Jer.31.31–34 and Isa.42.6; 49.8; 53.12. The death of Jesus appears primarily as the prophet martyr's gift of himself. Thanks to him, the new covenant will at last be realized.

In the light of this study, what significance can the Last Supper have for us today?

		[15]And he said to them, 'I have earnestly desired to eat this passover with you before I suffer; [16]for I tell you that I shall not eat it until it is fulfilled in the kingdom of God.' [17]And he took a cup, and when he had given thanks, he said, 'Take this, and divide it among yourselves; [18]for I tell you that from now on I shall not drink of the fruit of the vine until the kingdom of God comes.'	
[26]Now as they were eating, Jesus took bread	[22]And as they were eating, he took bread	[19]And he took bread, and	[23]The Lord Jesus, on the night when he was betrayed took bread,
and blessed, and broke it and gave it to the disciples and said, 'Take, eat; this is my body.'	and blessed and broke it, and gave it to them and said, 'Take; this is my body.'	when he had given thanks, he broke it and gave it to them saying, 'This is my body which is given for you. Do this in remembrance of me.'	[24]and when he had given thanks he broke it and said, 'This is my body which is broken for you. Do this in remembrance of me.'
[27]And he took a cup, and when he had given thanks he gave it to them saying, 'Drink of it, all of you,' [28]for this is my blood of the covenant which is poured out for many for the forgiveness of sins.	[23]And he took a cup and when he had given thanks he gave it to them and they all drank of it. [24]And he said to them, 'This is my blood of the covenant which is poured out for many.	[20]And likewise the cup after supper saying, 'This cup is the new covenant in my blood which is poured out for you.'	[25]In the same way also the cup after supper, saying, 'This cup is the new covenant in my blood. Do this, as often as you drink it, in remembrance of me. [26]For as often as you eat this bread and drink this cup, you proclaim the Lord's death until he comes.'
[29]I tell you I shall not drink again of this fruit of the vine until that day when I drink it new with you in my Father's kingdom.'	[25]Truly, I say to you I shall not drink again of the fruit of the vine until that day when I drink it new in the kingdom of God.'		

The Our Father

Christian prayers

Matthew 6.9–13	Joint liturgical translation	Luke 11.2–4

9 Our Father who art in heaven,
   Hallowed be thy name.
10 Thy kingdom come,
   Thy will be done,
   On earth as it is in heaven.
11 Give us this day our daily bread;
12 And forgive us our debts,
   As we also have forgiven our debtors.
13 And lead us not into temptation
   But deliver us from evil.

Our Father in heaven
hallowed be your name,
your kingdom come,
your will be done,
on earth as in heaven.
Give us today our daily bread.
Forgive us our sins
as we forgive those who sin against us.
Do not bring us to the time of trial
but deliver us from evil.

2 Father,
   hallowed be thy name.
   Thy kingdom come.

3 Give us each day our daily bread;
and forgive us our sins,
4 for we ourselves forgive every one
who is indebted to us;
and lead us not into temptation.

The text of this prayer is sometimes difficult: the word translated 'daily' is in fact found only here in Greek literature and there is some dispute as to its exact meaning; the phrase about temptation is obscure. The texts of Matthew and Luke differ: fidelity to the thought of Jesus seemed more important to the disciples than an exact reproduction of his words.

Compare these two texts with each other and with the joint liturgical text. Note the similarities and the differences.

Our Father who art in heaven: what is suggested by this use of the first person plural, the association of proximity (Our Father) with transcendence (in heaven)? The word Father doubtless reproduces the Abba, the intimate term, which characterizes the attitude of Jesus and the first Christians (Mark 14.36; Rom.8.15; Gal.4.6).

How do we 'hallow' God? See Ezek.20.41; 36.20f.

Thy kingdom come: what are we asking? Look again at p.65.

What is God's will? See e.g. Matt.18.14; Eph.1.9–10; I Tim.2.4; John 6.39–40.

What is the general purport of these three petitions (Luke clearly felt that they amounted to just one)?

Bread. For the different possible meanings of the word for 'daily' look at the notes in your Bible or a commentary or word book. What is this bread? Simply earthly food? Or also the bread of the kingdom?

Forgiveness. This is the essential characteristic of both Jew and Christian: because God has pardoned us, we ourselves cannot but pardon others.

Temptation. We are not asking God not to put us to the test, as he tested Abraham (Gen.22.1) or his people (Deut.8.2), but that he will not allow us to enter a temptation which is too strong for us.

Look at the context. Why do Matthew and Luke think Jesus taught this prayer? What is the theme developed next in Matt.6.14–15; Luke 11.5–13?

Other prayers

The New Testament has preserved a large number of prayers. You might read them and study some of them. Here is a list.

Magnificat: Luke 1.46–55
Benedictus: Luke 2.68–79
Nunc dimittis: Luke 2.29–32
The prayer of the community in Acts 4.23–31
Hymns either composed by Paul or collected by him:
   Phil.2.6–11; Col.1.12–20; Eph. 1.3–9; 3.4–21;
   I Tim.4.16; 6.15–16; II Tim.2.8; 2.11–13;
   Heb.13.20–21.
The hymn in I Peter 1.3–9
The various liturgical acclamations in the book of Revelation.

8 The Apocalypse: The Book of Revelation

Christ in majesty. The royal portal of Chartres (thirteenth century)

The Book of Revelation, the Apocalypse, is a book of fire and blood in the image of our world. We find it disconcerting. Here everything seems strange: the style, the imagery, the logic. But confronted with a painting which is not figurative, we should not ask, 'What does that represent?', but rather, 'What impression does that make on me?' That is also true of apocalyptic books. However, we shall find it useful to have some keys which will help us to find a way into them.

An apocalypse

This book and the book of Daniel are the only apocalypses in the Bible, but at the time apocalyptic was a very common genre in Judaism. For its precise characteristics see *How to Read the Old Testament*, pp. 89–90. Here is a summary of the essential features.

In a time of crisis, to maintain the faith and hope of believers, an author tries to unveil the end of history, to remove the veil (Latin *re-velare*, Greek *apo-kaluptein*) which hides the end of time. This revelation is both pessimistic about the present (our world is in the grip of evil, incurably), and optimistic about the future (in the end, God will emerge victorious and recreate this world).

Using the technique of the long jumper, the author goes back and pretends to be an illustrious person from the past: in this way he can 'announce' the immediate future (between the time in which he is supposed to have lived and his present) and the ultimate future, for which he has less information. This forces him to use blurred imagery! Thanks to the run-up which he has given himself, he has the possibility of discovering the way in which God usually directs history, and can derive from it basic laws which he uses when he envisages the future. Or, to use another image, the author carries out a study in trajectory.

The author of Revelation was probably writing about 95–100, and pretends that he is writing about 60.

A prophetic book

Because this is a Christian apocalypse, the literary genre is substantially changed. The Christian recognizes Jesus as the Messiah: so with him the end of history has come. Jesus is the key to interpreting the world. This book, while using the procedures of apocalyptic, is also above all a prophetic book.

The author does not conceal himself under a false name; he calls himself John, and locates himself on Patmos. He presents himself simply as a witness to the living Christ.

He is apparently pessimistic about the present, and looks towards the new creation of our old world at the end of time. However, the Christian cannot but be an optimist: he knows that Christ is the victor and that he is already at work in the world. Like the prophets, therefore, the author tries to interpret present history and discover its hidden meaning.

A liturgy

Worship is the place where from now on one encounters the Lord as he will be at the end. The sacraments henceforth make him present in our daily life. This is the joyful certainty which the liturgy proclaims and celebrates. And we shall see that the author takes up the Jewish liturgy to express his message of hope.

The author

Is this the man who wrote the Fourth Gospel? There are plenty of reasons (style, thought) for answering this question either way. We can keep to the tradition which identifies the two authors, but in the end the question is of only secondary importance.

Sealed letters. Elephantine papyri (Egypt, about 400 BC)

105

The Book of Revelation as a Whole

Why not begin by reading Revelation straight through? Many passages will seem obscure, but that doesn't matter. If you go into the museum in Angers, on the Loire, where there is an exhibition of Lurçat's tapestries, *Le Chant du Monde*, 'The Song of the World', you will be disoriented and astounded: the significance of many of the details may escape you, but you will be 'living' the Apocalypse.

All the same, here are some pointers which may prove useful. Some are fairly certain, for example the division into three main sections. Others are less so, like the title or the organization of the central part. Use them if they are a help, but don't feel obliged to accept them all.

In its present form the book appears as a meditation on the church: the life of the church depends on God who is Lord of history, on Jesus the faithful witness, and the Spirit who prays in it.

1. The incarnate church. 1–3

After some introductory words (1.1–3), John addresses the seven churches of Asia. Seven is a symbolic number expressing totality. So he is addressing the church, but the incarnate church as it is in local congregations, with their faults and their virtues. This is not the ideal church of which one dreams, but the very human church as we know it, made up of our fears, our sins and our weak desire to serve the Lord.

The vision of the Son of man (1.9–20) is a clear indication that the life of the church unfolds in the presence of the glorified Christ (1.20).

These chapters, which are quite easy, are essential: it is partly thanks to them that the others avoid being abstract, and concern us.

2. The committed church. 4–20

This is where the Apocalypse proper begins – and with it our difficulties!

We see the church fighting and struggling with the problems of its time and of all time. These are of two kinds: the church's relationship with Judaism (4–11) and the confrontation between the church and totalitarian political powers (12–20).

(a) The church and Israel. 4–11
What is the relationship between the church which feels itself to be the 'new Israel', the true people of God, and the Judaism which is fighting against it? John replies: the church is indeed the 'small remnant' of Israel, those who are faithful to God while believing in Jesus, but a people which is open to all nations.

The heavenly liturgy. 4–5
This section begins with a grandiose vision of God, the Lord of history, reigning in the centre of the cosmos, and of the Spirit (4). The Lamb, Christ sacrificed but living, has the power to open the seven scrolls of the Old Testament, each one sealed with a seal (5).

Events seen from 'heaven'. 6.1–8.1
The vision of the seven seals gives us the hidden, 'heavenly' meaning of the events which will be narrated later.

You might spend some time on this vision of the people of God at the end of time. It is made up of the elect coming from two different directions.

Some come from Judaism (7.1–8). They are 144,000, that is to say, not a number limited in a ridiculous way, as certain sects think, but on the contrary, a countless multitude. Twelve is the number for Israel (because of the twelve tribes), and the elect are twelve squared (12 × 12) multiplied by 1,000.

The others come from the Gentile world (7.9–17). Here John abandons cipher language to say plainly that they are a vast, innumerable crowd.

The mediaeval 'mysteries'

In the mystery plays which were acted outside mediaeval churches, there were hardly any changes of scene: one saw simultaneously, on one side earthly events, and on the other the heavenly court judging those events.

John already seems to make use of this procedure. In his imagery he presents an event and then the invisible meaning it has for faith. So the events brought about by the opening of the seven seals (6–7) are followed by others brought about by the successive soundings of the seven trumpets (8–11). These are not extra facts, but the two sides of the same events, visible and concealed.

Events experienced on earth. 8.6–11, 19

The sounding of the seven trumpets announcing the disaster which is to come is not an addition to what has gone before: now we see the earthly side of things. This transition from Israel to the church has been marked by the terrible catastrophe of the ruin of Jerusalem in 70: Israel is cast out and trampled under foot by the Gentiles (11.1–2). However, the church, following on from the two élite witnesses of the Old Testament, Moses and Elijah (11.6), and above all from Jesus (11.7–12), takes the message to the ends of the earth.

The episode of the small book which is eaten (10) here anticipates something that will be taken up in ch. 14.

(b) The church and the totalitarian powers. 12–20

The vision of the woman and the dragon (12.1–6) marks a turning point. It presents the essentials of what is to come: the church gives birth to the Messiah on calvary; Jesus is glorified and Satan defeated. He tries to harm the church, but God protects it. The following visions develop this overall view.

The forces involved. 12.7–14.5

Here again, we first see the hidden object of the struggle: in 'heaven', Michael fights against the dragon, i.e. God is victor over evil (12.7–18).

Specifically, on earth this is translated into the struggle between the powers inspired by Satan and those who are faithful to the Lamb. The evil powers are represented by two beasts: the beast from the sea (13.1–10), the symbol of totalitarian empires (at that time Rome), and the beast from the earth who enters its service (13.11–18), the symbol of the ideologies at the service of totalitarian empires. Facing them are the Lamb and those who follow him (14.1–5).

The announcement of judgment. 14.6–19.10

This is made in four stages.

- First, there is a proclamation of the gospel of judgment (14.6–13). This passage takes up ch. 10, presenting the little book, the gospel. This judgment is the ruin of Babylon, i.e. Rome and all the totalitarian empires, and rest for the faithful.
- However, the victory of the faithful lies the other side of the passion: the martyrs are the clusters of grapes trampled in the winepress (14.14–20). But victory is certain and can already be celebrated (15).
- The downfall of the totalitarian empires (16–17), who are represented by Babylon, the great whore.

- Two songs celebrate the result: the lamentation over Babylon (18) and the triumph song of the elect (19.1–10).

The final victory of the Messiah. 19.11–20.15

This is again presented on two levels.

- in 'heaven', Christ appears, his garments red not with the blood of his enemies but with his own blood (see *How to Read the Old Testament*, p. 104, the 'cursing Psalms');
- on earth, we have the 'thousand years' of the history of the church.

3. The transfigured church. 21–22

After these chapters of fire and blood, the finale, like the final chorus to a hymn to joy, introduces us to the peace of paradise, the paradise of Genesis. However, John tells us that this is not nostalgia for a lost golden age, but hope set before us.

The church comes down from heaven. That indicates that it both is the earthly church in which we live and at the same time has been remade entirely by God. Taking up the great vision with which the Bible begins, this church recreated by God really becomes the kingdom of God, the city in which he establishes his dwelling place with the Lamb, the cosmic kingdom in which all peoples will be at home and in which God is all in all.

However, this is still only a 'vision': it is both that which is already dimly experienced in the church of today and that towards which it journeys and which it must bring nearer. The Spirit, too, does not cease to inspire its prayer: 'Oh, yes! Come, Lord Jesus!'

Numerical symbolism

Seven is the perfect figure, symbolizing fullness.
Three and a half (half seven) signifies imperfection, suffering, a time of trial and persecution. Be careful! Three and a half can appear in many forms, but its symbolic value remains the same: so three and a half, or a time, times and half-a-time (perhaps $1 + 2 + \frac{1}{2}$), or three and a half years, have the same significance as three and a half days, or forty-two months, or 1260 days.
Twelve signifies Israel (because of the twelve tribes).
Four signifies the world (the four points of the compass)
A thousand is an incalculable quantity.

Some Texts from Revelation

🦊 Letters to the churches. 1–3

These letters are all constructed along the same lines:

- The address of the letter (the name of the church);

- the Christ who sends it is designated by an image taken from the opening vision (1.9–20);

- an examination drawing up a balance sheet of failings and virtues and calling for conversion;

- a refrain ends each letter: 'Hear what the Spirit says to the churches', and a gift is promised to the one who conquers, a gift which will be taken up again in the final vision (21–22).

When you read these letters, try to find this structure. Then you might study one letter in detail or look at them all, keeping an eye open for two features:

The particular situation of a church is the place in which it lives out its faith. The examination in each letter in fact often alludes to a particular feature of the city (in Laodicea, for example, there was a famous medical school which made eye ointment) or an event which marked it out (for example, Sardis was captured several times by an enemy 'coming like a thief'). Look at the notes in your Bible or in a commentary. So the specific situation is rather like a sign of the times which the community has to decipher.

The coming of Christ in worship. Reread the different gifts given to the conqueror (at the end of each letter). If you put these back in the context of Jewish and Christian writings of the time, you will see that most of them are allusions to the sacraments. The white robes (3.5), the crown (2.10; 3.11) and the new name (2.17) allude to baptism, and the manna (2.17), the fruits of the tree of life (2.7) and the banquet (3.20) allude to the eucharist.

You might also look at the relationship between these gifts and the summary of them at the end, in chapters 21–22. You will see similarities there, but also a difference: the letters envisage regular liturgical celebrations in the communities, while Rev. 22 envisages above all the last Supper, the last Easter, when Christ will finally come as judge and saviour. However, already, in worship we are invited to the table of this Lord where he gives himself to us.

A reconstruction of the altar of Zeus at Pergamum (third century BC). The 'throne of Satan' in Rev. 2.13 may be an allusion to this.

🦊 The great eucharist. 4–5

Read this text carefully; it is one of the finest in the book. Who are the main characters? What are they doing? What is the relationship between them? What places do we find?

References to the Old Testament in your Bible or in a commentary will help you to discover the meaning of certain images. Here are the main ones. The elders (or old men), those who hold authority in the people of God, form a kind of presbytery round God and recall the elders around the bishop in the liturgy. The four living creatures (or animals) represent the created world with its four horizons: they form God's throne. The seven lampstands probably signify the Holy Spirit. The book is the Old Testament, which remains sealed, incomprehensible, until Jesus opens it.

Note the songs of praise. Who are they praising? Why? Note the paradox which expresses the mystery of Christ well: a lion is announced, and what appears is a lamb as though slain (4.5–6).

What is the relationship between heaven and earth? Between God-lamb-spirit and the universe-humanity?

It seems that here we are midway between the Jewish liturgy and our eucharistic prayers.

The morning office in the Jewish liturgy contains three great benedictions which serve as a framework for the recitation of the Shema, which plays the part of our Creed. The first celebrates God as Creator, and the community unites itself with the hymn of the angels, chanting the Sanctus (see the extract in the box on the following page). The second thanks God for the love which he has shown to his people by giving them the Law (see the extracts in How to Read the Old Testament, p. 100). After the recitation of the Shema (see How to Read the Old Testament, p. 57), the third praises God for the redemption once achieved at the time of the Exodus, the pledge of the redemption which he has still to accomplish.

The liturgy in Rev. 4–5 follows the same pattern. Try to discover the elements in it: praise to God the Creator, to Christ who opens the book of the Law that he enables us to understand, to the Lamb of the Exodus accomplishing the definitive exodus and making his people a kingdom of priests who offer up the world's praise.

Look at the eucharistic prayers in use at your church: can you find the same features in them?

♉ The woman crowned with stars. 12.1–6

Chapter 12 is virtually a summary of the whole book. It is important to get a good idea of the main characters.

- Who is the dragon? See 12.9.
- Who is the child? The quotation in v. 5 will help you. To which event from the life of Jesus is Ps. 2 applied in the New Testament (see *How to Read the Old Testament*, p. 102)?
- Who is the woman? Before answering, think of what you have just discovered about the child. Then reread Isa. 54.1; 66.7; John 16.21,22 (see p. 97, and *How to Read the Old Testament*, p. 90, 'Daughter of Zion')?
- What is the fate of this woman (12.13–14)? What does the desert suggest (for numerical symbolism see p. 107)?

It looks as though here we have a summary of the paschal mystery and the situation of the church, involved in an exodus until the end of time. Can you make this more precise? What significance does it give to Christian life?

> *Blessed art thou, O Lord our God, King of the universe, who formest light and createst darkness, who makest peace and createst all things. Who in mercy givest light to the earth and to them that dwell thereon, and in thy goodness renewest the creation every day continually. How manifold are thy works, O Lord! In wisdom thou hast made them all. . . Be thou blessed, O Lord our God, in the heavens above and on earth below. Be thou blessed, our Rock, our King and our Redeemer, Creator of holy beings, Praised be thy name for ever; Creator of ministering spirits, all of whom stand in the heights of the universe, and with awe proclaim in unison aloud the words of the living God and everlasting King. All of them are beloved, pure and mighty; and all of them in dread and awe do the will of their Master; and all of them bless and praise, glorify and reverence. . . the Name of the Divine King. . . in tranquil joy of spirit, with pure speech and holy melody they all respond in unison, and exclaim with awe: 'Holy, holy, holy, is the Lord of hosts: the whole earth is full of his glory.' And the Ophanim and the holy beings, with a noise of great rushing, upraising themselves towards the Seraphim, thus over against them offer praise and say: 'Blessed be the glory of the Lord from his place.'*
>
> Blessing from the Jewish liturgy: the Yozer

♉ The transfigured church. 21–22

These chapters are magnificent. Why not read them simply for enjoyment, to savour their poetry and religious depth?

To go further, you will have to see how they show that all the expectation of the Old Testament will one day be satisfied, and that it is already in the course of realization. At the end of this course through the Bible, at the same time it might be a good test of what knowledge of the Bible you have acquired! The great mass of references in the margin of your Bible might discourage you, so give priority to certain themes.

The second creation is like the first, but minus the serpent and sin. In reading Gen. 2–3, see what is taken up and what is superseded (Gen. 2.9; 3.9).

It realizes the announcement of a new creation made by the prophets in the exile: see Isa. 65.17–19; 66.22. In this new creation, there is no more death, no more crying, no more tears. The curse from Genesis has been done away with: see Isa. 25.8; 35.10; 40.2; Gen. 3.2. That is also expressed by the disappearance of the sea, the resort of the powers of evil.

This holy city is a continuation of the earthly church (Jerusalem) and the cosmos, but they are completely recreated (coming down from heaven). It is the abode of God among men, hoped for in II Sam. 7.14; Isa. 7.14; Ezek. 37.27; Lev. 26.11–12. It is the bride of Christ radiant with light: Isa. 52.1; 60; 61.10. Isaiah described the ramparts of this city (Isa. 54.11) and Ezekiel reconstructed its Temple (Ezek. 40). But in this city with twelve gates (one for each apostle, the foundations of the church, though its only real foundation is the Christ, I Cor. 3.11), there is no longer a Temple, for God is all in all.

This new paradise, set before us as a task to be performed and a gift to be received from God, is irrigated by the spring of living water flowing from the side of the Lamb who was slain, a spring which has a name: the Holy Spirit. See Ezek. 47.1–12; Zech 13.1–3; John 19.34 (p. 97).

And all this is already present through the prayer of the church and the Spirit, and is already given in the sacraments to those who conquer.

The Christ of the Apocalypse

The background to this page of text is the royal portal of Chartres: the whole of Revelation is there. Stone saints with ecstatic smiles, and vaulting reaching silently upwards, on which angels and elders sing, all lead us towards one central point: Christ in majesty, enthroned on the universe of the four living beings forming the cross for the tympanum. Only the Christ is represented, because he has a human face. The Father and the Spirit are invisibly present.

Someone. . .

When the heavens open, John sees a throne. And on the throne, victorious. . . . There is no name. A participle without a subject. For God cannot be named. However, he is the only one who can be enthroned over creation, because he is the Creator. And before him, the universe, stretching to Ezekiel's four horizons, is transformed into Isaiah's seraphim to proclaim his praise. Even more, he is the God of the exoduses: who is and was and is to come (1.4). One would have expected the phrase to end 'and is to be', 'Is to come' introduces him into history. He is the one who goes with us through all the events of which scripture speaks. And finally, in his Son, he comes to us.

The Christ

The lamb as though slain. . . This is almost Jesus' proper name, which sums up his whole mystery. The lamb is this man, Jesus of Nazareth, still bearing what are now the glorious marks of his struggle on the cross and wearing the garment stained with the blood that he has shed (19.13). But he is standing, as a result of the resurrection, glorified at the very heart of God, whose throne he shares. The Spirit with the seven flames, the radiance of the life of God, has become the light which gives him inner light, and through these seven eyes allows him to see all things in the light of God (5.6). The second person of the Trinity is a man who takes into his glory all humanity, from the elect of Israel to the Gentile world – and the cosmos which reflects his radiance.

He is the paschal lamb whose sacrifice at the time of the Exodus brought about the people's salvation, the lamb whose blood sealed the covenant. Seen through the evocation of the new exodus hymned by Isaiah, this lamb is the suffering servant of Isa. 53,

whose death suffered as a sacrifice became a light and a covenant for all people. In him mankind can at last become the priestly people who give significance to the whole world, involving it in the praise of the God who has saved it.

However, paradoxically this lamb becomes the shepherd, Ezekiel's shepherd (34.23), who is none other than God pasturing his flock with loving care (Rev. 7.16–17).

Son of man: that is how Jesus appears to John in his first vision (1.12–20). Here is that mysterious being announced by Dan. 7 and awaited at the end of time: Jesus is at the same time a priest in a white robe and a king with a golden girdle; his white hair suggests his eternal youth, his voice is powerful, and nothing escapes his eyes, burning flames penetrating the depths of men's hearts. In his mouth the word of God is a sharp sword, separating good from evil.

Like God, he is the first and the last, the alpha and the omega. His resurrection is the gateway to true life. From now on this living being possesses the keys of Hades: he has forced the gates of the abode of the dead, and Christian existence becomes a wait for the true life.

Jesus can be the faithful witness as seen by Second Isaiah because he has entered the divine secret. In him we know the invisible God. What cannot be known has taken the countenance of a man, and from now onwards his beauty is reflected on all human faces, for the disciple must bear witness to him in the world after his example. For Second Isaiah, the martyr bears witness even more by his words than by his death.

Jesus is the faithful companion who knocks at our door and invites himself to dine with us, so that he can invite us to sit with him on his throne (3.14, 21).

The Spirit

As a sevenfold flame burning ceaselessly before the image of God, Christ's seven-eyed gaze, the Spirit is above all the one who tells us the words of Christ: every letter sent by the Christ ends with the words 'Hear what the Spirit says' (1–3). Like a mother, the Spirit invites us to rest (14.13). Above all, it keeps the church faithful to Christ; it is the love which murmurs in the bride's heart those words which it needs must say, 'Oh, yes! Come, Lord Jesus.'

'According to the scriptures'

Often in the course of this reading of the New Testament we have referred to the scriptures, to what for us has become the Old Testament. What I said at the end of *How to Read the Old Testament* (it's worth re-reading pp. 109–111 of that book) should now be clearer to you: the scriptures formed the cultural and religious milieu of the first Christians as they did that of the Jews. They enable us to enter to some degree into their world of symbols, to discover what could be suggested to them by expressions which are at first sight trivial, like 'the third day', or everyday people and things, like the shepherd and the vine.

Even more profoundly, the scriptures are and remain the expression of God's promise and man's expectation. For the disciples as for us, Jesus makes sense only in the context of this promise, and as a response to our expectation.

To convince ourselves further of this, if there is any need, we are going to go back to some texts that we have already studied, and look at one more.

Words filled with meaning

We all have words which, because of our education, our reading or certain events, carry a meaning which is important to us but which others who have not undergone the same experience will not always be able to see immediately.

The way in which the Jews and the first disciples were familiar with scripture means that for them some words were pregnant with a meaning which we find difficulty in discovering, especially as our translations do not always succeed in conveying every aspect of the word. Here are two instances.

Luke begins his account of the ascent to Jerusalem like this: 'As the time drew near when Jesus would be taken up into heaven, he made up his mind and set out on his way to Jerusalem' (9.51, Good News Bible). The way in which this translation reads doubtless suggests Jesus' determination and courage, and inclines us towards a psychological translation. That is why translations like this, however lively and attractive on the surface, have their drawbacks. Fortunately the RSV is much more literal and at least enables us to glimpse a further dimension. It replaces 'made up his mind' with 'set his face', a strange expression which in fact occurs in one of Isaiah's Servant poems. Although he is persecuted and people spit in his face and pull at his beard, the servant sets his face so as not to yield, because the Lord comes to his aid. Thus the prime concern of this passage is not psychological, as the Good News Bible suggests, but theological. Luke is not interested in states of mind, but is rather expressing his conviction that Jesus was the Servant of Isaiah, that he knew that he was responsible for his mission and that he would not weaken, despite suffering, because the Lord came to his aid.

In the introduction to the account of the passion, Matthew makes Jesus himself announce his imminent death. Then he continues: 'Then the chief priests and the elders gathered in the palace of the high priest. . .' (Matt. 26.3). We get the impression that here we have a simple account. However, the Jerusalem Bible gives four references in the margin. The first, John 11.47–53, sends us back to the more detailed account in John. The three others are stranger: Ps. 2.1–2; Acts 4.25–27; Ps. 31.14. In all three we find the same verb, gather. We may also note that the other evangelists do not use it in their accounts of the passion (except for Luke 22.66, where it appears in the singular), but that Matthew uses it again in 26,57; 27.62; 28.12 to describe the gathering of the high priests against Jesus. And we find it again in Acts 4.25–27, where this time there is a quotation of Ps. 2. So we are led to think that in choosing this verb, Matthew too wanted to allude to the same psalm. And if this is correct, the whole meaning of the passion is illuminated.

As he begins his account, Matthew senses a difficulty: he wants to narrate the passion of Christ, but how can his readers follow it? If Jesus was truly the Messiah, how could he have been rejected by the Jewish authorities who were established by God to recognize this Messiah when he came? By saying that they gathered together, just like the enemies in Ps. 2, against God and his Messiah, Matthew declares: if they rejected him, this was because they were the evil one of whom the psalm (and Ps. 31) speaks. So Jesus is the Messiah. And if now he is in process of living out the first strophe of the psalm – the gathering of the enemies against him – we can be certain that the other strophes will also be realized: God will intervene and establish his Messiah, Jesus, as Lord over all the world.

Realities filled with meaning

A person or event from the past can be filled with meaning in order to express something of the reality that we experience today. Of a child, we might say, 'he's the very image of his father', or, in another case, 'That's where she met her Waterloo'.

Similarly, the Jews and the first Christians discovered in their past history people (Moses, David, Elijah) or events (the Exodus, the return from exile) which could give meaning to their everyday life. However, the way in which this came about was more profound and more complex than ours. For us, people and events are instances, simple images. For them, these really did bear a meaning, a hope: in some way they expressed, or lived out in advance, what would only really appear at the end of time or in Jesus Christ. They are more than examples: they are types or mock-ups (see *How to Read the Old Testament*, p. 111). That is why this way of taking up the scriptures is often called typology.

Unfortunately, it is impossible to say more about this extremely important aspect here. We shall have one instance of it as we study the annunciation to Mary: Luke presents Mary as the daughter of Sion and Jesus as Son of David. However, you should note (or remind yourself of) the way in which Jesus is presented as the new Adam (Rom. 5.12ff.; Luke 3.38, see p. 82), the new Moses (see pp. 72, 76), the new Elijah (see p. 88), the stone rejected and made the cornerstone (Ps. 118, see p. 91), the Temple, the Son of Man.

🐱 The annunciation to Mary. Luke 1.26–38

The account of an annunciation

Read this text and note the different parts of which it is made up. Then read the annunciation to Zechariah (Luke 1.5–25) and the annunciation to Gideon (Judges 6.11–24). You will find there the same pattern, the same features, the same questions. So Luke is taking up a well-known literary genre here, and that is illuminating: when it was used, it was meant to stress not the virtues or the psychology of the person involved, but the mission entrusted on behalf of the people of God.

If there is a common mould, are the sayings of the angel and Mary perhaps original? Compare them with the texts of the Old Testament which are in boxes alongside: putting them in the mouth of the angel is a way for Luke of saying who Mary and Jesus are in the divine plan.

For Luke, who is Mary?

The daughter of Zion. The angel takes up the oracle from Zephaniah, or others very similar to it like Joel 2.21–27; Zech. 2.14–17; 9.9–10. If he presents Mary as the daughter of Zion, at the end of time, what mission is he assigning to her? How does that concern us personally (see How to *Read the Old Testament*, p. 61)?

The new name given to Mary comes from a verb which only appears one other time in the New Testament, in Eph. 1.6, where it is applied to the church at the end of time. How does that illuminate the role assigned to Mary as a figure of the church?

The mother of Emmanuel: Isa. 7.14.

The first of the believers at the beginning of a new people, just as Abraham was through his faith (Gen. 18.14).

So Luke is primarily interested, not in Mary's psychology or her privileges, but in her mission among the people of God, in the church. Try to be more specific about this mission.

For Luke, who is Jesus?

Son of David or *Son of the Most High*. He is the Emmanuel of Isa. 7.14, and above all the Son of God in the sense of being the Son of David enthroned as king in II Sam. 7 (*How to Read the Old Testament*, p. 42).

Thus Jesus fulfils the expectations of Israel. However, Luke goes on, he does so in a more remarkable way than one might ever imagine. In fact he is:

Son of God. The verb overshadow (Hebrew *shakan*) appears only in a few Old Testament texts and has a very strong sense: God comes to inhabit his temple in person. This verb led to the word Shekinah, which expresses the real presence of God in the midst of his people (see p. 74 on the subject of Matt. 18). The only true temple is therefore from now on the womb of Mary, and the word Son of God (v. 35) has quite a different meaning from Son of the Most High (v. 32).

Try to be more specific, at the end of this study, in showing how his use of scripture allows Luke to express his faith, discovered in the light of Easter, and allows us to know that this adventure concerns us too.

1. Presentation of the scene and the people involved

26 *In the sixth month the angel Gabriel was sent by God to a city of Galilee named Nazareth,*
27 *to a virgin betrothed to a man whose name was Joseph, of the house of David;*
and the virgin's name was Mary.

2. Salutation by the angel

28 *And he came to her and said,*
'Hail, O favoured one,
the Lord is with you.'

3. Reaction

29 *But she was greatly troubled at the saying,*
and considered in her mind what sort of greeting this might be.

4. The angel's message

30 *And the angel said to her,*
'Do not be afraid, Mary,
for you have found favour with God.'
31 *And behold, you will conceive in your womb and bear a son, and you shall call his name Jesus* (the Lord saves).
32 *He will be great,*
and will be called the Son of the Most High;
and the Lord God will give to him the throne of his Father David,
33 *And he will reign over the house of Jacob for ever; and of his kingdom there will be no end.'*

5. Questions leading to a new message

34 *And Mary said to the angel,*
'How can this be,
since I have no husband?'
35 *And the angel said to her:*
'The Holy Spirit will come upon you,
and the power of the Most High will overshadow you;
therefore the child to be born
will be called holy, the Son of God.

6. A sign is given

36 *And behold your kinswoman Elizabeth in her old age has also conceived a son;*
and this is the sixth month with her who was called barren.
37 *For with God nothing will be impossible.'*
38 *And Mary said, 'Behold I am the handmaid of the Lord; let it be to me according to your word.'*

7. The angel goes away

And the angel departed from her.

He has freely bestowed grace on us in the Beloved.
Eph. 1.6

Zephaniah 3.14–16

Rejoice, daughter of Zion, the king of Israel, the Lord is in your midst.

Do not fear, O Zion. The Lord your God is in your midst, a warrior who gives victory.

Isaiah 7.14

The virgin shall conceive and bear a son, and shall call his name Emmanuel.

II Samuel 7

I will make for you a great name, like the name of the great ones of the earth. . .
I will be his father and he shall be my son. . .
I will establish the throne of his kingdom.
Your house and your kingdom shall be made sure for ever before me; your throne shall be established for ever.

Exodus 40.35
Num. 9.18,22

The cloud abode upon it and the glory of the Lord filled the tabernacle.

Gen. 18.14

God said to Abraham,
'Is anything too hard for the Lord?'

'Must . . .'

Some texts might give the impression that Jesus is not free, that his life is written in advance in these scriptures so that he has only to realize it: 'The Son of man must be delivered up.' 'The scripture must be fulfilled' (Luke 24.7; Acts 1.16). This is not a matter of obligation, but of interpretation.

Think of someone who exclaims, 'That had to happen.!' She doesn't mean, 'That was fated, there was nothing anyone could have done about it,' but rather, 'It was in the logic of things, as a result of a whole series of earlier attitudes or events.' To understand the event, she interprets it by going back into the past, and now – but only now – it becomes clear that things couldn't have ended otherwise.

To understand how the one who was now recognized as Messiah and Son of God could have been rejected by his people and finally condemned to death, Christians put his death in the logical context of his life, his attitudes and the position he took up over against the established powers, for God and for the poor. And they had to acknowledge that the message of this Messiah was so different from what was expected that things had to happen like this. However, they went back still further, into scripture, to locate this life and this death in the logic of God's attitude. When we studied the kingdom of God (pp. 65,78), we saw that God is not neutral, that he is on the side of the oppressed, and because of that he too was rejected by his people. So they interpreted the fate of Jesus in the light of the fate of the persecuted righteous man in the Psalms, the suffering servant of Isaiah. Such is God's character, such is that of Jesus, that he had to be rejected and die.

It is probable that the disciples simply carried on an interpretation that was begun by Jesus. It sometimes happens that someone can attach meaning to an event which he in fact hopes will not happen.

In all probability, at the beginning of his mission Jesus thought that he could fulfil it in a happy way and that the Jews would accept his message. And then he had to consider the evidence: he was upsetting too many people; things would turn out badly (see p. 85 again). Jesus did not want to die (he even fled to escape death, John 11.54). However, in faithfulness to his mission he had to face up to death and therefore, in advance, give it meaning. And he found this meaning by meditating on the scriptures: he went up to Jerusalem as the Suffering Servant of Isaiah (see p. 111) and put his death in the train of that of the prophets (the parable of the murderers in the vineyard, p. 91).

The scriptures or Jesus?

Like the Jews, the first Christians assiduously reread the scriptures, looking for a meaning in their life. Their methods of interpretation were the same, yet everything was different.

For the Jews, scripture came first: the Jews were the servants of scripture and related it to the present in order to find a specific way of putting it into practice. 'My life is the Law,' Paul could say. For Christians, the risen Jesus was henceforth the centre, the key to everything. In order to understand his mystery and his mission better, they put it in the context of scripture, which was thus also made to serve Christ: 'My life is Christ.'

We can see the errors of a certain kind of Christian apologetic which relies on the argument from prophecy. Jesus, people might say, fulfilled the prophecies: that proves that he is God. They start from the scriptures to arrive at Jesus. The first Christians started with Jesus and went back to the scriptures. Here is an example. According to Matt. 26.15, Judas was paid thirty pieces of silver; that fulfilled the 'prophecy' of Zech. 11.12. Mark and Luke simply write that 'they agreed to give him money'. Matthew is trying to understand: he sees that Jesus was rejected by his people just as God himself had been. By making the text more specific with his reference to Zechariah, Matthew is not intending to give historical information (we don't know how much Judas received) but theological teaching: Jesus is God himself, rejected by his people.

By doing this, the disciples are opening up a way to us: to give meaning to our life in the service of Christ, we too should put it in the context of scripture.

In this way we rejoin the profound apocalyptic movement. In making a study of a trajectory (see p. 105), Revelation invites us to pick up our roots in the past, the past of the people of God, of Jesus Christ, and to discover there the trajectory which today we need to extend by our lives, in faithfulness to our history and in the freedom of the Spirit.

The Beginning of the Gospel

The beginning ... what a strange title for a conclusion! The double sense of this word will help us to complete this course through the New Testament by looking in two directions. Beginning in fact signifies a point of departure and a gateway on to the future.

The starting point of the gospel is clearly Jesus of Nazareth. What can we really know about him through the texts of the New Testament?

Jesus made a future for the gospel: these New Testament texts, and also the life of Christians for two thousand years. Is the gospel closed? Can we continue to write it today?

1. Jesus, the Beginning of the Gospel

Look back on the course which we have just covered. Perhaps we began it with the idea that the Gospels would put us in direct touch with Jesus, even if we did not actually say so: we thought that by opening them, we would hear his words as though they had been recorded on tape, and would see him as though in a photograph. It's clear at the end of this study that things are not as simple as that: we have neither recordings nor films of Jesus.

Have we lost anything by that? I feel sure that you will have discovered, by contrast, everything that we've gained. We do not have words or photographs which are accurate but none the less incomprehensible because their meaning escapes us: authentic witnesses hand the words and actions of Jesus on to us and interpret them at the same time. So the New Testament introduces us to a living community, and it is with that community that we are invited to make this encounter with the Lord Jesus.

However, perhaps another question arises: through these interpretations can we really get back to the very person of Jesus of Nazareth?

Easter is not a wall

Fortunately the time is past – I'm thinking, roughly speaking, of a period between 1920 and 1950 – when scholars, astonished at rediscovering the importance of the Christian communities and their interpretative work, claimed that Easter is a wall behind which we cannot go. They thought that while the New Testament gives us a good account of the disciples' faith in the risen Christ, it no longer allows us to know the Jesus of history.

After several decades, scholars have come back to more sensible positions. Easter is not a wall but a prism, which reveals the splendours of the mystery of Jesus. Through this prism we can really rediscover Jesus of Nazareth.

Just to reassure you, if that is necessary, and possibly to encourage you to look at some of the more learned commentaries, I shall list some of the criteria which scholars have produced to help us rediscover the authentic words or actions of Jesus. We shall spend a short while on the results they have achieved.

How do we arrive at Jesus of Nazareth?

Two criteria above all are used, and they must be taken together: originality and similarity.

Originality is assessed in connection with what came before and what went afterwards. If Jesus declares in a Gospel that God is our Father, he is not being original in relation to Jewish belief. The Old Testament already said as much, so it is probable that Jesus also said so; however, this phrase could also have been attributed to him because it was common at the time. On the other hand, if Jesus addresses God as 'Abba', using a much more familiar term, almost equivalent to 'Daddy', the familiarity is original: a Jew would not have dared to invent it.

After Easter, Jesus was recognized to be the Christ, the Lord, the Son of God. When Thomas says on the evening of Easter Day, 'My Lord and my God', we can read this as the church's faith: the words are not original in relation to what was believed after Easter. On the other hand, if Jesus declares, 'Even the Son does not know the hour of judgment', we find ourselves confronted with a phrase which would seem to contradict the faith of the church: if Jesus is God, he ought to know everything. This is an original phrase which the disciples would have preferred to suppress rather than to invent. Similarly, the church would not have dared to invent a scene like that of the agony in Gethsemane where one who was now recognized to be Son of God could be seen weeping bitterly and being afraid of death, or that in which he comes to receive the baptism of John, which was a baptism for sinners.

Similarity also works on two levels. There must be a certain coherence between what is said of Jesus and what is known of his day. If a modern text tells us that Napoleon reviewed his armies as they marched past the Eiffel Tower, we know that it is a fiction. When Jesus says, 'Do not go into their synagogues', we know that the phrase has been edited after there has been a separation between Christians and Judaism: Jesus should in fact say 'the synagogues', as we would talk about going to church: to say 'We're going to their church' suggests a division between us and those who go there regularly.

There must also be a certain coherence between the words of Jesus or his attitudes. The Gospel of Thomas (a Gnostic account from the second century) ends with this exchange: Simon Peter says, 'Let Mary (Magdalene) go out from among us, because women are not fit to live.' Jesus says, 'I will make her male so that she shall be a living spirit like you men; every woman who becomes a male will enter into the kingdom of God.' Such a phrase has a strange ring in view of what we know of Jesus: it is surely not authentic. Or when the Arabic Childhood Gospel of Jesus (a seventh-century writing) shows us the child Jesus killing on the spot a friend who has bumped into him and made him fall over, we know that this is completely out of character with the way in which Jesus performed miracles and the love he showed for all men.

Scholars use other criteria: these are the chief ones. However, we should note the results of their research: it has succeeded in establishing that certain words and actions may well be attributed to Jesus. However, it does not claim in any way that the other sayings or actions whose authenticity cannot be established in the same way do not come from Jesus. This research can affirm certain points: it does not claim at all to deny those which it cannot affirm in the same way.

The main stages in the life of Jesus

Without going into details about the actions and attitudes of Jesus, we can take it that the main features of his life are assured.

Jesus began his mission with the baptism which he received at the hands of John. Perhaps he was John's disciple for a while, and then separated from him.

In Galilee, Jesus preached the imminent coming of the kingdom of God. Crowds followed him enthusiastically, recognized him as a prophet and perhaps as the Messiah. However, their expectation was so ambiguous, filled with nationalistic hope, that Jesus disappointed them. Gradually these crowds left him. The pressure from his opponents grew more severe. Jesus guessed that to continue as he was doing was likely to bring him to a violent end.

He then went up to Jerusalem – several times, if we are to believe John. His attacks on the religious system, with the Temple at its centre, aroused more and more antagonism from his opponents. His way of behaving towards sinners, the people who did not observe the Law, and women and his very free way of interpreting the Law with authority, to restore it to its primitive purity (for example, the law of the sabbath), led to his rejection.

Religious authorities among the people (not all of them) condemned him to death. They succeeded in getting the Jerusalem crowds behind them. They delivered Jesus to the civil power for execution. Pilate sought to free him, less concerned for justice than anxious to cross the desires of the authorities. In the end he yielded. Jesus died on 7 April 30 (or, by another reckoning, 3 April 33).

'True God and true man'

To ask, 'What awareness did Jesus have of himself and his mission?' may court an amazing answer. Since he is God, he knew everything. However, some texts do allow us to ask this question; for example, there is one in which Jesus declares his ignorance of the day of judgment (Mark 13.32).

Here we are confronted with a mystery; here we can only hang firmly on to both ends of the thread without knowing how they are to be brought together: Jesus is fully God and he is also fully man.

When faced with a mystery, we are always tempted to neglect one aspect or at least to favour another. And the way in which we begin necessarily leads us to stress one aspect. For centuries, theology has deliberately been framed in terms of 'from above, downwards': it presents the mystery of the Son of God made man; so we begin from the affirmation that Jesus is God, to show that he was also fully man. Contemporary theology tends rather to be 'from below, upwards': it recognizes that Jesus is fully man, and in the Gospels looks for those features in his actions and his words which show a special and unique relationship with the Father, in which we can see his divinity.

The first disciples above all stressed the divine aspect. For those who had known Jesus and lived with him, it was clear that he was a man as they were. What they had to show was that this man was God.

Later on in the history of the church, and recently in Christian education as well, this was the starting point for disciples: Jesus is God. Hence the recent reaction: there has been all the more stress that he is man. That could lead to excesses, like the theological development called 'theology of the death of God', or certain popular representations in which Jesus is no more than a hero, a revolutionary or a close friend. However, avoiding one extreme should not lead us to the other.

So the Christian affirms very carefully, with the New Testament and the whole tradition, that Jesus is Son of God from the first moment of his conception. To ask what awareness Jesus might have had is not to doubt this faith; it is simply to attempt to locate it in the growth of this person who was fully man.

It has always been accepted that Jesus grew up, that he was hungry and cold, that he suffered, that he learned to talk and to pray. But to be man – as we are even more aware today – means also to be free, to have a choice, to look for one's way, to take chances. If Jesus was fully man, he had a psychology, freedom, like ours.

We saw earlier (p. 114) that Jesus probably first thought that his mission would be successful simply as a result of his preaching; confronted with opposition, he must then have envisaged the possibility of his violent death and attached a meaning to it. He was not acting out a comedy in the garden of the agony when he was coming to terms with his passion, believing according to the Pharisaic faith which he shared that God would raise him up at the end of time on the third day. A human comparison may help us here. We know that a new-born baby is a 'man', but he or she becomes aware of the fact only gradually; and throughout our existence, events and reflection allow us to discover better who we are and what our task is. We might think that it was the same with Jesus. Fully Son of God from the time of his conception, helped by the great experiences which God vouchsafed him, like the baptism and the transfiguration, and by the power which he discovered that he had of curing bodies and transforming hearts, he gradually became aware of the fact.

In affirming in this way that Jesus experienced our human condition 'in all things save sin', we are not minimizing his divinity, but are getting a better view of this divine humility of a God who became man, fully man, that we might become God.

Non-Christian Texts about Jesus

We know Jesus through the Gospels. Few secular texts say anything about him. There is nothing surprising in that: they did not have reporters or journalists in those days, and sadly the death of a Jew in an obscure corner of the Roman empire was an all too common occurrence. Secular writers only began to show an interest when the movement which Jesus launched showed its strength and seemed likely to put the very Empire in peril (see *How to Read the Old Testament*, p. 32, 'What is a historical event'). Here are the main texts.

About 110, Pliny the Younger, proconsul in Asia Minor, wrote to his friend the emperor Trajan to tell him how he was treating Christians. Christians were multiplying to such a degree that pagan temples were deserted. He did not go out looking for Christians, but when they were denounced, he imposed the death penalty on them if they persisted in their faith.

Some explained that they had ceased to be Christians . . . They maintained that the amount of their fault or error had been this, that it was their habit on a fixed day to assemble before daylight and recite by turns a form of words to Christ as a god; and that they bound themselves with an oath, not for any crime, but not to commit theft or robbery, or adultery, not to break their word, and not to deny a deposit when demanded. After this was done, their custom was to depart, and to meet again to take food, but ordinary and harmless food . . .

I have found nothing but an absurd superstition.

About 115, the Roman historian Tacitus describes Nero's persecution of the Christians, after the great fire of Rome in 64.

Christus, from whom the name had its origin, suffered the extreme penalty during the reign of Tiberius at the hands of one of our procurators, Pontius Pilate, and a deadly superstition, thus checked for the moment, again broke out not only in Judaea, the first source of the evil, but also in Rome, where all things hideous and shameful from every part of the world meet and become popular . . .

About 120, another Roman historian, Suetonius, wrote this in his *Life of Claudius*:

Since the Jews constantly made disturbances at the instigation of Chrestus, he expelled them from Rome.

Thus Christians were confused with Jews and Christ was taken as an agitator from among them (conpare this text with Acts 18.2).

He makes another brief allusion in his *Life of Nero*:

Punishment was inflicted on the Christians, a class of men given to a new and wicked superstition.

Flavius Josephus is a Jewish historian who first fought against the Romans and then entered their service. He died in Rome about 98, having written several works presenting Judaism to the Romans.

A passage from the *Jewish Antiquities* speaks of Jesus. This text has come down to us in different forms, and Christian hands have clearly been at the original text. The version given here has some chance of being earlier than the others; it can be found in the *Universal History* composed in Arabic, in the tenth century, by Agapius, bishop of Hierapolis.

About this time arose Jesus, a wise man, who did good deeds and whose virtues were recognized. And many Jews and peoples of other nations became his disciples. Pilate condemned him to be crucified and to die. However, those who had become his disciples preached his doctrine. They related that he had appeared to them three days after his crucifixion and that he was alive. Perhaps he was the Messiah in connection with whom the prophets foretold wonders.

Alexamenos worships his god
An anti-Christian caricature scratched on a wall in Rome (end of the second century or beginning of the third). It shows a figure at prayer in front of a crucified figure with an ass's head.

2. Can we Write the Gospel Today?

Are the Gospels, the New Testament, a closed book?' Can we continue to write them today? This question will help us to understand what the canon is and how it has been formed.

The canon of the New Testament

'Canon' and 'testament' are strange words, which prompt us to look at them in rather closer detail.

Canon, from a Greek word signifying rule, denotes in various contexts the ideal norm. In the fifth century BC a Greek sculptor wrote 'On the canon', i.e. the exact proportions of the human body. The 'canon of virtues' drawn up by ancient philosophers suggested how to live a moral life. 'Canon law' is the law which serves as a rule for Catholics. The 'canon of scripture' is the catalogue of books recognized by a church as the rule of its faith.

You should not confuse the canonicity of a book (the fact that it is included in this canon) with its authenticity. An authentic book is one which has been written by the author to whom it is attributed. The conclusion of Mark (16.9–20) is not authentic (it was not written by the author of the Gospel, but added later); it is, however, canonical.

The Greek Bible translated the Hebrew word denoting the covenant by *diatheke*, which indicates the arrangements made between two parties. At the beginning of the third century, Tertullian translated *diatheke* by the Latin word *testamentum*, which produces the English word testament.

The canon of the New Testament was formed gradually, by trial and error; some books were accepted and others were rejected.

Collections of books must have been made at an early stage: first of all there was a collection of Paul's letters (already indicated by II Peter 3.15), then probably a collection of Gospels and Catholic Epistles (James, I and II Peter, I, II, III John, Jude).

In the second century, the delimitation of the canon was speeded up as a reaction to two kinds of heresy: the Gnostics produced various Gospels (like those found at Nag Hammadi in Egypt, which include the Gospel of Thomas) and false apostolic letters. At the other extreme, Marcion, in Rome round about 150, rejected the Old Testament and part of the New.

The canon as we now have it was almost fixed between 150 and 300. Evidence from this period includes the Muratorian Canon (named after Muratori, who discovered it), an eighth-century manuscript giving a list of books accepted in Rome about 180, the writings of Irenaeus (who died about 202), Terutllian (died 220), Clement of Alexandria (died before 215) and Origen (died in 254).

These lists correspond almost exactly with the present-day canon: books sometimes disputed are Hebrews, James and I and II Peter. On the other hand, other books like the Didache, the Shepherd of Hermas and the Gospel of Peter were sometimes included. The canon was fixed in the fourth century, with a few minor differences, depending on churches.

In the Greek church, Eusebius of Caesarea (who died in 340), recognized the present-day canon except for Revelation. However, in 367 Athanasius fixed the canon of the Old and New Testaments as we have it today.

In the Syrian church, the official version, the Peshitto, does not have II Peter, II and III John, Jude and Revelation.

In the Latin church, Jerome, who translated the Bible into Latin between 384 and 395 (the Vulgate), adopted Athanasius' list.

What is the basis for the choice of the canon?

Several criteria played a part in the admission or rejection of books: they had to be of apostolic origin and be Catholic or universal, i.e. accepted in all the churches. These criteria played their part, but they are not enough to form the basis of our canon: some books then thought to have been written by the apostles were written at a later stage by their disciples.

So the ultimate criterion is that because the church is animated by the Holy Spirit, it has felt that certain books 'edify' it, build it up, and others do not. The recognition of the canon as all the inspired books which lay a foundation for faith is itself an act of faith in the Spirit which guides the church. The canon is now closed: the revelation has been made. Does that mean that we no longer need to write the gospel for our day?

The Text of the New Testament

'Do we have the original text of the Gospels or the New Testament? What is the basis of the text that we have in our Bibles?' These are questions which people often ask.

In fact, we have hardly any original texts from antiquity at all. One of the rare examples is a letter written by Simon bar Cochba, leader of the Jewish revolt in 135 (see p. 121). Usually we only have copies. Thus the earliest manuscripts of the works of the Latin poet Virgil date from four centuries after him; thirteen centuries separate Plato from the manuscripts of his writings, and in the case of the Greek poet Euripides this goes up to sixteen centuries.

We are in a much better position with the New Testament. We have thousands of manuscripts, some of which are very old.

These manuscripts are written either on papyrus (the fibres of a plant) or parchment (the skin of sheep, goats or calves). They can either be scrolls or, more often, in the form of a codex (leaves sewn together like our modern books). Until the ninth century they were written in majuscules (or in uncials, i.e. capital letters), without separation between the letters; thereafter they were also written in minuscules.

Here are some important periods in the transmission of the text of the New Testament.

Down to the fourth century

Even at the end of the second century, people were disturbed about differences between manuscripts. At Alexandria, scholars made a recension, i.e. from different manuscripts they tried to establish the text that they thought came closest to the original. This 'Alexandrian recension' spread throughout the Empire.

The Greek text was translated into Latin (the Old Latin or the Itala, between 160 and 180), Syriac and Coptic.

From this period we still have:
the Rylands papyrus
(see p. 9);
Bodmer papyrus II, about 200, from Egypt: fourteen chapters from John (the beginning of John is in the box opposite);
three Chester Beatty papyri, from about 250: these contain passages from the Gospels, from Paul and from Revelation.

From the fourth to the sixth century

The great complete manuscripts of the New Testament, written on parchment, date from this period:

Vaticanus (middle of the fourth century);
Sinaiticus (middle of the fourth century);
Alexandrinus (beginning of the fifth century);
Codex Ephraem (fifth century);
Codex Bezae (fifth century), which has only the Gospels and Acts. The text of Acts differs somewhat from the usual text;

Sinaiticus. Heb. 13,24-25

Freer Codex (fifth century), which has only the Gospels.

At the beginning of the fifth century a new recension was made in Byzantium. This established itself as the common version (the Koine) in all Greek-speaking churches.

The text of the versions was unified: in 382 St Jerome produced the Vulgate (Latin). The Peshitto (Syriac) and the Armenian version date from the fifth century.

From the sixth century to the Renaissance

A great many copies were made in the monasteries.

Renaissance: fifteenth and sixteenth centuries

Greek manuscripts came over into the West after the capture of Constantinople in 1453.

The Alcala Polyglot, edited by Cardinal Ximenes, the work of a conscientious scholar, was begun in 1502 and published in 1522. To keep it out (competition was strong even in those days), in 1516 Erasmus published a text which was established in six months on the basis of only six manuscripts. The printer Robert Estienne revised the Erasmus text on the basis of Alcala. Theodore of Beza took up the fourth edition of Estienne; this is the Received Text, which was used down to the end of the nineteenth century.

From the middle of the nineteenth century

In 1859, Tischendorf discovered Sinaiticus and published Vaticanus. These are the two manuscripts which serve as the basis for the text of our Bibles as we now have it.

Differences between manuscripts are only in points of detail. Although we do not have the original texts, we can trust the copies that we have.

Writing the Gospel today?

After following this course, we have probably had to give up rather naive ideas like: the apostles listened to Jesus, wrote down his words and actions, and after Pentecost set off for their mission to the world, Gospels under their arms... Jesus gathered together disciples, founded his church which existed before the Gospels and gave them their shape...

We have followed this course because it matches what seems to have happened. However, our approach does have an important consequence for us today.

If we had photographs and recordings of Jesus, we would be condemned to repetition, to taking them as a model to be reproduced.

If the Jesus whom the New Testament presents to us was discovered slowly by Christian communities, through their lives and their reflections, we have a future opened up to us. Our communities, today, have to continue this work of discovering Jesus through our life and our questions. The life of our churches today, the face of the Risen Christ which they show to the world, are the Gospels that we write today.

In common with many other texts, the Epistle to the Ephesians, in a passage which we studied on p. 37, reminds us of the work of Christian communities: to build up the body of Christ until it achieves its perfect form. That is what the glorified Lord has equipped his church to do, and he needs that church: the Holy Spirit and the various ministries are the gifts which he gives it. Christians must 'give birth' to Christ in the world (Rev. 12.1–6; John 16.21–22; see p. 109). And their life, expressed in countless writings, from personal or liturgical prayers to innumerable testimonies, are the Gospel of the twentieth century.

However, there is a basic difference between these 'Gospels' which we produce and the writings of the New Testament. The latter are recognized as the word of God; they form the rule of faith for Christians of all times and all places. With them, revelation comes to an end: God has told us everything in his Son. Our 'Gospels' do not tell us anything more; they simply show the way in which the first message resounds in a particular part of the world in a particular century; so they are not universal. Furthermore, they are valid only to the extent that they produce the same sound as the first writings, for which they provide today's harmony.

So Christians are not condemned to the passive reproduction of a model: they are invited to give birth to Christ in the world, to discover, in faithfulness to the first message, the countenance of the Risen Christ for our world.

Autograph letter of Simeon bar Cochba, leader of the second Jewish revolt in AD 135.

If You Want to Know More . . .

As far as possible, I have deliberately avoided referring to other books in this work; you can manage very well by using it on its own, along with a good Bible. However, if you want to explore further, you will find the following books useful.

Reference books

A wealth of information about the content of the Bible can be found in two dictionaries: James Hastings, *Dictionary of the Bible*, T. & T. Clark, and the five-volume illustrated *Interpreter's Dictionary of the Bible*, Abingdon Press. Two convenient atlases are Lucas Grollenberg, *Shorter Atlas of the Bible*, Penguin Books, and the *Oxford Bible Atlas*, edited by H. G. May, Oxford University Press: each has an illustrated text as well as the maps. There are many commentary series, with a separate volume for each book (or groups of books in the case of the smaller works in the New Testament). Three very useful series for the New Testament are the New Clarendon Bible, published by Oxford University Press, which has illustrations; the Black's New Testament Commentaries, published in England by A. & C. Black and as the Harper New Testament Commentaries in the USA by Harper and Row; and the Cambridge Bible Commentaries, published by Cambridge University Press. The Pelican New Testament Commentary series, now published by SCM Press and Westminster Press, is incomplete, but has some important volumes in it. Big one-volume commentaries are, of course, predominantly concerned with the Old Testament because that is so much bigger; they also contain articles on general topics. There are three good ones to choose from: *The Jerome Biblical Commentary*, edited by R. E. Brown, J. A. Fitzmyer and R. E. Murphy, Geoffrey Chapman and Prentice Hall; *The New Catholic Commentary on Holy Scripture*, edited by R. C. Fuller, Leonard Johnston and Conleth Kearns, Nelson; and *Peake's Commentary on the Bible*, edited by M. Black and H. H. Rowley, Nelson. A synopsis of the Gospels is a very important book to have; the most convenient is Burton Throckmorton, *Gospel Parallels*, Nelson. A concordance will help you to trace the use of words and phrases, and to look up passages about whose location you are unsure; the most up-to-date one is Clinton D. Morrison, *An Analytical Concordance to the Revised Standard Version New Testament*, Westminster Press and SCM Press.

Background information

C. K. Barrett, ed., *The New Testament Background: Selected Documents*, SPCK
    This contains translations of a wide variety of works of every kind from the time of the New Testament, giving some impression of thoughts and practices at the time.

Joachim Jeremias, *Jerusalem in the Time of Jesus*, SCM Press and Fortress Press
    A classic work, reconstructing from Jewish sources what Jerusalem must have been like.

Josephus, *The Jewish War,* Penguin Books
    This is the most accessible and readable translation of the work of a Jewish historian who survived by joining the Roman side and wrote a history of events leading to the capture of Jerusalem.

Eduard Lohse, *The New Testament Environment,* SCM Press and Abingdon Press

Bo Reicke, *The New Testament Era*, A. & C. Black and Fortress Press
    Two comprehensive accounts of the historical background and religious ideas which underlie the New Testament.

Samuel Sandmel, *The First Century in Judaism and Christianity*, Oxford University Press

Samuel Sandmel, *Judaism and Christian Beginnings*, Oxford University Press
    A Jewish scholar offers his perspective on the beginnings of Christianity and provides an important correction to many ideas we too easily accept uncritically.

Geza Vermes, *The Dead Sea Scrolls in English*, Penguin Books
    A translation with comments of the most important discoveries.

Geza Vermes, *The Dead Sea Scrolls*, SCM Press and Fortress Press
    An account of their discovery and of the most important consequences for biblical studies.

General works

T. G. A. Baker, *What is the New Testament?* SCM Press
    A compact introductory study dealing with questions of authority, etc.

Alan T. Dale, *New World*, Oxford University Press
    A basic, illustrated guide.

W. D. Davies, *Invitation to the New Testament*, SPCK and Doubleday
    Written for the author's teenage daughter.

Floyd V. Filson, *A New Testament History*, Westminster Press and SCM Press
    A simple history extending from the time of the Maccabees to the early church.

R. M. Grant, *A Historical Introduction to the New Testament*, Fount Books and Simon and Schuster
    A good non-technical study with a wealth of information, lucidly presented.

A. M. Hunter, *Introducing the New Testament*, SCM Press and Westminster Press
A basic guide to questions of date, authorship and the content of books.

C. F. D. Moule, *The Birth of the New Testament*, A. & C. Black and Harper & Row
An account of the circumstances leading to the formation of the New Testament.

Stephen Neill, *The Interpretation of the New Testament 1861–1961*, Oxford University Press
A riveting account of the rise of New Testament criticism.

Norman Perrin, *Introduction to the New Testament*, Harcourt, Brace
A textbook written along new lines.

R. Spivey and D. Moody Smith, *Anatomy of the New Testament*, Collier-Macmillan
A comprehensive analytical study of the content of the New Testament.

Robert C. Walton (ed.), *A Basic Introduction to the New Testament*, SCM Press and John Knox Press (American title: *Bible Study Source Book: New Testament*)

Easter and the Resurrection

R. E. Brown, *The Virginal Conception and the Bodily Resurrection of Jesus*, Geoffrey Chapman and Paulist Press
A discussion of the evidence using the techniques of biblical criticism.

C. F. Evans, *Resurrection and the New Testament*, SCM Press
A thorough discussion of the idea of resurrection and its significance throughout the New Testament.

Willi Marxsen, *The Resurrection of Jesus of Nazareth*, Fortress Press
A rather controversial but extremely stimulating approach.

Norman Perrin, *The Resurrection Narratives: A New Approach*, Fortress Press
The theological significance of the stories in Matthew, Mark and Luke.

U. Wilckens, *Resurrection*, St Andrew Press and John Knox Press
Biblical testimony to the resurrection: an examination and explanation.

Paul and his letters

William Barclay, *The Mind of St Paul*, Fount Books and Harper and Row
A portrait drawn from his letters.

Günther Bornkamm, *Paul*, Hodder & Stoughton and Harper & Row
A detailed all-round study which relates to his theology and his biography.

F. F. Bruce, *Paul: Apostle of the Free Spirit*, Paternoster Press and Eerdmans (American titles: *Paul: Apostle of the Heart Set Free*)
An examination of the main themes of his thought.

W. D. Davies, *Paul and Rabbinic Judaism*, SPCK and Fortress Press
A pioneering study in the connection between Paul's thought and what we know of contemporary Judaism.

Lucas Grollenberg, *Paul*, SCM Press and Westminster Press
A highly attractive account, perhaps the best introductory book.

A. M. Hunter, *The Gospel according to St Paul*, SCM Press and Westminster Press
The theology of St Paul and its meaning today.

John A. T. Robinson, *Wrestling with Romans*, SCM Press and Westminster Press
A good way of getting down to detailed study of one of Paul's letters.

Krister Stendahl, *Paul among Jews and Gentiles*, SCM Press and Fortress Press
Argues that we should beware of assessing Paul by the wrong standards.

Mark and miracles

C. F. Evans, *The Beginning of the Gospel*, SPCK
An introduction to the purpose and construction of the Gospel.

R. P. Martin, *Mark, Evangelist and Theologian*, Paternoster Press and Zondervan
Shows how Mark's thinking is related to that of Paul.

D. E. Nineham, *Saint Mark*, Penguin Books
One of the best New Testament commentaries in any language and an ideal introduction.

R. H. Fuller, *Interpreting the Miracles*, SCM Press and Westminster Press
Particularly concerned with their theological significance.

Ernst and Marie-Luise Keller, *Miracles in Dispute*, SCM Press and Fortress Press
A fascinating history of the understanding of miracles.

Matthew and the Sermon on the Mount

W. D. Davies, *The Sermon on the Mount*, Cambridge University Press
An analysis of its content.

H. Benedict Green, *The Gospel of Matthew*, Oxford University Press
Perhaps the most useful commentary on the Gospel.

E. Schweizer, *Good News according to Matthew*, SPCK and John Knox Press
Another useful guide in the form of a commentary.

Luke and parables

John Drury, *Tradition and Design in Luke's Gospel*, Darton, Longman and Todd
A provocative and questioning study.

E. Haenchen, *The Acts of the Apostles*, Blackwell and Westminster Press
A big book, but surprisingly easy to understand if you pick and choose, and very illuminating

I. H. Marshall, *Luke, Historian and Theologian,* Paternoster Press and Zondervan
  A study of Luke, his thinking and his approach to history.
Neil Richardson, *The Panorama of Luke,* Epworth Press
  Perhaps the best approach to the Gospel and Acts; readable and clear in its explanations.
A. M. Hunter, *Interpreting the Parables,* SCM Press and Westminster Press
  A good popular book.
Joachim Jeremias, *Rediscovering the Parables,* SCM Press and Scribner
  A popular version of the most famous book ever written on the subject.

Lucas Grollenberg, *Jesus,* SCM Press and Westminster Press
  A vividly readable study by the distinguished Dutch Dominican.
Geza Vermes, *Jesus the Jew,* Fount Books and Fortress Press
  Against a Jewish background by a distinguished Jewish scholar.
None of these books is difficult to read. It would be well worth going through each of them and comparing the portraits they give.

The Synoptic Gospels

Some useful books which deal with all three Synoptic Gospels (and in some cases with the Gospel of John as well) are: William Barclay, *The Gospels and Acts,* SCM Press and Westminster Press; F. W. Beare, *The Earliest Records of Jesus,* Blackwell (a companion to *Gospel Parallels*); A. E. Harvey, *Companion to the Gospels,* Oxford University Press; Keith Nickle, *The Synoptic Gospels,* SCM Press and John Knox Press.

John and worship

There is a richer collection of commentaries on the Gospel of John than on virtually any other book of the Bible; somehow the book seems to bring out the best in modern writers. They are not necessarily easy, but they will more than repay the time and effort you spend on them. Among the distinguished authors are R. E. Brown, E. C. Hoskyns, Barnabas Lindars and John Marsh: they will point you to yet others. More general books are A. M. Hunter, *According to John,* SCM Press and Westminster Press, O. Cullmann; *The Johannine Circle,* SCM Press; Ernst Käsemann, *The Testament of Jesus,* Fortress Press; and C. H. Dodd, *The Interpretation of the Fourth Gospel,* Cambridge University Press. For the letters see especially J. L. Houlden's commentary in the Black New Testament series. Worship, even worship in New Testament times, is a vast subject, and it is impossible to give a list of books about it here; a good starting point is J. D. G. Dunn, *Unity and Diversity in the New Testament,* SCM Press and Westminster Press. Commentaries on Revelation are also helpful here: see the series mentioned above.

The beginning of the Gospel . . .

And here is the most difficult task of all! At least you should look at:
C. H. Dodd, *The Founder of Christianity,* Fount Books
  A portrait by a very famous English New Testament scholar.

PALESTINE in the first century
■ Fortresses

ROMAN EMPERORS	JUDAEA SAMARIA IDUMAEA	GALILEE PERAEA	ITURAEA TRACHONITIS	ABILENE	PRIESTS	JESUS and the CHRISTIAN COMMUNITY	PAUL: his life	his letters	OTHER WRITINGS
AUGUSTUS	HEROD THE GREAT 37 – 4								
	ARCHELAUS	HEROD ANTIPAS	HEROD-PHILIP II		6				
	6 exiled to Gaul				10 Annas	?6 Birth of JESUS	Between 0 and 10, born at Tarsus		
	8 Coponius Ambibolus	divorces and marries Herodias, wife of Herod-Philip I	marries Salome, daughter of Herod-Philip I and Herodias						
	12 Amnius Rufus				15 Eleazar				
14	15 Valerius-Gratus				18		between 15 and 25, studies at JERUSALEM, with Gamaliel		
TIBERIUS	26 PONTIUS PILATE		34 dies childless		Caiaphas	JOHN THE BAPTIST / Baptism of JESUS / Death and resurrection			
	36 Marcellus M.				36 Jonathan	36? Martyrdom of Stephen	37 Call. Preaches in Arabia, JERUSALEM TARSUS		
37 CALIGULA					37 Theophilus				
	39 Exiled to Lyons								
41	41	HEROD AGRIPPA 1			41 Simeon	42 Death of James, Peter in prison	43 Barnabas goes to look for Paul in Tarsus Ministry in ANTIOCH with Barnabas,		
	44				44 Matthias		44 'famine' visit to Jerusalem		
CLAUDIUS	44 Cuspius Fadus						45 – 48 First mission: Cyprus and Derbe Paul goes to the 'Council'		
	46 Tiberius Alexander				46 Elionaeus				
	48 Vintidius-Cumanus				48	end 49 – 50 'Council of JERUSALEM'			
54	52 Antonius FELIX marries Drusilla sister of Berenice	HEROD AGRIPPA II and his 'sister' BERENICE					50 – 52 Second mission: Antioch to Athens. Stays at CORINTH	51 I-II Thessalonians	
NERO	60 Porcius FESTUS				58 Ananias		53 – 58 Third mission. EPHESUS (2 – 3 years) Macedonia, Corinth (winter 57 – 58)	57? Philippians I-II Corinthians	JAMES I PETER
					Ishmael Joseph Annas II Jesus Joshua Matthias Phinehas		58 – 60 In prison in Caesarea (Felix-Festus), visit of Agrippa and Berenice	Galatians, Romans	
	62 Albinus						61 – 63 Prison in ROME. Spain? Macedonia	63 Colossians, Ephesians Philemon	HEBREWS MARK
68 Galba	64 Gessius Florus						65		
69 Otho	66 Jewish Revolt						66 – 67 Prison in ROME, MARTYRDOM	Timothy, Titus	
70 Vitellius									
VESPASIAN	TITUS captures JERUSALEM								MATTHEW LUKE – ACTS JUDE
79 TITUS									II PETER
81 DOMITIAN									JOHN, I – III JOHN REVELATION
96									

Analytical Index

Jesus

King, 63, 99
Lamb, 110
Lord, 37, 52, 54, 71, 76, 88
Martyr, 87
Messiah (or Christ), 58, 60, 63, 64, 65, 75, 76, 96, 111
New Adam, 51, 53
New Elijah, 85
New Moses, 85
Priest, 53
Prophet, 88
Saviour, 76, 85
Servant, 54, 63, 85
Son of David, 58, 60, 62, 112
Son of God, 58, 60, 63, 64, 71, 75, 76, 85, 99, 100, 112
Son of Man, 58, 63, 64, 75, 76, 100, 110
Word (Logos), 98

Holy Spirit, 19, 32, 51, 55, 81, 88, 97, 99, 109, 110, 119

Church

and kingdom of God, 70
in Matthew, 69
in Revelation, 106, 108
Two images, 46, 52
Various aspects, 32, 48, 84, 119

Groups, institutions

Baptists, 28
Diaspora, 25, 54
Elders, 27
Essenes, 28, 93
Festivals, Jewish, 30
Godfearers, 28
Jamnia (or Jabneh), 31, 69
Levites, 27
Nazarenes, 28
Pharisees, 27, 28, 31, 45, 69
Priests, 27
Proselytes, 28
Publicans, 27
Sabbath, 30, 61
Sadducees, 27, 28
Samaritans, 28
Sanhedrin, 30
Scribes, 27
Synagogues, 30
Zealots, 28

Some themes

Appear, make visible, 37, 39–41

Ascension-exaltation, 39
Baptism, 51, 55
Beatitudes, 65, 78
Catechesis, 12, 24, 55, 77–80
Celebration, worship, 13, 24, 36–37, 57, 93, 101–104, 108
Christian action, morality, 47, 48, 55–57
End of time, 71
Eucharist, 40, 63, 75, 87, 96, 102
Exaltation, see *Ascension*
Forgiveness, 56, 61, 76, 104
Gnosis, 93, 116, 119
Kerygma, see Preaching
Kingdom, reign of God, 65, 70, 77, 89, 92
Mary, 86, 112
Morality, see Christian action
Preaching, kerygma, 13, 23, 34, 39
Resurrection, 33–44
Scriptures, 42, 70, 81, 111–114
'Third day', 36
Universalism, 58, 69, 81

Literary questions

Allegory, 89
Apocalypse, 21, 54, 71, 105
Calling, accounts of, 20, 61
Canon of Scripture, 31, 119
Controversy, 20, 61
Gospel, 18, 57
Koine (common Greek), 82
Midrash, 21, 74
Miracle, 20, 65–68
Narratives, 21, 38
Parable, 20, 89–92
Recension, 120
Synopsis, 15, 16–17
Targum, 37
Theophany, 20
'Tool box', 21
'Tracing paper', 19, 69, 81
Type 'mock up', 72
'Upheaval', 67, 71, 75

Jewish texts

Parable of Rabbi Bun, 90
Prayer from the Jewish liturgy, 109
Philo (on Ex. 20.18), 84
Targum on Hos. 6.1, 36
Targum on Num. 24.17, 74
Targum on Ps. 68, 37
Testament of Levi. 60

The Synoptic Gospels: Texts Studied

Other Texts Studied

Table of Contents

The Books of the Bible

Abbreviations, and the pages in this book on which they are mentioned

Old Testament

(The Deutero-Canonical books are printed in italics)

Amos	Amos	Judith	Judith
Bar.	*Baruch*	I Kings	I Kings
I Chron.	I Chronicles	II Kings	II Kings
II Chron.	II Chronicles	Koh.	Koheleth
Dan.	Daniel	Lam.	Lamentations
Deut.	Deuteronomy	Lev.	Leviticus
Eccles.	Ecclesiastes (also called Koheleth)	*I Macc.*	*I Maccabees*
		II Macc.	*II Maccabees*
Ecclus.	*Ecclesiasticus* (also called *Sirach*)	Mal.	Malachi
		Micah	Micah
Esther	Esther	Nahum	Nahum
Ezra	Ezra	Neh.	Nehemiah
Ex.	Exodus	Num.	Numbers
Ezek.	Ezekiel	Obad.	Obadiah
Gen.	Genesis	Prov.	Proverbs
Hab.	Habakkuk	Ps.	Psalms
Hag.	Haggai	Ruth	Ruth
Hos.	Hosea	I Sam.	I Samuel
Isa.	Isaiah	II Sam.	II Samuel
	(I Isaiah, chs. 1–39)	*Sir.*	*Sirach*
	(II Isaiah, cha. 40–55)	S. of S.	Song of Songs
	(III Isaiah, 56–66)	Tob.	Tobit
Jer.	Jeremiah	*Wisd.*	*Wisdom*
Job	Job	Zech.	Zechariah
Joel	Joel		(I Zechariah, chs. 1–8
Jonah	Jonah		(II Zechariah, chs 9–14)
Josh.	Joshua	Zeph.	Zephaniah
Judg.	Judges		

New Testament

Acts	The Acts of the Apostles 23, 34, 44, 81–88	Luke	The Gospel of Luke 81–88
		Mark	The Gospel of Mark 58–64
Apoc.	The Apocalypse: also called the Revelation of St John the Divine (see below)	Matt.	The Gospel of Matthew 69–76
		I Peter	I Peter 53
Col.	Colossians 52	II Peter	II Peter 53
I Cor.	I Corinthians 49, 50, 56	Phil.	Philippians 47. 49
II Cor.	II Corinthians 49, 50	Phlm	Philemon 52
Eph.	Ephesians 52	Rev.	The Revelation of St John the Divine (also called Apocalypse) 105–110
Gal.	Galatians 49, 50		
Heb.	Hebrews 53		
James	James 53	Rom.	Romans 49, 51
John	The Gospel of John 93–100	I Thess.	I Thessalonians 48
I John	The First Letter of John 98	II Thess.	II Thessalonians 48
II John	II John	I Tim.	I Timothy 52
III John	III John	II Tim.	II Timothy 52
Jude	Jude 53	Titus	Titus 52